Created and editied by

Susan Morris

Bernice McCarthy

4MAT® is a registered trademark of Excel, Inc.

ISBN 0-9608992-5-1

Table of Contents

Middle School

English

Foreign Language

Guidance

History

Language Arts

Interdisciplinary

Mathematics

Physical Education

Science

Social Studies

Table of Contents

High School

The purpose of this book is to help people use 4MAT. It was written by teachers for teachers. The instructional plans included are the work of creative professionals. They were chosen for their diversity of content, clarity of concept, generalizable appeal, creative methods of instruction, and incorporation of 4MAT principles. Most importantly, the authors reported that these plans had a positive impact on teaching and learning in their classrooms.

The task of choosing these plans was a most pleasurable one; it is gratifying to see how much we have all learned since the previous editions of 4MAT in Action were published in 1983 and 1990. And it is, indeed, a pleasure to note that this third edition of exemplary 4MAT plans demands two separate volumes: the first for grades K - 6, and the second for grades 7 - 12.

We are indebted to the teachers who contributed to this collection. We gratefully dedicate this book to them.

Susan Morris
Bernice McCarthy
Spring 1995

The 4MAT System

The 4MAT System: A Cycle of Learning

Major premises of 4MAT

1

- Human beings perceive experience and information in different ways.
- Human beings process experience and information in different ways.
- The combinations formed by our own perceiving and processing techniques form our unique learning styles.

2

- There are four major identifiable learning styles.
- They are all equally valuable.
- Learners need to be comfortable about their own unique learning styles.

3

- Type One Learners are primarily interested in personal meaning. Teachers need to create a reason.
- Type Two Learners are primarily interested in the facts as they lead to conceptual understanding. Teachers need to give them facts that deepen understanding.
- Type Three Learners are primarily interested in how things work. Teachers need to let them try it.
- Type Four Learners are primarily interested in self-discovery. Teachers need to let them teach it to themselves and others.

4

- All learners need to be taught in all four ways, in order to be comfortable and successful part of the time while being stretched to develop other learning abilities.
- All learners will "shine" at different places in the learning cycle, so they will learn from each other.

5

- The 4MAT System moves through the learning cycle in sequence, teaching in all four modes and incorporating the four combinations of characteristics.
- The sequence is a natural learning progression.

6

- Each of the four learning modes needs to be taught with both right- and left-brain processing techniques.
- The right-mode-dominant learners will be comfortable half of the time and will learn to adapt the other half of the time.
- The left-mode-dominant learners will be comfortable half of the time and will learn to adapt the other half of the time.

7

- The development and integration of all four modes of learning and the development and integration of both right- and left-brain processing skills should be a major goal of education.

8

- Learners will come to accept their strengths and learn to capitalize on them, while developing a healthy respect for the uniqueness of others and furthering their ability to learn in alternative modes without the pressure of "being wrong."

9

- The more comfortable we are about who we are, the more freely we learn from others.

Teaching to All Four Learning Styles Using Right- and Left-Mode Techniques

Remember,
each of the four learning style types
has a quadrant, or place,
where s/he is most comfortable,
where success comes easily.

The Imaginative Learners, those who fall
in quadrant one,
prefer to learn through a combination
of sensing/feeling and watching.

The Analytic Learners, those who fall
in quadrant two,
prefer to learn through a combination
of thinking through concepts and watching.

The Common Sense Learners, those who fall
in quadrant three,
prefer to learn by thinking through concepts
and trying things out for themselves,
by doing.

The Dynamic Learners, those who fall
in quadrant four,
prefer to learn by sensing/feeling and doing.

The 4MAT System is designed so all four types of learners are comfortable some of the time and challenged some of the time.

We continue to understand the 4MAT cycle in deeper ways.

What follows is the result of our experiences since the first edition of 4MAT in Action.

We continue to make discoveries about 4MAT.

The most important ongoing affirmation is that 4MAT is more difficult than it looks.

and the second is that some steps are more difficult than others.

4MAT requires major attitudinal shifts in the way we think and feel about teaching.

These attitudinal shifts are necessary in order to produce:

- Learning environments where all learners have an equal chance to learn;
- Learning environments where motivation is considered the primary task of the teacher;
- Learning environments where non-trivial concepts form the instructional base;
- Learning environments where the skills that are taught are related to concepts and have immediate usefulness;
- Learning environments where learners are encouraged to speak in their own voices while attending to and honoring the voices of others;
- Learning environments where learners are led to the delight of self-discovery;
- Learning environments where alertness is fostered by teaching to all four learning styles using right and left mode techniques;
- Learning environments where learners are assessed according to the multiple ways knowledge can be represented;
- Learning environments that not only honor but also celebrate the diversities of learners.

Let us begin by going around the circle once again.

Quadrant One: Integrating Experience with the Self

A process from Concrete Experience to Reflective Observation.

Sensing/Feeling to Watching/Reflecting.

All learners go through all of the quadrants, but quadrant one appeals most to Imaginative Learners. The favorite question of the Imaginative Learner is "Why?" You must create an experience through which learners discover their own reasons for learning.

The Type One Imaginative Learner's most comfortable place is the upper right corner of the model.

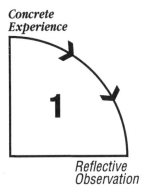

Concrete Experience

1

Reflective Observation

Teacher's Role - Motivator/Witness
Method - Simulation, Discussion

The goals that are emphasized in the first quadrant are focusing and generating skills, making meaning, observing, visualizing, imagining, inferring, connecting, diverging, listening, interacting, honoring subjectivity, and reflecting. In Quadrant One, students may be engaged in activities such as sharing personal reflections and autobiographic episodes, relational thinking, journal entries, brainstorming, mindmapping, drawings, group discussions, simulations, study teams, exit slips and self-assessment. Teachers may assess student performance through observation of student interest and engagement, level of student excitement, students' abilities to own their own message and acceptance of each other's ideas, individual authenticity and willingness to present ideas they are not yet sure of, the frequency of student-initiated ideas, analysis of products resulting from student discussion or the quality of journal entries.

The Quadrant One Steps

Step One

Create An Experience
Type One, Right Mode Learner most comfortable
Teacher's Role - Motivator
Method - Discussion
Question to be answered - Why?
Create a reason

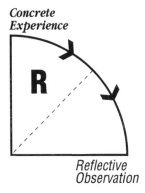

Concrete Experience

R

Reflective Observation

In Quadrant One we create a reason. We answer the question "Why?"

Begin by Creating an Experience. The Right Mode, Quadrant One Step.

The objective is to allow the learners to enter into the experience, to engage them, and to integrate the experience with personal meaning. Remember, the right mode jumps right into the experience, and the left mode stands back and analyzes what happened.

Imbue the experience with meaning so learners are able to see connections from their own experience. Richard Gibboney of the University of Pennsylvania School of Education comments on objectives and meaning: "Objectives must be valuable now, in their own immediate having."

A majority of teachers with whom we have worked report that this step is very difficult. They seem to struggle to create a concrete experience, something that can be apprehended or perceived on a direct and immediate level by the learners, something that connects to the learners' own experience and is therefore valuable to them now.

The 4MAT Steps in Depth

When we encounter teachers who have this difficulty, and they are in the majority, we begin by asking them what they are teaching. In other words, we go immediately to the Second Quadrant in order to find out the concept they are teaching.

They answer, for example, "Capital letters."

We then ask, "What is the concept underlying capital letters?"

And to our amazement we are usually met by silence, and a most uncomfortable silence.

If capital letters differentiate between generalities and specifics, then one can easily construct experience based on this concept. The students know, for example, that they like to be called by their names, John, Jane, etc., rather than "the girl in the red sweater" or "the boy in the grey shirt." They can understand the concept of generalities versus specifics when you point out to them how they like to be called by their names, how they like to be specified. Tell them there is a method for specifying in written form, and it is capital letters.

In addition, you can give the students the experience of a world where capital letters are not used, and have them discuss and with luck discover the reason for capital letters, a reason that connects to their own experience.

But the more serious question remains: how can the teacher help learners make the connection to meaning, the purpose and usefulness of the underlying concept, the glue that holds it together, the reason that makes sense, if the teacher does not know what it is?

In order to "Create a Concrete Experience," you must understand the concept.

Jerome Bruner speaks to this:

"When we try to get a child to understand a concept . . . the first and most important condition, obviously, is that the expositors themselves understand it. I make no apology for this necessary point. To understand something well is to sense wherein it is simple, wherein it is an instance of a simpler general case . . . to understand something is to sense the simpler structure that underlies a range of instances, and this is notably true in mathematics."

We teach skills in boxes. Somehow these skills have become ends in themselves, isolated entities, and have become separated from their meaning.

Without meaning, there is no understanding. It is like memorizing words in a foreign language without knowing what they mean, a frustrating and foolish task.

In order to Create an Experience, you must know the concept.

The problem graphically illustrated is this:

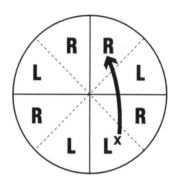

The Concept is the key!

Our system has taught us to break things down, to look at the parts.

We must return to the whole picture.

Teachers need to motivate their learners to want to learn what they are about to teach. We felt the difficulty we would encounter in Quadrant One was that some teachers would not agree that motivation was their primary task.

In some cases that has been true. The following conversation took place during the first break in one of our workshops. The speaker was a high school science teacher on a faculty in a Midwestern city. He moved in quickly and with great intensity.

"Motivating students is not my job. That's an outrageous notion."

I replied, "Then whose job is it?"

He answered, "It's their job, the students, I mean. It's their responsibility to be motivated when they come to my class. And it's their parents' job to make sure they stay that way."

I asked, "Then what is your responsibility?"

He answered, "To give them information."

I replied, "Then they don't need you. A good text, a good computer program could do just as well."

So we continue to meet some teachers who operate under the assumption that they are only required to teach motivated learners, learners who enter their classrooms excited and curious about the content to be taught. These teachers do not accept the idea that the art of teaching is arousing curiosity, creating excitement, answering the question "Why?" Motivation is the purpose of the Concrete Experience, the Right Mode Step of Quadrant One.

But, in order to design the Concrete Experience, a teacher needs to know the concept to be taught. Without the proper grasp of the concept, one cannot create a meaningful Concrete Experience. Somehow it takes the knack of grasping the idea of something in a way that connects to meaning. It is the core idea formed by mentally combining all the characteristics and particulars into a useful construct.

We are convinced this process is whole-brained, simply because we must analyze the parts while seeing the whole.

The Calculus lesson presented in this book (see page 342) is a perfect example of this grasping. The Quadrant One, Right Mode experience created by the authors constitutes the essence of the concept of maximal/minimal optimization, the objective of the lesson. The students are given wrapping paper and gift boxes to be wrapped. Their task is to wrap a maximal number of packages using a minimal amount of paper—a relatively common, everyday task that taps the heart of the calculus concept of this unit. It is the simplicity inherent in the meaning that connects the concept to understanding. Note that the Bruner quote ends with the statement, "to understand something is to sense the simpler structure that underlies a range of instances, and this is notably true in mathematics."

When the teacher truly understands the concept, the creation of the concrete experience simply becomes a matter of translating the concept into the language of the students, the language the students would use if they were attempting to explain the same thing.

In Literature, it is particularly important for the teacher to identify the concept which is exemplified by the literary work being studied. In other words, the teacher is not just teaching the literary work which the learners will read, but rather a significant concept is identified which all of the learners can relate to their own lives. Lynn Dieter uses the concept of "Choices" to engage her students in

the study of A Man for All Seasons. (See page 276) She begins by involving them with Scruples® questions that demand individual moral judgements, creating an immediate connection between her students' life experiences and the theme of the literary work they will read and study in this unit

The Concrete Experience must embody the essence of the concept at a simpler level, in order to prepare the students for the complexities that lie ahead as they move around the circle. Herein lies the right mode aspect - the concept gestalt coupled with the personal experience, the experience that connects to the self.

The right mode seems to engage the sense of relationship. It seems to embody a natural, intuitive way of thinking. We need to encourage intuitive ways of thinking, as "our left brains have become too stiff with technique, far from the scanning eye."

We believe one of the biggest stumbling blocks in designing the Quadrant One, Right Mode Step is the inability to translate the concept into a simple structure, in language learners can understand and relate to, and in a manner that connects to their personal lives.

We now move on to Step Two.

Step Two

Reflecting on Experience
Type One, Left Mode Learner most comfortable
Teacher's Role - Witness
Method - Discussion
Question to be answered - Why?
Create a reason

Concrete
Experience

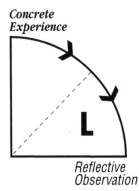

L

Reflective
Observation

The 4MAT Steps in Depth

The left mode aspect of reflecting on experience lies in the quality of analysis. Now the learners examine the experience. The method is discussion, which is the method in the first quadrant, but the focus has changed. The learners are now asked to step outside the experience and look at its parts.

Teachers do not seem to encounter much difficulty with this step, although there are two things to guard against: one, getting too technical in the analysis, and two, attempting to introduce new material. It appears when teachers construct a meaningful concrete experience, they have no difficulty helping learners to reflect on that experience. The experience itself flows into the quality of the reflection.

Notice this ease of operation when you read the lesson units included in this book. Teachers have made creative use of cooperative learning strategies, mindmapping, classification charts, and teacher-led discussion to enable their learners to reflect on their personal feelings and experiences.

Quadrant Two: Concept Formulation

A process of learning from Reflective Observation to Abstract Conceptualization.

Reflecting/Watching to Developing Concepts.

All of the students go through this process, but Quadrant Two appeals most to the Analytic Learners.

The Type Two Learner's most comfortable place is the lower right corner of the model.

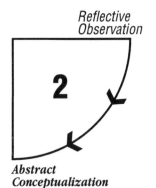

Reflective Observation

2

Abstract Conceptualization

Teacher's Role - "Teacher"
Method - Informational

The first quadrant is "create a reason" and the second is "teach it to them."

The second quadrant and those that follow are also divided into right- and left-mode techniques. The development of both right- and left-mode functioning continues throughout the learning cycle. Some of our students are right-mode dominant, some are left-mode dominant, but all need to develop both types of processing skills.

Reflective Observation
(Watching/Reflecting)

Right Mode Techniques

2

Left Mode Techniques

Abstract Conceptualization
(Thinking/Developing Concepts)

The goals that are emphasized in Quadrant Two are reflecting, seeing relationships, developing idea coherence, conceptualizing, defining, patterning, classifying, comparing, contrasting, being objective, discriminating, planning, constructing theoretical models, and acquiring knowledge. In the second quadrant, students may be engaged in activities such as non-verbal representations of connections, essays, spatial non-representations; creating analogs, metaphors, and clusters; outlining; using fish, venn and tree diagrams; discussions; oral exams and research; constructing theoretical models; objective tests, exit slips, and self-assessment. Teachers may assess student progress by checking for concept congruence (oral or written), quality of concept maps showing linkages between ideas, descriptions of reasoning; quality of planning steps; identification of criteria; ability to break into parts; evidence of theoretical understanding; and essays showing understanding of knowledge presented.

Quadrant Two has been discussed above in the context of the relationship between the Concrete Experience and the concept to be taught, but we need to examine concept formulation more carefully, as it is the essence of Quadrant

Two, as well as the core of the entire unit plan. It leads directly to practice and personalization in Quadrant Three, and on to self-discovery in Quadrant Four. The degree to which the "Why?" of the first quadrant is answered affects the understanding of the "What?" of the second quadrant; so also the "What?" of the second quadrant has an impact on the success of the third and fourth quadrants.

As we move into Quadrant Two, we are leading students from the specific personal reality to the theoretical conception. We now need to deepen student understandings of how the concept can be examined in the abstract, at the theoretical level. We are integrating the Concrete Experience (Right Mode, Quadrant One) and the analysis of the experience (Left Mode, Quadrant One) into a deeper understanding of the concept.

If Steps One and Two in Quadrant One have embodied the essence of the concept, then the students are ready to move to Quadrant Two.

You begin with the Right Mode step, possibly the most critical step in the learning process.

The Quadrant Two Steps

Step Three

Integrating Observations into Concepts
Type Two, Right Mode Learner most comfortable
Teacher Role - "Teacher"
Method - Informational
Question to be answered - What?
Teach it to them

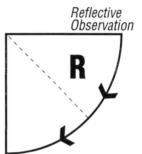

Reflective Observation

R

Abstract Conceptualization

The right mode step of Quadrant Two attempts to deepen reflection; it is an integrating step. We have come to see this step as the key to the learners' internalization of their need for further understanding of the concept at hand. It is the place where they link their personal, subjective experience with the objective, analytic world of the content at hand.

The poetry plan by Diane Rizzetto on Robert Frost's "The Mending Wall" is an excellent example of the process of Step Three, a deepening of the conceptual understanding, through the creation of visual analogs portraying "walled in" or "walled out." (See page 10) This Step Three activity enables the learners to tap into and deepen the richness of what they already know about the concepts being studied.

When you design Step Three, Quadrant Two, the Right Mode Step, look for another medium, another way of looking at the concept that engages the senses while simultaneously affording the opportunity for more reflection. Remember you are moving the learners from the concrete to the abstract, and Reflective Observation is the gateway. You want to create an activity that causes them to mull over the experience and reflection just completed

The 4MAT Steps in Depth

in Quadrant One and assists them in formulating and deepening their understanding of the concept, the purpose of Quadrant Two.

Step Four

Developing Theories and Concepts
Type Two, Left Mode Learner most comfortable
Teacher Role - "Teacher"
Method - Informational
Question to be answered - What?
Teach it to them

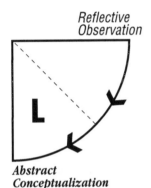

Reflective
Observation

L

Abstract
Conceptualization

The left mode step of Quadrant Two takes your learners to the heart of conceptual information. Be sure "the subject matter does not swamp the learner with information easily available elsewhere, but rather information is given selectively to assist in learner inquiry." We are not interested in rote memory, the antithesis of thinking. We are stressing information that relates to the core of the concept. Many of the unit plans in this book demonstrate Step Four activities in which creative teachers have gone beyond traditional lecture accompanied by the text to teach content to their learners.

In her Algebra I unit on algebraic properties, Shari Wilson has her students viualizing, demonstrating, kinesthetically "being," or drawing the operation of each of the algebraic functions as they are presented by the teacher. This is preliminary to the students performing each function as part of a traditional algebraic formula. (See page 331). Another good example of interactive instruction is Karen Dietrich's Biology unit teaching the structure of DNA (page 363). In addition to the traditional lecture with overheads, blackboard, and text, she has her students experiment with alcohol and egg whites as well as use pop beads to more fully

demonstrate the structure of nature's building blocks.

The Fourth Step is to "teach it to them." The choices of content must be related to the concept and engender further learner inquiry.

Quadrant Three: Practice and Personalization

A process of learning from Abstract Conceptualization to Active Experimentation.

Thinking/Developing Concepts to Doing/Trying it Themselves.

All of the students continue on through this process, but Quadrant Three appeals most to the Common Sense Learners.

The Type Three Learner's most comfortable place is the lower left corner of the model.

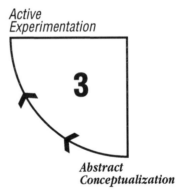

Active
Experimentation

3

Abstract
Conceptualization

Teacher's Role - Coach
Method - Facilitation

Common Sense Learners rely heavily on kinesthetic involvement to learn, using body senses as a focus for understanding. They need to try it. They are concerned with finding out the answer to the question, "How does this work?" They are anxious to try it themselves. They edit reality. The teacher's role is to provide the materials and the encouragement necessary for a "trying things out" environment.

Abraham Maslow speaks of growth as taking place subjec-

The 4MAT Steps In Depth

tively "from within outward." He comments on the healthy child as follows:

"... (s)he tends to try out his (her) powers, to reach out, to be absorbed, fascinated, interested, to plan, to wonder, to manipulate the world. Exploring, manipulating, experiencing, being interested, choosing . . .

(This) lead(s) to Becoming through a serendipitous way, fortuitously, unplanned, unanticipated. Spontaneous, creative experience can and does happen without expectations, plans, foresight, purpose or goal."

In commenting on the relationship between safety and growth, Maslow goes on to say:

"Apparently growth forward customarily takes place in little steps, and each step forward is made possible by the feeling of being safe, of operating out into the unknown from a safe home port (emphasis ours) of daring because retreat is possible... Now, how can we know when the child feels safe enough to dare to choose the new step ahead? Ultimately the only way in which we can know is by his choice which is to say only he can ever really know the right moment when the beckoning forces ahead overbalance the beckoning forces behind, and courage outweighs fear. Ultimately the person even the child must choose for himself. Nobody can choose for him too often, for this itself enfeebles him, cutting his self-trust, and confusing his ability to perceive his own internal delight in the experience, his own impulses, judgments, and feelings, and to differentiate them from the interiorized standards of others."

Maslow speaks eloquently of choices encouraged by a safe environment. We emphatically agree. We do not believe learning can take place without learners being allowed to make choices, to explore, to manipulate, to experience. These activities are often found in primary schools, but exploration, manipulation, and experimentation in the higher grades and post-secondary learning environments is frequently limited to reading another book or writing another essay, activities that appeal to only a small percentage of our learners.

The four quadrants in the 4MAT System move from teacher-initiated to learner-initiated activities. In Quadrant One (Steps One and Two), the teacher is the initiator, the primary actor. S/he plans and implements the experience as well as the reflective discussion that follows the experience. In Quadrant Two, the teacher is the information giver; first in Step Three by linking the experience and the reflection into the concepts to be taught,

and second (Step Four) by teaching the material and skills.

"Apparently growth forward customarily takes place in little steps, and each step forward is made possible by the feeling of being safe, of operating out into the unknown from a safe home port..."

This changes as we move into Quadrant Three. The third quadrant is where the learners become active, more self-initiating. Learners become the primary actors even more in Quadrant Four.

In the first quadrant the teacher creates a reason.

In the second quadrant the teacher teaches it to them.

In the third quadrant the teacher lets them try it themselves.

The teacher's role in the third quadrant is one of coach/facilitator. The crucial teaching skill in this quadrant is organizational, to gather the materials needed for manipulation and to set up the encouraging environment needed so the learners can try it themselves. Without the active involvement of the learners, schooling at all levels is a sterile overlay, an externally applied act, satisfying the teacher perhaps (after all, s/he's working), but not involving the students in any meaningful way.

So, the emphasis in the third quadrant (and the fourth) is on learner activity.

The learners take the concepts and skills that have been taught and try them. The goals that are emphasized in Quadrant Three include resolving contradictions, managing ambiguity, computing, collecting data, inquiring, predicting, recording, hypothesizing, tinkering, measuring, experimenting, problem-solving, and making decisions.

The 4MAT Steps in Depth

Students may be engaged in activities such as field work and lab work, adapting new knowledge for personal usefulness, conversations with teacher and peers, demonstrations, worksheets, chapter questions, and essays; puzzles, diagrams, computer experiments, interviews, exit slips, and self-assessment. Teachers may assess student progress by looking for evidence of learner authenticity, student ability to integrate knowledge into life (usefulness), flexibility of thought, contingency logic and reasoning, manageability and timelines for projects, project choice parameters, reflective notes about content, essays or problems requiring multiple methods of solution, accuracy and thoroughness.

The third quadrant is also divided into Left and Right Mode Techniques.

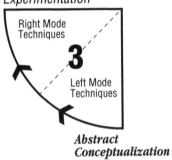

Active Experimentation

Right Mode Techniques

3

Left Mode Techniques

Abstract Conceptualization

Note that Left Mode techniques come first in the third quadrant.

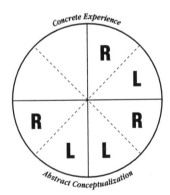

Concrete Experience

R

L

R

R

L

L

Abstract Conceptualization

This is because of the proximity to the Abstract Conceptualization dimension. As we move into Quadrant

Three (Step Five) the learners react to the "givens" presented in Quadrant Two, but in a more fixed, prearranged way than in Step Six.

Quadrant Three: Practice and Personalization

Step Five

Working on Defined Concepts
(Reinforcement and Manipulation)
Type Three, Left Mode Learner most comfortable
Teacher Role - Coach
Method - Facilitation
Question to be answered - How does this work?
Let them try it
Comments on Step Five

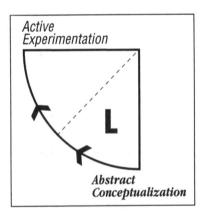

Active Experimentation

L

Abstract Conceptualization

In Step Five, the students react to the givens. They do worksheets, use workbooks, try fixed lab experiments, etc. These materials are used to reinforce the concepts and skills taught in Quadrant Two. A good workbook of prepared exercises can be used in Step Five. This is a traditional step, as is Step Four. Sad to say, Steps Four and Five in the 4MAT Model constitute the bulk of what transpires in many traditional learning environments and what is recommended in many teacher's manuals.

Note that these two steps, Steps Four and Five, are left-mode techniques. Step Four appeals to the Analytic left-mode-learners, and Step Five appeals to the Common Sense left mode learners. One can easily see the value of these two steps for all learners, but exclusive teaching in this way handicaps all learners. Schools must stop teaching exclusively in these two steps if we are to individualize in any meaningful way.

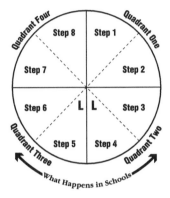

Good unit plans have learners really practice what they are learning. In the Literature unit on "Rich in Love,"(page 191) after answering quiz questions and filling worksheets on figurative language and identifying quotes, students are asked to additionally apply their learning with visual metaphors for characters and a new possible epilogue for the end of the story. Likewise in the unit on Elizabethan Theater (page 19) Maureen Adams checks her students understanding of this literary period by having them develop Elizabethan action cartoons using couplets representative of the literature of the times. Both of these examples ask students to go a step further in their application of what they have learned.

The left mode characteristic of Step Five lies in the reaction to givens. The learners have been taught a skill or a concept, and now they are asked to manipulate materials based on those skills/concepts. They are still adapting to experts; they are still working on prescribed materials. They have begun. But the creative stepping out, the adding something of their own, the applying their own uniqueness to the material, comes in Step Six, the right mode step of Quadrant Three.

Step Six

Messing Around
(Adding Something of Themselves)
Type Three, Left Mode Learner most comfortable
Teacher Role - Coach
Method - Facilitation
Question to be answered - How does this work?
Let them try it.

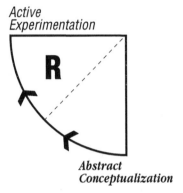

Real integration begins with Step Six.

The learners are "adding something of themselves," "messing around," and making the material theirs.

The right mode characteristic of Step Six is in the integration of the material and the self, the personal synthesis, as well as in the opportunity for learners to approach the content in their own most comfortable way. The right mode Common Sense Learners are most comfortable in Step Six.

To return to Maslow:

"If the child can choose the experiences which are validated by the experience of delight, then he can return to the experience, repeat it, savor it to the point of repletion, satiation or boredom. At this point he shows the tendency to go on to more complex, richer experiences and accomplishments.

. . . Such experiences not only mean moving on, but have a feedback effect on the Self, in the feeling of certainty (This I like; that I don't for sure); of capability, mastery, self-trust, self-esteem."

The skills materials given in Step Five should afford learners the opportunity to practice what they have learned, to try it themselves. Workbook pages can never be substituted for conceptual learning; rather they complement and reinforce the concepts. We are concerned about the amount of workbook pages being used in the schools we visit. It appears that many times they are used to teach the concepts, rather than to reinforce the concepts. If this is true, it indicates that teachers are bypassing Quadrant Two and going directly to skills and drills without the conceptual underpinnings so necessary for understanding.

We ask the reader to ponder any classroom learning situation in which learners are required to complete workbook pages as the major emphasis of the class. Our experience indicates that this is the case in a great many classrooms. The workbook has become the concept lesson.

To return to Gibboney again:

"... skills and drills must be related to thought. Information is never severed from thoughtful doing. And thinking and doing are inseparable."

Creative teachers provide their learners with the opportunity to extend what they have learned through making project choices and individualizing their own experimentation. In good lesson plans, the teacher may keep in mind individual learning style characteristics when planning activities for the learners to select. Good teachers also require their learners to maintain ownership over the quality of the work they choose to do; Step Six of a 4MAT unit is the ideal place for the teacher and students to agree upon the rubrics that will be used to assess the final product created by the learners. Likewise, learners may appreciate the opportunity to choose either to work cooperatively in a team or to work alone on a project to be shared later with the group.

Bob Bates' mathematics unit on Measures of Central Tendency is a good example of multiple student options for applying what they have learned in their own lives. They choose a topic to explore and have the choice of creating a story, a picture, a diagram/chart, or of conducting a survey. Likewise, the Driver's Education plan written by Washington-Lee High School teachers (see page 221) provides for real-life extension of classroom learning when students tabulate driving infractions at a busy intersection and make safe driving posters for use in a school-wide Safe Driving Week.

In other words, the drills you design must prepare the students to move from the Abstract Conceptualization of Quadrant Two to the Active Experimentation of Quadrant Three. "Without testing, ideas do not flow from the abstract to the real (the equally important realm of experience.)"

Step Six begins to move the students into Self-Discovery. Maslow speaks of delight, *"experiences which are validated by . . . delight."* The word describes Self-Discovery beautifully.

Actor-director Richard Benjamin, speaking of his experience at La Guardia Performing Arts School, epitomizes the delight of learning in this mode:

It was . . . the luckiest thing that ever happened to me. It was a longer (school) day, but they couldn't get the kids out of there."

This is active thinking. This is learning by doing, and its essence is problem solving.

"We solve a problem or make a discovery when we impose a puzzle form on a difficulty to convert it into a problem that can be solved in such a way that it gets us where we want to be. That is to say, we recast the difficulty into a form that we know how to work with - then we work it. Much of what we speak of as discovery consists of knowing how to compose a workable kind of form on various kinds of difficulties. A small but crucial part of discovery of the highest order is to invent and develop effective models or puzzle forms. It is in this area that the truly powerful mind shines. But it is surprising to what degree perfectly ordinary people can, given the benefit of instruction, construct quite interesting and what, a century ago, would have been considered greatly original models.

Of only one thing am I convinced: I have never seen anybody improve in the art and technique of inquiry by any means other than engaging in inquiry."

We cannot lead our learners to inquiry by using workbook pages as the major thrust of our lessons. We must motivate them by answering the question "Why?"; we must teach it to them by answering the question "What?"; we must lead them from the abstract to the real by answering the question "How does this work?"; and we must allow them the delight of self-discovery by building in the question "If?"

"Much of what we speak of as discovery consists of knowing how to impose a workable kind of form on various kinds of difficulties."

Quadrant Four: Integrating Application and Experience

A process of learning from Active Experimentation to Concrete Experience.

Doing/Trying It Themselves to Sensing/Feeling.

All of the learners go through this process, but Quadrant Four appeals most to the Dynamic Learners.

The Type Four Dynamic Learner's most comfortable place is the upper left corner of the model.

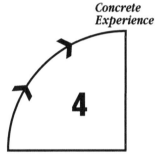

Teacher's Role - Evaluator/Remediator/Co-Learner
Method - Self-Discovery

The goals that are emphasized in Quadrant Four are creating, identifying constraints, revising, creating models, coming to closure, editing, summarizing, verifying, synthesizing, re-presenting, reflecting anew, re-focusing, and evaluating. Students are actively engaged in editing processes (revising, refining); error analyzing; concluding; taking a position; assessing the quality of their evidence; creating, collaborating, verifying, and summarizing; syntheisizing original performances; preparing and presenting exhibitions and/or publications; exit slips, and self-assessments. Teachers may be assessing students by reviewing portfolio selections, student products, field notes, exhibits, first and second drafts, their use of "best" experts, the quality of oral/visual presentations (appropriateness, sensitivity to feedback, originality, relevance to a larger audience), quality of new insights and questions,willingness to push limits, and ability to extend concepts and ask new questions.

Quadrant Four Steps

Step Seven

Analyzing for Usefulness or Application
Type Four, Left Mode Learner most comfortable
Teacher's Role - Evaluator/Remediator/Co-Learner
Method - Self-Discovery
Question to be answered - If?
"Let them teach it to themselves and to someone else"

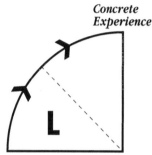

Now we move into Quadrant Four, where the learners deepen the initiative they began in Step Six. Here they refine the uniquely personal things they have done. If we have done our job well, the impetus to explore, to manipulate, to choose now comes from them. They have been freed to go beyond the objectives themselves. The teacher can now evaluate and remediate; and the learners can evaluate themselves, their learning, and refine and edit their own work. The students are truly learning from each other.

Comments on Step Seven

This is the step where the learners are asked to analyze what they have planned as their "proof" of learning. The left-mode characteristic of Step Seven lies in the analysis of the planning. This analysis should be based on:

1. Relevance to the content/skills

2. Originality

3. Excellence

Step Seven requires the learners to apply and refine in some personal, meaningful way what they have learned. As you will see in the lesson plan samples in this book, there are many different ways to achieve this step. The students (as well as peers and the teacher) will be involved in editing and refining the work that has been done so far, analyzing for strengths and weaknesses, taking a position, and productive self-assessment. Many kinds of choices are possible.

Teachers should move their students to usefulness, and it is immediate usefulness. Students are now capable of going beyond the objectives themselves to personal interest based on the combined experience in Quadrant One, the knowledge in Quadrant Two, and the practice leading to personalization in Quadrant Three. The learning is being extended outward into their lives.

Step Eight

Doing It Themselves and Sharing What They Do With Others
Type Four, Right Mode Learner most comfortable
Teacher's Role - Evaluator/Remediator/Co-Learner
Method - Self-Discovery
Questions to be answered - How can I apply this? What can this become?
Let them teach it to themselves and to someone else

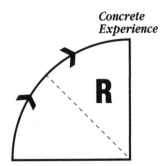

Concrete Experience

R

Active Experimentation

In the last step of the lesson unit, Step Eight, the learners share what they have learned with each other, and perhaps with the wider community at large. This is the place where students truly are asked to stand and speak in their own voices as they share in their own best way what it is they each have learned from the cycle of the unit they experienced. So we return to synergy, where we began. But there is a difference, a great difference (if we have done our job). We have given our learners the skills to discover for themselves whether or not what we have taught is worth knowing.

"We may well ask of any item of information that is taught or

that we lead a child to discover for (her) himself whether it is worth knowing. I can think of only two good criteria and one middling one for deciding such an issue: whether the knowledge gives a sense of delight and whether it bestows the gift of intellectual travel beyond the information given, in the sense of containing within it the basis of generalization. The middling criterion is whether the knowledge is useful. It turns out, on the whole,. . . that useful knowledge looks after itself. So I would urge that we as school (wo/men) let it do so and concentrate on the first two criteria. Delight and travel, then.

. . . It seems to me that the implications of this conclusion are that we opt for depth and continuity in our teaching, rather than coverage, and that we re-examine afresh what it is that gives a sense of intellectual delight to a person who is learning."

And so . . .
we move our students
from the usefulness
of Quadrant Three,
to the delight
of Quadrant Four.

We lead them to Self-Discovery;
we take them
back around the circle
in ever-increasing complexity.

The cycle begins again with energy generated by the cycle just completed.

The 4MAT Steps In Depth

It seems to me that good teachers do four things well:

They instill a love of learning,
They make the difficult easy,
They help us believe in ourselves—
  that the impossible is possible,
  that we can help change our world.
And they give us an awareness of the need to honor each other.

So go forth and teach.
And most of all, teach your students to celebrate diversity.

For our culture has a way of giving us ladders when we need trees,
reason when we need myth, and separateness when we need unity.
In the music of the universe, there is harmony.

For when you teach your students to celebrate diversity,
you will give the gift of grace.
The grace to blend all that is, was, and shall be.

And God will go with you.

Bernice McCarthy based on Bob Samples[1][2]

Footnotes:

1. McCarthy, Bernice, *The 4MAT System: Teaching to Learning Styles with Right/Left Mode Techniques.* Barrington, IL: Excel, Inc., 23385 Old Barrington Road, 60010. 1980, 1987.

2. Gibboney, Richard A., *Toward Intellectual Excellence: Some Things to Look for in Classrooms and Schools (TIE),* Graduate School of Education, University of Pennsylvania, 3700 Walnut Street, Philadelphia, PA 19104-3688. 1982. Page 10.

3. Bruner, Jerome S., *On Knowing: Essays for the Left Hand.* Belknap Press of Harvard University Press, Cambridge, MA. Second Printing, 1980. Paperback, pages 105-106.

4. *ibid.*, page 8.

5. Gibboney, Richard A., *op. cit.* page 14.

6. Maslow, Abraham H., *Toward a Psychology of Being.* Second Edition. NY: Von Nostrand Reinhold Company. 1968. Chapter Four.

7. *ibid.*

8. Gibboney, Richard A., *op. cit.* page 23.

9. Atwater, Carol, "Special Schools," *USA Today,* Wednesday, April 13, 1983. Section 3D.

10. Bruner, Jerome S., *op. cit.*, page 94.

11. *ibid.*, pages 108-109.

12. Samples, Bob, *Mind of Our Mother.* Reading, MA: Addison-Wesley Publishing Company. 1981.

Compare/Contrast

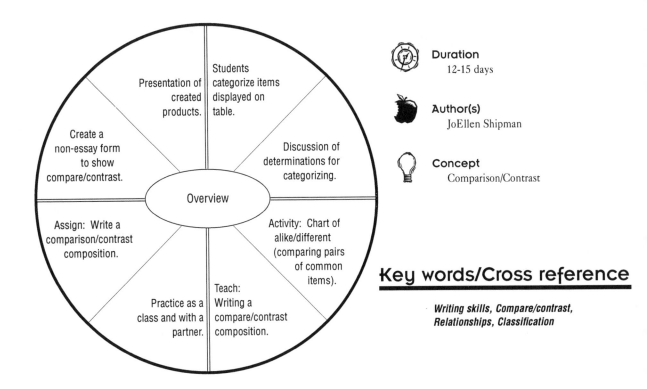

Overview

- Students categorize items displayed on table.
- Presentation of created products.
- Create a non-essay form to show compare/contrast.
- Assign: Write a comparison/contrast composition.
- Practice as a class and with a partner.
- Teach: Writing a compare/contrast composition.
- Activity: Chart of alike/different (comparing pairs of common items).
- Discussion of determinations for categorizing.

Duration
12-15 days

Author(s)
JoEllen Shipman

Concept
Comparison/Contrast

Key words/Cross reference

*Writing skills, Compare/contrast,
Relationships, Classification*

Overview

Objective
The student will write a comparison/contrast composition showing critical analysis of the chosen subjects.

About the Author
JoEllen Shipman, teacher of 7th and 8th grade English, Reading, and Social Studies at McCullouch Middle School in Marion, Indiana.

Required Resources
Array of items for compare/contrast exercise; video clip for compare/contrast ad exercise

Quadrant 1—Experience

 ## Right Mode—Connect

Students categorize items displayed on table.

Objective
Each student will categorize items through his/her analysis of their similarities and differences.

Activity
The teacher should randomly arrange on a table in the classroom as many items as possible from three or four of the following given lists (or develop others to use). Have students group the items into categories (either physically or on paper).

Fruits	Writing Equip.	Sewing Items	Dental Needs
apple	ink pen	straight pin	toothbrush
orange	pencil	safety pin	toothpaste
grape	typing paper	needle	mouthwash
banana	quill	spool of thread	floss

Hair Care	Measuring Devices	Sports Eqp.	Craft Supp.
comb	measuring spoon	softball	yarn
hairbrush	measuring cup	ballbat	clay
shampoo	thermometer	tennis racket	watercolors
conditioner	tape measure	tennis shoes	frame

Assessment
Participation in the activity.

 ## Left Mode—Examine

Discussion of determinations for categorizing.

Objective
Students will analyze the skills and determiners they used in the preceding categorizing activity.

Activity
Class discussion of determinations for categorizing which should include:
1) Are all items in each group alike?
2) How did you decide how to group items?
3) How are items within a group different?
4) When or why do we group them differently?
5) Is one particular set of groupings correct?

Assessment
Participation in the class discussion.

Quadrant 2—Concepts

 ## Right Mode—Image

Activity: Chart of alike/different (comparing pairs of common items).

Objective
The student will understand adaptations and uses of comparison/contrast.

Activity
1) Teacher skit of a commercial comparing two products (such as "Cheer" and "Brand X") to illustrate one common use of comparison/contrast. 2) Discuss being a good comparison shopper and how this relates to comparison/contrast writings. 3) Partner activity: chart of alike/different (comparing pairs of common items) to complete and discuss.

Assessment
Completion of assigned chart.

 ## Left Mode—Define

Teach: Writing a compare/contrast composition.

Objective
The student will understand the concepts and skills used in writing a comparison/contrast composition.

Activity
Textbook information presented and discussed:
A) Sample writing, B) Definition, C) Assignments, including work on evaluating whether to compare or contrast and on writing for particular audiences and purposes, D) Brainstorm composition uses (book reviews, movie critiques, "Describe Your Favorite Season or Holiday" -type of writing assignments, social studies topics such as countries or leaders, science such as results of experiments or classification of rocks or elements, etc.).

Assessment
Successful completion of individual assignments.

Compare/Contrast

Quadrant 3—Applications

 ### Left Mode—Try

Practice as a class and with a partner.

Objective
Students will practice comparison/contrast skills together.

Activity
1) Compare a pen to a pencil together in class (or paper/pencil versus chalk/chalkboard) after teacher modeling of a comparison such as an apple to an orange. Do a Venn Diagram, then write a rough draft together of two or three paragraphs. 2) With a partner, choose two animals or famous people to compare. Brainstorm, complete a Venn Diagram, then write a rough draft of a Comparison/Contrast composition.

Assessment
Involvement in the assigned activities and completion of the Venn Diagram and the rough draft assigned.

 ### Right Mode—Extend

Assign: Write a comparison/contrast composition.

Objective
Student will write a comparison/contrast composition.

Activity
Assign composition writing: topic choices include books, movies, sports, middle school vs. elementary, and well-known personalities. Students will write individual compositions, but will work with partners for brainstorming, revising, and proofreading.

Assessment
Final draft of composition will be graded according to class-developed criteria.

Quadrant 4—Creations

 ### Left Mode—Refine

Create a non-essay form to show compare/contrast.

Objective
Each student will create a non-essay form to show comparison/contrast.

Activity
1) Class discussion of some possible ways to present the concept of comparison/contrast in non-essay form, such as debates, commercials, a chart of similes and metaphors, billboards, panel discussions, audio presentation of musical compositions, or shopping for a melon.
2) Assign: each student is to create a non-essay form to show comparison/contrast.

Assessment
Successful completion of non-essay comparison/contrast project.

 ### Right Mode—Integrate

Presentation of created products.

Objective
The student will present his/her non-essay comparison/contrast representation to the class.

Activity
Individual presentations to the class of created forms to show comparison/contrast.

Assessment
Requirements: 1) Completion of class presentation, 2) Non-essay form, and 3) Clearly shows comparison and contrast.

Following Written Directions

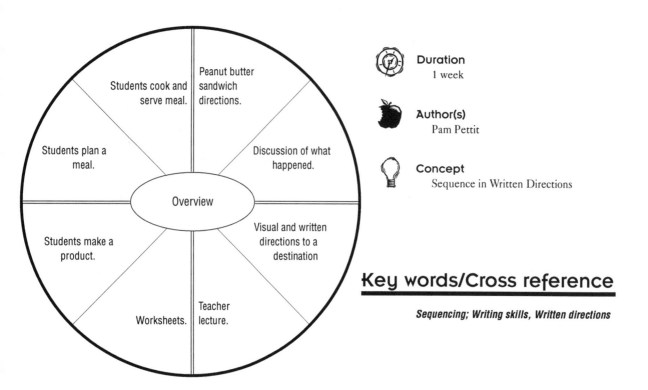

Students cook and serve meal.

Peanut butter sandwich directions.

Students plan a meal.

Discussion of what happened.

Overview

Visual and written directions to a destination

Students make a product.

Worksheets.

Teacher lecture.

Duration
1 week

Author(s)
Pam Pettit

Concept
Sequence in Written Directions

Key words/Cross reference

Sequencing; Writing skills, Written directions

Overview

Objective
Students will learn the importance of sequence in creating and following written directions.

About the Author
At the time this was first published in 1983, Pam Pettit was a reading teacher at McHenry Community High School, McHenry, IL

Required Resources
Peanut butter, jelly, bread, knives, lots of paper towels.

Author's Notes
These students are enrolled in study skills classes because of their repeated failure in mainstreamed classes. A primary reason for their failure is consistent inability to follow directions.

Following Written Directions

Quadrant 1—Experience

 ### Right Mode—Connect

Peanut butter sandwich directions.

Objective
To aid students' understanding of the importance of following written directions accurately.

Activity
Students are instructed to write out directions for making a peanut butter and jelly sandwich. Each student will then make a sandwich following another student's direction. Students will then consume their sandwiches.

Assessment
Students' participation.

 ### Left Mode—Examine

Discussion of what happened.

Objective
To understand the importance of following directions.

Activity
To understand the importance of following directions.

Assessment
Quality of discussion.

Quadrant 2—Concepts

 ### Right Mode—Image

Visual and written directions to a destination.

Objective
To enlarge student understanding of the need to follow directions.

Activity
Each student creates and shares with a partner sequenced visual and written directions to follow to another room in the school, a classmate's home, etc. Students report the steps necessary to follow the map; what worked and what didn't.

Assessment
Arrival at their destination.

 ### Left Mode—Define

Teacher lecture.

Objective
To enhance student awareness of the variety of situations in which understanding of written directions is essential.

Activity
Teacher lecture on following of written directions.

Assessment
Objective test of the above.

Quadrant 3—Applications

 ### Left Mode—Try

Worksheets.

Objective
Reinforcement and practice of above skills.

Activity
Worksheets include: following directions on a map, unscrambling a series of tasks, following test directions.

Assessment
Successful completion of worksheets.

 ### Right Mode—Extend

Students make a product.

Objective
Reinforcement of the concepts by making a product.

Activity
Students will complete one of the following: build a model, napkin folding, make a kite, etc., following written directions.

Assessment
Quality of projets.

Quadrant 4—Creations

 ### Left Mode—Refine

Students plan a meal.

Objective
To give students the experience of working together, planning, following directions, for a common goal.

Activity
Students will work together in planning a meal. Each course will require an unfamiliar recipe. A time schedule is developed along with the shopping list.

Assessment
Student involvement.

 ### Right Mode—Integrate

Students cook and serve meal.

Objective
To follow through with a plan and share results with classmates.

Activity
Following recipes, each student will prepare one course for the meal.

Assessment
Quality of finished product.

Heroes in Greek Mythology

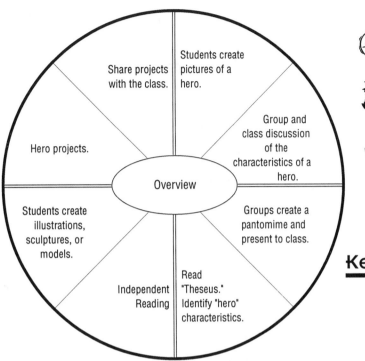

Share projects with the class.

Students create pictures of a hero.

Group and class discussion of the characteristics of a hero.

Hero projects.

Overview

Students create illustrations, sculptures, or models.

Groups create a pantomime and present to class.

Independent Reading

Read "Theseus." Identify "hero" characteristics.

 Duration
2 weeks

 Author(s)
Carole L. Lutes

 Concept
The Hero in Greek Mythology

Key words/Cross reference

Theseus, Twelve Labors of Hercules, Hero, Greek Mythology

Overview

 Objective
To understand the concept of the hero in Greek Mythology and read the exploits and adventures of Hercules and Theseus.

 About the Author
Carol L. Lutes teaches at Dodd Junior High School, Cheshire, CT. She is a participant in the Cheshire 4MAT Implementation Project, led by Jennifer Soloway and Patricia DiGiacomo.

 Required Resources
Markers, colored pencils and drawing paper

 Bibliography
"Theseus" Enjoying Literature. MacMillan Literature Series, New York, MacMillan Publishing Company, 1985.
"The Labors of Hercules" Counterpoint in Literature. Glenview, Illinois, Scott, Foresman and Company, 1976.

Heroes in Greek Mythology

Quadrant 1—Experience

 ### Right Mode—Connect

Students create pictures of a hero.

Objective
To create an experience that allows each student the opportunity to characterize a hero.

Activity
Teacher distributes markers, colored pencils, and drawing paper and asks each student to draw a picture of a hero. Students will create pictures based upon their perceptions of a hero.

Assessment
Student interest and involvement.

 ### Left Mode—Examine

Group and class discussion of the characteristics of a hero.

Objective
To analyze the experience.

Activity
Teacher will divide the students into groups of four. Using each student's picture, the group will make a list of the characteristics they have included in their pictures—i.e., strength, size, etc. Each group will share their lists with the entire class, and the teacher will chart the list of characteristics developed by the class.

Assessment
Teacher observation of participation in the group and group social skills. Quality of class discussion and the lists from each group.

Quadrant 2—Concepts

 ### Right Mode—Image

Groups create a pantomime and present to class.

Objective
To clarify the concept of the hero.

Activity
In groups of four or five, create a pantomime that highlights one or more characteristic of a hero. Present to the class and class must guess the characteristic. (Characteristics may be assigned using the class list as a resource.)

Assessment
Ability to work together and individual contribution to the group.

 ### Left Mode—Define

Read "Theseus." Identify "hero" characteristics.

Objective
To read *"Theseus"* and point out characteristics of the hero in Greek mythology.

Activity
Directed reading of *"Theseus"*: Highlight "heroic" characteristics of Theseus. Discuss the elements of the myth such as setting, characterization, plot, point of view and theme. Compare Greek hero to student heroes.

Assessment
Teacher checks for student understanding of the myth and the characteristics of a hero.

Heroes in Greek Mythology

Quadrant 3—Applications

 ### Left Mode—Try

Independent Reading

Objective

To further develop student ability to read and analyze a "hero" myth.

Activity

Independently, students will read *"Twelve Labors of Hercules"* and list activities or examples from the myth that illustrate that Hercules is a hero.

Assessment

Quality of students' understanding and accuracy of their lists.

 ### Right Mode—Extend

Students create illustrations, sculptures, or models.

Objective

To apply what has been learned.

Activity

To stress the concept of a hero, each student will illustrate, create a sculpture, or construct a model for *"Theseus"* or *"Hercules"* emphasizing a heroic moment.

Assessment

Quality of illustration, sculpture, or model.

Quadrant 4—Creations

 ### Left Mode—Refine

Hero projects.

Objective

To extend what has been learned.

Activity

Student will complete a hero project:
1) Write an original myth about a hero of student's own creation.
2) Choose a hero or heroine in Greek mythology and stage a "This is Your Life" program.
3) Pretend Hercules was assigned a 13th labor; describe his task and how he accomplished it.
4) Predict the outcome of a conflict between Hercules and Theseus.

Assessment

Quality of student effort.

 ### Right Mode—Integrate

Share projects with the class.

Objective

To share what has been learned.

Activity

Students will present hero projects to the class.

Assessment

Quality of student presentation, written and/or oral.

Poetry - Mending Wall

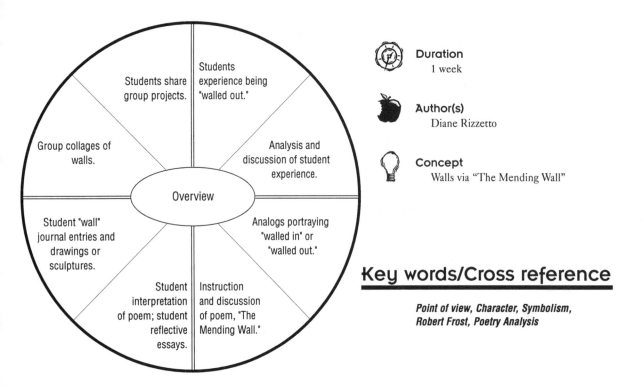

Students share group projects.

Students experience being "walled out."

Group collages of walls.

Analysis and discussion of student experience.

Overview

Student "wall" journal entries and drawings or sculptures.

Analogs portraying "walled in" or "walled out."

Student interpretation of poem; student reflective essays.

Instruction and discussion of poem, "The Mending Wall."

Duration
1 week

Author(s)
Diane Rizzetto

Concept
Walls via "The Mending Wall"

Key words/Cross reference

Point of view, Character, Symbolism, Robert Frost, Poetry Analysis

Overview

Objective
Students will use the concept of feeling "walled-in and walled-out" to explicate the poem, *The Mending Wall.*"

About the Author
Diane Rizzetto is an educational consultant who has been involved in education for over twenty years. She previously was chair of the English Department at Head-Royce School, in Oakland, CA, where she currently resides.

Required Resources
Cookies for some of the class; illustrations (ideally slides) of New England countryside

Bibliography
"Symbol Builder: Robert Frost" American Literature Survey: Course Outline. Villa Maria, PA: Center for Learning, 1979.

Poetry - Mending Wall

Quadrant 1—Experience

 ### Right Mode—Connect

Students experience being "walled out."

Objective

To create an experience or feeling of being "closed out" or "closed in."

Activity

Teacher divides class into 4 groups, approximately 4 students per group. Distribute cookies to students in the following ways:

"Group One—because you are near the board, you may each have one cookie."

"Group Two—because you are near the door, you may each split one cookie."

"Group Three—because you are in the middle of the room, you may have one cookie for your whole group." Group Four is ignored by the teacher.

For about five minutes, teacher simply shows pictures and talks about the New England landscape, with a focus on how hilly, wooded, and full of rocks it is, and on the piled stone walls which keep cows in. Winter scatters the stones; each spring, farmers must rebuild the stone walls.

Author's Notes

This activity is taken from the text, American Literature Survey: Course Outline.

Assessment

Curiosity of students, particularly those in Group Four who received no cookies.

 ### Left Mode—Examine

Analysis and discussion of student experience.

Objective

To analyze the experience.

Activity

Teacher leads class discussion with a focus on how students felt when they did or did not receive the cookies. Hopefully responses will include mention of feeling "closed out" or "closed in." Teacher charts responses on board. Have students had similar real-life experiences where they felt this way?

Assessment

Quality of discussion and relevance of student contributions.

Quadrant 2—Concepts

 ### Right Mode—Image

Analogs portraying "walled in" or "walled out."

Objective

To clarify and deepen the idea of "fencing" or "walling."

Activity

Each group creates a visual analog portraying the feeling of being walled in or walled out.

Assessment

Teacher observation of group social skills; depth and quality of analogs.

 ### Left Mode—Define

Instruction and discussion of poem, "The Mending Wall."

Objective

To read and analyze the poem, *"The Mending Wall,"* by Robert Frost.

Activity

Teacher and students read the poem together. Discuss the elements of the poem such as point of view, character, symbolism.

Assessment

Teacher checking for student understanding of poem and poetic elements.

Quadrant 3—Applications

 ## Left Mode—Try

Student interpretation of poem; student reflective essays.

Objective

To further develop student ability to analyze a poem.

Activity

1. One half of the class responds as the narrator: "The fence is used to..." copying from the text lines to complete the statement. The other half of the class responds as the neighbor in the same way. Students share their interpretations with each other, as teacher charts collective responses.
2. Students individually write paragraph essays responding to the questions, "What wall, other than the physical one, exists between the narrator and the neighbor?" and "Why do people create walls?" Give examples.

Assessment

Quality of student analysis of poem and depth of paragraph essays.

 ## Right Mode—Extend

Student "wall" journal entries and drawings or sculptures.

Objective

To apply what has been learned.

Activity

Students will keep wall journals for a week from which creative writing assignments will be generated. They will create individual wall drawings or sculptures with expressions of what they wall in or out.

Assessment

Quality of journal writing and accompanying illustrations or sculptures.

Quadrant 4—Creations

 ## Left Mode—Refine

Group collages of walls.

Objective

To extend what has been learned.

Activity

Given the question: "Do good fences make good neighbors?", in cooperative groups students will create collages of pictures and magazine or newspaper articles which are examples of real or symbolic walls. Each group develops a statement in response to the question to accompany its collage.

Assessment

Ability to work together and individual contributions to the group effort.

 ## Right Mode—Integrate

Students share group projects.

Objective

To share what has been learned. To further express feelings.

Activity

Student groups share final projects with rest of class either orally, in dramatic form, or as an art form.

Assessment

Quality of student efforts, written and/or oral presentations.

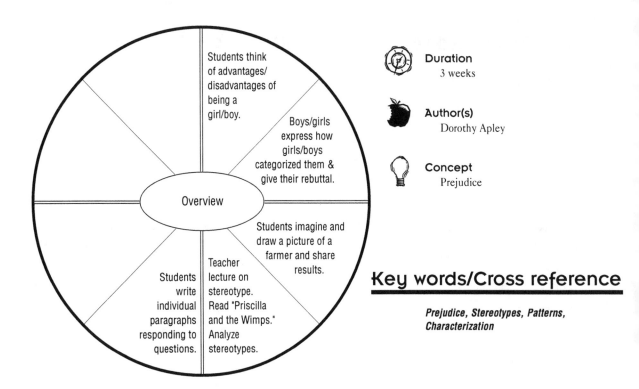

Overview

Students think of advantages/disadvantages of being a girl/boy.

Boys/girls express how girls/boys categorized them & give their rebuttal.

Students imagine and draw a picture of a farmer and share results.

Teacher lecture on stereotype. Read "Priscilla and the Wimps." Analyze stereotypes.

Students write individual paragraphs responding to questions.

Duration
3 weeks

Author(s)
Dorothy Apley

Concept
Prejudice

Key words/Cross reference

Prejudice, Stereotypes, Patterns, Characterization

Overview

Objective
To connect students to the concept of Stereotypes and how it affects us in our lives and viewpoints of others.

About the Author
Dorothy Apley teaches English at Geneva High School, Geneva, NE.

Required Resources
Story, *"Priscilla and the Wimps"*

Quadrant 1—Experience

 ## Right Mode—Connect

Students think of advantages/ disadvantages of being a girl/boy.

Objective

To connect students with their own experiences with stereotype.

Activity

Only girls can talk. Think one minute of advantages of being a boy, and of disadvantages of being a boy. Brainstorm, writing answers on the board. Then girls cannot talk while boys think of advantages of being a girl, and disadvantages of being a girl. Brainstorm, writing answers on the board.

Assessment

Quality of student participation and involvement.

 ## Left Mode—Examine

Boys/girls express how girls/boys categorized them & give their rebuttal.

Objective

To analyze the experience.

Activity

Teacher leads class discussion. Boys are allowed to express how the girls have categorized them and give their rebuttal, agreeing or disagreeing. Girls are then allowed to express how the boys have categorized them and give their rebuttal.

Assessment

Quality of discussion and relevance of students' contribution.

Quadrant 2—Concepts

 ## Right Mode—Image

Students imagine and draw a picture of a farmer and share results.

Objective

To deepen understanding of categorizing groups.

Activity

Students are asked to imagine a picture of a farmer, including his clothes, home, vehicle, etc. Students draw a picture and share results, noting similarities in their concept of a farm—white wooden house, overalls, etc.

Assessment

Quality of students participation and sharing and noting similarities in their pictures.

 ## Left Mode—Define

Teacher lecture on stereotype. Read "Priscilla and the Wimps."
Analyze stereotypes.

Objective

To read and analyze the short story, *"Priscilla and the Wimps."* To develop student knowledge of stereotype.

Activity

Teacher lecture on stereotype (over simplified opinion that ignores individuality and puts people into categories). Read *"Priscilla and the Wimps."* Analyze stereotypes in story.

Assessment

Student note-taking and teacher checking for understanding.

Stereotypes (1 of 2)

Quadrant 3—Applications

 ### Left Mode—Try

Students write individual paragraphs responding to questions.

Objective
To further student ability to understand how we stereotype.

Activity
Students write individual paragraphs, responding to the questions, "Who was stereotyped in *"Priscilla and the Wimps?"* and "What stereotypes have you encountered in your own life?" and "Why do you think people stereotype others?" Be sure to give specific examples.

Assessment
On task student behavior in writing and depth of paragraphs.
This will spiral into the concept of prejudice and *Roll of Thunder Hear My Cry*.

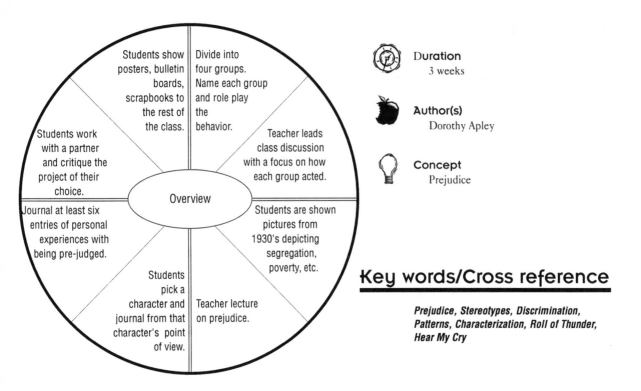

Overview

- Students show posters, bulletin boards, scrapbooks to the rest of the class.
- Divide into four groups. Name each group and role play the behavior.
- Students work with a partner and critique the project of their choice.
- Teacher leads class discussion with a focus on how each group acted.
- Journal at least six entries of personal experiences with being pre-judged.
- Students are shown pictures from 1930's depicting segregation, poverty, etc.
- Students pick a character and journal from that character's point of view.
- Teacher lecture on prejudice.

Duration
3 weeks

Author(s)
Dorothy Apley

Concept
Prejudice

Key words/Cross reference

Prejudice, Stereotypes, Discrimination, Patterns, Characterization, Roll of Thunder, Hear My Cry

Overview

Objective
To connect students to the concept of Stereotypes and how it affects us in our lives and viewpoints of others.

About the Author
Dorothy Apley teaches English at Geneva High School, Geneva, NE.

Required Resources
Student text, *Roll of Thunder Hear My Cry*

Quadrant 1—Experience

 ### Right Mode—Connect

Divide into four groups. Name each group and role play the behavior.

Objective
To create an experience of categorizing groups.

Activity
Divide into four groups. Name each group one of the following: Snakes, The Underworlds, The Hills, and The Kings. Each group will role play the behavior, dialogue, and describe the dress or other distinguishing features that they think members of a group with this name would display.

Assessment
Involvement of the students in the experience.

 ### Left Mode—Examine

Teacher leads class discussion with a focus on how each group acted.

Objective
To analyze the experience.

Activity
Teacher leads class discussion with a focus on how each group acted according to its name. Two names give us a good connotation. Two names give a bad connotation. Students share what they judged the other groups would act like just by knowing the name of the groups. Which group would they like to be a member of and why.

Assessment
Quality of student contributions.

Quadrant 2—Concepts

 ### Right Mode—Image

Students are shown pictures from 1930's depicting segregation, poverty, etc.

Objective
To clarify and deepen the meaning of being judged according to what group you are in.

Activity
While listening to song, "Roll of Thunder, Hear My Cry," students are shown pictures from 1930's depicting segregation, poverty, etc.

Assessment
Students' contributions to discussion.

 ### Left Mode—Define

Teacher lecture on prejudice.

Objective
To understand concepts of prejudice and discrimination and read and analyze the book, *Roll of Thunder Hear My Cry.*

Activity
Teacher lecture on prejudice. (Stereotyping leads us to pre-judge a person before we really know him or her. When we act on prejudice, it is discrimination.) Students read the book *Roll of Thunder Hear My Cry,* noting examples of prejudice against the Logan family.

Assessment
Student note-taking and involvement in discussion.

Quadrant 3—Applications

Left Mode—Try

Students pick a character and journal from that character's point of view.

Objective
To deepen students' understanding of the content and concepts in the book.

Activity
Students pick a character and journal from that character's point of view. Students develop the character, describing his/her outside and inside characteristics and reactions to events in the novel. Students create similes such as the following: T.J. is like an alley cat. Each student writes an extended metaphor about the character of his/her choice.

Assessment
Quality of students writing and contributions to the class discussion.

Right Mode—Extend

Journal at least six entries of personal experiences with being pre-judged.

Objective
Refocus on concept of prejudice.

Activity
1) Journal at least six entries of personal experiences with being pre-judged. Start with the leading, "I pre-judged someone when . . . or I was pre-judged when . . .".
2) Research individuals who fought prejudice and write an essay describing this individual and how he/she fought discrimination.
3) Create a scrapbook of news articles that contain examples of prejudice or articles that describe situations in which discrimination is being fought. The student must write what the article is about and who or what is being discriminated against.
4) Create a bulletin board or poster depicting prejudice or write song lyrics from the points of view of one of the characters in the book.

Assessment
Quality of student work.

Quadrant 4—Creations

Left Mode—Refine

Students work with a partner and critique the project of their choice.

Objective
To extend what has been learned.

Activity
Students work with a partner and critique the project of their choice. Partners then select a living example of an adult who has been pre-judged or discriminated against. This person must be interviewed, analyzing how, when, where, and why he/she was pre-judged or discriminated against.

Assessment
Student contribution in peer critiquing and depth of interview.

Right Mode—Integrate

Students show posters, bulletin boards, scrapbooks to the rest of the class.

Objective
To share what has been learned.

Activity
Students show posters or bulletin boards, scrapbooks or read essays or journal entries to the rest of the class. Students also share what they found the most interesting about the individual whom they interviewed.

Assessment
Quality of student efforts, written and/or oral presentations.

Timelessness of Theater

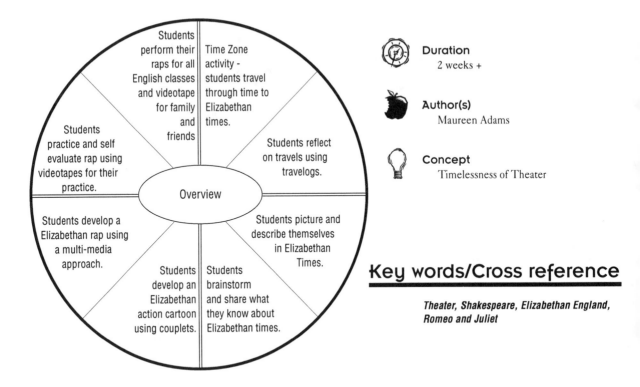

Students perform their raps for all English classes and videotape for family and friends

Time Zone activity - students travel through time to Elizabethan times.

Students reflect on travels using travelogs.

Students practice and self evaluate rap using videotapes for their practice.

Overview

Students develop a Elizabethan rap using a multi-media approach.

Students picture and describe themselves in Elizabethan Times.

Students develop an Elizabethan action cartoon using couplets.

Students brainstorm and share what they know about Elizabethan times.

Duration
2 weeks +

Author(s)
Maureen Adams

Concept
Timelessness of Theater

Key words/Cross reference

Theater, Shakespeare, Elizabethan England, Romeo and Juliet

Overview

Objective
To reinforce the timelessness of theater through an introductory exploration of Shakespeare and his world.

About the Author
Maureen Adams is a Teacher Development Consultant for Killeen Independent School District in Killeen, TX.

Required Resources:
Science Fiction Music (*2001, Star Trek, Star Wars,* etc.).
Renaissance Music (harp, flute or Celtic music are examples).
Stage Lights/Strobe (optional but desired).
Travel Log (teacher-constructed journal for students to use to record/draw reflections).
Bard of Avon (book by Stanley/Vennemea - in print, can be ordered by any bookstore).
Shakespeare's Insults - Wayne S. Hill (in print, can be ordered by bookstore).

Elizabeth and Essex (film 1939 - check your local Blockbuster).
Society For Creative Anachronism or actors from community theater or local college. Janet Mendenhall (817) 526-7310 - Brian Vega (817) 698-1474. These people will help find your local chapter of SCA plus they helped me with quadrant one and are a literal warehouse of info. Well worth the phone call.
Romeo and Juliet Rap (tape) - Teacher's Discovery, TVE Division, 1100 Owendale, Suite G, Troy, MI 48007.
Resource People: Campus Technologist/Campus Librarian, Campus band or choir director.

Bibliography
Books for Kids:
Garfield, Leon. *Shakespeare Stories* (NY: Schocken Books, 1985).
Haines, Charles. *William Shakespeare and His Plays* (NY: Franklin Watts, 1968).

Hodges, C. Walter. *Shakespeare's Theatre* (NY: Coward/McCann Inc., 1964).

Stewart, Philippa. *Shakespeare and His Theatre* (Wayland Pub., 1973).

Society For Creative Anachronism: The Known World Handbook (Nationwide Printing).

Books for Teachers:

Byson, Bill. *The Mother Tongue: English and How It Got That Way* (NY: William Morrow, 1990).

Fido, Martin. *Shakespeare* (NY: Peter Bedrick Books, 1985).

Folger Shakespeare Library, Volunteer Decents: Shakespeare For The Young.

Fraser, Russell. *Young Shakespeare* (NY: Columbia University Press, 1988).

Rowse, A.L. *Shakespeare the Man* (NY: Harper & Row, 1973).

Schoenbaums. *William Shakespeare: The Globe and The World* (NY: Folger Shakespeare Library, 1979).

Quadrant 1—Experience

 ## Right Mode—Connect

Time Zone activity - students travel through time to Elizabethan times.

Objective
To connect and pique student's interest in Elizabethan Times.

Activity
Students enter a time zone (your room—strobe lights if possible). Play sci-fi music if possible—*2001. A Space Odyssey* or *Star Wars* theme music as you take students back to Elizabethan Times. Music should gradually fade from sci-fi to Elizabethan Music as you reveal an Elizabethan setting with members of the Society for Creative Anachronism in full garb with props and weapons. They unfreeze from their position and launch into a sword fight followed by a discussion of life in Elizabethan Times, allowing time for questions by the students. If members of Society for Creative Anachronism are not available, contact local community theaters, college or high school theater groups for talent or costumes.

Assessment
Questions and discussion are invited and encouraged.

 ## Left Mode—Examine

Students reflect on travels using travelogs.

Objective
To give students the opportunity to reflect and image their time travel experience.

Activity
Students are given a travel log in which to draw or comment on their thoughts and observations about their time travel adventure. Students are invited to share their discoveries.

Assessment
Travel log entries.

Quadrant 2—Concepts

Right Mode—Image

Students picture and describe themselves in Elizabethan Times.

Objective

To extend the experience of the time travel into their own personal experience.

Activity

Play Elizabethan Music and then show a clip from the 1939 movie, *"Elizabeth and Essex"* starring Bette Davis and Errol Flynn. Now have students imagine themselves in Elizabethan Times. Then have them draw a picture of themselves and write what a typical day would be like for them in Elizabethan Times. (Provide fru-fru of all sorts for drawings.) Teacher does a picture to share also. Students and teacher share pictures and writing.

Assessment

Students reflect in their travel log while teacher reads from *Bard of Avon*.

Left Mode—Define

Students brainstorm and share what they know about Elizabethan Times.

Objective

To define specific knowledge gained and challenge students to use this knowledge.

Activity

Play Elizabethan Music. Divide students into groups. Have students brainstorm everything they know about Elizabethan Times to include William Shakespeare. Students share their insight and information gained. Use groups for this activity. Teacher then reads from *Bard of Avon* and *Romeo and Juliet* to show the language of Elizabethan Times as compared to modern times.

Assessment

Students reflect in travel logs. Teacher dismisses class using a Shakespearean couplet: "Take thy faces hence."

Quadrant 3—Applications

Left Mode—Try

Students develop an Elizabethan action cartoon using couplets.

Objective

To try a new experience using knowledge gained.

Activity

Play Elizabethan Music. Read excerpts from *Romeo and Juliet*. Give students appropriate selections of couplets to read to each other (from *Romeo and Juliet*). Divide students into groups. Give each group a few couplets to transform into an Elizabethan Action Cartoon. Use chart paper and markers. Groups post and share their toons. Teacher points out the rhythm of the couplets and challenges students to re-read their toons while the rhythm is tapped out.

Assessment

Toons that are created and reflections in travel logs.

Right Mode—Extend

Students develop an Elizabethan rap using a multi-media approach.

Objective

To extend the student' experience so it truly becomes their own.

Activity

Review life in Elizabethan Times–focus on language using the book *Shakespeare Insults*. Revisit couplets and extend discussion to modern day rap and how rap is similar to the language of Shakespeare in terms of rhythm and using the language of the common man. Play *Romeo and Juliet* rap and have students tap out rhythms as they did for the couplets. Now divide students into groups and challenge them to create a rap of their own depicting a day in the life of Shakespeare. They may use couplets for their rap if they wish. Provide percussion instruments so students can choose to be a writer, musician or performer.

Assessment

Reflect in travel logs and raps.

Timelessness of Theater

Quadrant 4—Creations

 ### Left Mode—Refine

Students practice and self-evaluate rap using videotapes for their practice.

Objective
To refine and evaluate students' work (rehearse-practice-videotape).

Activity
Students practice their raps for each other. Group input and self-evaluations. Groups now choreograph movement for their raps. Videotape for self-evaluation.

Assessment
Videotape and reflect in travel log.

 ## Right Mode—Integrate

Students perform their raps for all English classes and videotape for family and friends.

Objective
To integrate, to share, and to celebrate student's work with peers and community.

Activity
Students publish and perform their raps for all English classes. A final videotape is made so students can share with family and friends outside of school.

Assessment
Students hand in travel logs and return via music to the 20th century.

Where the Red Fern Grows

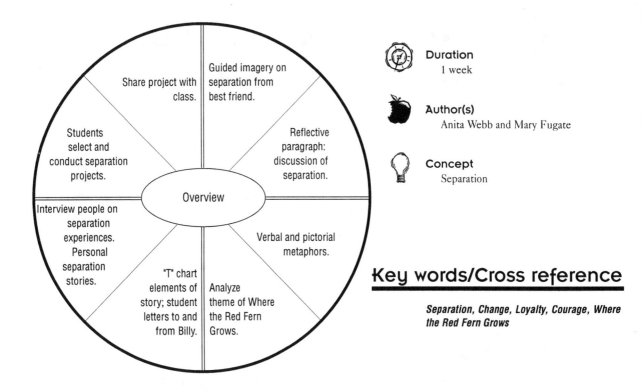

- Guided imagery on separation from best friend.
- Reflective paragraph: discussion of separation.
- Verbal and pictorial metaphors.
- Analyze theme of Where the Red Fern Grows.
- "T" chart elements of story; student letters to and from Billy.
- Interview people on separation experiences. Personal separation stories.
- Students select and conduct separation projects.
- Share project with class.

Overview

Duration
1 week

Author(s)
Anita Webb and Mary Fugate

Concept
Separation

Key words/Cross reference

Separation, Change, Loyalty, Courage, Where the Red Fern Grows

Overview

Objective
Students use the concept of Separation to read and understand the book, *Where the Red Fern Grows*.

About the Authors:
At the time this plan was first published, Mary Fugate was Principal of Trailridge Middle School, Shawnee Mission School District, Lenexa, KS. In addition she has nineteen years experience as an elementary principal, elementary classroom teacher, and math resource teacher.

Anita Webb taught English at Trailridge Middle School. She also has more than an additional twenty-five years classroom teaching experience at the elementary level.

Mary and Anita are both certified 4MAT System Trainers for their school district.

Bibliography
Rawls, Wilson. *Where the Red Fern Grows*. Published in Prentice Hall Literature. Englewood Cliffs, NJ: Prentice Hall, 1989.

Quadrant 1—Experience

Right Mode—Connect

Guided imagery on separation from best friend.

Objective

To connect students to the experiences of separation in their own lives and the changes that separation brings.

Activity

Teacher conducts guided imagery. Students imagine their best friend is moving away: 3000 miles away. They may never see each other again. They recall memories of their times together. How do their lives change with their friend now gone? Students are encouraged to add images of their own to the teacher's guided experience.

Assessment

Involvement of students in the experience and their contributions to it.

Left Mode—Examine

Reflective paragraph: discussion of separation.

Objective

To analyze the experience of separation.

Activity

Students write a reflective paragraph expressing their feelings when separation occurs. They are encouraged to share their paragraphs with the class in discussion. Teacher extends discussion of separation to elicit other examples from students' lives: divorce, death of a loved one (even a pet), moving from elementary school to middle school, examples from current events. Teacher introduces the book, *Where the Red Fern Grows,* and the theme of separation which runs throughout the story. Focus is on the bond that forms in relationships.

Assessment

Quality of discussion and relevance of student contributions.

Quadrant 2—Concepts

Right Mode—Image

Verbal and pictorial metaphors.

Objective

To clarify and deepen the concepts which run through the story.

Activity

In cooperative learning groups, students create verbal and pictorial metaphors:
"Separation is..."
"Loyalty is..."
"Trust is..."
Each group member contributes individually; the group creates a chart to include all contributions for display to the rest of the class.

Assessment

Teacher observation of group social skills; depth and quality of metaphors.

Left Mode—Define

Analyze theme of Where the Red Fern Grows.

Objective

To analyze the book for theme; to cite examples of separation and how Billy deals with the death of Old Dan.

Activity

Students read *Where the Red Fern Grows.* Review the details of the bond between Billy and his dogs. Elicit from students examples of separation in other stories. Small group discussion: Does character influence how different individuals accept/process feelings brought about by separation? Students list Billy's thoughts and actions when Old Dan dies.

Assessment

Small group contributions to large group. Teacher checking for student understanding of novel.

Quadrant 3—Applications

 ## Left Mode—Try

"T" chart elements of story; student letters to and from Billy.

Objective
To further explore the aspect of separation as a form of change.

Activity
1. Whole group lists adjustments people make when separation (change) occurs.
2. In cooperative learning groups, students create a "T" chart: on right side cite changes Billy made to accept the dogs into his life; on the left side changes when they died. Share "T" charts with whole class.
3. Students discuss how adjustments help them cope and continue with healthy lives when change/separation occurs. Share with whole group.
4. Students will each write a letter to Billy concerning the death of his dogs, and another letter from Billy to them.

Assessment
Quality of "T" charts and letters to/from Billy; contribution to whole group.

 ## Right Mode—Extend

Interview people on separation experiences. Personal separation stories.

Objective
Refocus on aspects of separation.

Activity
1. Students will identify one person to interview for personal experiences with separation. They must identify their subject; make an appointment; prepare appropriate questions, including a focus on coping strategies and necessary adjustments.
2. Students will write a personal separation story of their own giving examples from their own lives of how the betrayal of loyalty and trust is a form of separation. A final paper will be prepared comparing their own experiences with those of their interviewee.

Students will choose one project to be done alone or with a team:
1. Select a scene from the novel dealing with separation that would be appropriate for dramatic presentation. Prepare dialogue and practice for sharing with the class.
2. Role play separation and the changes it causes. Portray adjustments which lead to a level of comfort.
3. Create an illustration or collage of separations, adjustment, comfort.
4. Write a paper reacting to T.S. Eliot's statement, "To make an end is to make a beginning."

Assessment
Quality of reflective writing. Quality of project plans.

Quadrant 4—Creations

 ## Left Mode—Refine

Students select and conduct separation projects.

Objective
To extend what has been learned.

Activity
Working alone and in peer groups, students will critique, edit and refine first drafts of projects. Teacher will provide guidance as final drafts are created.

Assessment
On-task behavior of students; quality of project plans and revisions.

 ## Right Mode—Integrate

Share project with class.

Objective
To share what has been learned. To further express feelings.

Activity
Students share final projects with rest of class.

Assessment
Quality of student efforts, written and/or oral presentations.

Concert Band

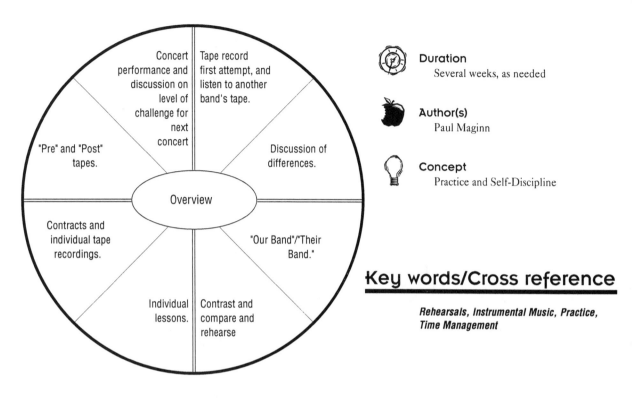

Overview

Concert performance and discussion on level of challenge for next concert

Tape record first attempt, and listen to another band's tape.

"Pre" and "Post" tapes.

Discussion of differences.

Contracts and individual tape recordings.

"Our Band"/"Their Band."

Individual lessons.

Contrast and compare and rehearse

Duration
Several weeks, as needed

Author(s)
Paul Maginn

Concept
Practice and Self-Discipline

Key words/Cross reference

Rehearsals, Instrumental Music, Practice, Time Management

Overview

Objective
Students will learn the importance of regular, disciplined, independent practice for optimal group performance.

About the Author
At the time this plan was written, Paul Maginn was an instrumental music teacher in the Webster Central School District, Webster, NY.

Required Resources
Cassette recorder/player for taping band practice sessions.

Bibliography
Band piece used:
Chattaway, Jay, *"Captain Video."* William Allen Music, Inc. Marlow Heights, Maryland 20748.

Concert Band

Quadrant 1—Experience

 ### Right Mode—Connect

Tape record first attempt, and listen to another band's tape.

Objective

Students will develop a deeper awareness of the need for more practice at home on their instruments.

Activity

On the first day of band, the teacher will place a tape recorder in front of the class with the speakers facing the students. Hand them copies of a medium/hard piece of music with which they are unfamiliar: an energetic piece. The band will do a quick warm-up. The teacher will then have the band play the unfamiliar piece from beginning to end, while s/he tapes the attempt. The students will then listen to themselves on tape. Next they will hear the tape of another middle school band playing the same piece well.

Assessment

Quality of student participation.

 ### Left Mode—Examine

Discussion of differences.

Objective

Students become aware of how to contrast two different renditions of the same piece for polish and professionalism.

Activity

The teacher will conduct a class discussion covering the following topics: The good characteristics of each tape (they must identify what they did do well); the students' general feelings as they listened to the two bands; the potential of middle school students for playing an instrument, and what it takes to play well.

Assessment

Quality of the discussion and conclusions reached.

Quadrant 2—Concepts

 ### Right Mode—Image

"Our Band"/"Their Band."

Objective

To integrate personal listening with analysis and conceptual development.

Activity

Using the chalkboard, the teacher makes two columns: one is headed "Our Band," the other is headed, "Their Band." The students will analyze the tapes using the following procedure:

1. Determine differences in the two bands in specific sections of the music.
2. Indicate dynamic changes, rhythmic differences, and basic texture variations.
3. Analyze the intent of the composer in each section of the piece.
4. Using the piece as an example, the teacher will make sure the students comprehend note values and their dynamics.

Assessment

The students will rehearse the piece in sections demonstrating improvement, comprehension of note values, and the dynamics.

 ### Left Mode—Define

Contrast and compare and rehearse.

Objective

To integrate personal listening with analysis and conceptual development.

Activity

Continuation of activities begun in Quadrant Two Right Mode.

Note:

The method used by Mr. Maginn in this quadrant is whole brained, a simultaneous right/left approach. This combination seems to work very well in this lesson.

Assessment

The students will continue to rehearse the piece in sections demonstrating improvement, comprehension of note values, and the dynamics. Teacher gives written quiz covering these topics taught.

Concert Band

Quadrant 3—Applications

 ### Left Mode—Try

Individual lessons.

Objective

Students master the music in the correct style with proper dynamics and rhythm.

Activity

During the week's lessons, the teacher coaches the students in groups of four and five.

Assessment

Student progress and eagerness during lessons.

 ### Right Mode—Extend

Contracts and individual tape recordings.

Objective

Students learn to manage their practice time. Students experience their own individual improvement over time.

Activity

Students will contract daily practice time with the teacher.

Students will be required to tape record their playing at home at the beginning of their practice, and retape at the end of their time. Teacher will give input as to improvement, and ask students to comment on the same.

Assessment

Commitment to practice contracts and personal improvement.

Quadrant 4—Creations

 ### Left Mode—Refine

"Pre" and "Post" tapes.

Objective

Students will again analyze the progress the entire band has made in mastering the piece.

Activity

The teacher will once again record the band playing the entire piece. Students will then listen to the "pre" and the "post" tapes. Students will analyze the band's improvement. The teacher will emphasize the obvious connection between individual improvement and the entire band's improvement.

Assessment

Quality of final tape and student contribution to discussion and analysis.

 ### Right Mode—Integrate

Concert performance and discussion on level of challenge for next concert

Objective

Students experience the presentation of their music in a concert setting. Students plan their next concert based on their expertise.

Activity

The students will present their band in concert. (This presentation could also be recorded.) And the students will discuss the level of challenge they feel they can handle for their next concert.

Assessment

The concert performance and the level of challenge the students choose.

Art Preservation

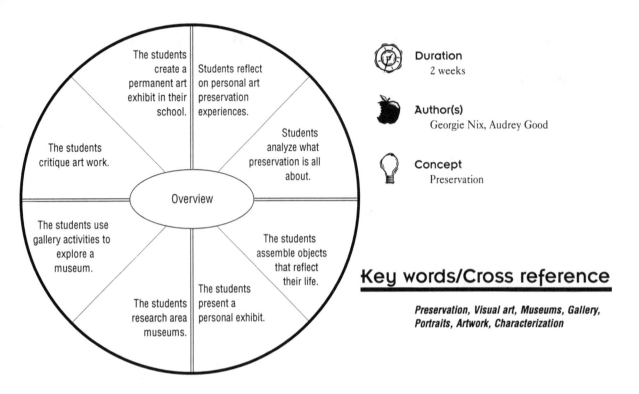

The students create a permanent art exhibit in their school.

Students reflect on personal art preservation experiences.

The students critique art work.

Students analyze what preservation is all about.

Overview

The students use gallery activities to explore a museum.

The students assemble objects that reflect their life.

The students research area museums.

The students present a personal exhibit.

Duration
2 weeks

Author(s)
Georgie Nix, Audrey Good

Concept
Preservation

Key words/Cross reference

Preservation, Visual art, Museums, Gallery, Portraits, Artwork, Characterization

Overview

 Objective
Students will explore the importance of preservation in a society.

 About the Authors
Georgie Nix and Audrey Good have taught Visual Arts and Performing Arts at Franklin Regional Junior High in Murrysville, Pennsylvania for more years than they would like to admit.

 Required Resources
Prints of famous artworks, telephone books, local newspapers, local museums, unglazed ceramic tiles, underglazes, brushes.

 Bibliography
Art and Man magazines.

Art Preservation

Quadrant 1—Experience

 ### Right Mode—Connect

Students reflect on personal art preservation experiences.

Objective
Working as a large group, the students will discuss the whys and ways they have experienced art preservation.

Activity
In preparation for this class, students will be invited to bring examples of their own elementary school artwork or projects that have been saved.
The students will:
1. Look at examples of elementary artwork.
2. Discuss the ways we save early art efforts (refrigerator art).
3. Discuss how art teachers display artwork.
4. Try to remember any elementary art experiences that they are particularly fond of.
5. Discuss why their individual art pieces have been saved and preserved.

Assessment
Engage students in remembering their early art efforts and their experience with art preservation.

 ### Left Mode—Examine

Students analyze what preservation is all about.

Objective
Working in small groups, the students will brainstorm about the concept of preservation.

Activity
The students will use paper charts to analyze:
1. Why people save.
2. What people save.
3. Where people save.
4. How people save.
5. When people save.

Assessment
A student spokesperson from each group will present information from their chart to the class.

Quadrant 2—Concepts

 ### Right Mode—Image

The students assemble objects that reflect their life.

Objective
As an introductory activity to assembling a personal exhibit, the teacher will give a presentation on an exhibit of personal items that reflects his/her life.

Activity
Learning to assemble and present a collection, the students will:
1. View a presentation by the teacher, and
2. As a homework assignment, assemble a museum collection from objects in their lives. The students will chose eight of their personal objects that show something about our culture, their lifestyle or a particular interest. The students will be asked to explain the tales their treasures tell about them.

Assessment
Quality of student collections.

 ### Left Mode—Define

The students present a personal exhibit.

Objective
The students will set up a display of their exhibit. As in museum collections, the students will create cards that give specific information about their objects.

Activity
The teacher will give individual instruction to the students as they:
1. Write a group heading card that titles their collection.
2. Write a group label card that explains the intent of their collection.
3. Write individual label cards that give the specific information about each object in their collection.

Assessment
Each student will assume the role of a museum critic. They will select one of the student collections and write a review about it.

Quadrant 3—Applications

 ## Left Mode—Try

The students research area museums.

Objective

The student will research the specifics of the different types of museums in the local area.

Activity

Working in small groups, the students will use phone books to research:
1. The names and types of local museums.
2. The location, hours and admissions fees of area museums.
3. The titles of people responsible for preserving museum work.
4. What each museum is responsible for.

Assessment

Each group will complete a form that records their research findings.

 ## Right Mode—Extend

The students use gallery activities to explore a museum.

Objective

The students will use a variety of gallery activities as they explore a local museum.

Activity

During a field trip to a local museum, students will work individually or with a partner to complete the following gallery activities:
1. A Scavenger Hunt—Go "in search of" specific objects located in the exhibit.
2. Portrait Personality—Draw a sketch of one of the portraits shown in the gallery and then write an invented biography about the subject.
3. Taking A Closer Look—Draw an enlarged portion of a part of a painting, then exchange their drawing with their partner and try to find the original painting in the gallery.

Assessment

Students on-task behavior in gallery activities.

Quadrant 4—Creations

 ## Left Mode—Refine

The students critique artwork.

Objective

The students' will critique an exhibit.

Activity

Using a "gallery" of art prints, the students will be asked to indicate their feelings about each work by placing a series of tokens in front of each print. The tokens express:
1. I like it
2. I hate it
3. The best in show.
4. The hardest to make
5. The best idea
6. I want to take it home

Assessment

The students' willingness to analyze and reflect on the artwork in an exhibit.

 ## Right Mode—Integrate

The students create a permanent art exhibit in their school.

Objective

The students will make art a permanent part of their school.

Activity

1. Using graph paper, students will draw a 5"x5" geometric design.
2. Students will color their designs using colored pencils.
3. Students will transfer their designs to an unglazed ceramic tile.
4. Using underglazes, the students will fill in each color of their design.
5. Ceramic tiles will be fired in a kiln.
6. Completed tiles will be installed in the school.

Assessment

The students will create a ceramic tile to be installed in the school as part of a ceramic quilt.

Self-Expression

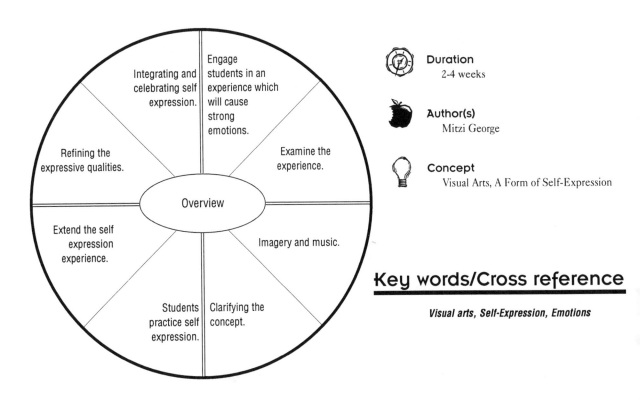

Integrating and celebrating self expression.

Engage students in an experience which will cause strong emotions.

Refining the expressive qualities.

Examine the experience.

Overview

Extend the self expression experience.

Imagery and music.

Students practice self expression.

Clarifying the concept.

 Duration
2-4 weeks

Author(s)
Mitzi George

 Concept
Visual Arts, A Form of Self-Expression

Key words/Cross reference

Visual arts, Self-Expression, Emotions

Overview

Objective
The student will identify, clarify, and illustrate the concept of self-expression through the visual arts.

About the Author
Mitzi George is a middle school art teacher in Lake Charles, LA. She works for the Calcasieu Parish School System. Ms. George has twelve years of teaching experience on all levels of the educational spectrum.

 Required Resources
Tape player, musical tapes, slides or pictures of reproductions from various artists, old magazines, newspapers, scissors, glue, paint, brushes, etc.

Self-Expression

Quadrant 1—Experience

 ## Right Mode—Connect

Engage students in an experience which will cause strong emotions.
Creating the mood.

Objective

The student will identify the need for self-expression and role play an incident which will engage them into the thought process of self expression.

Activity

Create an incident which will cause strong reaction in the students. Discuss the feelings experienced. Small groups develop a role play identifying the issue and feelings experienced. Play music in background. Share skits.

Assessment

Student participation in small groups and overall class.

 ## Left Mode—Examine

Examine the experience.
Examining the issue and responses.

Objective

The students will list and discuss the issues which arise from the skits. The students will also reflect on and identify their own personal feelings toward the issue.

Activity

Have class list issues which arose from skits. Discuss how the students perceived the issue, how they felt during the experience, what caused the issue to be an issue. Have students identify the issue with a color. On newsprint, have them write the responses.

Assessment

Student participation.

Quadrant 2—Concepts

 ## Right Mode—Image

Imagery and music.

Objective

The students will identify emotional responses to musical rhythms and sounds. The student will illustrate their responses.

Activity

Play a tape of instrumental music. Ask students to listen with their eyes closed for one minute and identify emotions which correlate with the music. Give each student a sheet of large paper, paint, and brush. Have students respond to the music using paint and brush, changing brush strokes, line, shape, pattern, and color as the music's mood changes.

Assessment

Student work.

 ## Left Mode—Define

Clarifying the concept.

Objective

The student will identify, define, and discuss the concept of visual expression.

Activity

Lecture on the artist as historical recorder, social critic, or prophet. Show examples of work from artists such as Picasso, Jose Clemente Orozco, Chagall, Kollowitz, etc. Discuss the ways these artists used their mediums to express anger, social injustices, fear, etc.

Assessment

Quiz.

Quadrant 3—Applications

 ### Left Mode—Try

Students practice self-expression.

Objective

The student will brainstorm issues which are of concern to them. The student will select one issue and develop a thematic collage to express that issue.

Activity

Have students brainstorm issues which they feel strongly about. Have them identify the issue and emotion with a color theme. Then ask them to identify some images which will convey the message. Have them illustrate their work in the form of a collage using magazines, newspapers, found objects, etc. Play music as students work.

Assessment

Student work.

 ### Right Mode—Extend

Extend the self-expression experience.

Objective

The student will illustrate visually a social comment.

Activity

Have the student take the same issue and extend their concept into a social commentary. Ask the student to develop an original drawing, painting, or sculpture using their emotional response and message.

Assessment

Student work.

Quadrant 4—Creations

 ### Left Mode—Refine

Refining the expressive qualities.

Objective

The students will evaluate and describe the quality of work done.

Activity

Have students share their work in class. Ask each member of the class to choose a piece they like and write a description, including the message they received from it. Then have the students share responses with the artist. Have each student take their own piece and do a critique deciding if anything needs to be reworked. Allow them time to rework.

Assessment

Written work and self-critiques.

 ### Right Mode—Integrate

Integrating and celebrating self-expression.

Objective

The students will incorporate their work into a final show to be viewed by the public.

Activity

Have students arrange an art show of their work: The students design a title and logo, invitations, the space to be displayed. Arrange the mailing list and invitations. Decide/arrange refreshments and any music to be played during the reception. The show opens— CELEBRATE!

Assessment

Public response, student response.

Visual Perception

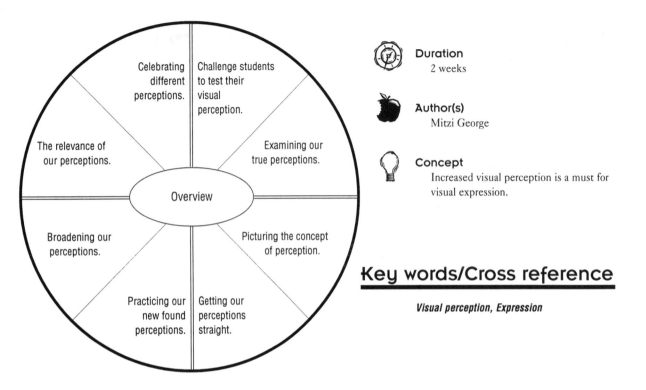

Celebrating different perceptions.

Challenge students to test their visual perception.

The relevance of our perceptions.

Examining our true perceptions.

Overview

Broadening our perceptions.

Picturing the concept of perception.

Practicing our new found perceptions.

Getting our perceptions straight.

Duration
2 weeks

Author(s)
Mitzi George

Concept
Increased visual perception is a must for visual expression.

Key words/Cross reference

Visual perception, Expression

Overview

Objective
To identify, clarify, define, and illustrate the importance of increasing visual perception.

About the Author
Mitzi George is a middle school teacher in Lake Charles, LA. She has twelve years of experience in art education through a wide spectrum of the educational arena.

Required Resources
Slides or photos of a variety of objects, paper bags, a variety of small objects, a variety of natural objects (can be the same as before), illustrations from DaVinci's sketchbooks of drawings, paper, drawing medium.

Quadrant 1—Experience

Right Mode—Connect

Challenging the student to test their perception.

Objective

The student will identify the need for increasing visual perception.

Activity

The teacher develops slides or pictures of ordinary objects in close-up and unusual positions. Show the slides/pictures of the objects without disclosing what the items are. Have students write down what they think the object is. Then give each student a closed paper bag containing an unidentified object. Do not allow students to look in bag. Have them slip their hand into the bag and handle the object. Have them draw what they think the object looks like.

Assessment

Student work.

Left Mode—Examine

Examining our true perceptions.

Objective

The students will identify and discuss their perceptions of what they experienced as opposed to what they actually experienced.

Activity

Show the slides and help students to identify the objects or pictures. Give each student a magnifying glass and allow them to examine the object in the bag. Have them compare and contrast their perception of the object and the actual object.

Assessment

Participation.

Quadrant 2—Concepts

Right Mode—Image

Picturing the concept of perception.

Objective

The students will illustrate the concept of perception.

Activity

Have students further examine the object they had in their bag. Instruct them to do a drawing of the object looking at the details of the object through a magnifying glass. Play instrumental music as students work. Compare and contrast the two drawings the students have done. Did their perceptions of the object change?

Assessment

Student work and participation.

Left Mode—Define

Getting our perceptions straight.

Objective

The student will identify and discuss the need for increasing visual perception.

Activity

Lecture on the need for increased visual perception. Discuss the need for eye-hand coordination. Show examples from DaVinci's sketchbook of objects being drawn in a variety of positions in order to familiarize the artist with the object. Discuss and demonstrate the various techniques for drawing.

Assessment

Quiz.

Visual Perception

Quadrant 3—Applications

Left Mode—Try

Practicing our new found perceptions.

Objective
The student will illustrate the use of visual perception.

Activity
Give each student a natural object to examine. Guide them through a contour drawing of the object, check for understanding pointing out needed details. Have the students change the direction of their object and do another drawing on their own. They may do several positions on one paper.

Assessment
Student work.

Right Mode—Extend

Broadening our perceptions.

Objective
The student will extend the concept of visual perception and apply their knowledge of self-expression to illustrate a theme.

Activity
Have students do a contour drawing of their hand. Then have them brainstorm all of the things their hands do for them. Ask them to identify one activity which is most meaningful to them. Illustrate that theme in a drawing. Play music as the students work. The picture must convey the theme and show a clear understanding of the importance the hand plays.

Assessment
Student work.

Quadrant 4—Creations

Left Mode—Refine

The relevance of our perceptions.

Objective
The student will analyze and critique their work.

Activity
Have students analyze their own work. On a sheet of paper, ask them to write a critique discussing their ability to look beyond the normal perception of an object or theme.

Assessment
Student's written critique and teacher critique.

Right Mode—Integrate

Celebrating different perceptions.

Objective
The student will integrate a variety of valid perceptions into one theme.

Activity
As a group, ask the students to examine the work and identify a theme that runs throughout the drawings. Have them arrange the pieces into a class quilt to be displayed in the school.

Assessment
Student/teacher reactions.

Visual Communication

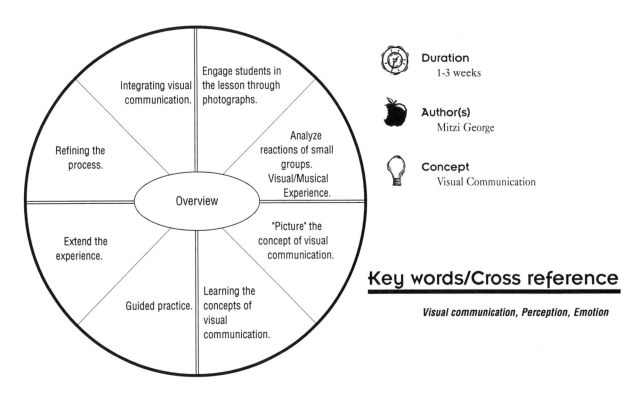

Duration
1-3 weeks

Author(s)
Mitzi George

Concept
Visual Communication

Key words/Cross reference

Visual communication, Perception, Emotion

Overview

Objective
The student will identify, discuss, and illustrate the concept of visual communication.

About the Author
Mitzi George is a middle school art teacher in Lake Charles, LA. She has had twelve years of teaching experience at all levels of the educational spectrum.

Required Resources
Rod Stewart recording *"Every Picture Tells a Story,"* tape player, slides or reproductions of artworks from Picasso, Van Gogh, etc., Polaroid cameras and film or zap shot camera. Various art materials, i.e., charcoals, pencils, ink, etc.

Visual Communication

Quadrant 1—Experience

Right Mode—Connect

Engage students in the lesson through photographs.

Objective

Students will identify and discuss the impact of visual images.

Activity

Have students bring photos of an earlier event in their life. Share the photo and tell about the event in small groups. Have students discuss another event not associated with the photo. Reflect on the differences in conversation and discuss.

Assessment

Determined by individual participation and group participation.

Left Mode—Examine

Analyze group reaction and provide a visual experience.

Objective

The student will discuss the ability of a picture to communicate messages through images.

Activity

Examine the students reactions in their small group discussions. Play the song "Every Picture Tells a Story" by Rod Stewart. Show slides of various artworks which evoke strong reactions and/or give a social comment.

Assessment

Student participation/reaction.

Quadrant 2—Concepts

Right Mode—Image

"Picture" the concept of visual communication.

Objective

The student will illustrate the concept of visual communication through photography.

Activity

Divide students into teams. Provide each team with a Polaroid or Zap shot camera. Direct team to take a picture which will convey a message or emotion. Pair each team with another team and let them share photo images. Have student choose a photo they reacted to strongly. Have the student write a paragraph describing the message or feeling they received from the photo.

Assessment

Participation and writing assignment.

Left Mode—Define

Learning the concepts of visual communication.

Objective

The student will identify the concepts of visual communication.

Activity

Lecture on key concepts and skills needed for visual communication: Eye-hand coordination, increased visual perception, understanding emotions. Show examples of Picasso, Van Gogh, A. Stieglitz, etc. Discuss the use of perspective, value, color, and stroke techniques to convey emotional responses. Demonstrate various ways mediums convey anger, fear, etc.

Assessment

Quiz.

Visual Communication

Quadrant 3—Applications

 ### Left Mode—Try

Guided practice.

Objective

The student will experiment and practice various techniques of drawing to convey emotions.

Activity

Guide students through the use of gesture and contour techniques. Have students practice. Demonstrate various mediums, i.e., compressed charcoal, vine charcoal, ebony pencil, pen and ink, brush and ink, ink and wash, etc. Have students experiment with expressing emotion: call out emotions and allowing them to respond visually. Give each student a subject matter/object to illustrate three times. Each illustration should convey a different emotion.

Assessment

Critique.

Right Mode—Extend

Extend the experience.

Objective

The student will illustrate the concept of visual communication.

Activity

Have the student brainstorm about topics they would like to make a social comment about. Then have them illustrate their feeling toward the subject. The illustration should reflect clearly the artist's view of the subject.

Assessment

Teacher critique.

Quadrant 4—Creations

 ### Left Mode—Refine

Refining the process of visual communication.

Objective

The student will critique their own work pointing out the strengths and weaknesses.

Activity

The student writes a critique of their own work. The student then presents the piece to class for a group critique. Focus on what topic is illustrated, does the image match topic, emotion involved; does the medium and technique used match the emotion or message, etc.

Assessment

Student participation and formal critique.

 ### Right Mode—Integrate

Integrating the visual communication process.

Objective

The student will incorporate their visual images with poetry to create a publication.

Activity

Each student is to select one drawing from the unit to illustrate a poem. The poem may either be original work or a personal favorite. Publish final arrangement of work.

Assessment

Overall product and presentation. Response of community.

Descriptive Language

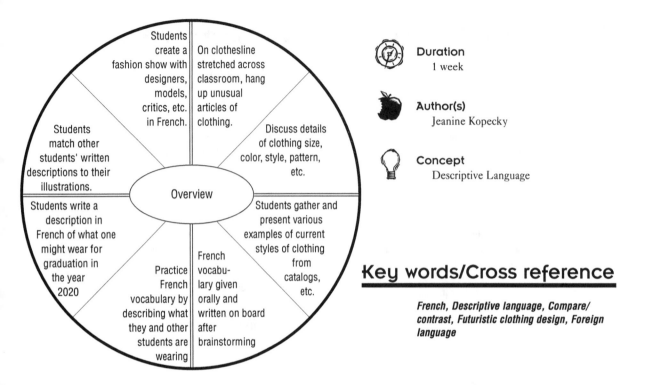

Students create a fashion show with designers, models, critics, etc. in French.

On clothesline stretched across classroom, hang up unusual articles of clothing.

Discuss details of clothing size, color, style, pattern, etc.

Students match other students' written descriptions to their illustrations.

Overview

Students write a description in French of what one might wear for graduation in the year 2020

Students gather and present various examples of current styles of clothing from catalogs, etc.

Practice French vocabulary by describing what they and other students are wearing

French vocabulary given orally and written on board after brainstorming

Duration
1 week

Author(s)
Jeanine Kopecky

Concept
Descriptive Language

Key words/Cross reference

French, Descriptive language, Compare/contrast, Futuristic clothing design, Foreign language

Overview

Objective
To enable students to describe and understand descriptions of articles of clothing in French. Students will be working in all four skill areas: listening, speaking, writing, and reading.

About the Author
Jeanine Kopecky teaches 7th grade exploratory French and 8th grade French I at Denison Middle School, Lake Geneva, Wisconsin.

Required Resources
Unusual and interesting articles of clothing, clothesline, magazines, catalogs.

Descriptive Language

Quadrant 1—Experience

 ### Right Mode—Connect

On clothesline stretched across classroom, hang up unusual articles of clothing.

Objective
Inspire students' interest in describing clothing.

Activity
Hang up interesting, unusual, and/or outdated articles of clothing on a clothesline stretched across the classroom. (I use old "hippie" clothes, goofy-patterned socks, etc.)

Assessment
Students have various reactions to the clothing: "Ooh-yuck!", "The tie-dye is cool!" "You wore those!?"

 ### Left Mode—Examine

Discuss details of clothing size: color, style, pattern, etc.

Objective
Encourage students to discuss what they observe.

Activity
Discuss details of clothing hanging on the line, i.e., colors, patterns, sizes, styles, textures, accessories.

Assessment
Students discuss what details they like and don't like.

Quadrant 2—Concepts

 ### Right Mode—Image

Students gather and present various examples of current styles of clothing from catalogs, etc.

Objective
Students relate clothing descriptions to current styles.

Activity
Students gather together examples of current clothing styles from catalogs, magazines, drawings, or what they themselves are wearing. They create poster-board collages with their selections.

Assessment
Students evaluate different styles, colors, etc.

 ### Left Mode—Define

French vocabulary given orally and written on board after brainstorming

Objective
To teach French vocabulary relating to clothing and descriptions of clothing.

Activity
1) Describe clothing on clothesline in French. 2) Hand out written descriptions in French and have students pin them to correct article of clothing on clothesline. 3) Brainstorm clothing articles with descriptions and list on board in French.

Assessment
Students identify clothing on clothesline by verbal cues to each other.

Descriptive Language

Quadrant 3—Applications

 ### Left Mode—Try

Practice French vocabulary by describing what they and other students are wearing.

Objective

To encourage students to practice newly learned vocabulary.

Activity

1) Students practice new vocabulary by describing what they are wearing. 2) Students take turns describing other students' clothing and listeners have to figure out whose clothing was being described.

Assessment

Students can apply learned vocabulary in real life situations.

 ### Right Mode—Extend

Students write a description in French of what one might wear for graduation in the year 2020.

Objective

To motivate students to experiment with new vocabulary in written descriptions.

Activity

1) Students will draw, illustrate, or paste-up cutouts of clothing that they would imagine wearing if they were graduating in the year 2020. 2) Students will write a brief description of their futuristic clothing using new vocabulary in French.

Assessment

Students are applying knowledge to new situations.

Quadrant 4—Creations

 ### Left Mode—Refine

Students match other students' written descriptions to their illustrations.

Objective

Recreation of new vocabulary by reading, comprehending and identifying another student's written description.

Activity

Students will each receive another student's written description of their 2020 graduation clothing and will try to match it to the correct illustration.

Assessment

Student comprehension of written description and application to current situation.

Right Mode—Integrate

Students create a fashion show with designers, models, critics, etc. in French.

Objective

To encourage students to communicate actively with new vocabulary.

Activity

Students create a fashion show with designers, models, critics, buyers, commentators, advertisers, and investors using French vocabulary.

Assessment

Everyone contributes their ideas and has a role in active communication using new vocabulary.

Career Exploration

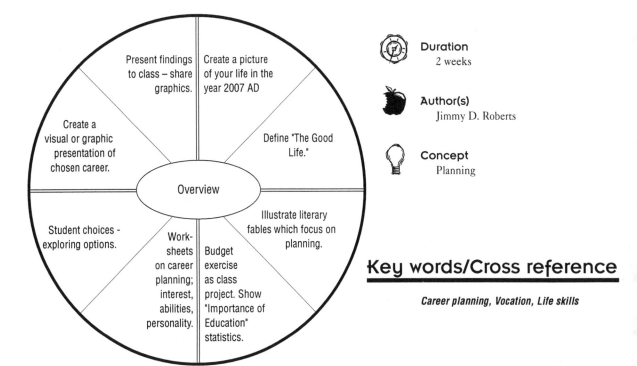

Present findings to class – share graphics.

Create a picture of your life in the year 2007 AD

Create a visual or graphic presentation of chosen career.

Define "The Good Life."

Overview

Student choices - exploring options.

Worksheets on career planning; interest, abilities, personality.

Budget exercise as class project. Show "Importance of Education" statistics.

Illustrate literary fables which focus on planning.

Duration
2 weeks

Author(s)
Jimmy D. Roberts

Concept
Planning

Key words/Cross reference

Career planning, Vocation, Life skills

Overview

Objective
To enable students to realize the importance of planning for the future and the importance of intro-spection to making career decisions.

About the Author
Jimmy D. Roberts is the Curriculum Coordinator for the Central Texas Tech Prep Consortium. Mr. Roberts has a Masters of Education in Curriculum and Instruction from Texas A&M University. He has worked as an instructional administrator since 1987. He is a certified in-house trainer of 4MAT for The Central Texas Tech Prep Consortium.

Required Resources
Department of Labor statistics; Career Exploration Curriculum worksheets; Career Success Tabloid (alternative - Occupational Outlook Quarterly); Regional Targeted Occupations List; Regional, State and National Labor Market Statistics.

Bibliography
Dothan City Schools, Career Development, Grades 7 & 8, Dothan Alabama, 1992. (Personal interest inventories are available from several educational publishers.)
Statistics can be found from several sources includ-ing the U.S. Census Bureau, the U.S. Department of Labor, the local and state employment commissions, local community colleges, and local Private Industry Councils.
Texas State Occupational Information Coordinating Committee, Career Successes, 1991.

Quadrant 1—Experience

Right Mode—Connect

Create a picture of your life in the year 2007 AD.

Objective

To have students think about their own futures; to foster introspection.

Activity

Describe with words or draw a picture to illustrate how you see yourself in the year 2007 AD. Students can draw a picture, create a mind map, or create a collage. As a class, the students create a life clock illustrating the relative amount of time spent in formal education, on the job, and in retirement.

Assessment

Participation; finished product—picture or word map. Have students verbalize importance of career planning based on their finished Life Clock.

Left Mode—Examine

Define "The Good Life."

Objective

To enable students to focus on the aspects of their life they view as important.

Activity

Class discussion to define "The Good Life" – What is important? What part does money play? Have the students make a class list of possible aspects of the good life. From the cumulative list, have the individual students prioritize a list reflecting their own personal values.

Assessment

Finished product: each student prioritizes an individual list taken from class definition of "The Good Life."

Quadrant 2—Concepts

Right Mode—Image

Illustrate literary fables which focus on planning.

Objective

To integrate the idea of planning with personal goals.

Activity

The teacher reads several very short pieces illustrating the importance of planning. Examples: *"The Grasshopper and the Ant," "Parable of the Ten Maidens," "Parable of the Wise and Foolish Builders," "Parable of the King Going Into Battle – Counting the Cost,"* or any short fable illustrating the importance of planning. Students working in groups develop a way of illustrating the need for planning through role play, model, collage, etc.

Assessment

Quality of projects.

Left Mode—Define

Budget exercise as class project. Show "Importance of Education" statistics.

Objective

To enable students to see the connection between financial needs and defined quality of life.

Activity

Have students do the budget exercise. Review statistics from Department of Labor; EDUCATION HELPS DETERMINE JOB SECURITY, STARTING SALARIES, and AVERAGE MONTHLY EARNINGS BY LEVEL OF EDUCATION.

Assessment

Check for understanding.

Quadrant 3—Applications

 ## Left Mode—Try

Worksheets on career planning; interest, abilities, personality.

Objective
To enable students to explore the components of a good career decision plan.

Activity
Worksheets on identifying interest, abilities, and personality.

Assessment
Students complete worksheet (informal inventories).

 ## Right Mode—Extend

Student choices - exploring options.

Objective
To enable the student to explore career options which are consistent with the personal inventories.

Activity
Students study personal inventories and find possible job fit through exploration of careers through in-house resources and personal interviews.

Assessment
Degree to which student selection meets identified interest, abilities, and personality – student defends choice.

Quadrant 4—Creations

 ## Left Mode—Refine

Create a visual or graphic presentation of chosen career.

Objective
To analyze the prerequisites for successful entry into chosen career.

Activity
Students will prepare a graphic presentation of the needs associated with a chosen career. The product should include education requirements, work environment, and specialized abilities needed. Students may work individually or cooperatively on career clusters.

Assessment
Degree of specificity and quality of graphic.

 ## Right Mode—Integrate

Present findings to class – share graphics.

Objective
To share what they have learned with others, to defend their choice based on personal reasons.

Activity
The students will make an oral presentation to the class about their findings and will provide informational handouts to other students to make a career exploration packet.

Assessment
Quality of handouts and oral presentations.

Planning for High School

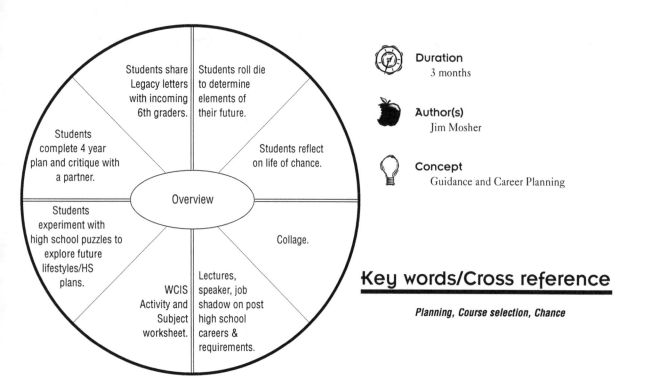

Students share Legacy letters with incoming 6th graders.

Students roll die to determine elements of their future.

Students complete 4 year plan and critique with a partner.

Students reflect on life of chance.

Overview

Students experiment with high school puzzles to explore future lifestyles/HS plans.

Collage.

WCIS Activity and Subject worksheet.

Lectures, speaker, job shadow on post high school careers & requirements.

Duration
3 months

Author(s)
Jim Mosher

Concept
Guidance and Career Planning

Key words/Cross reference

Planning, Course selection, Chance

Overview

Objective
To help students plan course selection for their high school four-year plans.

About the Author
Jim Mosher is a counselor at Edison Middle School in Janesville, WI.

Required Resources
Wisconsin Career Information System.

Quadrant 1—Experience

 ## Right Mode—Connect

Students roll die to determine elements of their future.

Objective
To help students sense the need for planning as a life skill.

Activity
Student(s) roll a die to determine the level of education, marital status, health, income and occupation and record their findings.

Assessment
Students record their chance findings.

 ## Left Mode—Examine

Students reflect on life of chance.

Objective
To have students discuss and reflect upon their present and future choices.

Activity
Discussion of previous experience. Describe your life chance. What do you like about your "life"? What do you dislike? What elements are within your control? Outside your control? What would you keep? What would you change? What would it be like if someone else made all your choices for you? Do you have a plan or are you gambling with your future?

Assessment
Quality of the discussion.

Quadrant 2—Concepts

 ## Right Mode—Image

Collage.

Objective
To help students see the relationship between learning and work.

Activity
Students will complete a collage of drawings, pictures and words depicting skills which the student possesses.

Assessment
Completion of collage and quality of insights to the relationship of learning and work.

 ## Left Mode—Define

Lectures, speaker, job shadow on post high school careers & requirements.

Objective
TSW: identify requirement for successful completion of high school and entrance requirements of post high school settings, i.e., the workplace, military, technical colleges, apprenticeship programs and four-year college programs.

Activity
Lectures, speakers (from a variety of post high school settings) and read DPI pamphlet.

Assessment
Quality of responses and questions.

Quadrant 3—Applications

 ## Left Mode—Try

WCIS Activity and Subject worksheet.

Objective

TSW: identify high school courses and levels of post high school training needed for five occupational areas of interest.

Activity

Complete worksheet on Weithted grading and quiz. Students will use the Wisconsin Career Information System print and software materials to complete a matrix worksheet listing occupations of interest and suggested high school courses.

Assessment

Completion of worksheets of information following the activity.

 ## Right Mode—Extend

Students experiment with high school puzzles to explore future lifestyles/HS plans.

Objective

TSW: explore how their decisions about courses, levels, co-curricular activities, work experiences, family life and leisure time interact to form a lifestyle.

Activity

1) Students will spend a half day shadowing a worker in a career interest area, a parent or conduct a phone interview of five workers. The student will identify knowledge and skills necessary for success on the job.
2) Working in pairs, students will take turns manipulating pieces of their high school puzzle to assemble a picture of their 9th grade year. Students will describe a typical day in high school. Students will share how they solve problems of time, space and priority. 3) Students will develop a four-year academic plan that reflects knowledge of self, graduation requirements and requirements for transition into the next setting.

Assessment

Enthusiasm, participation and a variety of problems discovered and solutions found.

Quadrant 4—Creations

 ## Left Mode—Refine

Students complete 4-year plan and critique with a partner.

Objective

To integrate knowledge of self and future options in a personally meaningful way.

Activity

Student will critique the four-year academic plan with a partner and then with the teacher or counselor.

Assessment

Does it meet the high school graduation requirement and the student's area of interest?

 ## Right Mode—Integrate

Students share Legacy letters with incoming 6th graders.

Objective

To share personal insights and knowledge of their middle school experience with 5th graders about to enter Edison Middle School.

Activity

Students will complete a "Legacy Letter" to a 5th grade student. Students will respond to "During my time in the middle school I have learned a lot about Edison and myself . . . I've had interesting experiences. . . I have grown and changed, too! . . . What I have learned may be helpful to you . . . Good luck!!! Letter will be shared with 5th graders.

Assessment

Completion of letter and enjoyment of the experiences.

The Great Depression

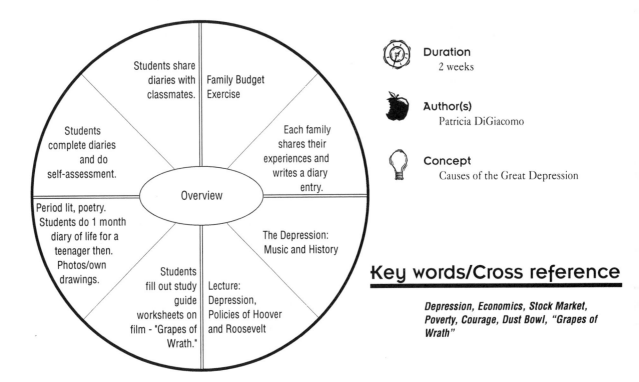

Students share diaries with classmates.

Family Budget Exercise

Each family shares their experiences and writes a diary entry.

Overview

The Depression: Music and History

Students complete diaries and do self-assessment.

Period lit, poetry. Students do 1 month diary of life for a teenager then. Photos/own drawings.

Students fill out study guide worksheets on film - "Grapes of Wrath."

Lecture: Depression, Policies of Hoover and Roosevelt

Duration
2 weeks

Author(s)
Patricia DiGiacomo

Concept
Causes of the Great Depression

Key words/Cross reference

Depression, Economics, Stock Market, Poverty, Courage, Dust Bowl, "Grapes of Wrath"

Overview

Objective
Students will only "feel" the Depression if they understand the impact on individual lives that such an economic upheaval causes.

About the Author
Patricia DiGiacomo teaches at Dodd Junior High School, Cheshire, CT. She is a certified 4MAT Trainer for her school district.

Required Resources
Music, poetry, magazines, and newspapers from the Great Depression era; video of *"The Grapes of Wrath;"* a version of the song, *"Brother Can You spare a Dime?"*

The Great Depression

Quadrant 1—Experience

Right Mode—Connect

Family Budget Exercise.

Objective
To enhance student's understanding of the ramification to their life of a sudden loss of income.

Activity
Students will work in small groups; each group will be a "family" which is given an income. They determine a budget. Then, their income abruptly stops. What happens? Prioritize budgets: What goes 1st, 2nd, 3rd?

Assessment
Participation.

Left Mode—Examine

Each family shares their experiences and writes a diary entry.

Objective
To have students understand the inevitable impact on individuals in a depression.

Activity
Each family shares their experience and writes a diary entry.

Assessment
List "feelings" about a young person's life in an economic disaster.

Quadrant 2—Concepts

Right Mode—Image

The Depression: Music and History.

Objective
To integrate the previous experience and reflections into the concept of economic, social, and political upheaval.

Activity
Teacher provides primary accounts of real people in Depression (newspapers, magazines, films, poetry). Play the song, "Brother, Can You Spare a Dime?"

Assessment
Refer back to your initial thoughts in Q1 - How do your "guesses" of life compare to the accounts given.

Left Mode—Define

Lecture: Depression, Policies of Hoover and Roosevelt.

Objective
To understand the specific causes of the Depression and to attempt to remedy the problems.

Activity
Lectures/readings of text and supplemental materials of causes. Focus on the administrations of Hoover and FDR - Domestic Policy.

Assessment
Test - objectives and essays.

Quadrant 3—Applications

 ## Left Mode—Try

Students fill out study guide worksheets on film - "Grapes of Wrath."

Objective
To reinforce information.

Activity
Students fill out worksheets; edit their class notes; and watch a version of the film, "Grapes of Wrath."

Assessment
Grade student work.

 ## Right Mode—Extend

Period lit, poetry. Students do 1 month diary of life for a teenager then. Photos/own drawings.

Objective
To integrate material with a personal experience of learning.

Activity
Students choose one of the following activities:
1) Diaries, (one month diary of life for a teenager during that time) gather and include photos/own drawings, or
2) Read and critique Depression literature, or
3) Do a Stock Market analysis as to what controls could have prevented the "crash".

Assessment
Teacher approval of topic.

Quadrant 4—Creations

 ## Left Mode—Refine

Students complete diaries and do self-assessment.

Objective
To analyze concepts taught within their own format.

Activity
Students will complete approved project according to contract.

Assessment
Teacher guide process (very little involvement).

 ## Right Mode—Integrate

Students share diaries with classmates.

Objective
To apply information to complex personal experiences.

Activity
Students share their project.

Assessment
Grade projects. Teacher: what next? The changing of role of government as America goes to war.

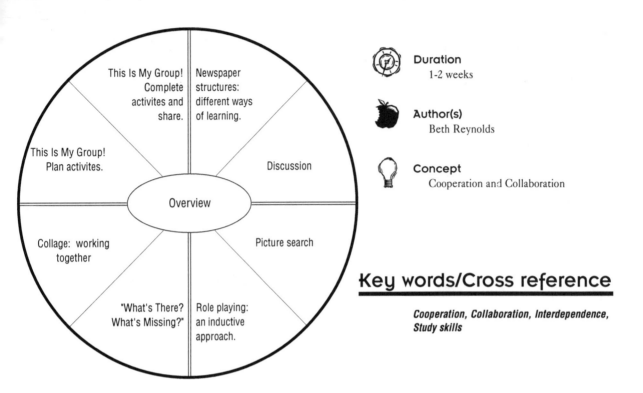

This Is My Group! Complete activites and share.

Newspaper structures: different ways of learning.

This Is My Group! Plan activites.

Discussion

Overview

Collage: working together

Picture search

"What's There? What's Missing?"

Role playing: an inductive approach.

Duration
1-2 weeks

Author(s)
Beth Reynolds

Concept
Cooperation and Collaboration

Key words/Cross reference

Cooperation, Collaboration, Interdependence, Study skills

Overview

Objective
By working together cooperatively we can improve our own learning as well as that of others.

About the Author
Beth Reynolds is a 7th grade Language Arts/Social Studies teacher at Nipher Middle School, Kirkwood, MO. She is a certified 4MAT Trainer.

Required Resources
Large stack of newspapers, pictures of people working together, magazines to cut up, markers, drawing paper, scissors, glue, craft paper for mural, embroidery floss (enough for one friendship bracelet per student), activity sheets: "What's There? What's Missing?" "Getting to Know You."

Bibliography
Johnson, David W., Johnson, Roger T., and Holubec, Edythe Johnson. *Cooperation in the Classroom.* Interaction Book Company: Edina, Minnesota, 1988.
Johnson, David W., Johnson, Roger T., and Holubec, Edythe Johnson. *Advanced Cooperative Learning.* Interaction Book Company: Edina, Minnesota, 1988.

Quadrant 1—Experience

 ## Right Mode—Connect

Newspaper structures: different ways of learning.

Objective
The student will experience two learning conditions—working alone and working as a member of a group; and will be able to compare/contrast the two to recognize the benefits of group work.

Activity
Different Ways of Learning. Students participate in the same activity first alone, and then in a small group—that of building a newspaper structure. Students are given a stack of newspapers with which they are directed to use in building the tallest structure possible. They are not allowed to use any other materials. Fifteen minutes are allotted for work time and students work at separate work stations. Once complete, students share structures. Explain to students that they will now participate in the same activity, but this time they will work as a member of a group rather than as an individual. Again, allow a work time and share once complete.

Assessment
Student ability to explain his/her experiences working alone and as a group member.

 ## Left Mode—Examine

Discussion.

Objective
The student will compare/contrast the two learning environments, naming benefits of each.

Activity
Discussion. Students are asked to analyze their experiences in a discussion:
- Compare the structures built each way. How are they alike? How are they different?
- What benefits did you notice as you worked alone? Together?
- What problems did you encounter each way?
- What special skills do you think you need when working with others? Did you experience any problems?
- How did you feel when working alone?
- How did you feel when working together?

Assessment
The student will be able to name the benefits of both working alone and working together in a written form: WHY work alone? WHY work together?

Quadrant 2—Concepts

 ## Right Mode—Image

Picture search.

Objective
The student will visually examine a set of pictures and work with others to generate a set of characteristics of group work.

Activity
Picture Search: What's the Difference? Working in groups, students compare pictures of people working in groups and others working alone. Together they generate characteristics seen, write them on paper, and share them with the class. (Magazine pictures work well, but need to be copied for all groups to see and therefore discuss the same situations.)

Assessment
The group list of characteristics can be used to check that students can identify characteristics of group work.

 ## Left Mode—Define

Role playing: an inductive approach.

Objective
Students will experience several scenarios which would be more effective if appropriate group skills were used.

Activity
Students role-play given situations designed to point to the need for group skills:

1) Students work alone on a given task, each completing each part of the task, i.e. write their names on the paper, write the answers on the paper, etc. Students then work in a group where there is a division of labor allowing for group roles.

Discuss. Highlight the group skill of working in roles.

2) Students begin working alone on a task sitting in desks arranged in straight rows facing the front of the room. They are then asked to work together on a task and are given time to do so. They are directed to first make a mess when moving together (make lots of noise, fight over how to arrange the desks, etc.).

Discuss. Highlight the need for moving into groups efficiently and being seated so that all group members can communicate directly with each other.

3) Students participate in a group activity where different group members display difficult behaviors: one is bossy, one refuses to work, one is a practical joker, etc.

Discuss. Highlight the need for all group members to participate.

Allow students to suggest other group skills for which they may have experienced a need. Make a list of these skills to work through one at a time as the year progresses. Leave space to add additional suggestions.

Assessment
Ask students, working in groups, to show a well functioning group by drawing a design on craft paper. Evaluate for the inclusion of the skills just discussed.

Quadrant 3—Applications

Left Mode—Try

"What's There? What's Missing?"

Objective

The student will evaluate given group situations for the use of both correct and incorrect group skills; the student will create an original description of a group showing both the use of correct and incorrect group skills.

Activity

"What's There? What's Missing?" Students complete the following activity sheet, evaluating each situation showing group work. Once finished, students then discuss their choices and together write additional descriptions. These are then presented to the class which evaluates the given situations.

"What's There? What' Missing?" Activity Sheet

In each of the following descriptions of group work, you will find some strengths and some weaknesses in how they do their tasks. In your group, discuss each and note 'what's there,' and 'what's missing.'

1. Ted, Nikki, and Sam are doing a worksheet together. They have only one copy. Ted is reading the problems, Nikki is writing answers, and Sam is preparing to tell the class their answers. As they work, Nikki keeps looking over Ted's shoulder, reading the problems before he does.

What's there?:

What's missing?:

2. Sandi, Nicole, and Jon have been assigned to the same group. They have gathered their things together and moved into a circle. Sandi and Nicole have covered their mouths and told secrets three times since the groups were announced. Jon sits ready to work.

What's there?:

What's missing?:

3. Steve, Jake, and Sam have been working on a group project for a class hour. They've all taken part in the project—both in assuming roles and in participating equally. The only problem they've had is in seeing each other. They are sitting in a row so only Jake can see both partners.

What's there?:

What's missing?:

4. Jaime, Zak, and Jason have fought all day. Jaime keeps blurting out the answers before Zak and Jason have had a chance to think. Zak and Jason have asked her to stop but she hasn't. Jaime says she is tired of doing all the work. Zak and Jason have told her to slow down and they'll help.

What's there?:

What's missing?:

5. Lisa's group is so proud of her! She's raised her spelling test scores and everyone gets an extra minute of break time. Bob and William have both praised her. Everyone feels great!

What's there?:

What's missing?:

Assessment

The accuracy and completeness of student evaluations on the activity and the creation of a like problem form the basis of evaluation for this activity.

Right Mode—Extend

Collage: working together.

Objective

The student will show the essentials of group work in a collage.

Activity

Class Collage: Working Together. Students work in small groups to complete a class collage. Each group is assigned one section of a large mural on which to show the essentials of group work. They may do so by cutting pictures from magazines, writing slogans, drawing pictures, writing riddles—in any way they may choose to complete their section of the mural. After allowing time for groups to work, ask each to present its interpretation to the class.

Assessment

Student creations showing the characteristics of group mechanisms form the evaluation component for this activity.

Quadrant 4—Creations

 ## Left Mode—Refine

This Is My Group! Plan activities.

Objective
The student will correctly apply the skills discussed to create the foundation of a well functioning group.

Activity
This is My Group! Students are assigned to cooperative groups which will be used throughout the unit. (I choose to assign my groups, but student-selected groups can also be used.) Each group is asked to complete the following tasks: 1) Interview each group member in order to get to know each other better. 2) Name the group. 3) Select a group mascot and three group colors. Groups are to be ready to introduce themselves to the whole class.

Assessment
The use of the skills discussed as necessary in good group work forms the basis of the evaluation for this activity as well as the final products in the following activity.

 ## Right Mode—Integrate

This Is My Group! Complete activities and share.

Objective
The student will work as a fully participating member of a group.

Activity
This Is My Group! Each group is allowed time to complete its tasks as given above. Interviews are conducted. Once names, mascots, and colors are chosen, groups are asked to create a group banner and friendship bracelets for each member using the group's colors. Celebrate the groups. Ask each to present itself to the class, introducing each member and explaining the group banner. These cooperative groups are to be used throughout the unit and can be evaluated at the end.

Assessment
Student application of productive group skills in completing and explaining the tasks, as well as their use of good group skills throughout the unit serve as an evaluation of this activity.

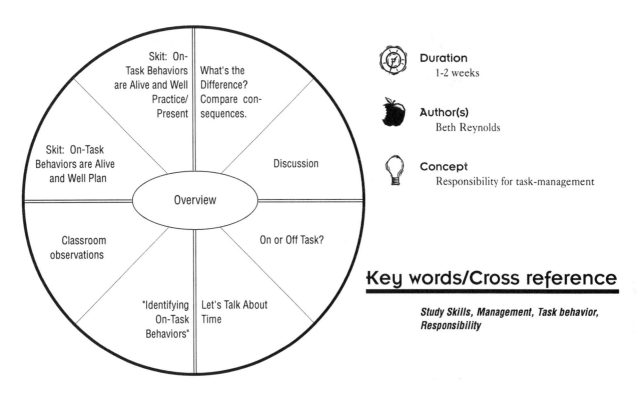

Duration
1-2 weeks

Author(s)
Beth Reynolds

Concept
Responsibility for task-management

Key words/Cross reference

Study Skills, Management, Task behavior, Responsibility

Overview

 Objective
On-task behavior during class times fosters academic achievement.

 About the Author
Beth Reynolds is a 7th grade Language Arts/Social Studies teacher at Nipher Middle School, Kirkwood, MO. She is a certified 4MAT Trainer.

 Required Resources
Vocabulary Skill Lesson: Overhead Terms and Examples, Quiz over same. Self-Assessment: What Do You Do During Class? Worksheets: On or Off Task? Identifying On-Task Behaviors. Monitoring Sheet: Self-Monitor and Reward Your On-Task Behavior.

 Bibliography
Good, Thomas L., Brophy, Jere E. *Looking in Classrooms.* Harper and Row: New York, 1984. pp. 30-35.
Hunter, Madeline. *Mastery Teaching.* TIP Publications: E1 Segundo, 1986. pp. 91-93.
Workman, Edward A. *Teaching Behavioral Self-Control to Students.* Pro-Ed: Austin, Texas, 1982.

Quadrant 1—Experience

 ## Right Mode—Connect

What's the Difference? Compare consequences.

Objective

The student will experience a situation in which academic outcomes are related to on- and off- task behaviors.

Activity

Students are divided into five groups which are then seated together. Each group is given a special set of directions to follow while the teacher instructs the class in a vocabulary lesson. These directions ask four groups to engage in off-task behaviors during instruction by talking to each other, writing notes, working on homework, or daydreaming. The fifth group is asked to pay close attention to the skill lesson. The lesson is then conducted and all students are given the same quiz at the end. These are scored and each group determines its average. Averages are written on the board as each group reads its directions to the rest of the class. Scores of each group are related to the behaviors displayed during the skill lesson.

Assessment

The student's ability to relate different on- and off- task behaviors to different academic outcomes will provide the basis for the evaluation of the effectiveness of this activity.

 ## Left Mode—Examine

Discussion.

Objective

The student will relate on- and off- task behaviors to classroom achievement.

Activity

Discussion. Students are asked to analyze the results of the above activity in a class discussion.

- Which groups did the best on the quiz? Why do you think this was so?
- Did anyone in the group talking to neighbors hear any of the lesson? How much did you hear?
- Did anyone who was daydreaming hear the lesson? . . . the note-writing group? . . . the homework group?
- What do you think interferes with learning in each different conditions?
- How did most students learn best?
- What does this say for the best behavior to have during class times?

Assessment

Student understanding of the experience is measured in his/her written response to the following question: WHY is academic success dependent on student behavior during class?

Quadrant 2—Concepts

Right Mode—Image

On or Off Task?

Objective

The student will label specific actions of fictitious students in given descriptions as positive or negative in terms of learning.

Activity

On or Off Task? Working in groups, students act out descriptions of fictitious students for the class. The class then discusses the behaviors shown, labeling them as 'helpful' or 'harmful' to given learning situations. At the end of the activity, the term 'on-task' is given for the helpful behaviors while the term 'off-task' is given to the harmful behaviors.

Assessment

The students' ability to classify the behaviors shown as 'on-task' or 'off-task' and their relation to classroom learning forms the basis of evaluation for this activity.

Left Mode—Define

Let's Talk About Time.

Objective

1) The student will be able to define 'on-task' and 'off-task' behaviors, give examples of each, and correctly classify given behaviors as such. 2) The student will be able to explain research findings related to on and off-task behaviors.

Activity

Let's Talk About It. Present students with information derived from educational research that shows the link between on-task behaviors and learning. Present the following questions, ask students to hypothesize the findings, and then share the actual results with the class. Let's Talk About Time - A Conversation Between a Student and an Educational Researcher.

1) Does the way time is spent in a classroom effect the amount of learning which I achieve?

Yes. In a study of 87 classrooms in 1980, those classes which did not engage in as much teacher instructed activity, did not achieve as much. Not only does student on-task behavior help learning, but the amount of time in which students are actually engaged—busy with—the learning activity effects the amount of material learned.

2) If a student only talks with others off and on, does it really hurt?

Yes. Frequent behaviors such as social interactions (talking to others) cut down on student achievement.

3) If the class is working in groups, can I talk to my friends?

Yes and no. Group activities have learning goals. Talking with group members about the assigned activity is an on-task behavior. Your teacher designs the learning activity so that by following the directions you can better achieve the learning goal. Talking to others in your group about the learning task is usually an important part of the directions. However, if you talk to your friends about something unrelated to the learning task, you are displaying an off-task behavior and your overall learning suffers. This is because you are not spending the needed time on the learning task.

4) A boy in my class is always goofing off telling jokes and getting the class to laugh. Is he hurting my learning achievement?

Yes. By disturbing the time which you have to work on a learning exercise, he is interrupting your learning time.

5) If we increase our math class time, will than mean that we will learn more math?

Maybe. The amount of time you spend in a class is not necessarily going to effect your overall learning rate. Researchers talk about something called 'student-engaged time' and claim that it is more important than the total amount of time spent in a class. Student-engaged time is the amount of time in which a student actively participates in a learning experience. That is, the time spent in a class when a student is not working on a learning task doesn't effect overall learning. If the added class time is to effect overall learning, it must be spent actively working on math. Therefore, more math time spent on math will help, but more math time used to socialize won't.

6) What if I spend a lot of time in math working on math problems, but I get them all wrong?

An educational researcher named Filby Fisher has introduced a new term, academic learning time, which takes accuracy into account. According to his research, learning occurs when a student spends time on learning exercises and does the work with a high level of success. This would seem to indicate that if you spent a lot of time doing problems to wrong way, and were never corrected, this added time wouldn't be helpful to your overall achievement. You would be well advised to check your work periodically to be sure that you're doing it right.

From this discussion, generate several lists of behaviors, those which are generally on-task behaviors and those which are off-task behaviors can be different if called for by the teacher in a learning situation. Write the lists on large paper and post for further consideration.

Assessment

Quality of student lists and ability to remain on-task (!) for the activities.

Quadrant 3—Applications

Left Mode—Try

"Identifying On-Task Behaviors."

Objective

The student will be able to identify both on- and off-task behaviors in given examples; will be able to assess his/her own behaviors for the same.

Activity

Identifying On-Task Behaviors. Students complete and discuss an activity sheet entitled, "Identifying On-Task Behaviors." Once complete, each student evaluates his/her own most frequent on and/or off-task behaviors. These assessments are to remain confidential. Students are asked to put them in a safe place so that they can check their progress in several weeks.

Assessment

Student mastery of on- and off-task behaviors is measured by their responses on the activity sheet.

Right Mode—Extend

Classroom observations.

Objective

The student will identify examples of on- and off-task behaviors in his/her daily classes.

Activity

Classroom Observations. Students are given observation sheets on which to record at least three examples each of on- and off-task behaviors. The directions ask students to watch for examples in team classes (in which team teachers would have been notified of the activity). Once observations are complete, group members are to share them and select their favorite examples from those noted. These are to be kept confidential between group members until they have completed the following activity and presented it to the class.

Assessment

Student observations on their activity sheets serve as a measure of student understanding of on- and off-task behaviors.

Quadrant 4—Creations

Left Mode—Refine

Skit: On-Task Behaviors are Alive and Well. Plan.

Objective

The student will create a skit showing both on- and off-task behaviors; will implement a system for self-monitoring and rewarding his/her own on-task behaviors.

Activity

On-Task Behaviors are Alive and Well. Working in small groups, students are to create skits showing examples of both on- and off-task behaviors. These skits should be set in a classroom (to be defined as any learning environment) and should show examples of behaviors shown by students of their own age.

Assessment

Evaluation of the planning phase becomes evident in the performing phase of this activity which follows.

Right Mode—Integrate

Skit: On-Task Behaviors are Alive and Well. Practice/Present.

Objective

The student will create and perform a skit showing on- and off-task behaviors in a learning setting; . . . will implement an on-task program to monitor and reward on-task behaviors.

Activity

On-Task Behaviors Are Alive and Well. Students practice and perform their skits for the class which discusses the on- and off-task behaviors shown in each. Once all skits are shown, introduce a 'Self-Monitoring and Reward' Program to the students. Explain that the purpose of the program is to help students become more aware of their behaviors during class times and to increase the percentage of time during which they are on-task. Go over the findings of Edward Workman in his book, Teaching Behavioral Self-Control to Students, briefly describing his belief that individuals are in control of their own behavioral self-control and have the power to improve themselves. Explain the basic mechanisms of the program: Students will each be given a weekly Self-Monitoring sheet. Explain that every class hour the alarm clock will go off once every twelve minutes, roughly dividing the class time in fourths. At the time the alarm sounds, students are to assess their own behaviors and answer the questions, "Am I on-task?". If they answer 'yes', they are to give themselves a point. If the answer is 'no', they are to skip the point that time. Each day the maximum number of points possible is four, and multiplied over the five days of a normal week, the maximum weekly points possible is 20. If a student earns 80% of the possible weekly points, or 16, he/she will be rewarded at the end of the week with a treat. (This treat can be any small reward—a piece of candy, ten minutes of free time, a pass to do only half of a homework assignment, etc.). The sheets should be set up and ready to go for the next day.

*** Note: When I first tried the self-monitoring program, I became very perplexed. I realized that many of the students were 'lying' on their sheets. That is, they gave themselves points when they didn't deserve them. However, the overall attention of the class was markedly improved. While the alarm was a disruption initially, we all got used to it and could almost mark sheets while we continued our activity. However, I still couldn't figure out why on-task behaviors were better overall while many of the students really didn't qualify for points when the alarm went off. A visiting principal helped me out. She explained that while some were not on-task when the alarm went off, they were put back on-task at that time. As a result, any student who was off-task was put back on. As a result, the overall class on-task behavior was much improved. It must be noted that this was first tried with a group of students which was comprised of top and bottom students with very few in the average range. Therefore, it contained a number of students who benefited from being put back on-task. Classroom observations help teachers too!

Assessment

Enjoyment of skits.

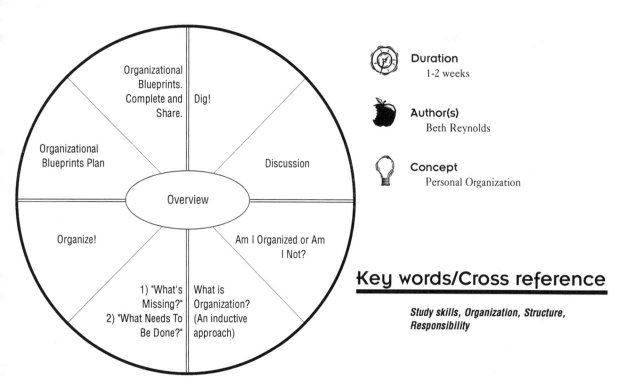

Duration
1-2 weeks

Author(s)
Beth Reynolds

Concept
Personal Organization

Key words/Cross reference

Study skills, Organization, Structure, Responsibility

Overview

Objective
Organization allows for the efficient storing and retrieval of items.

About the Author
Beth Reynolds is a 7th grade Language Arts/Social Studies teacher at Nipher Middle School, Kirkwood, MO. She is a certified 4MAT Trainer.

Required Resources
Student materials from locker. Activity sheets: What's Missing? What Needs to be Done? Large envelopes containing items written on notecards to develop an organizational blueprint for drawing paper, markers, student lockers and notebooks.

Quadrant 1—Experience

 ### Right Mode—Connect

Dig!

Objective

The student will experience the need for organization.

Activity

Dig! Ask the students to bring all of their school materials to class without telling them what they need them for. Once they are ready, commence with the following search. Explain that they have been asked to have certain materials with them at all times. In the following activity, materials will be named and every student who can come up with the item will earn a point. Points will be recorded and tallied at the end, with the student receiving the most points winning the game.

Suggested items: pencil, pen, eraser, blank lined paper, a math book, Language Arts homework from last night, notes from Social Studies on . . ., Language Arts journal, compass, colored pencils, Colonial America packet, etc. Talley the points to determine the winner.

Assessment

Student understanding of the importance for organization is measured in the following discussion.

 ### Left Mode—Examine

Discussion.

Objective

The student will experience and analyze the need for organization.

Activity

Dig! Discuss the activity. Ask students to propose the purpose of the activity. Why do you think we did this? Why is it important to be able to find your things? What happens in 'real life' when you can't find them? What happens if this is repeated over and over again? Can you think of a time in which this presented a problem for you? What do you call it when there is a place for everything and everything is in its place?

Assessment

The students show their understanding of the experience by writing an answer to the following question: WHY organize?

Quadrant 2—Concepts

 ### Right Mode—Image

Am I Organized or Am I Not?

Objective

The student will access his/her own understanding and application of organizational skills at school.

Activity

Am I Organized or Am I Not? Hand out drawing paper and ask the students to think about their lockers. Do they presently have a plan for organizing their materials? Ask them to draw their locker, locating all of the items mentioned in the 'Dig!' activity. Once complete, discuss their drawings. Did you really have a place for everything? Are there things you aren't sure where to look for? Do you think you once had a plan, but just haven't stuck to it? Can you describe your plan?

Assessment

Student answers to the discussion along with their locker layouts provide a means to evaluate their self-assessment of organizational skills.

 ### Left Mode—Define

What is Organization? (An inductive approach)

Objective

The student will be able to define and name critical attributes of organization.

Activity

An Inductive Look at Organization. Together discuss organization and what it means. 1) Students write definitions. 2) Share. List critical attributes. 3) Write a final definition. 4) Teacher generates examples, non-examples. Check student understanding. 5) Students write examples, non-examples and check each other.

Assessment

Correct identification of critical attributes; self-generated examples provide measure of mastery.

Quadrant 3—Applications

 ## Left Mode—Try

1) "What's Missing?"
2) "What Needs To Be Done?"

Objective

The student will be able to identify and solve given organizational problems.

Activity

Activity Sheets. Students work through and discuss the problems of fictitious students in the sheets: What's Missing? What Needs to be Done?

Assessment

Responses to the activity sheets provide a measure of student mastery of the above objective.

What's Missing?

In each of the following situations, a student is having difficulty with his/her school work because something is missing. Read each situation carefully and try to identify the missing thing. For each missing item, explain how better organization would prevent its loss.

1. Susan carefully wrote down her science assignment on a piece of notebook paper, folded it and stuck it in the front of her science book. She was supposed to make a list of at least five different types of adaptations which animals make to their environments and give the reasons for these changes. When she started to reach for her science homework assignment, Susan realized that she hadn't brought her book home because she didn't need it in order to complete her work. What is Susan missing and why? What could be done?

2. Juan grabbed his math book out of his locker as he ran to class. His friends had stopped him in the hall after the last class and had tried to tell him about the latest skateboards in the local bike shop. He was going to be late to class if he didn't hurry. When he reached for his math paper, Juan realized that he had his social studies notebook instead of his math notebook and the teacher wouldn't let him go to his locker. After class, he forgot to get his paper from his locker and turn it in. He kept forgetting and eventually he received a zero for the assignment. What had Juan failed to do? What should he have done?

3. Pam carefully completed her science insect collection, spending many hours carefully labeling and mounting her specimen. She was proud of her work

and turned it in expecting to receive an 'A' for her collection. When it was returned, her heart fell. There on the front was a note from the teacher explaining that she had not included the class, phyla, and Latin names of the insects. Her grade was a 'C'. Where had Pam gone wrong? What could she have done?

4. Samantha tried to find her worksheet for language in the back of her notebook. She knew she had completed it last night when she worked on her homework. However, she still hadn't found it when the teacher collected the papers and she didn't have one to turn in. What had Samantha missed doing organizationally? What should she have done?

5. Gary usually kept all of his things in his book bag. At the beginning of each class, he pawed through all of his possessions in order to find the book for that class. When he finally found the book, he still had to dig for his paper. By the end of the day, Gary was so tired of digging, he usually gave up. As a result, he frequently did not have a book to use during this fifth hour class and he didn't turn in any papers. Where did Gary go wrong? What could he do to solve his problems?

What Needs to Be Done?

In each of the following situations, a student needs to organize some part of his/her work or materials in order to better complete his/her work. Read each situation carefully and write down your suggestions for each student to help him/her become better organized.

1. Eric gathered all of his books together at the end of the day. Usually he stood in front of his locker for several minutes trying to remember his assignments for the night. Also he usually forgot to take at least one book home each night and so he failed to complete at least one assignment. What suggestions do you have to help Eric become better organized?

2. Tina picket up her book and opened it to the page which had been assigned for homework. She read the directions and carefully completed the assignment. When she was finished, she remembered she had to feed the dog. She left her books on her desk and got busy doing other things. In the morning she grabbed everything as she ran to catch the bus. When she got to school she realized that she had left her homework on her desk at home. What suggestions do you have to help Tina become better organized?

3. Latasha worked to complete all of her homework. When she was finished, she stacked it all up and put it in her science folder. The next day in math class,

she reached for her math assignment only to find that it wasn't in her science folder. What suggestions do you have to help Latasha become better organized?

4. Henry shook his head in dismay. The teacher had listed four papers on the board which he was to turn in today. Henry had been given these papers two weeks ago and had finished the first two. He hadn't realized that all four would be turned in today. What suggestions do you have to help Henry become better organized?

5. Sally's mother told her that she had to go to bed in one more hour. Sally wasn't sure that she could finish her social studies project by then. She had bought the poster board this afternoon and had started on the project after dinner. What suggestions do you have for Sally?

 ## Right Mode—Extend

Organize!

Objective
The student will create organizational blueprints for a given problem.

Activity
Organize! The students, using the steps in the planning process, create directions for organizing a locker. Their posters contain:
Title
How to Organize a Locker
Materials Needed:
Steps to Follow:
Caution!
Once posters are done, students trade and use the plans to organize their lockers. The effectiveness of the plans are then discussed.

Assessment
The organizational plans shown on the posters provide a measure of student mastery.

Quadrant 4—Creations

 ## Left Mode—Refine

Organizational Blueprints Plan.

Objective
The student will be able to apply organizational skills to a real life problem.

Activity
Organizational Blueprints. Together, students brainstorm things in their lives which need to be organized. These are then listed on the board. Possible answers include: locker, notebook, my room, CDs and CD stuff, baseball cards, clothes . . .. Students are then asked to select one area of their lives for which organizational plans can be developed. Once selected, students are to make organizational plans, or blueprints, for their related items. These plans are then to be turned into the type of poster designed for organizing a locker.

Assessment
Evaluation of the student's ability to apply these skills is based upon his/her final plans.

 ## Right Mode—Integrate

Organizational Blueprints. Complete and Share.

Objective
The student will be able to apply organizational skills to a real-life problem.

Activity
Organizational Blueprints. Students are given time to complete their plans. Once finished, plans are shared with the entire class.

Assessment
A measure of student mastery of organizational skills is made by evaluating their plans.

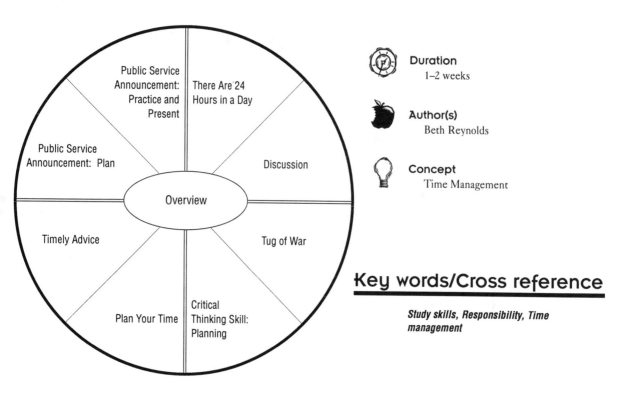

Duration
1–2 weeks

Author(s)
Beth Reynolds

Concept
Time Management

Key words/Cross reference

Study skills, Responsibility, Time management

Overview

Objective
The wise management of time allows you to do both those things you want to do and those things you need to do.

About the Author
Beth Reynolds is a 7th grade Language Arts/Social Studies teacher at Nipher Middle School.

Required Resources
Activity Sheets: 24 Hours in a Day, School Time, Daily/Weekly Schedule, The Perfect Saturday, Project Plans, Project Timeline, Monthly Schedule. Overhead: The Steps in Planning markers or crayons.

Bibliography
Good, Thomas L. and Brophy, Jere E. *Looking in Classrooms*. Harper and Row: New York, 1984.

Quadrant 1—Experience

 ## Right Mode—Connect

There Are 24 Hours in a Day.

Objective
The student will realize his/her normal expenditure of time in a day.

Activity
There Are 24 Hours in a Day. Begin this activity by asking students to close their eyes and go on a trip through a normal school day. Prompt their imagery by asking them to picture: . . . getting up in the morning . . . going through their morning routine . . . getting dressed . . . eating breakfast . . . leaving the house . . . traveling to school . . . arriving at school . . . going through their early morning routine . . . picturing themselves in their first hour class, second hour class . . . through the day . . . picturing themselves at lunch . . . at the end of the day . . . traveling home . . . going through their normal routine after school until dinner . . . eating dinner . . . going through their normal evening routine . . . getting ready for and going to bed.

Discuss the guided imagery trip. How many could easily picture a 'normal' day? Did anyone have trouble? Why? Did anything surprise you as you pictured it? Ask students to keep these images in their minds as they go through the following activity.

Pass out the '24 Hours in a Day' activity sheet. Explain that each piece of the 'pie' represents one hour in the day. Students are to fill out their expenditure of time during a 'normal' school day on this circle. Explain how to develop a key using color coding. Allow time for students to complete their wheels.

Assessment
A measure of the student's insight into his/her normal time expenditure is seen in his/her completed 24-hour wheel as well as his/her responses in discussion.

 ## Left Mode—Examine

Discussion.

Objective
The student will realize his/her normal expenditure of time in a day.

Activity
Discussion. Once the wheels are complete, discuss student findings. . . . How much time do you spend sleeping? After eliciting responses, show students that if they get the normal 8 hours of sleep each night, they are using 1/3 of their 24 hours in a day. . . . How much time do you spend in school? After rounding off the estimated time going to and from school as well as being in school, the average student at Nipher spends 7 hours a day at school when those 7 hours are added to the 8 spent sleeping, they represent 15 hours a day which are 'set in stone.' That is, students don't have much choice over how they spend these hours . . . How much time do you have left? Nine hours remain. All other daily activities fit into these nine hours . . . What other things do you have to do during a normal day? Think of chores, lessons, sports teams, personal hygiene, etc. Add up these times and subtract them from the nine hours which remained. The result represents the amount of time which the student has to spend in the way he/she likes.

Assessment
Student responses during the discussion provide a measure of his/her understanding of daily time allocations.

Quadrant 2—Concepts

 ## Right Mode—Image

Tug of War.

Objective
The student will relate his/her actions to a decision (conscious or unconscious) as to how time is allocated.

Activity
Tug of War. Provide students with a large rope to use in a tug of war. Explain that in this tug of war, the two sides are both found within our own heads. One side represents our desires. (Assign this to one end of the rope.) The other side represents our conscience which is telling us what we should do. (Assign this to the other end of the rope.) In other words, on one side we find the things we want to do and on the other we find the things we don't want to do.

Explain to the students that they are to listen to each situation and identify the thing the student wants to do and the thing s/he feels s/he should do. As each description is discussed, one student writes the thing desired on a sheet of paper and another writes the thing which needs to be done and stands on the corresponding side of the rope. They grab the ends of the rope and tug to show the interaction of the two.

After all situations are analyzed, ask the students to show how the rope might pull if . . . 1) a teacher called to tell your mom that you aren't finishing your homework. 2) tomorrow is a holiday. 3) you have tickets to a baseball game tonight. 4) grade cards come home in two weeks. 5) your older sister gets in trouble for not doing her work. 6) Christmas is next week. 7) your teachers talked with you today and asked you to do your best. 8) you got in a fight with your best friend. 9) your mom and/or dad is out of town. 10) you got an 'A' on a math test today. 11) you are tired because you didn't get enough sleep last night. 12) you have a lot of work to make up from being out of school sick last week. 13) you get mad at yourself because you forgot to bring home a book. 14) your favorite TV program is on tonight. 15) you want to get good grades.

Situation for the Tug of War

1. Teddy really likes to play soccer. He usually plays every day after school. Today he had to go to the dentist after school. Right now it's 8 o'clock. He's had dinner and doesn't have to go to bed until 10 o'clock. He knows he has a big project due tomorrow and he hasn't done much on it, but he really wants to play soccer. What is tugging at Teddy?

2. Maria has a special day in store for her today. After school her grandmother is coming to visit. She is going to take Maria shopping to buy her new clothes for her birthday. After shopping, they will return home where her mother is preparing a special birthday feast. Her family will celebrate her birthday. She'll open presents and blow out candles on a cake. Her special day will be over by 8 which leaves her plenty of time to do her homework, but she somehow doesn't want to do it. What is tugging at Maria?

3. Jessie has a lot of homework to do. It seems like she has something to do for every teacher. Since she hasn't done any homework for three nights, things have really piled up. If she starts right after she gets home, she might get done by ten o'clock tonight. Jessie just doesn't want to do it. She feels like crying. What is tugging at Jessie?

4. It's Wednesday and that means church day. Nickie knows that she has church class from 7 to 8:30 tonight. Right after school she has a piano lesson and then she has to baby-sit her little brother so her mother can take her older brother to his baseball practice. She knows she has an hour of homework to do tonight, but her favorite TV program comes on at 9. It lasts until 10 and that's when she has to be in bed. What is tugging at Nickie?

5. Justin hates to work. He's not particular. He doesn't like to do any kind of work—yard work, homework, housework—nothing. He just wants to play. It doesn't matter how much play time he's had, it's never enough—particularly if there's work to be done. What should be tugging at Justin?

6. Kay's team won the championship game today! They are the best volleyball team in their league. Kay was so worked up she couldn't get anything done before the game. She talked to friends on the phone and rode her bike around. After the game, the coach took the team out for pizza. They celebrated until 8:30. It was almost 9 before she got home. The day had taken its toll on her. She was beat. All she wanted to do was to go to bed, but there on her desk was an English assignment she knew she should do. What was tugging at Kay?

Assessment
Student responses will indicate whether or not s/he understands the time decision that is being made in each situation.

Left Mode—Define

Critical Thinking Skill: Planning.

Objective

The student will be able to develop time plans allowing for the completion both of those things he/she wants to do and those things he/she needs to do.

Activity

Critical Thinking Skill: Planning. Introduce the students to the critical thinking skill of planning. Work through the skill lesson fashioned according to the Deductive Thinking Plan which follows:

Critical Thinking Skill: Planning
Concept
Planning helps make a task more manageable by breaking it into parts which can be completed in segments over a period of time.
Objectives:
1. The student will be able to identify the steps included in the planning process.
2. The student will be able to analyze situations for the correct use of the planning process.
3. The student will be able to use the process to make long-term plans for completing a class project.

Materials:
'Planning' poster, modeling exercise material sample project assignment, 'The Perfect Saturday' worksheet, blank planning sheet, blank timeline sheet.

Procedure
1. Mental Set
Present the students with the following problem to solve in their groups. Explain that they are to imagine that they have been given the opportunity to invite six of their friends over on Saturday to celebrate their birthday. As part of their birthday gift, their parents have pledged to let them plan the perfect Saturday (within reason). However, part of the deal is that they do all the planning. The perfect Saturday will start at 10 a.m. and will go until 10 p.m. Plans have to account for all of this time. Everyone in the group will need to agree with the final choices. One list is to be completed for each group and a group member will be chosen at random to share the group's plans with the class.

After allowing a work time, share plans with the class. Post on the board. Ask students what services they will need (transportation), what resources they will need, how everyone will know when and where to meet, etc. Discuss some of the other things which need to be determined and have been omitted in the plans as they are now.

2. Rationale/Objectives
Explain to the students that developing and using good plans can help them better accomplish tasks more efficiently. One example of such a long-range task is an insect collection. The purpose of the following skill lesson is to help students learn the steps of the planning process and how to apply them.

3. Input
Have students turn to a partner and try to answer the question: What do you think is the first thing you should do when making plans? After several minutes, have groups volunteer their answers. Hand out a 'Perfect Saturday.' sheet to each group. Go over the steps to follow in developing good plans:

1) Decide what you want to do.
As you identify what you want to do, weigh the various alternatives to determine the one most to your liking. Then explain your choice to a friend as completely as possible, changing it where necessary. By the time you have finished this step, you should have a clear picture of what you hope to accomplish.
Turn to your partners. Complete this step for your perfect Saturday plans.
2) Make a list of all materials and resources which you will need to complete your project.
In your mind, review what you just decided to do, asking yourself, "What will I need?", every step of the way. Try to imagine all of the little things as well as the big ones. For example, if you are going to prepare breakfast, you will need not only food, but also cooking utensils and small items such as salt and pepper. Write down all of the things you will need. Turn to your partners. Complete this step for your perfect Saturday plans.
3) Next, carefully list all of the steps you will follow in the correct order to complete your task.
Be careful to include all of the things which you will need to do. Again, review what you have decided to do, asking yourself what to do next each step of the way. Write the steps in the order which you will follow.
Turn to your partners. Complete this step for your perfect Saturday plans.
4) Finally, make a list of all the things which could go wrong.
By considering the things which might come in the way of your successfully completing your project, you are developing a better idea of the specific problems which you might encounter. You will also automatically come up with possible solutions. You may want to make some changes in your plans here. You may also choose different alternatives if the one chosen doesn't work as you carry out your plan.
*** This is not to say that you know you will have problems.

It is rather a precautionary step which everyone needs to work through.

Turn to your partners and complete this step for your perfect Saturday plans.

4. Check for Understanding/Modeling

Once group plans are complete, one member of each group is randomly selected to share the group's plans with the next clockwise group. The receiving group should make sure that the plans are complete. All problems should be written down by a recorder and given to the visitor who is taking them back to the group which needs to make changes until the sharing group OK's the plans by signing them.

The teacher should monitor group work, checking that the plans are correct and that the groups are working well. Also let the students know that they will be monitored on the skill of having all group members participate and complete their roles.

5. Modeling/Check for Understanding/Guided Practice.

Return to the topic of long-range school assignments. Explain to the students that these steps can be used in planning to complete schoolwork. Go over several examples of such projects, at least one of which should be an actual assignment made on the team.

Ask students in their groups to make plans for completing a real assignment—plans which they think they could follow. Again, students are to complete one plan and will be selected at random to share the plans with the class. Plans are to be posted on the board as they are shared. They should then be compared/contrasted—How are they alike and how are they different? . . . and why? Introduce one final aid in completing long-range assignments—a timeline. Show students how to break the large task into smaller bits which can be done over time. These smaller bits can then be written on a calendar in order to show when they are to be done. Go over an example using a sample timeline on the overhead. Have students turn to their partners and make a timeline to follow. Once complete, students should all sign the final plans and timeline, indicating that they will use them to complete the long-range assignment. Group members will check each week to be sure that all group members are on time with their project parts. Introduce a final activity on time management. Working in groups, students are to design and perform a commercial which gives a public service announcement about the importance of time management. Brainstorm with the class the many people who would benefit from planning their time expenditure and how. Discuss ways to approach the commercial. Once groups have finished, have them present their skit to the class.

6. Closure

Ask students to finish the statement: I think that time management . .

Steps to Follow in Planning:

1. Decide what you want to do.
2. Make a list of all materials and resources which you will need.
3. List all the steps which you will follow in the correct order.
4. Make a list of the things which could go wrong.

The Perfect Saturday

Use the steps in the planning process in order to plan the perfect Saturday for you and a group of six friends to go from 10 o'clock in the morning until 10 o'clock in the evening. Write your plans below.

Step 1: Tell what you will do on your perfect Saturday.

_____
_____
_____
_____
_____

Step 2: List the materials and resources you will need.

_____
_____
_____
_____
_____

Step 3: List the steps in the order that you will need to follow.

_____
_____
_____
_____
_____

Step 4: List problems you might have.

_____
_____
_____
_____

Assessment

The student's completion of the plans for a "Perfect Saturday" provides a measure of his/her mastery of the concepts both of the planning process and of time management.

Quadrant 3—Applications

 ### Left Mode—Try

Plan Your Time.

Objective

The student will be able to use the planning process to make plans for spending time on a daily, weekly, and monthly schedule.

Activity

Plan Your Time. Introduce weekly time schedules. Share examples with the students and show them how to fill them out. Together go through the steps in the planning process as the schedule is completed.

Step 1: Describe what you are going to do. Develop a time plan to schedule daily plans for a week in order to fit in both those things I need to do and those things I want to do.

Step 2: List the materials you will need. I will need a weekly schedule form and pencil. I will also need to know all the obligations I have for the week, i.e., all scheduled lessons, chores, social engagements, etc.

Step 3: List the steps in order that you will follow. 1) Ask my mother to help me identify the obligations I have for the week. 2) Gather a schedule form, a pencil, and an eraser. 3) Enter my obligations onto my schedule first. 4) Fill in with the things I most definitely want to do. 5) Identify the remaining time as flexible time—left for free time, but available for other things if needed.

Step 4: Make a list of the things which might go wrong—and possible solutions for the problems. 1) I might have a lot of homework one night. Solution: use some of my flexible time. 2) I might have to baby-sit my little brother. Solution: adjust my flex time. 3) I might have to go to the dentist. Solution: skip ball practice. 4) I might have family company one evening. Solution: do my homework right after school.

Once plans are complete, help students to fill in a weekly schedule. Once weekly plans are made, introduce the subject of long-range planning. Brainstorm and list the types of projects which are completed over a week or more. Discuss the special problems which they may present. Show students how to use the planning process to help with long-range plans. Model the use of the process in a present assignment. Ask students to complete project plans and a monthly schedule for breaking down the identified tasks.

Assessment

The plans completed provide the basis for evaluation of student mastery of this quadrant's objective.

 ### Right Mode—Extend

Timely Advice.

Objective

The student will act as a specialist to solve sample time management problems.

Activity

Timely Advice. Return to the students mentioned in the tug of war activity. Working in teams, students are to select one problem, discuss possible solutions, list solutions on a chart showing how to alter a daily schedule to allow for needed changes, and share them with the class.

Assessment

The student will show his/her understanding of time management through solutions for given problems.

Quadrant 4—Creations

Left Mode—Refine

Public Service Announcement: Plan.

Objective
The student will identify a common time allocation problem and will create a public service commercial giving possible solutions to the problem.

Activity
Public Service Announcement. Working in groups, students are to identify a common time management problem shared by students in their age group. The group is then to present the problem and possible solutions in a public service commercial which is given to the class.

Assessment
An evaluation of student mastery of the objective follows the completion of the commercial.

Right Mode—Integrate

Public Service Announcement: Practice and Present.

Objective
The student will identify a common time allocation problem and give possible solutions for the problem in a public service commercial.

Activity
Public Service Announcement. Groups are to practice their skills and prepare all props needed. They then present their commercials to the class. The skits are videotaped for sharing with parents at Open House.

Assessment
The identification of a time management problem and the possible solutions given provide a measure of student mastery of the objective.

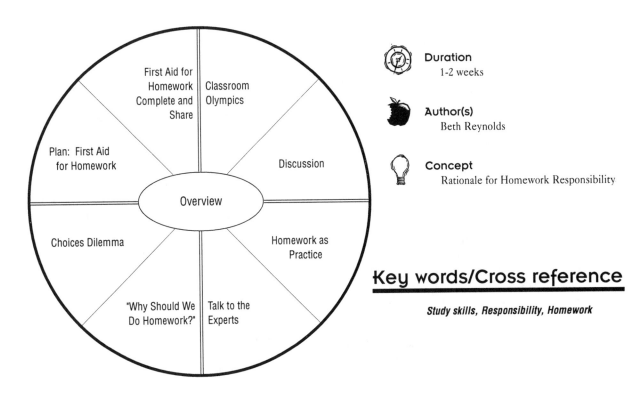

Duration
1-2 weeks

Author(s)
Beth Reynolds

Concept
Rationale for Homework Responsibility

Key words/Cross reference

Study skills, Responsibility, Homework

Overview

Objective
Homework provides practice—and practice makes perfect.

About the Author
Beth Reynolds is a 7th grade Language Arts/Social Studies teacher at Nipher Middle School, Kirkwood, MO. She is a certified 4MAT Trainer.

Required Resources
Classroom Olympics materials: pennies, cups, paper, trash cans, coins. Practice overhead activity sheet: Why Should We Do Homework?

Bibliography
Hunter, Madeline. *Mastery Teaching.* TIP Publications: El Segundo, CA, 1982.

Quadrant 1—Experience

 Right Mode—Connect

Classroom Olympics.

Objective

The student will experience a situation in which practice makes a difference.

Activity

Classroom Olympics. Working in three groups, students participate in a three part competition against two other groups. The three events are: 1) throwing paper wads into a trash can 12 feet away (3 tosses each). 2) dropping 10 pennies in a coffee cup over the shoulder (best of 2 tries each). 3) flipping and calling the toss of a coin (total of 5 tries).

Do not explain the competition to the students. Instead, tell them that they will be doing three different things during this class session. They are to read and follow the directions to any other. Hand out the following directions and work on student compliance.

Group 1: You are to visit the library to select an independent reading book. You must be back in class in 15 minutes. Allow these group members to leave.
Group 2: You are to write in your journals for seven minutes. At the end of this time, you will receive new directions.
Group 3: You are to meet me in the hall as soon as you finish reading these directions.
Get group 2 started and meet group 3 in the hall. Once there, quickly brief them on the activity and get them started practicing for the three events. Rotate them quickly through the activities. After seven minutes, meet group 2 in the classroom. Explain to them the three part competition which will take place shortly and allow them to practice for the three events for about five minutes. When the first group returns to class, direct everyone to be seated. Introduce the three part competition and explain that the three groups will comprise the competing teams.
Hold the competition. Average the scores of the teams in each of the events. Rank order the teams according to the results.

Assessment

Student understanding of the experience is indicated by statements made during the following discussion.

 Left Mode—Examine

Discussion.

Objective

The student will evaluate the results, determining the relationship between group performance and the amount of practice time afforded the group.

Activity

Discussion. Discuss the results of the Classroom Olympics. Was there any relationship between the scores and the practice times? If so, what was it? Why do you think this happened? What do you think might happen if some groups were given even more time to practice? What did the groups which practiced have to give up that the other groups got? Can you think of any other time you might have to give something up in order to get time to practice something? How does practice time relate to final scores? In what other areas in your life can this be seen?

Assessment

Measures of student understanding can be determined both from their answers during the discussion and their written answers to the following question: WHY practice?

Quadrant 2—Concepts

Right Mode—Image

Homework as Practice.

Objective

The student will be able to relate homework to academic achievement.

Activity

Homework as Practice. Students, working in small groups, are given multiple examples of homework assigned at different levels and in different classes. Each group is to carefully consider the assignments and decide what is being practiced. They are then to create a "Practice Poster" for each. For example:

Wanted: Accuracy in Recognizing Nouns:

Description: A noun is a part of speech naming a person, place, or thing.

Last Seen: Nouns are regularly seen in sentences. They appear in the sentences of the assignment below.

Reward: A successful learner; a pat on the back; a feeling of accomplishment; a good grade.

Assessment

Quality of student posters.

Left Mode—Define

Talk to the Experts.

Objective

The student will be able to name the benefits of work completion.

Activity

Talk to the Experts. Present the students with typical questions about homework asked by students their age. Discuss possible answers and then reveal the answers of the experts.

1. Does practice really always make perfect?

No. To improve your skills, you need to practice in a certain way. For one thing, you need to practice a short, meaningful chunk of material at a time. As you practice, you need to check to be sure that you're right. If you don't, you might practice—and therefore learn—the wrong thing. So as you work on your homework, you need to be concentrating on it, and checking yourself at short intervals.

2. How long should I spend each evening on homework?

It depends. Classes and teachers differ. Usually at the middle school level, you can count on about one to one and a half hours of homework a night. You might be advised to try to mix the types of work you have. That is, the more meaningful the work is and the better you concentrate on it, the more you learn. It's hard to concentrate on the same type of thing over a long time. Therefore, if you change the kinds of work you do, like work on a written assignment, switch to math problems, and then go back to another written assignment, you may get more out of your work.

3. Does doing the same thing over and over really help me to learn?

It does to a point. Research shows that when learning a new skill, you need to practice over and over again in different ways in the beginning. This is called 'massed' practice. You learn a great deal in a short period of time, but you tend to forget it after awhile. In order to remember the skill for a long time, you need to practice it again, but space the times you practice further and further apart. This is called 'distributed practice' and allows for long-term memory.

4. When should I check my work?

As often as possible. As you do your work, stop periodically and check to be sure you are doing the task correctly. Be sure that you listen to the teacher and check your work in class the next day. To practice without knowing whether or not you're doing the right thing, often does no good.

Assessment

Student answers to questions during the presentation provides a measure of their understanding of the material.

Quadrant 3—Applications

Left Mode—Try

"Why Should We Do Homework?"

Objective

The student will be able to explain the fundamentals of meaningful practice covered.

Activity

Why Should We Do Homework? Students complete the activity sheet giving answers to the importance of doing homework.

Name _____

Why Do Homework?

Answer the question, 'Why do homework?' to each student below.

1. John seems to know what's going on in class each day. He listens to the teacher explain how to do things, and watches her do sample problems on the board. Why should he do problems at home for homework?
2. Kim worked really hard on last night's homework. However, she missed all of the problems. Her teacher explained her mistake to her in class today. Why should she do more problems for homework?
3. Reggie loves to talk. He tried to listen during class, but he can't seem to pay close attention. There are just too many friends to talk to. Why does Reggie need to do his homework after class?
4. David has trouble finishing his homework on time. During math class, he's usually working on his language homework which is due the next period. And during language class, he often works on his science which is due next. Why does David need to do his homework at home?
5. Teddy and Max are good friends. They do most things together. They belong to the same baseball team. They hang out together. They eat lunch together and go most places together. They even do homework together. Teddy does the math homework and Max does language. Then they trade papers and copy. How are Teddy and Max both being cheated out of learning as much as they can? Why do they both need to do their own homework?

Assessment

Student responses to the activity sheet provide a measure of his/her mastery.

Right Mode—Extend

Choices Dilemma.

Objective

The student will create a visual presentation of conflicts which can occur to anyone completing homework.

Activity

Choices Dilemma. In small groups, students design a sculpture using themselves and labels made from paper, markers, pictures—whatever items are at hand—depicting the many things which tempt students away from homework. Together brainstorm a list of these things and write on the board. After allowing time for groups to work, have each present its sculpture to the class. Discuss the specific dilemmas shown in each.

Assessment

The conflicts presented by group sculptures provide the basis for measurement of the above objective.

Quadrant 4—Creations

Left Mode—Refine

Plan: First Aid for Homework.

Objective
The student will create strategies to ease the problems which may occur to keep one from doing homework.

Activity
First Aid for Homework. Working in small groups, students create plans to cure homework problems. In so doing, they address the problems shown in the sculptures, creating a pamphlet which suggests ways to alleviate them. Possible solutions might include using comfortable furniture, bright lighting, asking for help from parents, or just having the family dog nearby.

Assessment
The pamphlet created provides a measure of student learning.

Right Mode—Integrate

First Aid for Homework Complete and Share.

Objective
The student will create strategies to ease the problems which may occur to keep one from doing homework.

Activity
First Aid for Homework. Groups are given time to complete their pamphlets, after which they are shared. As a closing activity, students are asked to list the most common problems which they individually have. They then select two possible solutions for each and make a commitment to try at least one.

Assessment
Contributions to and quality of pamphlets.

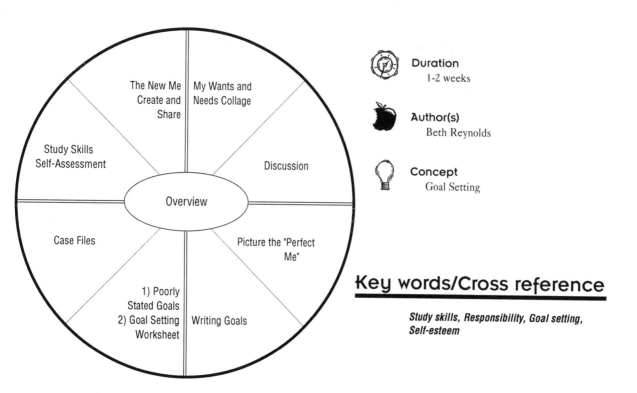

Duration
1-2 weeks

Author(s)
Beth Reynolds

Concept
Goal Setting

Key words/Cross reference

Study skills, Responsibility, Goal setting, Self-esteem

Overview

Objective
Academic achievement is possible for all students who make a commitment to try and to apply the necessary skills.

About the Author
Beth Reynolds is a 7th grade Language Arts/Social Studies teacher at Nipher Middle School, Kirkwood, MO. She is a certified 4MAT Trainer.

Required Resources
Drawing paper, construction paper, scissors, glue. Activity Sheets: The Things I Like to Do, The Things I Need to Do, Poorly Stated Goals, Making a Goal, Case Study Folders. Overhead: The 5 Conditions of a Good Goal.

Quadrant 1—Experience

 ## Right Mode—Connect

My Wants and Needs Collage.

Objective
The student will realize the many things he/she both wants to do and needs to do before making an effort towards balancing them in his/her life.

Activity
My Wants and Needs Collage. Each student is to make a collage in two parts, one showing the things which s/he likes to do, and the other showing the things s/he needs to do. Before beginning construction, together brainstorm lists of possible wants and needs. Wants might include playing basketball, talking on the phone, going ice skating, going to a movie or shopping, or even going on a vacation. Needs might include things such as walking the dog, cleaning his/her room, doing homework, washing dishes, baby-sitting little sister, or practicing piano. Point out that some things might be in both lists, such as walking the dog. Explain that the purpose of making the collage is to become more aware of the many things which students try to fit into their days. Go over various suggestions for making a collage including cutting pictures from magazines and cutting out letters to spell words. Allow time for students to work. After the collages are complete, ask each student to share his/hers with the class.

Assessment
Student collages and their descriptions which follow form the basis for evaluation.

 ## Left Mode—Examine

Discussion.

Objective
The student will be able to explain that both types of activities are important in life and that it is possible to plan time for both.

Activity
Discussion. Discuss student understandings which may have resulted from the activity.
1) What things of those shown could be done on a daily basis? . . . a weekly basis? . . . a monthly basis? . . . yearly?
2) Which of those things which you want to do would require resources such as money, transportation, or special equipment?
3) Which things would you like to do with your family? . . . your friends? . . . either?
4) Which do you have most control over? Least?
5) What things do you need to do that you tend to avoid? Why?
6) What ultimately leads to your doing them?
7) Which take a long time? . . . a short time?
8) Which do you do daily? . . . weekly? . . . monthly? . . . yearly?
9) Which of those things that you need to do, do you not mind doing?
10) What is the reason behind the need to do those things?
11) Is it possible to do both those things you want to do and those things you need to do?
12) Do you make a conscious effort to fit both in? Do you know how to plan to do this?

Assessment
Student contributions to discussion.

Quadrant 2—Concepts

 ## Right Mode—Image

Picture the "Perfect Me."

Objective

The student will explain that behaviors can be changed by setting goals and following through on them. These behaviors can make it possible to plan for time to do both the things we like to do and those we need to do.

Activity

Picture the "Perfect" Me. Ask the students to imagine what they would be like if they were "perfect" and were able to do both what they want to do and what they need to do in a normal day. Have them list all of the things they'd accomplish in just such a day. Then ask them to show such a day in a cartoon, showing each activity occurring at a definite time. Once complete have the students share their cartoons. Then discuss the topic:

1) Is it possible to really be "perfect" for any amount of time?

2) Can you learn to do things in new ways?

3) How could you do so?

Introduce the topic of goals and explain that once you know what behavior you want to change, you can do so by planning the change. Writing a goal to guide you can be a big step in the right direction.

Assessment

Student answers during discussion show their understanding of the objective.

 ## Left Mode—Define

Writing Goals.

Objective

The student will be able to develop well written goals: 1) Will be able to explain the five criteria of a well written goal. 2) Will be able to evaluate goals for these criteria.

Activity

Writing Goals. Introduce instruction by asking students to name all the goals they can think of. Discuss the critical attributes of a goal—something to aim for, a mark of success, the end result of a series of actions. Explain that goals can be found in places other than sports and that setting goals can help to change behaviors. Go over the five criteria of a well stated goal as given on an overhead. Give examples of goals which meet these criteria and others which don't. Model the correct way to write effective goals.

Five Conditions of a Good Goal:

1. It must be conceivable (can be put into words).
2. It must be possible for the person setting it.
3. It must be controlable (you need permission of others to involve them).
4. It must be measurable (you need to be able to say "Yes, I did it," or "No, I did not").
5. It must be stated with no alternative (no plan "B").

Assessment

Give students true/false statements about the five conditions of well stated goals. Ask them to hold thumbs up if the statement is true, and thumbs down if it is false. Discuss each.

Quadrant 3—Applications

 ### Left Mode—Try

1) Poorly Stated Goals 2) Goal Setting Worksheet

Objective

The student will be able to develop well written goals:
1) will be able to explain the five criteria of a well written goal; 2) will be able to evaluate goals for these criteria.

Activity

Poorly Stated Goals. After reviewing the five conditions of a good goal, have students complete the activity sheet, 'Poorly Stated Goals'. For each goal which is not well developed, ask students to rewrite it in an acceptable way.

Poorly Stated Goals:

Remember that all goals must meet five conditions in order to be effective:

1. A good goal must be conceivable.
2. A good goal must be possible for the person setting it.
3. A good goal must be controllable.
4. A good goal must be measurable.
5. A good goal must be stated with no alternative.

Write the condition which is not met in each of the following goals, making each a poorly stated goal. Write 'yes' next to each goal which meets all five conditions.

1. I will do my homework tonight. _____
2. I will win the US. Open Golf Tournament by June 30. _____
3. Tonight, I will either take out the garbage or watch TV before 10 P.M. _____
4. By the time I am twenty-one, I will discover something that will revolutionize the world. _____
5. I will invite Cathy over on Friday. _____
6. I will get an A on my science test on Friday. _____
7. I will get up in time to get to school by 8:15 on Monday morning. _____
8. I will buy my mother the neatest Mother's Day gift. _____
9. By 3:00 this afternoon, I will invite Cathy to my party. _____
10. I will be picked to be captain of something this year. _____

Make up a poorly stated goal to share with the class.

_____
_____
_____
_____
_____
_____

Assessment

Student scores on the paper indicate their mastery of the objective.

 ### Right Mode—Extend

Case Files.

Objective

The student will develop 'case studies' of students having problems for which goals are developed to help alleviate.

Activity

Case Files. Divide students into small groups for this activity. Each group is to be given a manila folder 'file' describing a student having academic problems. As a beginning activity, each group is to carefully study the file and develop a goal to help the student deal with his/her problems. These are then introduced to the class. Students then create a new student with new problems. They create their 'file' on easel paper which is then presented to the class. At the end of their presentation, the rest of the class develops a goal for him/her.

Case Studies:

- David is a bright, energetic seventh grade boy. Even though he's very smart, David doesn't get good grades in school. He pays good attention in all of his classes, but somehow he doesn't manage to get his homework done every night. Last quarter, David finished only 10 out of 25 math assignments. Consequently, David received a 'D' for math on his report card.

Can you write a goal for David to work towards?

- Juanita is a very small seventh grade girl. Every night she goes home with all of her books. She walks out of the door looking as if she'll fall over under all of the weight. However, inevitably Juanita receives low grades on her homework assignments. This happened just today with her math homework. Last night she did all of her work. However, as she tried to do the problems she realized that she didn't remember all of the steps to follow. When the teacher was explaining this in class, Juanita was reading a note from a friend. She had never seen the problem explained.

Can you write a goal for Juanita to work towards?

- Samantha is a very popular girl in the seventh grade. Each night at least four of her friends call her and they talk on the phone for half an hour each. Sometimes as many as six people call her! On those evenings her mother tends to get mad after Samantha's been on the phone for two hours. Samantha takes home all of her work each night. She knows how to do the work, but never seems to get around to it. Her grades on tests are good, but she doesn't get very good grades because she has so much incomplete work.

Can you write a goal for Samantha to work towards?

- Jake loves science and does very well in that class. When the teacher gives the class special experiments to try at home, Jake always tries them. He reads extra science books and studies hard for all of his science tests. He always finishes his science homework and is a ready participant in class discussions. However, by the time that Jake finishes doing all of this for science, he doesn't have time left for his other subjects. While he received an 'A' in science last quarter, his other grades were not so good. Jake's teachers in his other classes commented that while Jake seems to be capable of doing the work, he just doesn't.

Can you write a goal for Jake to work towards?

- Susan loves to talk. She talks to her parents at home. She talks to her friends on the bus. She talks to everyone at school. She talks during class discussions. She talks in the halls and in the cafeteria and in the gym even when no one can hear her. Susan has many interesting and funny things to say. Most people like to listen to her—at least for a while. The problem is that Susan likes to talk so much that she tends to do it all through her classes. Just today when she tried to write her language paper she realized that she had no idea of what to do. When she asked the teacher, she was given a brief explanation, but then the class time was up and she had to leave.

Can you write a goal for Susan to work towards?

- Jay really does try, but somehow he never manages to do things right. He always manages to write in pencil only to arrive in class and find that the teacher wanted the class to write in ink. Or he works on a map of North America only to find out that it was supposed to be a map of the world. The things

that Jay does, he does well. For example, his map was very neatly done. It just wasn't the right thing and so he didn't earn many of the possible points. Part of Jay's problem is that he dives right into a paper, thinking that he knows how to do it. Later he finds that he forgot to do something.

Can you write a goal for Jay to work towards?

- Jessie is so afraid that she will forget something that she carries everything around with her in a book bag. At the beginning of the year, her book bag was nice and neat. As the days went by, it became the collection place for everything she was given. By December, Jessie had in it every spelling test she had taken during the year, every handout given to her in science and social studies, as well as every math and language practice sheet returned to her. Her book bag was overflowing to say the least. However, Jessie was so afraid that she might forget something that she took it home every night and when she finished her homework, she put it in the book bag to take back to school. The big problem came about when the teacher asked her to take out her homework the next day. She could never find it.

Can you write a goal for Jessie to work towards?

Assessment

Student analysis of the case files and the goals written to solve the problem are used as a measure of mastery.

Quadrant 4—Creations

 ## Left Mode—Refine

Study Skills Self-Assessment.

Objective

The student will evaluate his/her academic and personal times and develop goals to meet any needs found.

Activity

Study Skills Self-Assessment. Have the students complete a Study Skills Self-Assessment to determine their academic needs. Discuss the results. Ask the students to further examine their free times to determine whether or not they are using them effectively. Once both are complete, have each student identify three areas in which to develop goals. Ask them to write goals and make a plan with their base groups to check their progress first every day, and later once a week.

Assessment

Student assessments and the goals which result provide a measure of their success in meeting the above objective.

 ## Right Mode—Integrate

The New Me Create and Share.

Objective

The student will create visual display of his/her 'old' self before applying goals and his/her 'new' self after the goals written take effect.

Activity

The New Me. For this activity, students actually 'create' a double-sided picture of themselves out of craft paper. To do so, they lay down on paper, their partners trace around their bodies, and they then 'dress' themselves with other paper. On one side, they are to create the person they were before the goals which they created take effect. On the other side, they create a visual display of the person they are after the goals are put into effect. They are to add details to the figures to show their feelings, the problems or successes which they are having, and the way others see them. For example, in the 'before' representation, they may put sunglasses on to disguise themselves, or hold a behavior referral in their hand. For the 'after' figure, they may add a new watch, a great report card, or a new smile. Once complete, the students share their figures, both the 'old' and the 'new' shapes. These are to be hung and shared and a small party held to celebrate their many successes.

Assessment

Student figures provide a visual measure of their understanding, but their feelings provide a measure of their hearts.

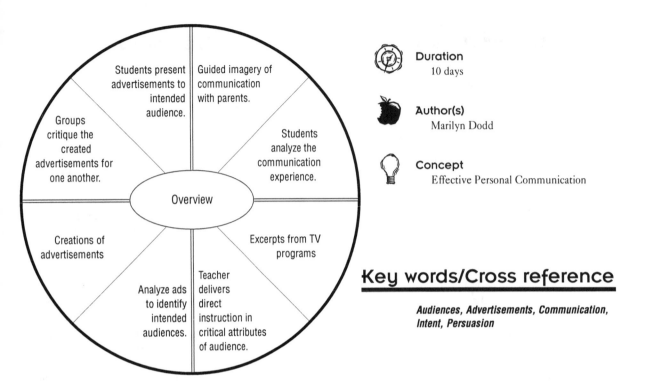
Communication/Audience

Students present advertisements to intended audience.

Guided imagery of communication with parents.

Groups critique the created advertisements for one another.

Students analyze the communication experience.

Overview

Creations of advertisements

Excerpts from TV programs

Analyze ads to identify intended audiences.

Teacher delivers direct instruction in critical attributes of audience.

Duration
10 days

Author(s)
Marilyn Dodd

Concept
Effective Personal Communication

Key words/Cross reference

Audiences, Advertisements, Communication, Intent, Persuasion

Overview

Objective
Students will learn strategies to know an intended audience to facilitate effective communication.

About the Author
Marlin Dod is a Reading Instructional Specialist in Pasadena Independent School District, Pasadena, TX. She is a participant in the Pasadena 4MAT Implementation Project and is a certified 4MAT Trainer.

Required Resources
Teacher-prepared guided imagery; teacher-prepared video clip of popular TV series appealing to teens.

Communication/Audience

Quadrant 1—Experience

 ### Right Mode—Connect

Guided imagery of communication with parents.

Objective

To create an experience to raise students' awareness of the importance of audience in communication.

Activity

Teacher conducts guided imagery. Students remember a time when they wanted a special favor from parents. Students recall which parent they approached, what time of day it was, where they were, what their tone of voice was, what kinds of words they used, what promises they made.

Assessment

Involvement of students in the experience.

 ### Left Mode—Examine

Students analyze the communication experience.

Objective

To analyze the experience of communication with parents.

Activity

Teacher leads class discussion of experience and charts students' responses on the chalkboard. Teacher extends discussion by asking why students selected the particular parent, time of day, etc. Teacher guides students to discover that their knowledge influenced their choices.

Assessment

Quality of discussion and relevance of student contributions.

Quadrant 2—Concepts

 ### Right Mode—Image

Excerpts from TV programs.

Objective

To extend the students' concept of audience to a broader context.

Activity

Students view teacher-prepared video clip exemplifying interpersonal communication from TV program that appeals to their age group. Students reflect on their feelings. Students create a visual metaphor of the communication connections.

Assessment

Quality of students' discussion of feelings elicited by TV program.

 ### Left Mode—Define

Teacher delivers direct instruction in critical attributes of audience.

Objective

To define, analyze, and categorize important aspects of audience.

Activity

Teacher lectures on the importance of recognizing the significant attributes of an intended audience. Working in groups of four, students identify and discuss appealing aspects of TV program and answer the following questions: 1) What knowledge does the creator of TV program have about the intended audience? 2) How do you know? Each group of students analyzes and categorizes the findings prior to developing a checklist of what communicators need to know about their audience. Groups compare checklists and revise appropriately to produce one comprehensive list.

Assessment

Completeness of checklist.

Quadrant 3—Applications

 ## Left Mode—Try

Analyze ads to identify intended audiences.

Objective
To apply checklist to written communications.

Activity
The teacher provides each group with four written advertisements intended for different audiences. In pairs, students analyze and evaluate the advertisements according to the checklist.

Assessment
Quality of students' evaluations of advertisements.

 ## Right Mode—Extend

Creations of advertisements.

Objective
To develop an advertisement for a specific audience to whom they want to "sell" something.

Activity
In groups of four, students develop an "advertisement" (a rap, a poster, a letter, or other medium of students' choice) about their school for fifth grade students.

Assessment
Quality of advertisements.

Quadrant 4—Creations

 ## Left Mode—Refine

Groups critique the created advertisements for one another.

Objective
To critique advertisements.

Activity
Student groups share advertisements with one another. Using audience checklist, viewing/listening groups critique presentations and make suggestions for improvement.

Assessment
Quality of effort put into activity.

 ## Right Mode—Integrate

Students present advertisements to intended audience.

Objective
To present advertisements to fifth grade students.

Activity
Students visit fifth grade classrooms and present advertisements to the students.

Assessment
Response of fifth grade students.

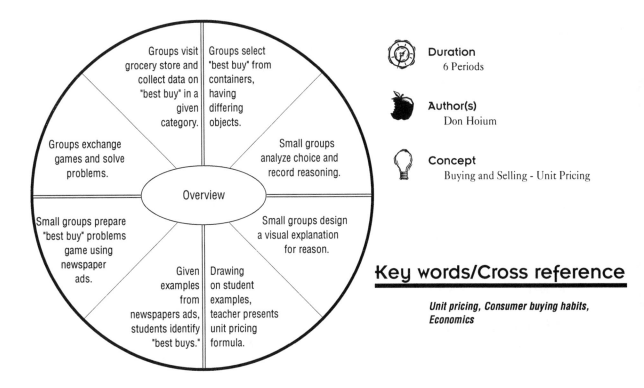

Groups visit grocery store and collect data on "best buy" in a given category.

Groups select "best buy" from containers, having differing objects.

Groups exchange games and solve problems.

Small groups analyze choice and record reasoning.

Overview

Small groups prepare "best buy" problems game using newspaper ads.

Small groups design a visual explanation for reason.

Given examples from newspapers ads, students identify "best buys."

Drawing on student examples, teacher presents unit pricing formula.

Duration
6 Periods

Author(s)
Don Hoium

Concept
Buying and Selling - Unit Pricing

Key words/Cross reference

Unit pricing, Consumer buying habits, Economics

Overview

Objective
This is the first of a three-wheel interdisciplinary unit. In this wheel, students experience an examination of unit pricing ($/quantity) in consumer buying habits.

About the Author
Don Hoium is a school psychologist for the Saskatoon Board of Education, Saskatoon, Saskatchewan, Canada. He is a certified 4MAT Trainer.

Required Resources
Mock product containers for Quadrant One; poster board and markers for Quadrant Two Right Mode; newspaper advertisements with prices.

Quadrant 1—Experience

 ### Right Mode—Connect

Groups select "best buy" from containers, having differing objects.

Objective

Students will attempt to identify best buys of identical products with differing volumes and prices.

Activity

Small groups of students are given three different sized containers with differing numbers of identical plastic blocks, with different prices labelled on each. They are asked to identify what is the "best buy."

Assessment:

Degree of involvement in activity.

 ### Left Mode—Examine

Small groups analyze choice and record reasoning.

Objective

Students analyze their choice above and identify a reason for it.

Activity

On a sheet of poster paper groups record a written reason for their "best buy" choice.

Assessment

Degree of involvement and detail in responses.

Quadrant 2—Concepts

 ### Right Mode—Image

Small groups design a visual explanation for reason.

Objective

Students create an illustration to support/explain/clarify written reason.

Activity

Groups produce an illustration on poster paper directly beneath written reason for "best buy" choice.

Assessment

Group participation and completion of imaging.

 ### Left Mode—Define

Drawing on student examples, teacher presents unit pricing formula.

Objective

Students explain the $/quantity formula.

Activity

Drawing on student examples, teacher identifies the best buy formula and provides additional examples.

Assessment

Student involvement and understanding of responses.

Quadrant 3—Applications

 ### Left Mode—Try

Given examples from newspapers ads, students identify "best buys."

Objective
Students complete "best buy" problems.

Activity
Students complete practice examples drawn from newspaper advertisements.

Assessment
Success with problems.

 ### Right Mode—Extend

Small groups prepare "best buy" problems game using newspaper ads.

Objective
Students prepare a grocery advertisement game.

Activity
In small groups, students prepare a print grocery advertisement with three groups of similar products of different sizes and prices. On the back of the ad, the best buys in each category are identified.

Assessment
Group involvement and detail in work.

Quadrant 4—Creations

 ### Left Mode—Refine

Groups exchange games and solve problems.

Objective
Students evaluate student ads to determine "best buys."

Activity
Groups exchange ads and try to identify "best buys" in each category.

Assessment
Degree of successful identification of "best buys."

 ### Right Mode—Integrate

Groups visit grocery store and collect data on "best buy" in a given category.

Objective
Students apply "best buys" formula in a grocery store setting.

Activity
In small groups, students select a product then visit a grocery store to collect data and produce a chart identifying various brands and the best buy available. Charts are then displayed in the classroom.

Assessment
Group involvement and detail in data collection analysis.

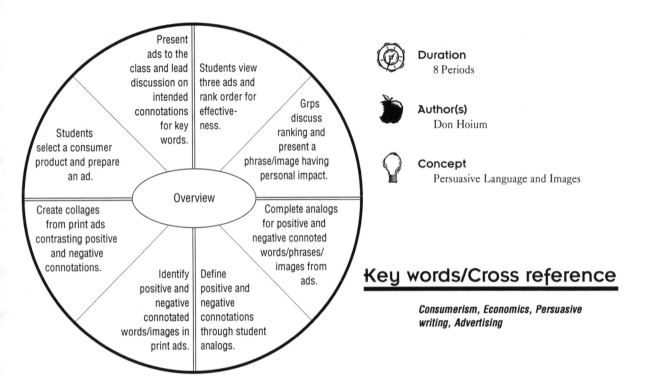

Present ads to the class and lead discussion on intended connotations for key words.

Students view three ads and rank order for effectiveness.

Grps discuss ranking and present a phrase/image having personal impact.

Students select a consumer product and prepare an ad.

Overview

Create collages from print ads contrasting positive and negative connotations.

Complete analogs for positive and negative connoted words/phrases/images from ads.

Identify positive and negative connotated words/images in print ads.

Define positive and negative connotations through student analogs.

Duration
8 Periods

Author(s)
Don Hoium

Concept
Persuasive Language and Images

Key words/Cross reference

Consumerism, Economics, Persuasive writing, Advertising

Overview

Objective
This is the second of a three-wheel interdisciplinary 4MAT unit. In this cycle, students will examine persuasive language and images through the use of advertising.

About the Author
Don Hoium is a school psychologist for the Saskatoon Board of Education, Saskatoon, Sask. Canada. He is a certified 4MAT Trainer.

Required Resources
Teacher prepared video clips of positive and negative TV advertisements; examples of printed positive/negative ads, materials for student projects cam corder, (if available), poster board, markers, etc.

Quadrant 1—Experience

 ### Right Mode—Connect

Students view three ads and rank order for effectiveness.

Objective
Students view consumer product advertisements (TV &/or Radio &/or print) and rank order for effectiveness.

Activity
View three ads and rank in order of personal impact.

Assessment
Extent of involvement in activity.

 ### Left Mode—Examine

Groups discuss ranking and present a phrase/image having personal impact.

Objective
Students reflect on ads and provide a reason for rankings and select a key image and/or phrase/word that most affected them.

Activity
In groups of three, discuss how they determined their rankings and then present a key image and/or phrase from the best ad.

Assessment
Quality of discussion and extent of image/phrase.

Quadrant 2—Concepts

 ### Right Mode—Image

Complete analogs for positive and negative connoted words/phrases/images from ads.

Objective
Students complete analogs for positively and negatively connected words/phrases/images drawn from previous discussion.

Activity
Present words/phrases/images drawn from student examples and have students complete analogs for both positively and negatively connoted words/phrases/images.

Assessment
Quality of analogs.

 ### Left Mode—Define

Define positive and negative connotations through student analogs.

Objective
Students define and provide examples of positive and negative connotations in language and/or images.

Activity
Through a class discussion based on the analogs created, definitions of positive and negative connotations are developed and examples offered.

Assessment
Extent of discussion and detail in definitions.

Quadrant 3—Applications

 ## Left Mode—Try

Identify positive and negative connotated words/images in print ads.

Objective
Students identify positively and negatively connoted words/images in print ads.

Activity
Students examine print ads and collect examples of positively and negatively connoted words and images.

Assessment
Clarity of selected images and words.

 ## Right Mode—Extend

Create collages from print ads contrasting positive and negative connotations.

Objective
Students create a collage of positively and negatively connoted words and images.

Activity
In pairs, students collect words/phrases and images from print ads and produce a collage contrasting positive and negative connotations.

Assessment
Quality and detail of collages.

Quadrant 4—Creations

 ## Left Mode—Refine

Students select a consumer product and prepare an ad.

Objective
Students plan and prepare a print, radio or TV advertisement for a product of their choice using effectively connoted words/phrases.

Activity
In pairs, students determine a consumer product and devise an advertisement using appropriately connoted words and images.

Assessment
Extent of planning and detail and quality of advertisements.

 ## Right Mode—Integrate

Present ads to the class and lead discussion on intended connotations for key words.

Objective
Students present advertisements to the class and discuss the connotations intended from key words/images.

Activity
Students present advertisements, lead discussion of intentions. Class completes reaction sheets to provide feedback to presenters.

Assessment
Quality of presentation and clarity of discussion.

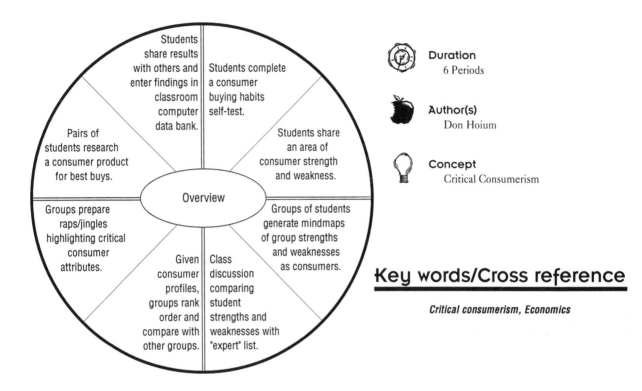

Students share results with others and enter findings in classroom computer data bank.

Students complete a consumer buying habits self-test.

Pairs of students research a consumer product for best buys.

Students share an area of consumer strength and weakness.

Overview

Groups prepare raps/jingles highlighting critical consumer attributes.

Groups of students generate mindmaps of group strengths and weaknesses as consumers.

Given consumer profiles, groups rank order and compare with other groups.

Class discussion comparing student strengths and weaknesses with "expert" list.

Duration
6 Periods

Author(s)
Don Hoium

Concept
Critical Consumerism

Key words/Cross reference

Critical consumerism, Economics

Overview

Objective
This is the third of a three-wheel interdisciplinary 4MAT unit. In this cycle, students will examine critical consumer attributes.

About the Author
Don Hoium is a school psychologist for the Saskatoon Board of Education, Saskatoon, Sask. Canada. He is a certified 4MAT Trainer.

Required Resources
Buying Habits Self-Test (see bibliography).

Bibliography
Burkman, E. (1976) *Individualized Science Instructional System: Buying and Selling.* Lexington: Ginn and Company

Quadrant 1—Experience

 Right Mode—Connect

Students complete a consumer buying habits self-test.

Objective
Students assess personal buying habits.

Activity
Students complete a consumer buying habits self-test and score results.

Assessment
Involvement in activity.

 Left Mode—Examine

Students share an area of consumer strength and weakness.

Objective
Students identify personal strengths and weaknesses as consumers.

Activity
Students use self-test results to determine an area of strength and weakness and share this with a small group.

Assessment
Quality of analysis and discussion.

Quadrant 2—Concepts

 Right Mode—Image

Groups of students generate mindmaps of group strengths and weaknesses as consumers.

Objective
Students create images representing consumer strengths and weaknesses.

Activity
In small groups, students generate mindmaps of group strengths and weaknesses as consumers.

Assessment
Extent of mindmapping.

 Left Mode—Define

Class discussion comparing student strengths and weaknesses with "expert" list.

Objective
Students recognize critical consumer attributes.

Activity
Drawing on mindmaps, teacher leads class in discussion to consolidate class listing of consumer strengths and then compares this to an "expert" list of consumer attributes.

Assessment
Student involvement in discussion.

Quadrant 3—Applications

 ### Left Mode—Try

Given consumer profiles, groups rank order and compare with other groups.

Objective
Students apply critical consumer attributes to identify good consumer profiles.

Activity
Given three consumer profiles, students in small groups rank them on the basis of critical attributes and compare findings with another group.

Assessment
Degree of application of critical attribute and involvement in discussion.

 ### Right Mode—Extend

Groups prepare raps/jingles highlighting critical consumer attributes.

Objective
Students personalize critical consumer attributes.

Activity
In small groups, students produce raps or jingles summarizing critical consumer attributes and present this to the class.

Assessment
Quality of raps and involvement in presentations.

Quadrant 4—Creations

 ### Left Mode—Refine

Pairs of students research a consumer product for best buys.

Objective
Students apply critical consumer attributes in researching a possible purchase.

Activity
In pairs, students select a consumer item of interest and use available resources (Consumer Reports Magazine, newspapers, local business, etc.) to determine the best buy.

Assessment
Extent of research.

 ### Right Mode—Integrate

Students share results with others and enter findings in classroom computer data bank.

Objective
Students share research results.

Activity
Students share results with two other pairs of students, then enter results in a classroom computer data bank to be used for class reference.

Assessment
Quality of presentation and detail of computer entries.

Math/Art=Symmetry

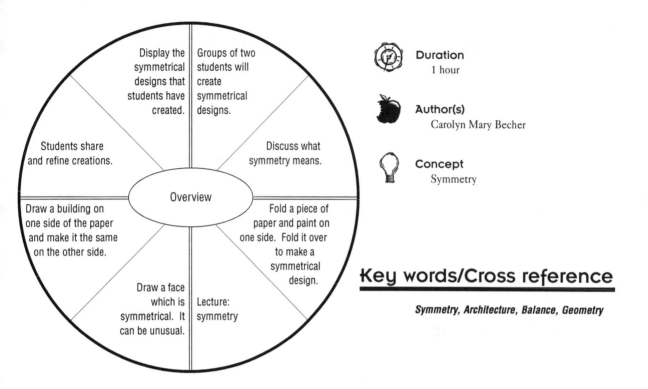

Display the symmetrical designs that students have created.

Groups of two students will create symmetrical designs.

Students share and refine creations.

Discuss what symmetry means.

Overview

Draw a building on one side of the paper and make it the same on the other side.

Fold a piece of paper and paint on one side. Fold it over to make a symmetrical design.

Draw a face which is symmetrical. It can be unusual.

Lecture: symmetry

Duration
1 hour

Author(s)
Carolyn Mary Becher

Concept
Symmetry

Key words/Cross reference

Symmetry, Architecture, Balance, Geometry

Overview

Objective
The students will identify what symmetry is.

About the Author
Carolyn Mary Becher is a middle school math teacher at Eden Valley Watkins High School, Paynesville, MN. She has developed particular expertise in using the visual arts to enhance mathematics instruction.

Required Resources
Art paper and tempera paint; ebony dark drawing pencils or crayons, popsicle sticks; scissors

Bibliography:
Grade 7 Mathematics Today, 2nd ed. by Janet S. Abbott, David Wells, Russel Jacobs, Joyce Light, Dr. Dennis W. Nelson, Mary Ann Shields, Rodney Thompson, Sara Tune, Harcourt Brace Jovanovich Publishers, 1987.
Art Talk, by Rosalind Ragans, Glencoe Publishing Company, 1988.

Math/Art=Symmetry

Quadrant 1—Experience

 Right Mode—Connect

Pairs of students will create symmetrical designs.

Objective
To create symmetry through body movement.

Activity
Students will work in groups of two. One student will make a design with his/her body and the other student has to pose with the same body configuration to create a unit that shows symmetry.

Assessment
Did the students' create a sculpture with their bodies that was symmetrical?

 Left Mode—Examine

Discuss what symmetry means.

Objective
To enhance the student's experience dealing with symmetry.

Activity
Students will discuss what "symmetry" means.

Assessment
Quality of discussion.

Quadrant 2—Concepts

 Right Mode—Image

Fold a piece of paper and paint on one side. Fold it over to make a symmetrical design.

Objective
To add more ideas to the concept of how symmetry works in math and art.

Activity
Students will fold a piece of paper in half and paint designs with tempera paint on one half of the paper and fold the wet paint over so it touches the other half of the paper to create a symmetrical design.

Assessment
Were the designs the same on both sides of the half of the paper?

 Left Mode—Define

Lecture: symmetry

Objective
To increase knowledge of the concept of symmetry.

Activity
The teacher gives a lecture defining symmetry. Symmetry in math and art separates a figure in a plane so that one part is an exact reflection of the other. The design is the same on both sides. Symmetry in art means formal balance. For instance, the Federal Reserve Building in Washington, D.C., shows symmetrical design (*Art Talk*, by Rosalind Regans, has some excellent visual examples).

Assessment
Students will take a test which has symmetrical and asymmetrical designs. The students will circle designs that are symmetrical.

Quadrant 3—Applications

 ### Left Mode—Try

Draw a face which is symmetrical. It can be unusual.

Objective
To reinforce what symmetry means by practice.

Activity
Students complete worksheet activities. Have students draw a face which is symmetrical.

Assessment
Is the face the same on both sides if you divide the face in half?

 ### Right Mode—Extend

Draw a building on one side of the paper and make it the same on the other side.

Objective
To combine lines and shapes to emphasize a man-made object that uses symmetry.

Activity
1. The students will fold a sheet of paper in half and draw half of a new style of building with an ebony dark drawing pencil or crayon on one half of the paper. Fold the paper over and use a popsicle stick and rub the paper to transfer the design to the other half of the sheet of paper. The design will look light so trace over the lines to make the darker to match what is on the other side of the paper.
2. Fold a sheet of paper in half and cut a shape by holding your finger-tips on the fold and cut the paper into a design. Unfold the paper to see the design. Students can decorate the design with lines and shapes that are the same on both sides of the fold. Students will give their design a name.

Assessment
Quality of drawings and degree of symmetry expressed.

Quadrant 4—Creations

 ### Left Mode—Refine

Students share and refine creations.

Objective
Students refine creations.

Activity
In small groups, students critique each others work for design and symmetry. They help each other with the names for their designs.

Assessment
Attention to the task and level of interest in each other's work.

 ### Right Mode—Integrate

Display the symmetrical designs that students have created.

Objective
To share ideas with others.

Activity
Students will display their work for others to see in the school.

Assessment
Quality of projects.

Graphing an Ordered Pair

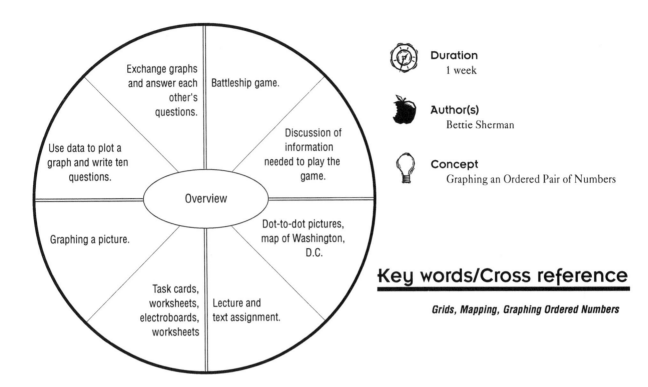

Duration
1 week

Author(s)
Bettie Sherman

Concept
Graphing an Ordered Pair of Numbers

Key words/Cross reference

Grids, Mapping, Graphing Ordered Numbers

Overview

Objective
Students will learn the strategies used in graphing ordered pairs of numbers.

About the Author
At the time this plan was written, Bettie Sherman was a mathematics teacher in Madison Local Schools, Mansfield, OH.

Required Resources
Blank 5-by-5grids for student "Battleship" game; teacher-prepared dot-to-dot type pictures and Washington, DC maps; teacher-prepared activities for guided practice; magazine pictures for display.

Graphing an Ordered Pair

Quadrant 1—Experience

 ### Right Mode—Connect

Battleship game.

Objective

To create an experience of graphing an ordered pair of numbers, given in a table.

Activity

Each team (2) gets a blank 5-by-5 grid in order to play a game of battleship.

Ship	Area Covered
Carrier	4 Coordinates
Battleship	3 Coordinates
Cruiser	2 Coordinates
Submarine	1 Coordinate

Explain that you have previously determined the position of four different ships on the grid. The students must try to locate each ship by naming coordinate points. Take turns (in teams) calling out coordinate points until all the ships have been located and identified. As points are called out, put an X where a ship or part of a ship is located and a circle around those points where there is no ship. The team that locates and identifies all the opponent's ships first is the winner.

Assessment

Group participation and interest.

 ## Left Mode—Examine

Discussion of information needed to play the game.

Objective

To enable the students to examine the power of graphing ordered pairs.

Activity

Discuss what the students have discovered so far about graphing ordered pairs. Ask: How did you understand the positions called out? Do we need some uniformity or rules? Is this (ordered pairs) a useful way of showing exact location? How do you think we could show negative numbers?

Assessment

Quality of discussion. Number of ideas generated.

Quadrant 2—Concepts

 ### Right Mode—Image

Dot-to-dot pictures, map of Washington, DC.

Objective

To provide activities that will broaden their experiences in graphing ordered pairs and reading ordered pairs.

Activity

Individual — Follow list of points to plot on worksheet. These will turn out dot-to-dot pictures of Snoopy, rocket ship, flower, etc.

Small Group — Give each team a map of Washington, DC, marked with points of interest. Letters equal distance on side, numbers on bottom. Find locations of various places. First team finished — 5 points. Each correct answer — 1 point.

Assessment

Quality and accuracy of individual pictures completed. Interest and participation of teams.

 ## Left Mode—Define

Lecture and text assignment.

Objective

To enhance their understanding of graphing ordered pairs. To enlarge their vocabulary.

Activity

Refer to the Battleship game in Quadrant One. Emphasize:

1. Graphs are ordered pairs.
2. The first number indicates the number of units moved to the right (or left) of 0. The second number indicates a move up or down.
3. A positive integer indicates a move to the right or up.
4. A negative integer indicates a move to the left or down.

Teacher lectures and illustrates on the overhead these concepts:

• Sample coordinates
• Ordered pairs of numbers
• Cartesian points
• Quadrants
• Integers
• X-axis
• Point of origin.

Also assign chapter on coordinate geometry in textbook.

Assessment

Objective test.

Graphing an Ordered Pair

Quadrant 3—Applications

 ### Left Mode—Try

Task cards, worksheets, electroboards, worksheets.

Objective
To give practice in plotting pairs of ordered numbers.

Activity
Teacher-made worksheets, electroboard, wheels of knowledge, and task cards.

Assessment
Quality and accuracy of above.

 ### Right Mode—Extend

Graphing a picture.

Objective
To allow students to make and play a game which will reinforce graphing Cartesian points.

Activity
1. Display a magazine showing a scene or emotion. Tell the students to think of one word that they think best describes the picture. Now think of a way to graph your word. Then tell what order to connect the points to form letters. Use your graph paper to set up a grid. Have other students figure out the word. Place the graphs around the magazine picture on a bulletin board. Students may find their own pictures and graph them the same way.

2. Find your own example of data that would be appropriate for a line graph. Then plot the information on your graph paper.

Examples:
- Use the weather report from a daily newspaper to make a line graph of daily temperature readings.
- Graph the stopping distance of a car at different speeds.
- Check newspapers, magazines, and reference books for ideas. After your graph is finished, write ten questions about your graph.

Assessment
Accuracy of list coordinates.

Quadrant 4—Creations

 ### Left Mode—Refine

Use data to plot a graph and write ten questions.

Objective
To edit and refine finished graph products.

Activity
Students evaluate each other's work. Teacher checks for quality of performance.

Assessment
Originality and quality of graphs and accompanying questions.

 ### Right Mode—Integrate

Exchange graphs and answer each other's questions.

Objective
To share the applications and uses of ordered pairs (graphs) with other students.

Activity
Students exchange graphs and answer each other's questions.

Assessment
Quality of sharing.

Integers

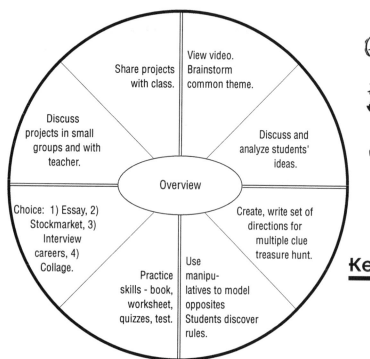

Share projects with class.

View video. Brainstorm common theme.

Discuss projects in small groups and with teacher.

Discuss and analyze students' ideas.

Overview

Choice: 1) Essay, 2) Stockmarket, 3) Interview careers, 4) Collage.

Create, write set of directions for multiple clue treasure hunt.

Practice skills - book, worksheet, quizzes, test.

Use manipulatives to model opposites Students discover rules.

Duration
1-2 weeks

Author(s)
Vera Hayes

Concept
Integers/Directionality

Key words/Cross reference

Integers, Rational numbers, Whole numbers, Zero, Distance, Direction, Symbol, Sequence

Overview

Objective
The students will relate opposite directions to integers. The students will add, subtract, multiply and divide integers and rational numbers.

About the Author
Vera Hayes is a middle school math teacher at Eisenhower Middle School, San Antonio, TX. She is a 4MAT trainer in the Northeast Independent School District.

Required Resources
Video on Directionality; chips as manipulatives, 2-colored counters or counters of different colors. (The video is teacher made. I video taped an outdoor elevator, children swinging, bread entering and popping up in a toaster, a ball bouncing vertically and horizontally, cars in traffic, numbers inside elevator as it went up and down, volume control indicator on car radio, football game, children on seesaw, shoppers on escalators, airplanes taking off and landing, a water fountain, and highway signs that indicate direction. The video allows for the motion and opposite directions to be seen in action.)

Bibliography
Focus on Pre-algebra by Mary Laycock,
Make it Simpler by Carol Meyer and Tom Sallee.

Quadrant 1—Experience

Right Mode—Connect

View video. Brainstorm common theme.

Objective
To create an image of distance, direction, and opposites.

Activity
View video illustrating opposite directions and indicating distance: up-down, north-south, east-west, above-below. Students brainstorm about common theme of video.

Assessment
Attentiveness to video, participation in brainstorming.

Left Mode—Examine

Discuss and analyze students' ideas.

Objective
To analyze video experience. Students will realize that every direction has an opposite, and direction includes distance. Therefore, there is a need for integers/rational numbers and zero.

Activity
Discuss/list/analyze students ideas - opposite direction, distance, need for numbers.

Assessment
Participation in discussion.

Quadrant 2—Concepts

Right Mode—Image

Create, write set of directions for multiple clue treasure hunt.

Objective
To deepen the connection between integers and their relationship to distance, direction, and opposites.

Activity
Create and write a set of directions for a multiple clue treasure hunt using a system of the group's own design. Directions will be written with signs and numbers - NO WORDS.

Assessment
Quality of teamwork and accuracy of understanding.

Left Mode—Define

Use manipulatives to model opposites Students discover rules.

Objective
To learn operations with integers/rational numbers.

Activity
Teacher uses positive/negative chips as manipulatives. Teacher models opposites, absolute value, adding, like/unlike signs, subtracting, multiplication, and division. Students "discover" rules.

Assessment
Participation with manipulatives, note-taking of examples.

Quadrant 3—Applications

 ## Left Mode—Try

Practice skills - books, worksheets, quizzes, tests.

Objective
To practice skills with integers.

Activity
Students practice skills using textbook exercises, worksheets and quizzes.

Assessment
Quizzes, tests.

Right Mode—Extend

Choice: 1) Essay, 2) Stockmarket, 3) Interview careers, 4) Collage.

Objective
To provide activities that will broaden students' experiences in using integers/rational numbers.

Activity
Choice: 1) Write essay "My Life as an Integer."
2) Select stock on U.S. Stock Exchange, follow its gains or losses for five days—a) Predict its course for next three days. b) Chart performance of $5000 investment for five days. 3) Interview stockbroker or career person who uses integers. 4) Create a collage of integers/rational numbers.

Assessment
Quality and accuracy of activities.

Quadrant 4—Creations

 ## Left Mode—Refine

Discuss projects in small groups and with teacher.

Objective
To give guidance and feedback to students' plans, to encourage, to refine.

Activity
In small groups, discuss projects. Teacher discusses projects with students.

Assessment
Participation, timelines.

Right Mode—Integrate

Share projects with class.

Objective
To share, to delight in what was learned.

Activity
Students' share essays, charts, predictions, interviews, or collages with class.

Assessment
Quality of sharing, enjoyment.

Measures of Central Tend.

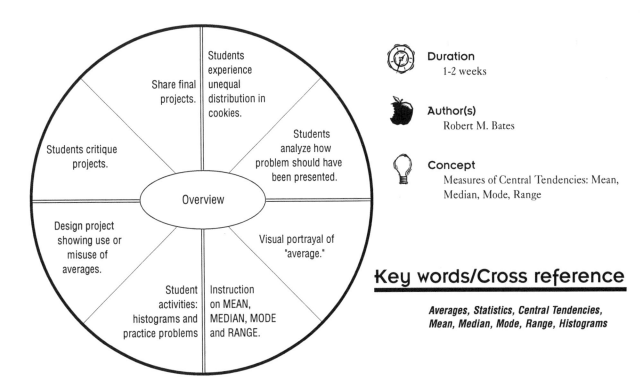

Duration
1-2 weeks

Author(s)
Robert M. Bates

Concept
Measures of Central Tendencies: Mean, Median, Mode, Range

Key words/Cross reference

Averages, Statistics, Central Tendencies, Mean, Median, Mode, Range, Histograms

Overview

Objective
Students will learn the measures of central tendency and how to compute them.

About the Author
Robert M. Bates, Ed.D., teaches mathematics in grades seven and eight at The Heath School, Brookline, MA. He has over twenty-five years teaching experience at the elementary and middle school levels. Bob has also served as an Associate Professor of Education at the post-secondary level.

Required Resources
Chocolate chip cookies for all students; art materials for student drawings; teacher-prepared overheads for direct instruction.

Measures of Central Tend.

Quadrant 1—Experience

 ### Right Mode—Connect

Students experience unequal distribution in cookies.

Objective
To connect "fairness" with "average" or "making things even."

Activity
The lesson begins with the question "How could we determine the average number of chocolate chips in a chocolate chip cookie (one measure of quality?)" When students suggest actually counting the chips in a sample and finding an average, distribute to pairs of students unequal piles of cookies with the condition that they may be eaten only when the task is completed.

Typically, those who are short-changed will demand/request either more cookies or a redistribution of those handed out. At this point, the piles are made equal by the latter method, including breaking them into parts. Then the original activity continues.

Assessment
Involvement of the students in generating suggestions for redistributing and sharing the cookies; students' ability/inability to find an average.

 ### Left Mode—Examine

Students analyze how problem should have been presented.

Objective
To list other situations in their lives in which students wanted to or did "level" things out.

Activity
Ask "Why do you feel better — or worse — about the restacking?" "What else could have been done?" "What was a situation in your own life where you had to make things right or even?"

Assessment
Student's ability to find an average and to suggest alternatives to the original lesson. Students' willingness to describe a parallel situation in their own lives.

Quadrant 2—Concepts

 ### Right Mode—Image

Visual portrayal of "average."

Objective
To draw an analogy between Baby Bear's "just right" porridge and the general idea of average (mean).

Activity
Recalling the story of Goldilocks, students are asked:
1. How is Baby Bear's porridge like the cookie stacks?
2. How is the porridge different from the cookie stacks?
3. How could ALL of the porridge be made "just right?"
4. Draw a picture (no words!) of "average."

Assessment
Students making the connection between the concept of "average" (mean) and making equal stacks of cookies. Students' ability to visualize "average."

 ### Left Mode—Define

Instruction on Mean, Median, Mode and Range.

Objective
To differentiate among Mean, Median (the middle number), Mode (the most frequent number) and the Range; to be able to determine each from a histogram.

Activity
Using overhead projector and transparencies, the teacher demonstrates the concepts. From a list of salaries of twelve employees of a company, a histogram is constructed. The four terms are defined and identified as more specific variations of the term average.

Assessment
Students complete a short quiz on another set of data by determining the mean, median, mode, and range.

Measures of Central Tend.

Quadrant 3—Applications

 ### Left Mode—Try

Student activities: histograms and practice problems.

Objective
To collect data, construct a histogram, and determine which measures of central tendency to use an average.

Activity
1. Heights of all seventh graders and of all eighth graders are determined. The information is put on a histogram by each student and the measures of central tendency are found.
2. Given a list of fictitious students and their allowances, students work in groups to find Mean, Median, Mode, and Range. The list should contain a fairly large range of allowances to be an effective demonstration. The students must decide which measure each person should use to persuade their parents that a raise in allowance is justified.

Assessment
The histogram determines whether or not each can find the measures. The group decisions show how they have understood the use of each measure.

 ### Right Mode—Extend

Design project showing use or misuse of averages.

Objective
To design a project/activity that shows the use —or mis-use — of averages.

Activity
Project choices could include:
1. Are "average" people "just right": looks, athletic ability, popularity, height, or are they mediocre?
2. Make a chart or draw a picture of the typical seventh grader.
3. Conduct an average/fair survey and propose a law that all families will give $x for an average allowance to be fair.
4. Design a league for basketball or football players of average height/weight. Specify your criteria for this design.
5. Show how sports statistics can be enlightening or misleading.
6. Make up (write, draw, tape, act out) a new Goldilocks story or make up a variation that uses "just right."

Assessment
Students can write a two or three sentence summary of their topic selection, including the means (story, diagram, picture, etc.) for presentation.

Quadrant 4—Creations

Left Mode—Refine

Students critique projects.

Objective
To assess the first draft of each student's project.

Activity
A cooperative learning activity in which students reflect on, and help assess, each other's projects after a first draft is done or an outline is constructed. Preferably, there would be no duplication of topics within each group.

Assessment
Working in cooperative groups, students assist each other in determining whether each group member's project includes:
1. Information on how and average is being applied or misused
2. A readable chart, picture, diagram or article presenting this information.

Right Mode—Integrate

Share final projects.

Objective
To create a title and present individual projects.

Activity
Sample titles could be discussed (e.g., "Yogi Bear — Smarter Than The Average Bear?"), but the main point is the actual presentation of the projects.

Assessment
The actual presentation of each project is judged on the basis of earlier criteria:
1. Information on average use or misuse is included.
2. Presentation through the selected means is clear and readable to the class.

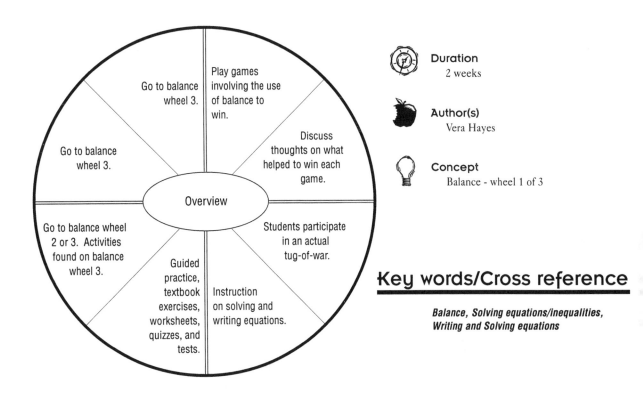

Duration
2 weeks

Author(s)
Vera Hayes

Concept
Balance - wheel 1 of 3

In the wheel diagram:

- Go to balance wheel 3.
- Play games involving the use of balance to win.
- Go to balance wheel 3.
- Discuss thoughts on what helped to win each game.
- Overview
- Go to balance wheel 2 or 3. Activities found on balance wheel 3.
- Students participate in an actual tug-of-war.
- Guided practice, textbook exercises, worksheets, quizzes, and tests.
- Instruction on solving and writing equations.

Key words/Cross reference

Balance, Solving equations/inequalities,
Writing and Solving equations

Overview

Objective
To understand the importance of balance in solving equations and inequalities.

About the Author
Vera Hayes teaches math at Eisenhower Middle School in North East Independent School District in San Antonio, Texas.

Required Resources
Games of balance, rope for tug-of-war, algebra tiles.

Bibliography
Algebra Tiles for the Overhead Projector by Hilde Howden.

Quadrant 1—Experience

 ## Right Mode—Connect

Play games involving the use of balance to win.

Objective

To make the student aware of the importance of balance.

Activity

Students will play one of the following games to illustrate balance: Twister, Hopscotch, Blockhead, Break-the-Ice, Barrel of Monkeys, Kerplunk, Jenga, relay races that involve balance such as book on head or egg in spoon. Students can build houses out of cards to see which group can build the tallest house.

Assessment

Participation in activities.

 ## Left Mode—Examine

Discuss thoughts on what helped to win each game.

Objective

To analyze the experience of playing the games. What is the winning factor in each game?

Activity

Students will write independently for 5 minutes expressing their thoughts about the activity or activities performed above. Students will then share their results as a small group. Finally, the activities will be discussed as a class.

Assessment

Participation in discussion.

Quadrant 2—Concepts

 ## Right Mode—Image

Students participate in an actual tug-of-war.

Objective

To deepen the connection between balance and the meaning of a balanced equation and the result when an action is taken on one side of an equation and not the other.

Activity

Students will participate in an actual tug-of-war using ropes borrowed from the P.E. department. Several arrangements of teams should be used to illustrate the differences in balance.

Assessment

Attentiveness to results when arrangements of teams are changed.

 ## Left Mode—Define

Instruction on solving and writing equations.

Objective

To provide instruction on:
1. Solving addition/subtraction and multiplication/division equations/inequalities.
2. Solving problems by writing one-step equations.
3. Writing and solving two-step equations/inequalities.
4. Solving problems by writing two-step equations.

Activity

Using algebra tiles or teacher made manipulatives, illustrate an equation. A balance scale and pattern blocks can illustrate the idea, or a transparency of a balance scale can simulate the same idea. Stress the idea that whatever is removed or added to one side of the equation must also be added or removed to the other side in order to maintain "balance." Relate this to the tug-of-war and how changing one side effected the other side.

Assessment

Participation with manipulatives, class participation, note-taking of examples.

Balance 1/3

Quadrant 3—Applications

 ### Left Mode—Try

Guided practice, textbook exercises, worksheets, quizzes, and tests.

Objective
To provide practice with solving equations/inequalities.

Activity
Students practice skills using textbook exercises, worksheets, and quizzes.

Assessment
Quizzes and tests.

 ### Right Mode—Extend

Go to balance wheel 2 or 3. Activities found on balance wheel 3.

Activity
Go to balance wheel 3 for activities. You may go to either balance wheel 2 or 3 at this time.

Quadrant 4—Creations

 ### Left Mode—Refine

Go to balance wheel 3.

Activity
Go to balance wheel 3.

 ### Right Mode—Integrate

Go to balance wheel 3.

Activity
Go to balance wheel 3.

Balance 2/3

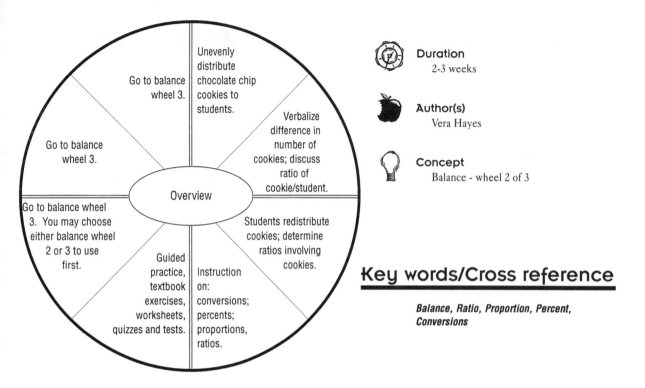

Go to balance wheel 3.

Unevenly distribute chocolate chip cookies to students.

Go to balance wheel 3.

Verbalize difference in number of cookies; discuss ratio of cookie/student.

Overview

Go to balance wheel 3. You may choose either balance wheel 2 or 3 to use first.

Students redistribute cookies; determine ratios involving cookies.

Guided practice, textbook exercises, worksheets, quizzes and tests.

Instruction on: conversions; percents; proportions, ratios.

Duration
2-3 weeks

Author(s)
Vera Hayes

Concept
Balance - wheel 2 of 3

Key words/Cross reference

Balance, Ratio, Proportion, Percent, Conversions

Overview

Objective
To teach students that the fractions, ratios, and proportions are used in their everyday lives.

About the Author
Vera Hayes teaches math at Eisenhower Middle School in North East Independent School District in San Antonio, Texas.

Required Resources
Chocolate chip cookies in plastic bags.

Bibliography
Math Textbook.

Balance 2/3

Quadrant 1—Experience

 ### Right Mode—Connect

Unevenly distribute chocolate chip cookies to students.

Objective
To introduce the idea of equal ratios and proportions.

Activity
Unevenly distribute chocolate chip cookies to students, purposely giving some students more than others. Instruct students not to eat or touch until everyone is served. (Cookies could be prepackaged in baggies.)

Assessment
Students' realizations and reactions to unequal distribution of cookies.

 ### Left Mode—Examine

Verbalize difference in number of cookies; discuss ratio of cookie/student.

Objective
To allow students to discuss equal proportions and analyze what needs to be done to correct the situation.

Activity
Students should quickly verbalize that the number of cookies each received are not equal. The food proportions are not equal. Discuss why and how to correct the situation. Students can determine the ratios of cookies to students, cookies to group, chocolate chips to cookie, etc.

Assessment
Participation in discussion.

Quadrant 2—Concepts

 ### Right Mode—Image

Students redistribute cookies; determine ratios involving cookies.

Objective
To have students actively show what equal ratios or proportions are by redistributing cookies.

Activity
Students redistribute cookies in equal proportions. Students can again determine ratios of chips to cookie, chips to groups, chips to class, chips to person, etc.

Assessment
Involvement in redistribution of cookies. Attentiveness to class activities.

 ### Left Mode—Define

Instruction on: conversions; percents; proportions, ratios.

Objective
To provide instruction on ratios, proportions and percents.

Activity
Teacher follows textbook activities in instruction on the above objectives.

Assessment
Student participation, note-taking of examples.

Quadrant 3—Applications

 ## Left Mode—Try

Guided practice, textbook exercises, worksheets, quizzes and tests.

Objective
To reinforce understanding through practice.

Activity
Students practice skills using textbook exercises, worksheets, and quizzes.

Assessment
Quizzes and tests.

 ## Right Mode—Extend

Go to balance wheel 3. You may choose either balance wheel 2 or 3 to use first.

Activity
Go to balance wheel 3 for activities. Balance wheel 3 may be used before balance wheel 1.

Quadrant 4—Creations

 ## Left Mode—Refine

Go to balance wheel 3.

Activity
Go to balance wheel 3.

 ## Right Mode—Integrate

Go to balance wheel 3.

Activity
Go to balance wheel 3.

Balance 3/3

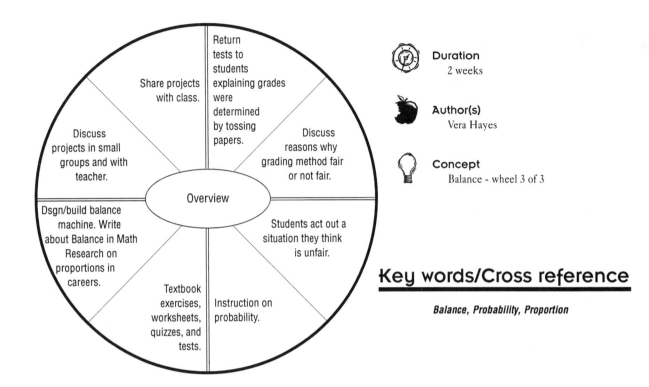

Duration
2 weeks

Author(s)
Vera Hayes

Concept
Balance - wheel 3 of 3

Key words/Cross reference

Balance, Probability, Proportion

Overview

Objective
The learner will relate balance to fairness and chances in probability.

About the Author
Vera Hayes teaches math at Eisenhower Middle School in North East Independent School District in San Antonio, Texas.

Required Resources
Set of previous tests.

Bibliography
The Good Time Math Event Book by Marilyn Burns.

Quadrant 1—Experience

 ## Right Mode—Connect

Return tests to students explaining grades were determined by tossing papers.

Objective
To create an awareness and meaning of fair in regard to the students' lives.

Activity
Before returning the previous or last test, explain to the students that you just ran out of time and were unable to grade them. In order to save time you have a plan for determining the grades very quickly: You will take the class set of tests and just toss them all in the same direction. The test that travels the farthest will receive a grade of 100 and the other tests will be graded proportionately to the distance it traveled.

Assessment
Students' reactions to and concerns about the new grading system.

 ## Left Mode—Examine

Discuss reasons why grading method fair or not fair.

Objective
To let the learner express his feelings about fairness.

Activity
Students will correctly assess the situation as not fair. Discuss the reasons why and what would be a fair method other than actual grading of the papers. They sometimes choose not to do their homework, can teachers choose not to grade? The discussion should lead into other fair and unfair situations.

Assessment
Participation in discussion and ideas about fairness.

Quadrant 2—Concepts

Right Mode—Image

Students act out a situation they think is unfair.

Objective
To let students connect "fairness" to situations that concern them.

Activity
In groups, students will choose a situation that they think is unfair and act it out for the class. Allow time for the students to plan and practice before performing for the class. Allow time for discussion after each performance.

Assessment
Attentiveness to performances. Quality of situations.

 ## Left Mode—Define

Instruction on probability.

Objective
To provide instruction on probability, permutations, and combinations.

Activity
Students can play the Fair Games from *The Good Time Math Event Book*. Instructional activities can be found in textbook.

Assessment
Participation in class activities.

Quadrant 3—Applications

 ## Left Mode—Try

Textbook exercises, worksheets, quizzes, and tests.

Objective
To practice working with probability.

Activity
Textbook exercises, worksheets, quizzes and tests.

Assessment
Quizzes and tests.

 ## Right Mode—Extend

Design/build balance machine. Write about balance in math. Research on proportions in careers.

Objective
To provide activities that will broaden students' experiences in using probability.

Activity
Students will select one of the following projects. Students should be given a timeline as to when the check/edit day will be and when the projects are due. Students should be informed as to grading procedures for the project.

1. Design and build a balance machine.
2. Write a report on the evidence of balance in mathematics.
3. Prepare a research report on the use of ratio and proportion in professional careers, i.e., Forensic Medicine, Architecture, Art, etc.
4. Create a story, poem, or video that illustrates balance.
5. Write the State Lottery Commission and find out what the probability (fairness) of each of the current lottery games is and how the probability is determined. The address can usually be found on a lottery ticket.
6. Student designed project to be negotiated and approved by the teacher.

Assessment
Quality and accuracy of activities.

Quadrant 4—Creations

 ## Left Mode—Refine

Discuss projects in small groups and with teacher.

Objective
To provide guidance and feedback to students' plans, to encourage, to refine.

Activity
In small groups, discuss projects. Teacher discusses projects with students.

Assessment
Participation, timeliness.

Right Mode—Integrate

Share projects with class.

Objective
To share, to delight in what was learned.

Activity
Students share their machines, reports, videos, poems or research with class.

Assessment
Quality of sharing, enjoyment.

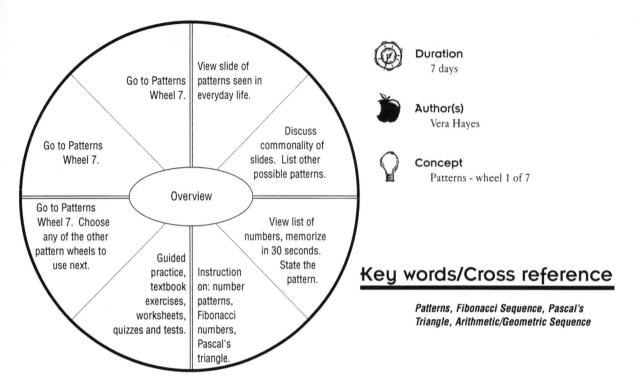

Go to Patterns Wheel 7.

View slide of patterns seen in everyday life.

Discuss commonality of slides. List other possible patterns.

Go to Patterns Wheel 7.

Overview

Go to Patterns Wheel 7. Choose any of the other pattern wheels to use next.

View list of numbers, memorize in 30 seconds. State the pattern.

Guided practice, textbook exercises, worksheets, quizzes and tests.

Instruction on: number patterns, Fibonacci numbers, Pascal's triangle.

 Duration
7 days

Author(s)
Vera Hayes

 Concept
Patterns - wheel 1 of 7

Key words/Cross reference

Patterns, Fibonacci Sequence, Pascal's Triangle, Arithmetic/Geometric Sequence

Overview

 Objective
To discover the many areas of math that are based on patterns.

About the Author
Vera Hayes is a math teacher at Eisenhower Middle School in the North East Independent School District in San Antonio, Texas.

 Required Resources
Teacher made slides of patterns—sewing patterns, stencils, computer programs, sheet music, patterns found in architecture, tessellations, radio towers with patterns of triangles used in construction, wall paper, checkerboards, wrapping paper, Visual Thinking transparencies from Scott Foresman. What picture comes next?

Bibliography
Exploring Math, grade 7 or 8, Scott Foresman.

Quadrant 1—Experience

 ### Right Mode—Connect

View slide of patterns seen in everyday life.

Objective

To make students aware that "patterns" come in various types.

Activity

Students will view slides of patterns seen in everyday life to illustrate different types of patterns: dress patterns, patterns in nature, in design, in music, in construction, in sports and in numbers. Music that has the same rhythm repeated throughout may be played as background music.

Assessment

Quality of reactions and participation of students.

 ### Left Mode—Examine

Discuss commonalty of slides. List other possible patterns.

Objective

To analyze reactions to slides. Students will realize that patterns exist everywhere.

Activity

Discuss with class the common element seen in all the slides. Students list other uses of or types of patterns.

Assessment

Participation in discussion.

Quadrant 2—Concepts

 ### Right Mode—Image

View list of numbers, memorize in 30 seconds. State the pattern.

Objective

To deepen the connection between patterns and their uses.

Activity

Show the number:
1,492,162,017,761,929,196,319,902,000 to students for 30 seconds. Ask them to memorize the number. (The key to memorization is a pattern of dates in history.) Ask successful students how they could memorize the number in such a short time. Using transparencies for visual thinking from Scott Foresman *7th or 8th grade, Exploring Math*, have students determine the next drawing in the visual patterns.

Assessment

Participation in class activity and discussions.

 ### Left Mode—Define

Instruction on: number patterns, Fibonacci numbers, Pascal's triangle.

Objective

To define and recognize patterns used in math.

Activity

Teacher presents lessons on: recognizing and continuing a number pattern, the Fibonacci sequence investigating and extending sequences generated by Pascal's triangle identifying number sequences as arithmetic, geometric, or neither finding missing terms in sequences.

Assessment

Student participation, note-taking and teacher checking for understanding.

Quadrant 3—Applications

 ### Left Mode—Try

Guided practice, textbook exercises, worksheets, quizzes and tests.

Objective
To practice skills in identifying and completing number patterns.

Activity
Students practice skills using textbook exercises, worksheets and quizzes.

Assessment
Quizzes and tests.

 ### Right Mode—Extend

Go to Patterns Wheel 7. Choose any of the other pattern wheels to use next.

Activity
Go to patterns wheel 7.

Quadrant 4—Creations

 ### Left Mode—Refine

Go to Patterns Wheel 7.

Activity
Go to patterns wheel 7.

 ### Right Mode—Integrate

Go to Patterns Wheel 7.

Activity
Go to patterns wheel 7.

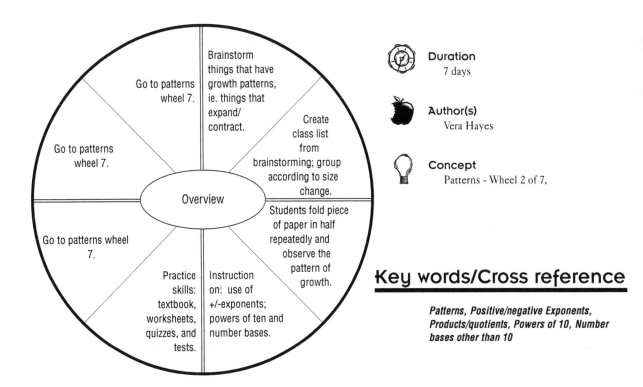

Duration
7 days

Author(s)
Vera Hayes

Concept
Patterns - Wheel 2 of 7,

Key words/Cross reference

Patterns, Positive/negative Exponents,
Products/quotients, Powers of 10, Number
bases other than 10

Overview

Objective
To develop an understanding that the use of exponents creates a pattern.

About the Author
Vera Hayes is a math teacher at Eisenhower Middle School in the North East Independent School District in San Antonio, Texas.

Bibliography
Math for Smarty Pants by Marilyn Burns, *Binary Power!* by John Veltman.

Quadrant 1—Experience

Right Mode—Connect

Brainstorm things that have growth patterns, i.e.. things that expand/contract.

Objective
To create an awareness of things that change in size.

Activity
Students brainstorm or cluster about things that have growth patterns, i.e.. things that expand or contract. Examples: interest on money is growth at a constant rate, Fibonacci's rabbits (from previous wheel), population growth, cells dividing in science class and the circles formed from dropping a stone into water. Depreciation on a car, the bounces of a ball dropped from high, or an echo as it fades out could be examples of growth decay or contraction.

Assessment
Student participation.

Left Mode—Examine

Create class list from brainstorming; group according to size change.

Objective
To analyze and categorize the list of growth patterns.

Activity
Create a class list from the brainstorming or clustering. Students analyze and group the items according to size change: was the change an exponential growth (multiplied or divided by the same number each time) or a constant change caused by adding/subtracting the same amount each time?

Assessment
Participation in discussion.

Quadrant 2—Concepts

Right Mode—Image

Students fold piece of paper in half repeatedly and observe the pattern of growth.

Objective
To deepen the understanding of exponential growth.

Activity
Each student will fold a piece of paper in half repeatedly and observe the pattern of growth. The pattern could be growth if the students are counting the number of rectangles being formed or exponential decay or contraction if considering the size of each rectangle after each fold.

Assessment
Attentiveness to results of folding.

Left Mode—Define

Instruction on: use of +/- exponents; powers of ten and number bases.

Objective
To define the use of exponents in our number system.

Activity
Teacher presents lessons on:
1. Using positive and negative exponents to write powers of 10 in standard and exponential form.
2. Finding products and quotients of power of 10.
3. Writing base 10 numbers in other number bases.
4. Writing number bases as base 10 numbers.

Assessment
Student note-taking and participation in class activities.

Quadrant 3—Applications

 Left Mode—Try

Practice skills: textbook, worksheets, quizzes, and tests.

Objective
To reinforce understanding by practice.

Activity
Students practice skills using textbook exercises, worksheets, and quizzes.

Assessment
Quizzes and tests.

 Right Mode—Extend

Go to patterns wheel 7.

Activity
Go to patterns wheel 7.

Quadrant 4—Creations

 Left Mode—Refine

Go to patterns wheel 7.

Activity
Go to patterns wheel 7.

 Right Mode—Integrate

Go to patterns wheel 7.

Activity
Go to patterns wheel 7.

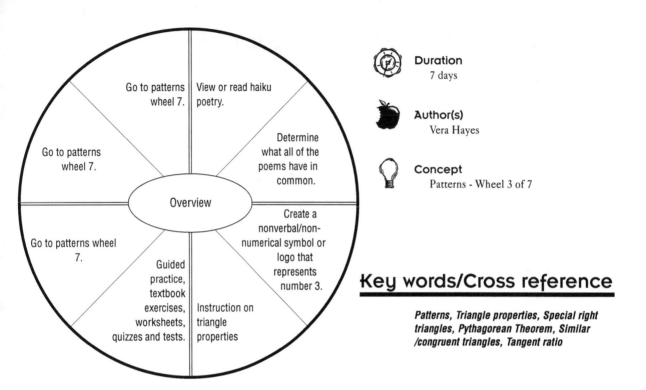

Duration
7 days

Author(s)
Vera Hayes

Concept
Patterns - Wheel 3 of 7

Key words/Cross reference

Patterns, Triangle properties, Special right triangles, Pythagorean Theorem, Similar /congruent triangles, Tangent ratio

Overview

Objective
To understand the patterns that exist with triangles, especially special right triangles.

About the Author
Vera Hayes is a math teacher at Eisenhower Middle School in the North East Independent School District in San Antonio, Texas.

Required Resources
A book of haiku poetry.

Bibliography
Cricket Songs, Japanese haiku translated by Harry Behn (Harcourt, Brace & World, Inc. New York).

1—Experience

Right Mode—Connect

View or read haiku poetry.

Objective

To create an awareness of the importance of the number 3.

Activity

Students view transparencies of haiku poetry. Do not introduce them as haiku. The students will hopefully recognize them as such. (You might inform the English teacher in advance that you will be working with haiku). Examples of haiku that can be used:

> A tree frog trilling
> softly, the first drop of rain
>   slips down the new leaves.
>   Rogetsu

>   Butterfly, these words
> from my brush are not flowers
>   only their shadows.
> Soseki

>   Well! Hello down there,
> friend snail! When did you arrive
>   in such a hurry?
> Issa

>   High on a mountain
> we heard a skylark singing
>   faintly, far below.
> Basho

>   A hungry owl hoots
> and hides in a wayside shrine...
>   so bright is the moon.
> Joso

>   Hop out of my way,
> Mr. Toad, and allow me
>   please to plant bamboo!
>   Chora

>   Broken and broken
> again on the sea, the moon
>   so easily mends.
> Chosu

Assessment

Quality of reactions and participation of students.

Left Mode—Examine

Determine what all of the poems have in common.

Objective

To analyze the commonality of the poetry.

Activity

In class discussion, students determine what all of the poems have in common. (3 lines with syllable pattern 5-7-5.)

(A haiku is a poem in three lines of five, then seven, then five syllables. It is made by speaking of something natural and simple suggesting spring, summer, autumn, or winter. There is no rhyme. Everything mentioned is just what it is, wonderful, here, but still beyond.)

Ask students what qualifies a poem as haiku? What stays consistent in haiku?

Assessment

Participation in discussion and quality of ideas.

Quadrant 2—Concepts

 ## Right Mode—Image

Create a nonverbal/non-numerical symbol or logo that represents number 3.

Objective
To deepen the students connection with the number 3.

Activity
Since the haiku had 3 lines consistently, students in groups of four will create a nonverbal/non-numerical symbol or logo that represents the number 3. Students will share their creations and explain.

Assessment
Quality of group work, level of interest.

 ## Left Mode—Define

Instruction on triangle properties.

Objective
To provide instruction on triangles.

Activity
Present lessons on:
1. Identifying similar triangles and using their properties.
2. Using the Pythagorean theorem.
3. Using relationships in special right triangles (30-60-90 and 45-45-90).
4. Using the tangent ratio.

Assessment
Participation in class, note-taking.

Quadrant 3—Applications

 ## Left Mode—Try

Guided practice, textbook exercises, worksheets, quizzes and tests.

Objective
To practice skills with triangles.

Activity
Students practice skills using textbook exercises, worksheets and quizzes.

Assessment
Quizzes and tests.

 ## Right Mode—Extend

Go to patterns wheel 7.

Activity
Go to patterns wheel 7.

Quadrant 4—Creations

 ## Left Mode—Refine

Go to patterns wheel 7.

Activity
Go to patterns wheel 7.

Right Mode—Integrate

Go to patterns wheel 7.

Activity
Go to patterns wheel 7.

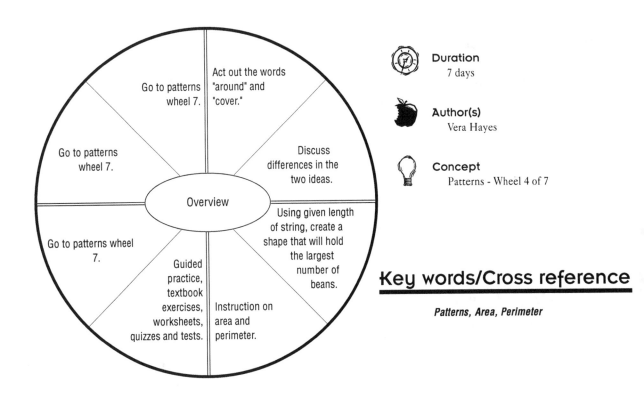

Go to patterns wheel 7.

Act out the words "around" and "cover."

Go to patterns wheel 7.

Discuss differences in the two ideas.

Overview

Using given length of string, create a shape that will hold the largest number of beans.

Go to patterns wheel 7.

Guided practice, textbook exercises, worksheets, quizzes and tests.

Instruction on area and perimeter.

Duration
7 days

Author(s)
Vera Hayes

Concept
Patterns - Wheel 4 of 7

Key words/Cross reference

Patterns, Area, Perimeter

Overview

Objective
The learner will view the formulas used in finding area and perimeter as patterns that are used repeatedly. There are patterns in the relationships of perimeter to area.

About the Author
Vera Hayes is a math teacher at Eisenhower Middle School in the North East Independent School District in San Antonio, Texas.

Required Resources
Beans and string.

Quadrant 1—Experience

Right Mode—Connect

Act out the words "around" and "cover."

Objective
To create an awareness between the meaning of "around" (perimeter) and "cover" (area).

Activity
In groups, students will act out the meaning of the words "around" and "cover." Allow students time to plan and practice before they perform for the class.

Assessment
Participation and group work.

Left Mode—Examine

Discuss differences in the two ideas.

Objective
To analyze the meanings of "around" and "cover."

Activity
Discuss the differences in the two words. Why and how do they differ? Why did your group choose to enact the concept in that manner?

Assessment
Participation in discussion.

Quadrant 2—Concepts

Right Mode—Image

Using given length of string, create a shape that will hold the largest number of beans.

Objective
To create an awareness that an equal distance around does not necessarily result in the same amount to cover.

Activity
Give each group a given length of string with which they are to create a shape that will hold the largest number of beans possible. Give each group beans with which to cover their shape. Is there a pattern in the results as far as the type of shape and the number of beans?

Assessment
Involvement in activity, group work.

Left Mode—Define

Instruction on area and perimeter.

Objective
To present instruction on finding area and perimeter and on the patterns in the relationship between the two as dimensions change.

Activity
Instructional activities on: 1) Finding perimeter and area of a plane figure involving circle, 2) Find the area and perimeter of parallelograms, triangles, trapezoids and irregular figures.

Assessment
Class participation, note-taking.

Quadrant 3—Applications

 ### Left Mode—Try

Guided practice, textbook exercises, worksheets, quizzes and tests.

Objective
To provide the learner with practice in finding area and perimeter.

Activity
Guided practice, textbook exercises, worksheets, and quizzes.

Assessment
Quizzes and tests.

 ### Right Mode—Extend

Go to patterns wheel 7.

Activity
Go to patterns wheel 7.

Quadrant 4—Creations

 ### Left Mode—Refine

Go to patterns wheel 7.

Activity
Go to patterns wheel 7.

 ### Right Mode—Integrate

Go to patterns wheel 7.

Activity
Go to patterns wheel 7.

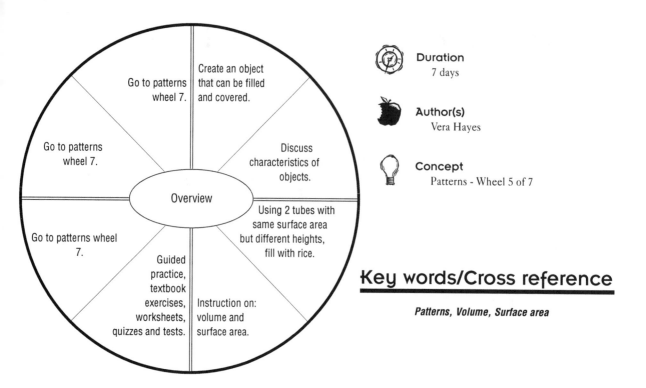

Duration
7 days

Author(s)
Vera Hayes

Concept
Patterns - Wheel 5 of 7

Key words/Cross reference

Patterns, Volume, Surface area

Overview

Objective
To view the formulas used in finding volume and surface area as patterns to follow.

About the Author
Vera Hayes is a math teacher at Eisenhower Middle School in the North East Independent School District in San Antonio, Texas.

Required Resources
Rice or beans, 5x8 inch cards, straws, toothpicks and/or craft sticks.

Bibliography
About Teaching Math, Marilyn Burns.

Quadrant 1—Experience

Right Mode—Connect

Create objects that can be filled and covered.

Objective

To create an awareness of volume and surface area.

Activity

In groups of four, students will create an object that they can fill up and cover up. The object will be created from either straws, toothpicks, or craft sticks.

Assessment

Participation, quality of work, and group work.

Left Mode—Examine

Discuss characteristics of objects.

Objective

To analyze objects to determine if they can be filled and/or covered.

Activity

Discuss the characteristic of each object that allows the object to be filled (3 dimensional, otherwise it would be just covered). What would be necessary to cover the object? (2 dimensions)

Assessment

Participation in discussion.

Quadrant 2—Concepts

Right Mode—Image

Using 2 tubes with same surface area but different heights, fill with rice.

Objective

To deepen the connection between filling up and the outside surface (cover) of a 3 dimensional figure.

Activity

Take two 5-by 8-inch cards and roll each into a tube, rolling one the short way and the other the long way. Tape them. Say to the class: "Suppose you filled each tube with rice or beans to compare how much each holds. Do you think each holds the same? If not, which one do you think holds more than the other? Why?"

Have the students make these predictions and write them down. Fill the longer tube with beans or rice. Place the filled tube inside the shorter tube to show the difference. Then pour the beans or rice from the longer tube into the smaller tube. Did the results match the predictions?

(Activity from *About Teaching Math*, by Marilyn Burns)

Assessment

Student participation and attentiveness.

Left Mode—Define

Instruction on: volume and surface area.

Objective

To provide instruction based on the concept that the formulas used in finding volume and surface area are patterns that we use repeatedly, no matter what the dimensions.

Activity

Present lessons on volume and surface area of geometric solids. The formulas used are patterns that we follow.

Assessment

Participation and notetaking.

Quadrant 3—Applications

 Left Mode—Try

Guided practice, textbook exercises, worksheets, quizzes and tests.

Objective
To provide practice in finding volume and surface area.

Activity
Guided practice, textbook exercises, worksheets and quizzes.

Assessment
Quizzes and tests.

 Right Mode—Extend

Go to patterns wheel 7.

Activity
Go to patterns wheel 7.

Assessment

Quadrant 4—Creations

 Left Mode—Refine

Go to patterns wheel 7.

Activity
Go to patterns wheel 7.

 Right Mode—Integrate

Go to patterns wheel 7.

Activity
Go to patterns wheel 7.

Patterns 6/7

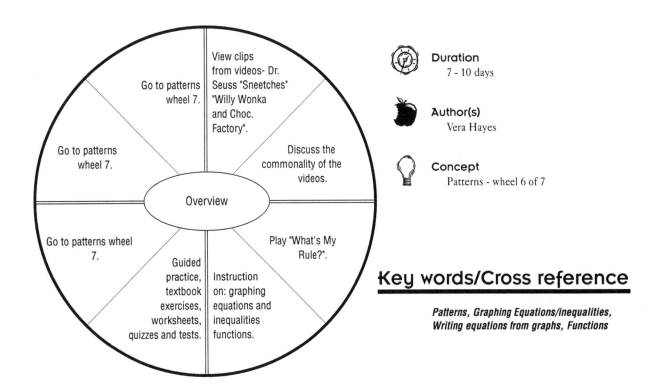

Go to patterns wheel 7.

View clips from videos- Dr. Seuss "Sneetches" "Willy Wonka and Choc. Factory".

Go to patterns wheel 7.

Discuss the commonality of the videos.

Overview

Go to patterns wheel 7.

Play "What's My Rule?".

Guided practice, textbook exercises, worksheets, quizzes and tests.

Instruction on: graphing equations and inequalities functions.

Duration
7 - 10 days

Author(s)
Vera Hayes

Concept
Patterns - wheel 6 of 7

Key words/Cross reference

Patterns, Graphing Equations/inequalities, Writing equations from graphs, Functions

Overview

Objective
To view functions as patterns.

About the Author
Vera Hayes is a math teacher at Eisenhower Middle School in the North East Independent School District in San Antonio, Texas.

Required Resources
Videos showing examples of machines in which input results in the same output. A teacher-made video could show a change machine, a tortilla machine, a french fry cutter, a washer or dryer with a window to view the clothes, a car wash, a toaster, a popcorn popper—all of these have an input upon which the same action is taken and then there is an output.

Quadrant 1—Experience

Right Mode—Connect

View clips from videos- Dr. Seuss "Sneetches" "Willy Wonka and Chocolate Factory".

Objective
To create an awareness that machines represent a pattern in the fact that the same action is taken on any input resulting in an output.

Activity
View clips from videos, "Sneetches" by Dr. Seuss and "Willy Wonka and the Chocolate Factory" or view a teacher-made video of machines in which there is input, an action taken and a resulting output. For example, change machines, coke machines, car washes, french fry cutters, tortilla machines, toasters, popcorn poppers, clothes dryers, washing machines.

Assessment
Attentiveness to video.

Left Mode—Examine

Discuss the commonality of the videos.

Objective
To determine the commonality of the videos.

Activity
Discuss the videos. Students determine commonalities.

In the "Sneetches," the sneetches were put into a machine and all had stars put on their stomachs. The same thing (pattern) happened each of them. There was an input and then there was an ouput after the same action was taken.

Assessment
Participation in discussion.

Quadrant 2—Concepts

Right Mode—Image

Play "What's My Rule?".

Objective
To deepen the connection between machines and functions/equations.

Activity
Play "What's My Rule" with the class. Teacher gives a number and the result of some operations on that number. Several examples will be given involving the same operation. Students will guess the "rule" or operations. The idea of the same operations being performed on the numbers is the pattern...the same thing that repeats.

Assessment
Participation in game.

Left Mode—Define

Instruction on: graphing equations and inequalities; functions.

Objective
To provide instruction on functions and graphing.

Activity
Present instruction on:
1. Graphing equations and inequalities on a number line.
2. Solving inequalities by graphing on a number line.
3. Graphing equations in two variables.
4. Writing equations for lines.

Assessment
Participation in class and notetaking.

Quadrant 3—Applications

 Left Mode—Try

Guided practice, textbook exercises, worksheets, quizzes and tests.

Objective
To provide practice in graphing and functions.

Activity
Guided practice, textbook exercises, worksheets, and quizzes.

Assessment
Quizzes and tests.

5 Right Mode—Extend

Go to patterns wheel 7.

Activity
Go to patterns wheel 7.

Quadrant 4—Creations

 Left Mode—Refine

Go to patterns wheel 7.

Activity
Go to patterns wheel 7.

 Right Mode—Integrate

Go to patterns wheel 7.

Activity
Go to patterns wheel 7.

Patterns 7/7

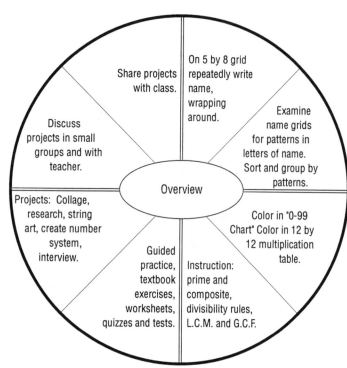

Share projects with class.

On 5 by 8 grid repeatedly write name, wrapping around.

Discuss projects in small groups and with teacher.

Examine name grids for patterns in letters of name. Sort and group by patterns.

Overview

Projects: Collage, research, string art, create number system, interview.

Color in "0-99 Chart" Color in 12 by 12 multiplication table.

Guided practice, textbook exercises, worksheets, quizzes and tests.

Instruction: prime and composite, divisibility rules, L.C.M. and G.C.F.

Duration
3 days (review for pre-algebra)

Author(s)
Vera Hayes

Concept
Patterns - wheel 7 of 7

Key words/Cross reference

Patterns, Number theory, Least common multiples, Greatest common factor, Divisibility rules, Prime/composite

Overview

Objective
To become aware of the patterns involved in multiplication, primes, divisibility rules.

About the Author
Vera Hayes is a math teacher at Eisenhower Middle School in the North East Independent School District in San Antonio, Texas.

Required Resources
Centimeter graph paper to write letters of names, 0-99 Chart for coloring, 12 x 12 Multiplication table.

Quadrant 1—Experience

Right Mode—Connect

On 5 by 8 grid repeatedly write name, wrapping around.

Objective
To create an awareness of patterns in grids and how patterns change with dimensions of grid.

Activity
Students will be given sheets of centimeter graph paper. Students will first cut out a 5 x 8 grid and repeatedly write their first names in the boxes, wrapping around as they reach the end of each line, until the entire grid is complete. The activity can be repeated with 6 x 7 grid, etc.

Left Mode—Examine

Examine name grids for patterns in letters of name. Sort and group by patterns.

Objective
To analyze patterns of letters in name grid.

Activity
Students examine the name grids for patterns in the letters of their names. Sort and categorize the grids by patterns. Analyze the effect of changing the size of the grid.

Assessment
Participation in discussion, attentiveness to their grid.

Quadrant 2—Concepts

Right Mode—Image

Color in "40-99 Chart" Color in 12 by 12 multiplication table.

Objective
To deepen the connection between patterns and our number system.

Activity
Students color the "0-99 Chart" a different color for each set of directions.
Set 1: Color all the numbers with both digits the same.
Set 2: Color all the numbers with digits that add to 8.
Set 3: Color all the numbers with first digits that are larger than the second digits.
Set 4: Color all the numbers with a 4 in them.
Set 5: Color all the even numbers.
Set 6: Color all the numbers with digits that add to 10.
What patterns appear?

Using a multiplication table (12 x 12), students color the multiples of 2, multiples of 3, and multiples of 5, each a different color and discover the patterns.

Assessment
Attentiveness to activity.

Left Mode—Define

Instruction: prime and composite, divisibility rules, L.C.M. and G.C.F.

Objective
To provide instruction of number theory stressing that the rules for divisibility and the multiples are patterns in number theory.

Activity
Present lessons on:
1. Determining prime or composite, factors.
2. Using rules of divisibility.
3. Finding greatest common factor.
4. Finding least common multiple.

Assessment
Participation and notetaking.

Quadrant 3—Applications

 ### Left Mode—Try

Guided practice, textbook exercises, worksheets, quizzes and tests.

Objective
To provide practice in using number theory skills.

Activity
Guided practice, textbook exercises, worksheets, and quizzes.

Assessment
Quizzes and tests.

 ### Right Mode—Extend

Projects: Collage, research, string art, create number system, interview.

Objective
To provide activities that will broaden students' experiences in the use of patterns.

Activity
Students will select one of the following projects. Students should be given a timeline as to when the check/edit day will be and when the projects are due. Students should be informed as to grading procedures for the project. This is a chance for the students to extend themselves into the concept.

1. Create a collage of "Patterns in our World" or a "Patterns in our World" book.
2. Research and write a report on patterns in one or more of the following areas: art, music, history, science, dance, athletics, etc. The area should be negotiated and approved by the teacher.
3. Create a string art design involving patterns.
4. Create an optical illusion with patterns using Fibonacci Numbers. (Fibonacci Art)
5. Create a number system other than base ten. Explain why you chose that number and how you would operate under that system.
6. Interview persons who use patterns in their work. Write a report on your interview or prepare a video or cassette recording.

Assessment
Quality and accuracy of activities.

Quadrant 4—Creations

 ### Left Mode—Refine

Discuss projects in small groups and with teacher.

Objective
To give guidance and feedback to students' plans, to encourage, to refine.

Activity
In small groups discuss projects. Teacher discusses projects with students.

Assessment
Participation, timeliness.

 ### Right Mode—Integrate

Share projects with class.

Objective
To share, to delight in what was learned.

Activity
Students share their projects.

Assessment
Quality of sharing, enjoyment.

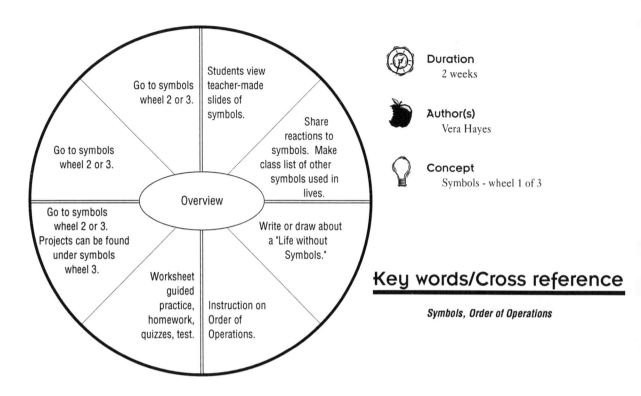

Duration
2 weeks

Author(s)
Vera Hayes

Concept
Symbols - wheel 1 of 3

Key words/Cross reference

Symbols, Order of Operations

Overview

Objective
To teach students the concept of symbols applies not only in math, but in their everyday lives.

About the Author
Vera Hayes teaches math at Eisenhower Middle School in North East Independent School District in San Antonio, Texas.

Required Resources
Math textbook with unit on Order of Operations. Slides of: sheet music, symbols of local businesses, college symbols, school symbols, restroom signs, Olympic symbol, medical symbol, religious symbols, symbols for editing, punctuation marks, clothing labels such as Polo, Guess, etc.

Quadrant 1—Experience

 ### Right Mode—Connect

Students view teacher-made slides of symbols.

Objective

To create an awareness of the varied number of symbols that are involved in our lives.

Activity

Show the teacher-made slides of symbols that can be found in the students' environment. Students will write their initial reaction to each symbol as it is shown.

Assessment

Quality of reactions and participation of students.

 ### Left Mode—Examine

Share reactions to symbols. Make class list of other symbols used in lives.

Objective

To analyze reactions to slides. Students will realize that symbols take the place of many words and may have different meanings to different people.

Activity

Students share their reactions to each symbol. Discuss the use of and our dependency on symbols. Make a class list of other symbols in our lives. What is the purpose of symbols in our lives?

Assessment

Participation in discussion.

Quadrant 2—Concepts

 ### Right Mode—Image

Write or draw about a "Life without Symbols."

Objective

To deepen the connection between symbols and our everyday lives.

Activity

In groups of four, students will write or draw about a situation illustrating "Life without Symbols" or "Why symbols are important." Students will share their work with the class.

Assessment

Quality of group work and participation.

 ### Left Mode—Define

Instruction on Order of Operations.

Objective

To provide instruction on the order of operations and evaluating expressions.

Activity

Introduce the lesson by having students interpret this sentence without punctuation—Paul said the teacher is very intelligent. Ask the students, "Who is intelligent?" Discuss the importance of punctuation in giving meaning to the statement. Relate this to the importance of symbols of operation in math and how the order affects the answer.

Topics to be taught: Order of Operations, Writing and Evaluating Expressions.

Assessment

Participation in class discussions and notetaking.

Quadrant 3—Applications

 ### Left Mode—Try

Worksheet guided practice, homework, quizzes, tests.

Objective
To practice skills with order of operations and evaluating expressions.

Activity
Students practice skills using textbook exercises, worksheets, and quizzes.

Assessment
Quizzes and tests.

 ### Right Mode—Extend

Go to symbols wheel 2 or 3. Projects can be found under symbols wheel 3.

Activity
Go to either symbols wheel 2 or symbols wheel 3 to find other mini wheels for this concept. Projects for the Symbols Concept are listed under symbols wheel 3.

Quadrant 4—Creations

 ### Left Mode—Refine

Go to symbols wheel 2 or 3.

 ### Right Mode—Integrate

Go to symbols wheel 2 or 3.

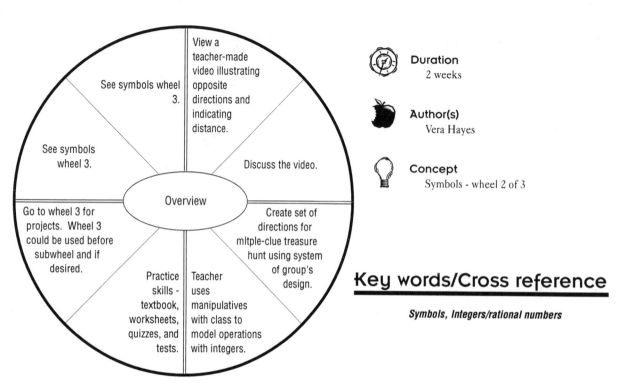

Duration
2 weeks

Author(s)
Vera Hayes

Concept
Symbols - wheel 2 of 3

Key words/Cross reference

Symbols, Integers/rational numbers

(Wheel contents:)

View a teacher-made video illustrating opposite directions and indicating distance.

See symbols wheel 3.

See symbols wheel 3.

Discuss the video.

Overview

Go to wheel 3 for projects. Wheel 3 could be used before subwheel and if desired.

Create set of directions for mltple-clue treasure hunt using system of group's design.

Practice skills - textbook, worksheets, quizzes, and tests.

Teacher uses manipulatives with class to model operations with integers.

Overview

Objective
The learner will view integers as opposite directions. The learner will perform operations with integers and rational numbers.

About the Author
Vera Hayes teaches math at Eisenhower Middle School in North East Independent School District in San Antonio, Texas.

Required Resources
Textbook

Bibliography
See Symbols Wheel 1

Quadrant 1—Experience

 ## Right Mode—Connect

View a teacher-made video illustrating opposite directions and indicating distance.

Objective
To create an image of distance, direction, and opposites.

Activity
View a teacher-made video illustrating opposite directions and indicating distance: roller coaster, ball bouncing, up/down, escalators, elevators, see-saw, children swinging, road signs, etc.

Assessment
Attentiveness to video, participation in brainstorming for commonality of video.

 ## Left Mode—Examine

Discuss the video.

Objective
To analyze video experience. Students will realize that every direction has an opposite and direction includes distance. Therefore, there is a need for integers/rational numbers and zero.

Activity
Discuss/list/analyze students' ideas about video—opposite direction, distance, need for numbers.

Assessment
Participation in discussion.

Quadrant 2—Concepts

 ## Right Mode—Image

Create set of directions for multiple-clue treasure hunt using system of group's design.

Objective
To deepen the connection between integers and their relationship to distance, direction, and opposites.

Activity
In groups, create and write a set of directions for a multiple-clue treasure hunt using a system of the group's own design—using signs and numbers. No words or letters are allowed. Groups should be allowed the freedom to leave the classroom to create an accurate set of direction to find the treasure on the school campus. Groups will exchange and follow clues to test their validity.

Assessment
Quality of teamwork and accuracy of understanding.

 ## Left Mode—Define

Teacher uses manipulatives with class to model operations with integers.

Objective
To provide instruction on operations and properties with integers.

Activity
Teacher uses positive/negative chips as manipulatives. Teacher models opposites, absolute value, adding like/unlike signs, subtracting, multiplication, and division. Students "discover" rules.

Assessment
Participation with manipulatives, notetaking of examples.

Quadrant 3—Applications

 ### Left Mode—Try

Practice skills - textbook, worksheets, quizzes, and tests.

Objective
To practice skills with integers and rational numbers.

Activity
Students practice skills using textbook exercises, worksheets and quizzes.

Assessment
Quizzes and tests.

 ### Right Mode—Extend

Go to wheel 3 for projects. Wheel 3 could be used before sub-wheel and if desired.

Activity
Go to symbols wheel 3.

Quadrant 4—Creations

 ### Left Mode—Refine

See symbols wheel 3.

Activity
Go to symbols wheel 3.

Assessment

 ### Right Mode—Integrate

See symbols wheel 3.

Activity
Go to symbols wheel 3.

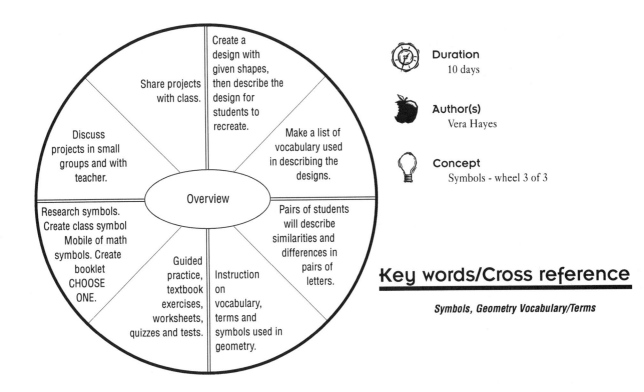

Share projects with class.

Create a design with given shapes, then describe the design for students to recreate.

Discuss projects in small groups and with teacher.

Make a list of vocabulary used in describing the designs.

Overview

Research symbols. Create class symbol Mobile of math symbols. Create booklet CHOOSE ONE.

Pairs of students will describe similarities and differences in pairs of letters.

Guided practice, textbook exercises, worksheets, quizzes and tests.

Instruction on vocabulary, terms and symbols used in geometry.

Duration
10 days

Author(s)
Vera Hayes

Concept
Symbols - wheel 3 of 3

Key words/Cross reference

Symbols, Geometry Vocabulary/Terms

Overview

Objective
To identify and use symbols and vocabulary used in geometry.

About the Author
Vera Hayes teaches math at Eisenhower Middle School in North East Independent School District in San Antonio, Texas.

Required Resources
Math Textbook

Bibliography
Humor in Math, National Council of Teachers of Mathematics.

Quadrant 1—Experience

Right Mode—Connect

Create a design with given shapes, then describe the design for students to recreate.

Objective
To create an awareness for the need for correct vocabulary in geometry.

Activity
Each pair of students will be given a set of geometric shapes with which to create a design. The student is to create the design behind a barrier so his partner cannot see the design. The partner is to describe the design well enough to the other person so that person can build exactly the same design. The partner cannot see what was designed, but may ask questions as directions are given. Change roles and try again.

Assessment
Participation in activity, attentiveness to partner.

Left Mode—Examine

Make a list of vocabulary used in describing the designs.

Objective
To analyze experiences and to become aware of need for the correct vocabulary in geometry.

Activity
Students will make a list of the vocabulary used in describing their designs. The lists will be combined into a class list to be posted in the room. Discuss why vocabulary is important.

Assessment
Number of words in list, participation with partner.

Quadrant 2—Concepts

Right Mode—Image

Pairs of students will describe similarities and differences in pairs of letters.

Objective
Students will become aware that geometry vocabulary is also used to describe things other than geometric designs.

Activity
Pairs of students will choose any two letters from the alphabet and describe their similarities and differences. Each pair of students will exchange their descriptions with another pair of students and they try to determine which letters are being described.

Assessment
Quality of work with partner, participation, effort in trying to give a complete description of each set of letters.

Left Mode—Define

Instruction on vocabulary, terms and symbols used in geometry.

Objective
To provide instruction on geometry vocabulary, terms and symbols.

Activity
Teacher will use activities in textbooks or activities of his/her own design.

Assessment
Class participation.

Quadrant 3—Applications

Left Mode—Try

Guided practice, textbook exercises, worksheets, quizzes and tests.

Objective
To provide the learner with practice to learn vocabulary used in geometry.

Activity
Guided practice, textbook, worksheets, and quizzes.

Assessment
Quizzes and tests.

Right Mode—Extend

Research symbols. Create class symbol. Mobile of math symbols. Create booklet. CHOOSE ONE.

Objective
To provide activities that will broaden students' experiences in the use of symbols.

Activity
Students will select one of the following projects. Students should be given a timeline as to when the check/edit day will be and when the project is due. Students should be informed as to grading procedures for the project. This is a chance for the students to extend themselves into the concept of "Symbols."

1. Considering the broad use of symbols in our daily lives, research the history of symbols in a specific area of use. Prepare a report either in poster or written form. (Examples: history of number system, geometric symbols, Braille, periodic table, traffic symbols, etc.).

2. Create a symbol that represents your math class. Display the symbol on a poster, write an explanation for the symbol for the class.

3. Find as many mathematical symbols as possible. Organize the symbols into "families" and display them in a mobile.

4. Create a booklet about symbols and the order of operations or integers as if it were a teaching tool for a younger student. You should "spice up" your work to make the booklet interesting!

5. Create a set of cartoons illustrating the order of operations, integers, mathematical symbols or geometry vocabulary. (Some examples can be found in the book *Humor in Math*).

6. Pretend you are an integer or a mathematical symbol. Write a story about your life.

7. Make a collage illustrating some idea about integers (opposite directions, ups-downs, opposite property, their uses, etc.). Choose one idea to illustrate.

Assessment
Quality and accuracy of activities.

Quadrant 4—Creations

Left Mode—Refine

Discuss projects in small groups and with teacher.

Objective
To give guidance and feedback to students' plans, to encourage, to refine.

Activity
In small groups, discuss projects. Teacher discusses projects with students.

Assessment
Participation, timelines.

Right Mode—Integrate

Share projects with class.

Objective
To share, to delight in what was learned.

Activity
Students share their projects with the class.

Assessment
Quality of sharing, enjoyment.

Transformations 1/4

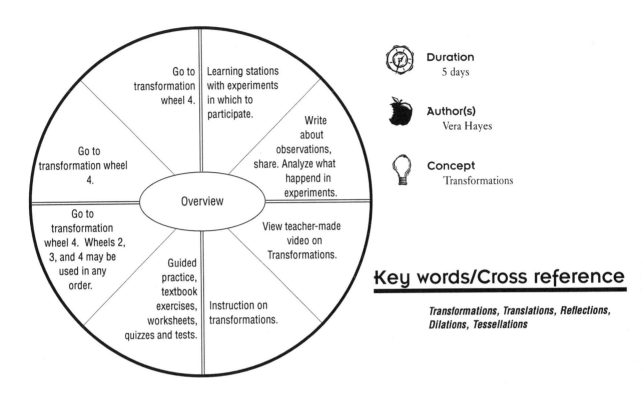

Overview

Go to transformation wheel 4.

Learning stations with experiments in which to participate.

Write about observations, share. Analyze what happend in experiments.

View teacher-made video on Transformations.

Instruction on transformations.

Guided practice, textbook exercises, worksheets, quizzes and tests.

Go to transformation wheel 4. Wheels 2, 3, and 4 may be used in any order.

Go to transformation wheel 4.

Duration
5 days

Author(s)
Vera Hayes

Concept
Transformations

Key words/Cross reference

Transformations, Translations, Reflections, Dilations, Tessellations

Overview

Objective
To create an awareness of transformations.

About the Author
Vera Hayes teaches math at Eisenhower Middle School in the North East Independent School District in San Antonio, Texas.

Required Resources
Experiments require the following: ice, whipping cream, egg white, paint, popcorn, sponges that enlarge when moist, mix master for beating egg white, popcorn popper.

Teacher-made video of transformations. Examples: video clips from Cinderella, Littlest Mermaid, Beetlejuice, Superman, Total Recall, Honey I Shrunk the Kids, Teen Wolf and others.

Quadrant 1—Experience

Right Mode—Connect

Learning stations with experiments in which to participate.

Objective
To experience transformations.

Activity
Divide class into groups. Assign one of the following experiments to each group.
1. Melting an ice cube.
2. Beating egg whites to stiff stage.
3. Mixing colors of paint.
4. Popping popcorn.
5. Placing the miniature sponges (found in craft shops for painting patterns) in water.

Assessment
Participation with group.

Left Mode—Examine

Write about observations, share. Analyze what happened in experiments.

Objective
To analyze the experiments.

Activity
Students will write about their observations, then share with the class. Analyze what happened and find the commonalities. (All are transformations)

Assessment
Participation in discussion.

Quadrant 2—Concepts

Right Mode—Image

View teacher-made video on Transformations.

Objective
To deepen the connection of transformations to changes.

Activity
View teacher-made video of "Transformations". See "Required Resources" for information.

Assessment
Attentiveness to video.

Left Mode—Define

Instruction on transformations.

Objective
To provide instruction on transformations.

Activity
Present lessons from textbook on translating, reflecting, rotating, and dilating figures in the coordinate plane.

Assessment
Participation and notetaking.

Quadrant 3—Applications

 ### Left Mode—Try

Guided practice, textbook exercises, worksheets, quizzes and tests.

Objective

To provide practice in transformation skills.

Activity

Guided practice, textbook exercises, worksheets, and quizzes.

Assessment

Quizzes and tests.

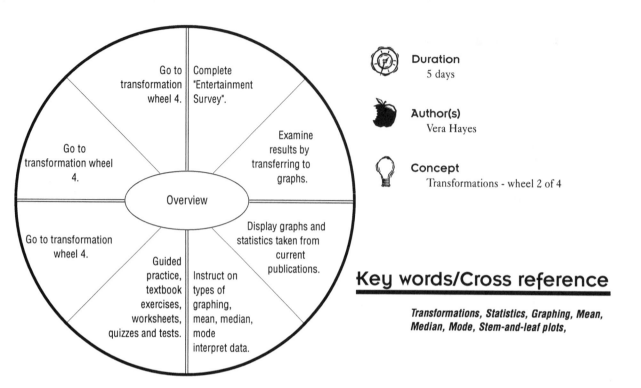

Duration
5 days

Author(s)
Vera Hayes

Concept
Transformations - wheel 2 of 4

Key words/Cross reference

Transformations, Statistics, Graphing, Mean, Median, Mode, Stem-and-leaf plots,

Wheel contents:
- Go to transformation wheel 4.
- Complete "Entertainment Survey".
- Examine results by transferring to graphs.
- Display graphs and statistics taken from current publications.
- Instruct on types of graphing, mean, median, mode interpret data.
- Guided practice, textbook exercises, worksheets, quizzes and tests.
- Go to transformation wheel 4.
- Go to transformation wheel 4.
- Overview

Overview

Objective
To view graphs as a transformation of data into an easy-to-read form.

About the Author
Vera Hayes is a math teacher at Eisenhower Middle School in the North East Independent School District in San Antonio, Texas.

Required Resources
Graphs and statistics from current publications, Entertainment survey.

Quadrant 1—Experience

 ### Right Mode—Connect

Complete "Entertainment Survey".

Objective
To gather data in which students will be interested.

Activity
Students will complete the Entertainment Survey individually. The entertainment survey is a set of questions with multiple choice answers from current entertainment. Questions are as follows:

Who is the funniest actress on TV?
Who would you rather play football for?
Which TV game show would you most like to appear?
Who is your favorite movie actor?
Which is the coolest TV show?
Which character on Beverly Hills 90210 would you most want to have as a best friend?
Would you rather be a superstar actor or a world-class athlete for a day?
Who's your favorite female singer?
Who is your favorite actress?
Favorite comedy series?
Which of the following movies would you most like to see turned into a theme park ride?
Who is the funniest actor on TV?
Which is funnier: Saturday Night Live, or In Living Color?

Assessment
Seriousness in answering survey.

 ### Left Mode—Examine

Examine results by transferring to graphs.

Objective
To analyze the data from the survey.

Activity
Examine the survey results by transferring the answers to graphs posted in the classroom. Class discusses graph results.

Assessment
Participation in completing graphs and discussion.

Quadrant 2—Concepts

 ### Right Mode—Image

Display graphs and statistics taken from current publications.

Objective
To deepen the connection between data and graphs as transformations of data.

Activity
Display examples of graphs and statistics taken from current publications.
Try to find graphs pertaining to topics that interest middle school students. Public libraries have business journals that contain great graphs. Discuss graphs as class.

Assessment
Participation and reaction to graphs.

 ### Left Mode—Define

Instruct on types of graphing, Mean, Median, Mode interpret data.

Objective
To provide instruction on statistics and graphing.

Activity
Present learning activities on:

- Using frequency tables and line plots to organize data and finding mean, median, and mode.
- Reading and making stem-and-leaf plots, box plots; and bar, broken-line and circle graphs and histograms.
- Interpreting data presented in graphs.

Assessment
Participation and notetaking.

Quadrant 3—Applications

 ### Left Mode—Try

Guided practice, textbook exercises, worksheets, quizzes and tests.

Objective
To provide practice in graphing skills.

Activity
Guided practice, textbook exercises, worksheets, and quizzes.

Assessment
Quizzes and tests.

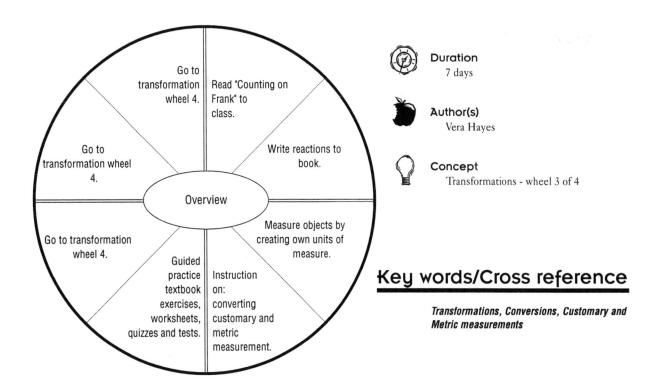

Duration
7 days

Author(s)
Vera Hayes

Concept
Transformations - wheel 3 of 4

Key words/Cross reference

Transformations, Conversions, Customary and Metric measurements

Overview

Objective
To view the conversion of measurements as transformations from one unit to another.

About the Author
Vera Hayes is a math teacher at Eisenhower Middle School in the North East Independent School District in San Antonio, Texas.

Required Resources
"Counting on Frank" by Gareth Sevens Childrens' Books.
Objects in the classroom to measure.

Quadrant 1—Experience

 ### Right Mode—Connect

Read "Counting on Frank" to class.

Objective
To create an awareness of different methods of measurement.

Activity
Read the childrens' book "Counting on Frank" to the class being sure the students have an opportunity to view the pictures.

Assessment
Attentiveness to story.

 ### Left Mode—Examine

Write reactions to book.

Objective
To analyze reactions to the book.

Activity
Students write their reactions to the book—the story of the measuring maniac.
Share students' reactions.

Assessment
Quality of responses.

Quadrant 2—Concepts

 ### Right Mode—Image

Measure objects by creating own units of measure.

Objective
To develop the understanding that objects can be measured with different units.

Activity
Give students object to measure by creating their own units of measure (cannot use inches, feet, centimeters, etc.). This activity leads to why we need conversions or transformation of measurements and why we use standard units of measure.

Assessment
Participation in measuring.

 ### Left Mode—Define

Instruction on: converting customary and metric measurement.

Objective
To provide instruction on converting measurements.

Activity
Present lessons on converting customary and metric measurements and on choosing the appropriate measurements.

Assessment
Participation and notetaking.

Transformations 3/4

Quadrant 3—Applications

 Left Mode—Try

Guided practice textbook exercises, worksheets, quizzes and tests.

Objective
To provide practice in converting measurement.

Activity
Guided practice, textbook exercises, worksheets, and quizzes.

Assessment
Quizzes and tests.

Transformations 4/4

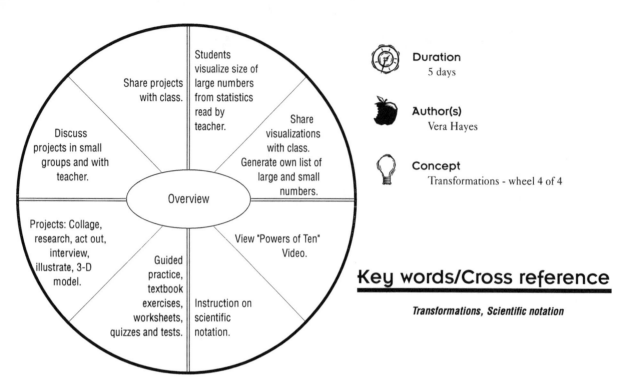

Duration
5 days

Author(s)
Vera Hayes

Concept
Transformations - wheel 4 of 4

Key words/Cross reference

Transformations, Scientific notation

Overview

 Objective
To view the writing of large/small numbers in scientific notation as a transformation.

 About the Author
Vera Hayes is a math teacher at Eisenhower Middle School in the North East Independent School District in San Antonio, Texas.

 Required Resources
Powers of Ten educational video or book.
List of large and small numbers—science books are a good source.

Bibliography
Powers of Ten by Phyllis and Phillip Morrison and Charles and Ray Eames.
ISBN # 0-7167-6003-7.

Transformations 4/4

Quadrant 1—Experience

Right Mode—Connect

Students visualize size of large numbers from statistics read by teacher.

Objective

To become aware of the use of very large/small numbers.

Activity

Read a list of large/small numbers either from statistics or science. Example: national debt, size of hydrogen atom. Have students visualize the size of these numbers as they are read.

Assessment

Attentiveness, response to numbers.

Left Mode—Examine

Share visualizations with class. Generate own list of large and small numbers.

Objective

To analyze reactions to numbers.

Activity

Students share their visualizations with the class and generate their own lists of large numbers and lists of small numbers and their uses. This could be a homework or research assignment.

Assessment

Participation in discussion.

Quadrant 2—Concepts

Right Mode—Image

View Powers of Ten Video.

Objective

To improve the students perception of large and small numbers.

Activity

View *Powers of Ten* video which illustrates the concepts of micro and macro sizes. There is also a book with that same title.

Assessment

Attentiveness to video.

Left Mode—Define

Instruction on scientific notation.

Objective

To provide instruction on scientific notation.

Activity

Present instruction on using scientific notation with large/small number and computing with scientific notation.

Assessment

Participation and notetaking.

Quadrant 3—Applications

 ## Left Mode—Try

Guided practice, textbook exercises, worksheets, quizzes and tests.

Objective
To provide practice with scientific notation.

Activity
Guided practice, textbook exercises, worksheets, and quizzes.

Assessment
Quizzes and tests.

 ## Right Mode—Extend

Projects: Collage, research, act out, interview, illustrate, 3-D model.

Objective
To provide activities that will broaden students' experiences in the use of transformations.

Activity
Students will select one of the following projects. Students should be given a timeline as to when the check/edit day will be and when the project is due. Students should be informed as to grading procedures for the project. This is a chance for the students to extend themselves into the concept of "Transformations".
When selecting a project, the student should be reminded to consider all types of transformations.

1. Make a collage of "transformations".
2. Write a research report on M.C. Escher.
3. Write and act out a transformation (as a group). This should be in the form of a commercial.
4. Interview a transformation. (This is a creative writing assignment about a character or object that transforms.)
5. Illustrate a transformation that has not been discussed in class.
6. Interview a professional that uses transformations in his work.
7. Make a 3-D model of a transformation.

Assessment
Quality and correctness of project.

Quadrant 4—Creations

 ## Left Mode—Refine

Discuss projects in small groups and with teacher.

Objective
To give guidance and feedback to students' plans, to encourage, to refine.

Activity
Discuss projects in small groups. Teacher discusses projects with students.

Assessment
Participation, timeliness.

 ## Right Mode—Integrate

Share projects with class.

Objective
To share, to delight in what was learned.

Activity
Students share their projects.

Assessment
Quality of sharing, enjoyment.

Gymnastics & Geography

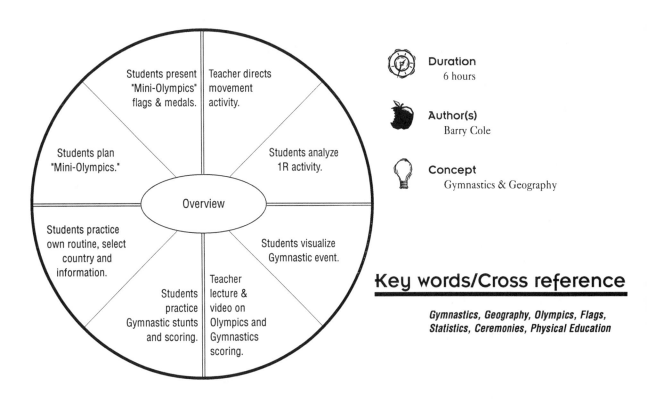

Duration
6 hours

Author(s)
Barry Cole

Concept
Gymnastics & Geography

The wheel diagram (clockwise from top right):
- Teacher directs movement activity.
- Students analyze 1R activity.
- Students visualize Gymnastic event.
- Teacher lecture & video on Olympics and Gymnastics scoring.
- Students practice Gymnastic stunts and scoring.
- Students practice own routine, select country and information.
- Students plan "Mini-Olympics."
- Students present "Mini-Olympics" flags & medals.
- Overview (center)

Key words/Cross reference

Gymnastics, Geography, Olympics, Flags, Statistics, Ceremonies, Physical Education

Overview

Objective
It is essential that we educate the whole child, the mind and the body. Assist students to make connections between the physical and intellectual aspects of learning. To insure that school subjects are interrelated because they are best comprehended when seen in relationship to one another.

About the Author
Barry Cole is a district resource teacher and staff developer at Montgomery Complex in Albuquerque, NM.

Required Resources
Library reference materials, gym mats, video of 1992 Olympic Gymnastic competition, rating sheet to score teams and individuals, world map, fabric, scissors, glue, cardboard or PVC tubing.

Quadrant 1—Experience

Right Mode—Connect

Teacher directs movement activity.

Objective

To connect students with what they know about body movement, cooperation, and Geography.

Activity

Create through movement, a tree, a ball, the world, a pyramid, the shape of the United States (whole class) and a star. Show students a card which has the outline of a country and have groups of students form the outline of the country.

Assessment

Students complete task.

Left Mode—Examine

Students analyze 1R activity.

Objective

Students analyze their experiences from 1R and establish connections to Gymnastics and Geography.

Activity

In groups, have students discuss: their observations, what happened, how what they previously knew helped them complete the tasks, how it relates to the sport of Gymnastics, and if any of them belong to Gymnastic schools or teams.

Assessment

Students ability to discuss, analyze and draw from their own experiences.

Quadrant 2—Concepts

Right Mode—Image

Students visualize Gymnastic event.

Objective

Have students visualize a Gymnastic event.

Activity

Play Aaron Copeland's "Fanfare for the Common Man." Ask students to visualize a strong teenager in white shorts and shirt. The teenager is on a gym floor with lots of people watching. The teenager starts to run across the floor, jumps into the air, and does two cart wheels, then a forward roll, stand on one leg and then does the splits. The people clap and cheer, some other people hold up cards with numbers on them. The people start to cheer and clap again.

Assessment

Make a drawing of some part of what they visualized.

Left Mode—Define

Teacher lecture & video on Olympics and Gymnastics scoring.

Objective

Learn the names and steps of various Gymnastic stunts. The Gymnastic point system used to evaluate a routine (simplified 10,9,8,7,6,5). The names of countries with Olympic level athletes.

Vocabulary:	Countries:
tuck	Belarus
roll	Japan
point	Russia
cartwheel	Romania
plant	United States
march	China
banner	Latvia

Activity

Teacher lecture on history, purpose, and function of Gymnastics, Olympics, and competition as ways to resolve differences. Show a video of the 1992 Olympic Gymnastic competition, analyze scoring by individuals, nations and medals won. Teach Gymnastic stunts.

Assessment

Students will score part of the video using a prepared rating sheet to check for understanding.

Gymnastics & Geography

Quadrant 3—Applications

 ### Left Mode—Try

Students practice Gymnastic stunts and scoring.

Objective
Provide guided practice of Gymnastic stunts and scoring.

Activity
Students in triads follow practice schedule going from station to station practicing identified stunt as well as scoring each other on rating sheet.

Assessment
Students compare and turn in rating sheets, shows proficiency in both Gymnastic stunts and scoring activity.

 ### Right Mode—Extend

Students practice own routine, select country and information.

Objective
To apply what has been learned.

Activity
Self select teams of 3 or 4, select a country to represent, develop own Gymnastic routine using individual and combination skills, select three interesting things about country, draw or make a flag of country you selected.

Assessment
Degree of cooperation and completion of tasks.

Quadrant 4—Creations

Left Mode—Refine

Students plan "Mini-Olympics."

Objective
Plan "Mini-Olympics."

Activity
Participate in drawing brackets, selecting teams for brackets and judges, elect team captain, decide time and location of "Mini Olympics," send invitations to parents and guests, tell other teams about your country and flag.

Assessment
Ability to complete above tasks.

 ### Right Mode—Integrate

Students present "Mini-Olympics" flag: & medals.

Objective
To share and enjoy what each student has learned.

Activity
Put on "Mini-Olympics." Enter alphabetically by countries, divide into assigned brackets, perform individual Gymnastic routines, record individual and team scores, award individual, team, and competitor medals (every child gets a medal, "every child is a winner").

Assessment
The student' enjoyment, enthusiasm and pride of their learning which has taken place.

Adaptations

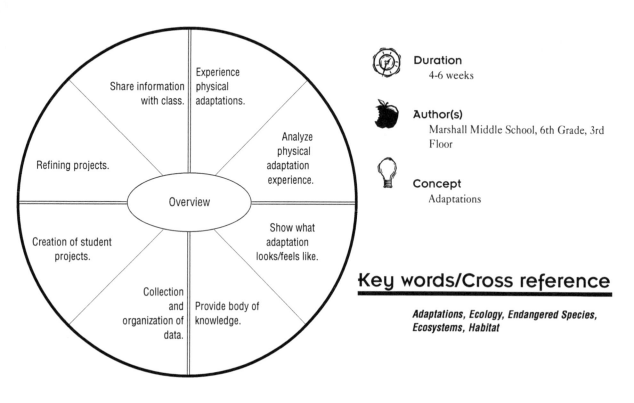

Duration
4-6 weeks

Author(s)
Marshall Middle School, 6th Grade, 3rd Floor

Concept
Adaptations

Key words/Cross reference

Adaptations, Ecology, Endangered Species, Ecosystems, Habitat

Overview

Objective

The student will analyze the relationships between animals and how they adapt to survive in their environment. The student will critique how adaptations help/hinder an animal's ability to survive in its natural surroundings. The student will judge how man's interference has affected nature's balance, and cause some animals to become endangered.

About the Author

Diane Buss is the Learning Support Teacher for Marshall Middle School. Mary Grace is the Reading/ Writing Specialist at Marshall Middle School. Joan Heinze, Wendy Manning, and Andrea Matthusen are members of the Third Floor Sixth Grade Team at Marshall Middle School, Janesville, WI.

Required Resources

"Endangered Species, pg. 6" *Ranger Rick's Naturescope*, Vol. 3, No. 3, 1987.
Endangered Species Picture Collections, American Teaching Aids, Minneapolis, MN.

Highlights Animal Books, Highlights For Children, Inc., 2300 West Fifth Ave., P.O. Box 269, Columbus, OH 43216-0269.
Discover Science, 1991, Scott Foresman, Glenview, IL. ch. 3, *"Change Through Time,"* pg. 64-84, *"Elk Ears"* p. 65 (or adapt from any science text that covers adaptations).
"Predators Pamphlet," 1989, National Wildlife Federation, 1400 16th St. N.W., Washington, DC 20036-2266
"Big Cats," p. 10-11, adapted from *"Cats of Many Colors,"* p. 18 of Naturescope Amazing Mammals II

Bibliography

"Copycat Page," pg. 15-18, *Ranger Rick's Naturescope, Endangered Species, Wild & Rare*, Vol. 3, No. 3, 1987.
"Habitat Is Home," pg. 31-33, *Ranger Rick's Naturescope, Endangered Species, Wild & Rare*, Vol. 3, No. 3, 1987.
Ranger Rick's Naturescope, Endangered Species, Wild & Rare, *"Ranger Rick's Endangered Species Index,"* pg. 64,

Adaptations

Vol. 3, No. 3, 1987.

"Exploring New Frontiers at Home," National Science and Technology Week, April 21-27, 1991.

Endangered Species, Evan Moore Corp., 1991 - Entire contents.

"Saving the Rhino," Junior Scholastic, Vol. 92, No. 6, Nov. 17, 1989. ISSN 0022-6688.

Scientific Encounters of the Endangered Kind, Good Apple, Inc. 1986 by Lynn Embry.

Zoobooks, San Diego Wild Life Park, Wildlife Education, Ltd. 3590 Kettner Blvd., San Diego, CA 92101.

Check with your librarian for a list of endangered species books.

Videos:

The Lorax, by Dr. Seuss (district owned at Madison School)

Discover the World of Science, *"Leech Farm," "Red Rough Lemur," "Manatee."*

National Geographic, *"Mountain Gorilla," "Keepers of the Wild," "Great Whales," "Noah, Keeper of the Ark."*

Scientific American Frontiers, *"Endangered Woodpeckers New Lease," "Restoring the Black Footed Ferret."*

Magazines:

Ranger Rick (copies that the students bring in for use).

Quadrant 1—Experience

Right Mode—Connect

Experience physical adaptations.

Objective
To create an experience for students to connect the purpose of physical adaptation.

Activity
Elk ears – Students construct elk ears from a pattern. They line up and hold the ear facing away from a person making light tapping noises. Distance is measured when students can no longer hear tapping. Repeat activity with ears turned to catch the tapping sound. Measure distance. Materials: construction paper, scissors, tape measure, elk ear pattern.

Assessment
Quality of student participation and observation.

Left Mode—Examine

Analyze physical adaptation experience.

Objective
Examine the Elk Ear Experience.

Activity
Analyze and discuss the individual differences in the listening activity, noting individual and group differences.

Assessment
Quality of student participation in discussion.

Quadrant 2—Concepts

 ### Right Mode—Image

Show what adaptation looks/feels like.

Objective
Portray the concept of Elk Ear Activity.

Activity
Students will show what adaptation looks/feels like through: collage, rap, poem, modeling, mime, etc.

Assessment
Quality of student production.

 ### Left Mode—Define

Provide body of knowledge.

Objective
To teach concept of adaptation.

Activity
Provide "acknowledged body of knowledge" related to the concept.
L.A. – Vocabulary - Spelling list words in L.A.
Science - Project Outline - Student research chosen animal and complete teacher made outline, i.e., - length, height, weight, color, eating habits, enemies, habitat, interesting facts, how does animal protect itself, how many were there, how many alive now, how do people hurt animals, what is being done to help animals.
Science - Lecture - From science textbook that contains adaptation or endangered species sections.
L.A. - Persuasive paragraph and oral interview - This is teacher generated to adapt to individual classes.
The persuasive paragraph needs to explain why it is important to save the species the students chose. They also need to explain how to save the species.
The interview involves two students, one asking questions which have been prewritten in generic form about any species. The other student is the expert on the species and answers the questions.

Assessment
Teacher verbal and/or written checking for student understanding.

Quadrant 3—Applications

 ### Left Mode—Try

Collection and organization of data.

Objective
Working on defined concepts.

Activity
Start research outline for Endangered Species (Science). Start persuasive paragraph (L.A.).
1.) Science - Big Cat Habitat/Coat of Many Colors:
Objective
To define camouflage. Describe how camouflage helps some predators survive.
Materials:
Copies of p. 11, from *Naturescope, Amazing Mammals* II, for each student. Animal and predator reference books, scissors, crayons, colored pencils, and markers.
Activity
Begin by discussing how certain colorations and markings can help predators sneak up on their prey. Also explain that spots, stripes, and other markings help to break up the outline of an animal's body. After the discussion, students research to match the five cat poems with the five given big cats. They then find photographs of cats and their habitat and color the cat in its habitat and glue the matching poem below cat or on the back.
2) Science - Animal Adaptations: Skill Sheet
Objective
To relate how animals use their unique adaptations to secure their food.
Materials:
Scott Foresman Science Workbook, p. 14.

Activity
To think individually or in a cooperative group about how the adaptations of each animal pictured on the skill sheet uses it's unique adaptations to help get its food.

Assessment
Quality of completed outline, completion of assignments.

Adaptations

 ### Right Mode—Extend

Creation of student projects.

Objective
To extend student's understanding of adaptation.

Activity
Create a brochure from independent research. Create a Habitat Range Map and a license plate for an endangered species. Finalize oral interview and persuasive paragraph.

Science
The brochure is to be designed like a travel brochure. A piece of 8-1/2" by 14" white paper is folded into thirds. Inside is information on why the species is endangered, a habitat range map, where to find more information with addresses, a plea for help, and the front cover should have a picture of the animal and a catchy title. Social Studies - Habitat Range Map is a map of the former and present range of the species. A key is necessary to depict the differences. This map should have a title, be neat and colorful, and may be mounted on construction paper for display. Teachers provide the necessary maps.

Science
A license plate form is completed by the students with the following: Title, year, picture of species, background habitat, and the continent or country either drawn or written.

Assessment
Participation, quality of work, completion of work, accuracy, and enthusiasm.

Quadrant 4—Creations

 ### Left Mode—Refine

Refining projects.

Objective
To demonstrate concern for the future using new learning.

Activity
Refine persuasive paragraph and oral interview.

Assessment
Quality of work, willingness, expression of ideas.

 ### Right Mode—Integrate

Share information with class.

Objective
To share and enjoy the products created.

Activity
Students share final presentations. Display students work in hallways and on bulletin boards. View the movie, "The Lorax" as a final celebration.

Assessment
Quality of completed projects, presentations, participation and enjoyment of learning.

Rotational Motion

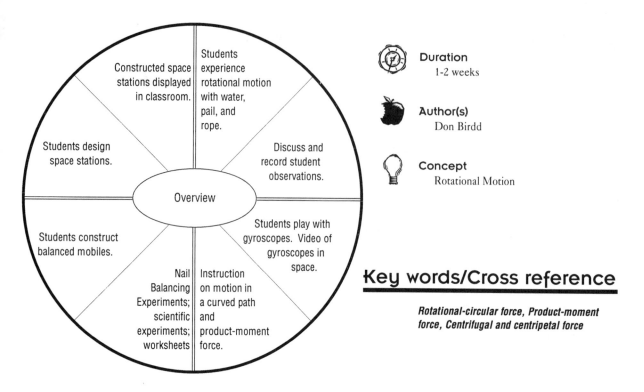

Constructed space stations displayed in classroom.

Students experience rotational motion with water, pail, and rope.

Students design space stations.

Discuss and record student observations.

Overview

Students construct balanced mobiles.

Students play with gyroscopes. Video of gyroscopes in space.

Nail Balancing Experiments; scientific experiments; worksheets

Instruction on motion in a curved path and product-moment force.

Duration
1-2 weeks

Author(s)
Don Birdd

Concept
Rotational Motion

Key words/Cross reference

Rotational-circular force, Product-moment force, Centrifugal and centripetal force

Overview

Objective
Students will learn the fundamental concept of rotational motion in physics.

About the Author
Dr. Donald L. Birdd is a Science Educator and Science Student Teacher Supervisor at Buffalo State College, Buffalo, NY. In addition, Don has fifteen years experience as a middle school and high school science teacher in schools in Wisconsin, Idaho, Colorado, and Kentucky. He is a certified 4MAT Trainer.

Required Resources
One-gallon pail of water on a cord; gyroscopes; twenty 16d nails for experiment; scientific company equipment: meter stick, weight hangers and weights, fulcrum (pivot) point; string, wooden dowel rods, paper clips and masking tape for student projects.

Bibliography
"Toys in Space." NASA Goddard Space Flight Center, Teacher Resource Laboratory. Greenbelt, MD 20771. Telephone: (301) 344-8570 or 344-7205. "NASA Aerospace Spinoffs: Twenty-five Years of Technology Transfer;" "NASA Spinoff - 1988;" and "NASA Spinoff - 1986." Superintendent of Documents, U.S. Government Printing Office, Washington, DC 20402.

Rotational Motion

Quadrant 1—Experience

 ### Right Mode—Connect

Students experience rotational motion with water, pail, and rope.

Objective

To create an experience where rotational motion of an object allows for the unexpected to happen. This should raise the question, "Why?"

Activity

After ensuring safety, teacher swings a 1-gallon pail of water on the end of a cord over his head in the classroom.

Assessment

Students' reactions and expectations. Teacher looks for prior experience with similar action or response of, "Wow, I wonder why the water did not spill out!"

 ### Left Mode—Examine

Discuss and record student observations.

Objective

To analyze student expectations and observations.

Activity

Using overhead/chalkboard, record, discuss and analyze student observations from the bucket of water experience.

Assessment

Ability of class to categorize their observations. Individual contributions to class effort.

Quadrant 2—Concepts

 ### Right Mode—Image

Students play with gyroscopes. Video of gyroscopes in space.

Objective

To extend students' understanding of circular motion on Earth and in space.

Activity

Students will "play" with gyroscopes and predict how they will behave in space. Students will observe video segment of how gyroscopes behave in space ("Toys in Space" produced by NASA, activities coordinated through National Science Teachers Association).

Assessment

Teacher observation of accuracy of student predictions.

 ### Left Mode—Define

Instruction on motion in a curved path and product-moment force.

Objective

To teach centrifugal and centripetal force as they affect motion of a body in circular motion.

Activity

Lecture on motion in a curved path. Discuss how students feel when a car they are riding in moves around sharp curves in a road. Ensure students have verbal and graphic representation of differences between centripetal and centrifugal forces. Discuss/identify product-moment force as another example of rotational/circular motion.

Assessment

Definition, spelling, and scientific literacy. Check student ability to use these terms contextually in a sentence.

Quadrant 3—Applications

 ## Left Mode—Try

Nail Balancing Experiments; scientific experiments; worksheets

Objective

To practice concepts of product-moment force.

Activity

1. Students balance 15-20 16d nails on the head of one 16d nail which has been pounded into the end of a 15 cm-long piece of 2 x 4.
2. Students use scientific company ordered equipment as follows: meter stick, weight hangers and weights, fulcrum (pivot) point, and teacher establishes a work sheet for students to determine product-moment force when given some variables (unknown mass).

Assessment

1. Accomplishment of nail balancing with appropriate written analysis/interpretation of WHY.
2. Accuracy in completing teacher-assigned inquiry/guided discovery lab worksheet.

 ## Right Mode—Extend

Students construct balanced mobiles.

Objective

To demonstrate rotational/counter-rotational motion using information learned.

Activity

Students are instructed to bring small "junk" item to class from home. They work in groups of four members. Each group is given seven pieces of string each 60 cm long, and three wooden dowel rods each 30-60 cm long. Boxes of paper clips and rolls of masking tape should be available for student use. Each group will construct a balanced mobile which will be suspended from the classroom ceiling.

Assessment

Construction of a balanced mobile.

Quadrant 4—Creations

 ## Left Mode—Refine

Students design space stations.

Objective

To have students learn about gyroscopic space platforms where humans could live and work.

Activity

Students will investigate several NASA publications available through the Government Printing Office which identify plans for humankind in space. They should focus their research on space and its potential products. (NASA SPIN-OFF PRODUCT BOOKS ARE AVAILABLE FROM THE GOVERNMENT PRINTING OFFICE) As a result of their research, student groups will design space stations which will satisfy living and research needs which they believe are important.

Assessment

The level of student involvement; the design plans for construction of a space station model.

 ## Right Mode—Integrate

Constructed space stations displayed in classroom.

Objective

To have students construct a model of their own space station design.

Activity

Students construct their space station models and hang them from the classroom ceiling. Products are presented and explained to the class.

Assessment

Quality of completed product and presentation.

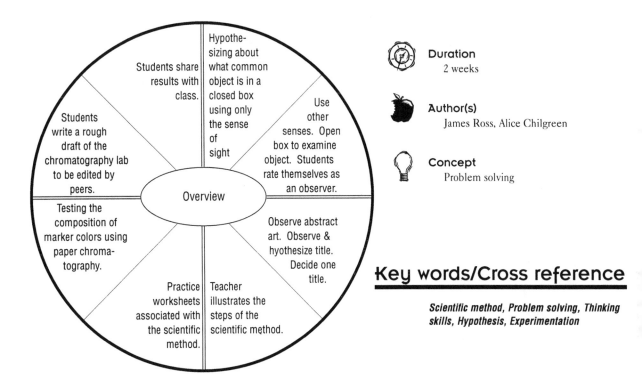

Overview (center)

Circle segments (clockwise from top):
- Hypothesizing about what common object is in a closed box using only the sense of sight
- Use other senses. Open box to examine object. Students rate themselves as an observer.
- Observe abstract art. Observe & hyothesize title. Decide one title.
- Teacher illustrates the steps of the scientific method.
- Practice worksheets associated with the scientific method.
- Testing the composition of marker colors using paper chromatography.
- Students write a rough draft of the chromatography lab to be edited by peers.
- Students share results with class.

Duration
2 weeks

Author(s)
James Ross, Alice Chilgreen

Concept
Problem solving

Key words/Cross reference

Scientific method, Problem solving, Thinking skills, Hypothesis, Experimentation

Overview

Objective
To develop the use of the scientific method for problem solving.

About the Author
James Ross is a Grade 8 Science Teacher at Mc Culloch Middle School, and
Alice Chilgreen is a Grade 8 Science/Math Teacher at Justice Middle School, Marion Community Schools, Marion, IN.

Required Resources
Array of "mystery boxes," abstract art prints, materials for scientific method experiment (suggestion: pendulum), Water color markers for chromatography experiment.

Quadrant 1—Experience

 ## Right Mode—Connect

Hypothesizing about what common object is in a closed box using only the sense of sight.

Objective

To illustrate the limitation of sight as an observer.

Activity

Place a box containing a mystery object in front of the student. Instruct them not to touch the box, but list five things that could not be in the box and five things that could possibly be in the box.

Assessment

The student notes are checked for participation.

 ## Left Mode—Examine

Use other senses. Open box to examine object. Students rate themselves as an observer.

Objective

To practice observation with the other senses.

Activity

Tell the student to pick up the box and observe it with senses other than sight. Hypothesize about what object is in the box. Open the box to check hypothesis. In a group activity, decide what is involved in good observation. Have the students rate themselves on a scale of 1-5 on their ability to make a good observation.

Assessment

Participation will be determined by the quality of student responses.

Quadrant 2—Concepts

 ## Right Mode—Image

Observe abstract art. Observe & hypothesize title. Decide one title.

Objective

To acknowledge differences in perception and relate to an individual's concept of the world.

Activity

Present students with 3 or 4 abstract works of art. Tell them to observe carefully and hypothesize about titles. In small group discussions, the students will compare observations to select one title.

Assessment

The student responses will be checked for diversity of ideas.

 ## Left Mode—Define

Teacher illustrates the steps of the scientific method.

Objective

To teach the scientific method.

Activity

The teacher will demonstrate an experiment which illustrates the steps of the scientific method. Any experiment which clearly demonstrates carefully to observe, hypothesis formation, experimentation, data collection, analysis and a conclusion is appropriate. Example: an experiment to determine the period of a pendulum.

Assessment

Notes from the demonstration will be checked for thoroughness and clarity.

Quadrant 3—Applications

 ### Left Mode—Try

Practice worksheets associated with the scientific method.

Objective
To practice skills associated with the scientific method.

Activity
Teacher directed activities that develop skills associated with the scientific method: observation, hypothesis, formation, experimentation and drawing conclusions.

Assessment
Individual papers are selected for grading.

Right Mode—Extend

Testing the composition of marker colors using paper chromatography.

Objective
To use the scientific method to solve a problem.

Activity
The students will test the composition of water color markers using paper chromatography.

Assessment
The teacher will check the results of the chromatography experiment.

Quadrant 4—Creations

 ### Left Mode—Refine

Students write a rough draft of the chromatography lab to be edited by peers.

Objective
To organize lab data into a lab report.

Activity
Students will write a rough draft of their chromatography lab. In small groups they will edit and refine each other's lab reports. Each group member must make at least one suggestion for improving each report.

Assessment
The rough draft will be evaluated in group activity.

Right Mode—Integrate

Students share results with class.

Objective
To share final reports.

Activity
The students will share their rough drafts and finished drafts with the larger group.

Assessment
Presentation and grading of the final lab report.

Sound Waves

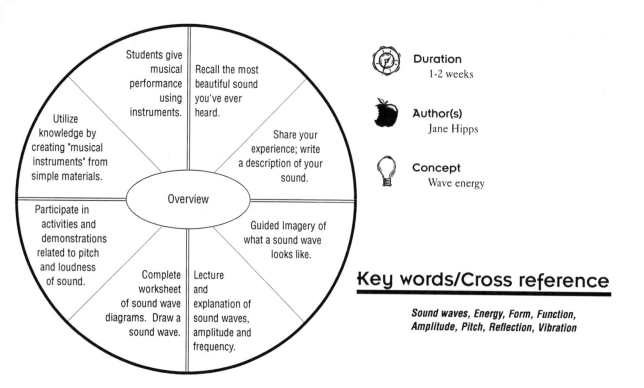

Duration
1-2 weeks

Author(s)
Jane Hipps

Concept
Wave energy

Key words/Cross reference

Sound waves, Energy, Form, Function,
Amplitude, Pitch, Reflection, Vibration

Overview

Objective
Students will understand that sound consists of
wave energy which has form and function.

About the Author
Jane B. Hipps is an Instructional Specialist at
Western Technical Assistance Center, Canton, N.C.
She is a certified 4MAT Trainer.

Required Resources
Tin cans, large rubber balloons, rubber bands, small
mirrors, rubber cement, flashlights, gallon plastic
tanks, tuning forks, soda straws, water and glasses,
combs and wax paper, rulers.

Sound Waves

Quadrant 1—Experience

 ### Right Mode—Connect

Recall the most beautiful sound you've ever heard.

Objective

To introduce students to the concept of sound by relating it to personal experience.

Activity

Guided imagery of the most beautiful sound you have ever heard.
Content for Guided Imagery: "Close your eyes and try to remember the most beautiful sound you have ever heard in the natural world. Note the setting (pause) any colors or smells you may have associated with the sound (pause). How did you feel? (pause) Imagine if that sound could talk and tell you its origin and purpose. You have two full minutes from now."
Materials: None

Assessment

Student concentration and participation.

 ### Left Mode—Examine

Share your experience; write a description of your sound.

Objective

Students share, compare and contrast their experience. Students write a brief description of their sound.

Activity

"Gather together in groups of four and tell each other all you can about your sounds and experiences associated with your sound. What are the similarities and differences between the sounds you selected? After the sharing and discussions, write down a description of your sound on the index card provided. Include in your description its quality, degree of loudness, pitch and source."
Materials: 3" x 5" index cards

Assessment

Ability to share and discuss information with others; quality of descriptive writing.

Quadrant 2—Concepts

 ### Right Mode—Image

Guided Imagery of what a sound wave looks like.

Objective

Students will experience an understanding of wave energy from a concrete example to a more abstract application.

Activity

Guided imagery of what a sound wave looks like. (Use an audio tape of the ocean in the background.)
Content for Guided Imagery: "We are going to use guided imagery again to continue our exploration of sound. Please close your eyes and listen. This time we will explore how sounds might look if we could actually see them and how sounds travel. (Pause 15 seconds. Allow students to concentrate on ocean sound.) Pretend that you are at the ocean watching waves travel along the surface of the water. When there is little wind and the water is calm, the waves lap softly to the shore, touch the sand, and recede back into the ocean. With greater force of wind, the waves hit the shore with more vigor.
Sound is also believed to travel in waves. It travels through air, water and solid materials in a wave-like motion. Suppose you hear someone call to you from a distance. The voice sounds are traveling to you through the air. Suppose you are swimming under water with a friend. This friend has a small rock in each hand. He hits the rocks together and you can hear this sound, locate your friend and swim toward him. Sound can travel through liquids.
Take yourself back in history and you are with a tribe of Plains Indians. You place your ear to the ground and listen for the vibrations of a buffalo herd as it moves swiftly across the plains. A rumbling of the earth lets you know that a herd of buffalo is heading your way. Sounds travel through solid materials.
Imagine my voice moving toward you in a series of waves. As I speak, the sounds travel in waves toward you. The sound of my voice is traveling to you through air. (Speak loudly) As I increase the volume of my voice, these waves cover a wider span of space. (Speak softly) As I decrease the volume of my voice, these waves cover a narrower span of space. (Speak in normal volume, high pitch) As I increase the pitch of my voice, these waves vibrate more times per second. (Speak in normal volume, low pitch) As I lower the pitch of my

voice, the sound waves vibrate fewer times per second. If I were speaking in a wide open space toward a rock cliff, we might hear an echo (pause—say softer) an echo, an echo of my voice as the sound waves hit the rock cliff and return." (pause for approximately 30 seconds and allow the students to listen to the sound of ocean waves)
Materials: Tape recorder, tape of ocean waves.

Assessment

Students keep eyes closed and appear to concentrate on the guided fantasy.

Left Mode—Define

Lecture and explanation of sound waves, amplitude and frequency.

Objective

Students will learn the basic concepts of sound waves.

Activity

Teacher explains the concept of sound waves—amplitude, frequency. Demonstrate a sound wave by using a slinky. (Reference 2, p. 508) Explain compressional waves—compressions and rarefractions, wavelength. Explain that sounds of higher pitch have more vibrations per second; sound of lower pitch have fewer vibrations per second. Louder sounds have greater amplitude, more energy. Softer sounds have less amplitude, less energy.

References: 1) Discover Science, (6th Grade Text); Scott Foresman and Company, 1989, pp. 240-243. 2) Physical Science, (High School Text); Prentice Hall, 1991, pp. 495-534. 3) Focus on Physical Science, (High School Text); Merrill Publishing Company, 1989, pp. 415-422.

Materials: Slinky

Assessment

Student attentiveness, asking and answering of questions.

Quadrant 3—Applications

Left Mode—Try

Complete worksheet of sound wave diagrams. Draw a sound wave.

Objective

Students will demonstrate their knowledge of sound waves by completing a worksheet to determine amplitudes and pitches. They will also draw their "most beautiful sound" (Quadrant One) according to amplitude and pitch.

Activity

Place a copy of "Name that Sound" on the overhead. Give each student or pair of students a copy of the worksheet, "Name that Sound." Have the student complete the sheet independently or with a partner. Once students have completed the task, go over their answers. Have students then draw a sound wave of "their most beautiful sound." Have them discuss their drawing with a partner to determine accuracy of their illustrations. The instructor should move among the students to determine their understanding of how waves can be visualized.

Materials: Worksheet "Name that Sound"—one per student or one per group of two students. Transparency of "Name that Sound."

Assessment

Accuracy of answers on worksheet, accuracy of drawing of their "most beautiful sound."

References: Sound, Workshop Leader's Guide, Operation Physics, American Institute of Physics.

Right Mode—Extend

Participate in activities and demonstrations related to pitch and loudness of sound.

Objective

Students gain a richer understanding of sound by participating in demonstrations and doing hands-on activities related to pitch and loudness of sound.

Activity

Activities and Demonstrations:
Demonstration: 1) Student can "see" sound waves through a demonstration by observing reflected light off

a vibrating membrane.

Materials: Tin can (13 oz. coffee can) with both ends removed, large rubber balloon (neck removed), rubber band, small mirror, rubber cement, flashlight.

Construction: Cover one end of open can with balloon and secure the balloon with a rubber band. Glue small mirror in the center of stretched balloon. One student holds the can. Another student holds the flashlight so that light is reflected off the mirror onto a screen. The student holding the can then yells loudly into the can. The vibration of the rubber balloon should be "visible" by observing the movement of the reflected light.

Note: By having several cans and flashlights, students can experiment with sound vibrations and reflected light; thus, this becomes a hands-on activity as well as a demonstration.

Activity 1:

Students can observe compressions and rarefractions of sound waves in water.

Materials:

Clear one gallon plastic tanks, tuning forks.

Instructions: Hit tuning fork on thickest part of hand palm, and dip tuning fork perpendicular to the surface of the water. The water will initially spray the tank and perhaps the student, but by looking quickly and carefully at the water around the tuning fork, bars of compressions and rarefractions can be observed. The students may have to repeat this activity several times to see what they are supposed to see.

Activity 2:

Hit a tuning fork on the thickest part of the palm of the hand. Listen to the tuning fork. Hit the tuning fork again and place the end of the fork to the table. Compare the volume of sound of the tuning fork in the air to the volume of the tuning fork against the table (solid material).

Materials:

Tuning forks, desks or tables.

Assessment

When asked, students should know that 1) sound creates vibrations, 2) sound waves consist of compressions and rarefractions, and 3) sound travels better (has greater volume) in solid material than air.

Quadrant 4—Creations

Left Mode—Refine

Utilize knowledge by creating "musical instruments" from simple materials.

Objective

Students will utilize their knowledge of sound by creating "musical" instruments from simple materials. They will then evaluate them according to pitch (pitches) and loudness.

Activity

Students will create their own sound maker from 1) soda straws (1 pitch instruments or multi-pitch instruments, 2) water and drinking glasses (bells, chimes), 3) combs and wax paper (kazoos), 4) rubber bands (string instruments), or 5) rulers (percussion instruments). Have students consider the amplitude and pitch of their instruments. Have students compare and contrast the pitch and amplitude of their instruments with those of other students. Have students graph themselves from instruments of loudest to highest pitch. Have students explain how their instruments work.

Materials: Rubber bands, rulers, combs, wax paper, soda straws (various diameters), drinking glasses with various amounts of water, mallets for striking glasses.

Assessment

Students will understand how to create "instruments" of various pitches and amplitude. Students will gain an understanding of how these instruments work.

Right Mode—Integrate

Students give musical performance using instruments.

Objective

Students will use their instruments in a creative way.

Activity

In groups of eight, students will use their created instruments to practice a known or original song (composition) for the rest of the class.

Materials: Instruments created from Quadrant Four, Left Mode.

Assessment

Students will, hopefully, either verbally or non-verbally, express satisfaction and joy over a creative experience and a well understood concept.

Tree Life Cycles (1 of 2)

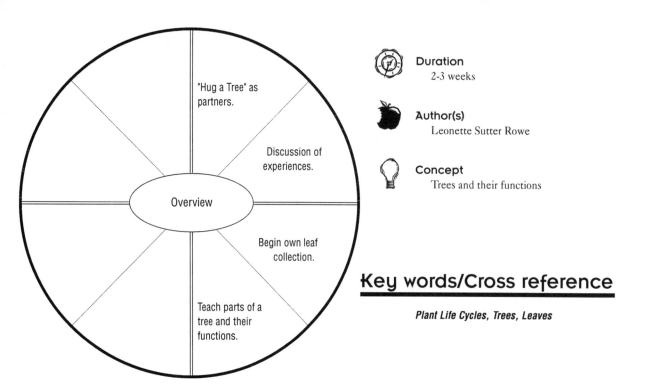

"Hug a Tree" as partners.

Discussion of experiences.

Overview

Begin own leaf collection.

Teach parts of a tree and their functions.

Duration
2-3 weeks

Author(s)
Leonette Sutter Rowe

Concept
Trees and their functions

Key words/Cross reference

Plant Life Cycles, Trees, Leaves

Overview

Objective
Students will learn basic tree characteristics.

About the Author
At the time this plan was written, Leonette Sutter Rowe was a 6th grade teacher in Green Local Schools, Smithville, OH.

Required Resources
Blindfolds for student partners.

Quadrant 1—Experience

 ### Right Mode—Connect

"Hug a Tree" as partners.

Objective

To experience and observe a living tree. To enhance observational skills.

Activity

Teacher assigns student pairs. After appropriate safety instructions and guidelines are clear, each pair of students takes a blindfold. One student in each pair blindfolds his/her partner and leads the "blind" student through the woods to a particular tree. The "guide" student then helps the "blind" student explore the tree and feel its uniqueness. The "guide" student asks questions like: Is the bark rough or smooth? Are there plants growing on the tree? Is the circumference of the trunk bigger or smaller than your waist? When the "blind" student is finished observing the tree, the "guide" student leads her/him back to where they began using an indirect route. The blindfold is removed, and the student tries to find the tree. When the tree is found, the partners switch roles and repeat the activity.

Assessment

Partner participation, adherence to guidelines, and responsibility for accomplishing the task.

 ### Left Mode—Examine

Discussion of experiences.

Objective

To pool observations. To discuss what makes all trees alike and what is unique about individual trees.

Activity

Students discuss their experiences in the "Hug a Tree" activity. List similarities and differences among trees on class charts.

Assessment

Quality of the discussion and accuracy of the lists.

Quadrant 2—Concepts

 ### Right Mode—Image

Begin own leaf collection.

Objective

To broaden the students' experience with one tree to trees in general.

Activity

Instruct students to begin their own leaf collections. Begin the collecting exercise with them. Model for the students the correct identification, collection, and pressing techniques.

Assessment

Participation, adherence to guidelines, and responsibility for accomplishing the task.

 ### Left Mode—Define

Teach parts of a tree and their functions.

Objective

To teach the parts of a tree and their functions.

Activity

Lecture with accompanying visual aids. Include the following terms: deciduous, conifer, root, trunk, bark, cambium, phloem, xylem, branch, leaf, blade, stem, photosynthesis, chlorophyll. Assign readings in text.

Assessment

Objective quiz.

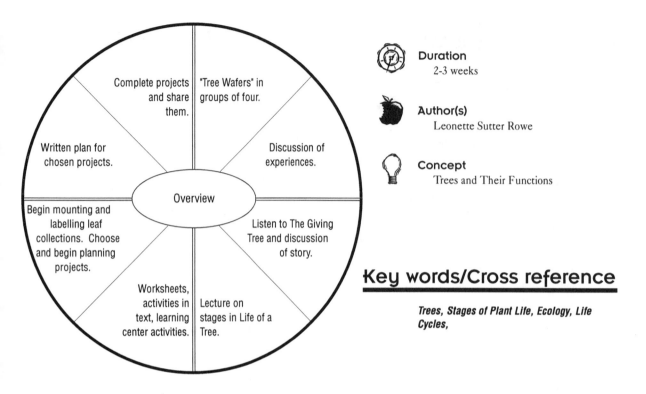

Circle diagram (clockwise from top):
- "Tree Wafers" in groups of four.
- Discussion of experiences.
- Listen to The Giving Tree and discussion of story.
- Lecture on stages in Life of a Tree.
- Worksheets, activities in text, learning center activities.
- Begin mounting and labelling leaf collections. Choose and begin planning projects.
- Written plan for chosen projects.
- Complete projects and share them.

Center: Overview

Duration
2-3 weeks

Author(s)
Leonette Sutter Rowe

Concept
Trees and Their Functions

Key words/Cross reference

Trees, Stages of Plant Life, Ecology, Life Cycles,

Overview

Objective
Students will learn the stages of tree life cycles.

About the Author
At the time this plan was written, Leonette Sutter Rowe was a 6th grade teacher in Green Local Schools, Smithville, OH.

Required Resources
Tree wafers (cross-sections of tree trunks);

Bibliography
Dunn, Rita and Kenneth, Teaching Students Through Their Individual Learning Styles: A Practical Approach. Reston Publishing Company, Inc. Prentice-Hall Company, Reston, Virginia. 1978, pp. 319-325, 329-338, 339-341.

Silverstein, Shel, *The Giving Tree*. Harper & Row, Publishers, New York, New York, 1964.

These are wonderful self-correcting materials for learning new concepts, as well as for reinforcing and practice. They are for tactile and visual students, as well as great fun for all students. Electroboard: pages 339-341; Task cards: pages 329-338; Learning circles: pages 319-325.

This lesson plan was included in the original 4MAT in Action.

Quadrant 1—Experience

Right Mode—Connect

"Tree Wafers" in groups of four.

Objective

To examine a cross section of a tree trunk.

Activity

Teacher assigns students to groups of four and gives each group a tree wafer (cross section of a tree trunk), straight pins, small paper labels, and a pen. Students examine the rings closely to identify which year each ring was made.

Students then pretend they are the tree from which the cross section was taken. By placing pins with labels in several of the rings, they indicate important events in their (the tree's) life. They may mark years when there was a dry spell, drought, injury from a moving vehicle, or removal of surrounding trees.

Students then add pins with labels at appropriate years for significant events in their own lives as human friends of this tree.

Assessment

Group participation and quality of time-line on tree trunk cross section.

Left Mode—Examine

Discussion of experiences.

Objective

To pool observations. To discuss the factors which may affect the way that a tree grows and, thus, alter the color and form of the rings.

Activity

Groups share their time-lines and explain why they placed pins at certain points for important events in the life of the tree.

Assessment

Quality of the discussion. Were the students involved in the discussion? How many ideas were generated? Did the students honor each other?

Quadrant 2—Concepts

Right Mode—Image

Listen to The Giving Tree and discussion of story.

Objective

To formulate the concepts of growth and development of a tree through another medium.

Activity

Students listen as teacher reads The Giving Tree. In the discussion that follows, emphasis is placed on visual imagery, feelings that were aroused, the sequence of events, and the main idea.

Assessment

Quality of students' responses.

Left Mode—Define

Lecture on stages in Life of a Tree.

Objective

To teach the stages in the life of a tree.

Activity

Lecture with accompanying visual aids. Include the following: bud, flower, fruit, cone, seed, embryo, seedling, terminal bud, life cycle.

Review growth and decay in terms of the following: rainfall, drought, sunshine, shade, fire, insects, disease, birds, mammals, storms, and the lower forms of life which hasten decomposition.

Assessment

Objective quiz.

Quadrant 3—Applications

 ### Left Mode—Try

Worksheets, activities in text, learning center activities.

Objective
To practice and reinforce the concepts.

Activity
Begin rotation at learning center with activity cards and tactile-kinesthetic activities (manipulative bulletin board on tree identification, learning circles and electroboard on basic vocabulary).

Assessment
Quality of written work and participation in T-K activities at the learning center.

 ### Right Mode—Extend

Begin mounting and labeling leaf collections. Choose and begin planning projects.

Objective
To reinforce and personalize students' learning by allowing them to choose an activity that explores some facet of trees.

Activity
Students begin mounting and labeling their leaf collections. Students continue their rotation through the learning center activities. Students choose one activity from the following:

- Make a sketchbook of trees showing each tree's shape, leaf, flower, and fruit.
- Tape an original poem about trees.
- Create a display showing the uses of wood from different kinds of trees.
- Pantomime the life cycle of a tree.
- Choose appropriate music and perform this pantomime to music.
- Do research to find out why some trees lose their leaves in autumn and others stay green all winter. Share the results of your research through a written report or a poster.
- Do research to find out why leaves change color in autumn. Collect samples of leaves that are changing color. Share your research and observations with your classmates through a written and/or oral report.

Assessment
How well the students go about the task of mounting and labeling the leaves for their collections. How well the students go about the task of selecting a project.

Quadrant 4—Creations

 ### Left Mode—Refine

Written plan for chosen projects.

Objective
To enhance student ability to plan and work systematically on a project.

Activity
Each student will write a contract for her/his chosen project specifying materials needed, resources to be used, concepts to be explored, and date of completion.

Note: Students continue mounting and labeling their leaf collections and rotating through the learning center activities.

Assessment
Quality of the written plans.

 ### Right Mode—Integrate

Complete projects and share them.

Objective
To increase student ability to work independently and to complete work they have begun. To provide an opportunity for students to share what they have learned and to learn from each other.

Activity
Students complete their projects and share them with their classmates through a display, an oral presentation, or a creative performance.

Assessment
Faithfulness to contract, quality of completed projects, participation, and sharing.
The scope of the contracted projects will determine the number of additional days needed.

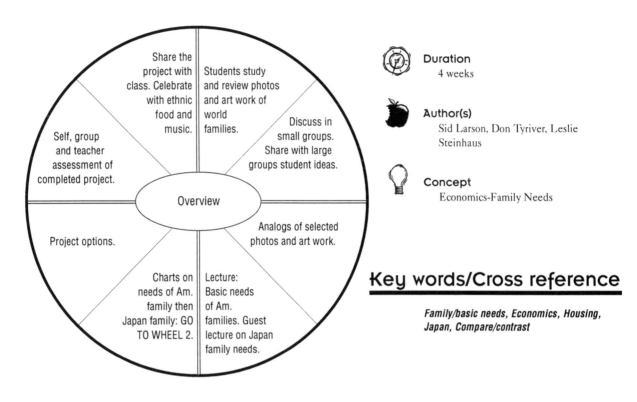

Overview

- Share the project with class. Celebrate with ethnic food and music.
- Students study and review photos and art work of world families.
- Discuss in small groups. Share with large groups student ideas.
- Self, group and teacher assessment of completed project.
- Analogs of selected photos and art work.
- Project options.
- Charts on needs of Am. family then Japan family: GO TO WHEEL 2.
- Lecture: Basic needs of Am. families. Guest lecture on Japan family needs.

Duration
4 weeks

Author(s)
Sid Larson, Don Tyriver, Leslie Steinhaus

Concept
Economics-Family Needs

Key words/Cross reference

Family/basic needs, Economics, Housing, Japan, Compare/contrast

Overview

Objective
Students will design a project that encompasses the common characteristics of world families' basic economic needs.

About the Authors
Sid Larson is a Reading/Writing Consultant; Don Tyriver is Principal of Edison Middle School, and Leslie Steinhaus is Assistant Superintendent of Curriculum/Staff Development in the School District of Janesville, Janesville, Wisconsin.

Required Resources
Photos of family members engaged in daily activities. The best source would be in your media center. Art work can be of your choosing that also shows families engaged in life's daily activities. Artwork use in the unit was Thomas Hart Benton's "Cradling Wheat" and "Roasting Ears" and Picasso's "Gourmet" and "Tragedy."

Bibliography
Textbooks (not required for the Unit) *Mathematics Plus*, HBJ, 1992.

Quadrant 1—Experience

Right Mode—Connect

Students study and review photos and artwork of world families.

Objective
Students view family members in different settings around the world through photographs and artwork.

Activity
1) Using a random assortment of photos of family members engaged in daily activities(6-8) from around the world, rotate the photos among the students. Have the students create a 4-column heading on their paper with the following criteria for viewing: country, continent, what are you seeing (observing)?, and personal question or comments. Each student will take approximately 45 seconds to complete the information on each photo. Move to 1 L activity and then return to #2.
2) Have the students review the works of art—Benton "Cradling Wheat" and "Roasting Ears" and Picasso— "Gourmet" and "The Tragedy". Have students study the print and make a 3-column heading on their paper with the following criteria: title of print, what students saw in print and personal questions or comments about the print. (Move to 1R and complete part 2)

Assessment
Quality of engagement and completion of the headings.

Left Mode—Examine

Discuss in small groups. Share student ideas with large groups.

Objective
Students discuss and analyze family needs through photos and works of art.

Activity
(Post photos on bulletin board or easel) 1) In triads have student discuss their information on each of the photo. Discuss information from activity as a class. Have the students write a summary statement in which they complete the following statement: I think the topic of our next unit is_____because_____. How is this like your own family? Why?
2) Complete the same activity as above with photos. Beam the following question to the class-Which print fits comfortably with the photos? Why? Students chose the Benton print, as the print that fit. (Unanimously students chose "The Tragedy" as the print that didn't fit stating the print shows a family who is unhappy, not doing anything and have nothing, no resources, needs not being met, etc.)

Assessment
Student participation and interest in the discussion.

Quadrant 2—Concepts

Right Mode—Image

Analogs of selected photos and art work.

Objective

Using analogs have student draw their feelings about selected photos and artwork.

Activity

Give direction on how to draw an analog. Have students draw their feelings/emotions using analogs. Have student draw an analog on each of the following: Roasting Ears, China rice paddy, Native American (from preceding unit), The Tragedy, Native Americans today, Gourmet, American family today, Bush people. Upon completing have students in their triads answer the following questions; "Are any of the analogs similar?" "Can you see connections between and among the photos and the works of art?" Share triad discussions with class as a whole. (Teacher then directs discussion about where people live and how it influences their lives. With teacher direction and from student responses a definition of economics evolves.

Assessment

Student participation and enthusiasm and the quality of drawings.

Left Mode—Define

Lecture: Basic needs of American families. Guest lecture on Japanese family needs.

Objective

Students identify the common basic needs of families in the USA, Japan, France, Germany, and/or Spanish speaking country.

Activity

Using the definition derived from student participation and a brainstorming activity, students come up with the following categories (or similar categories): clothing, housing, entertainment, transportation, food, and tools/utensils. Students are given an advanced organizer to chart each category and room to write information under each category. The teacher lectures and pulls information from students about American families under each category. The teacher gives students the percent of income American families spent on each of these areas.

Have a guest lecturer from Japan (or a country of your choosing). Have students complete a chart on Japan using the same categories listed above. The presentation could include slides which depict the basic needs of families in that country.

Assessment

Attention and participation in activities and checking for understanding using whole group and individual responses.

Quadrant 3—Applications

 ## Left Mode—Try

Charts on needs of American. family then Japanese family.

Objective
Students will complete the charts on the American and Japanese families.

Activity
Have students complete their charts working in their triads and sharing information with each other. Students will complete a compare and contracts Venn Diagram on American and Japanese families using the information gathered from charts on basic needs. Complete a graph showing the percent of family income spent on each of these needs in both countries. Students will make a natural and political map of Japan. Students will take a quiz over the materials on Japan and the USA.

Assessment
Completion of charts, political and natural feature map of Japan, graph and the score on the quiz.

Go to Wheels 2, 3, and 4 before continuing with the Quadrant Three, Right Mode activities, which are the culmination of this unit.

 ## Right Mode—Extend

Project options.

Objective
TLW design a project that reflects his/her choice of a country around the world with the perspective of the family 's basic needs.

Activity
In triads have students choose one country from around the world that has not already been studied by the class. After choosing a country, student should select one of the following projects—1) a collage, 2) a mobile, 3) a travel brochure to their country. In addition to this project, student must include a chart on basic needs of the country, a venn diagram that compares and contrasts the country with one already studied by the class, a graph showing information about the country using data and statistics found during research, and a political and natural feature map of the country of choice.

ENRICHMENT: 1) students could study the impact on families in their local communities whose basic needs are not met including service organizations which serve needy families. 2) Submit a project of your choosing to the teacher for approval. It must include the chart, graph, political and natural feature map and venn diagram.

Assessment
Completion of the project, quality of the project, and student participation.

Quadrant 4—Creations

Left Mode—Refine

Self, group and teacher assessment of completed project.

Objective

The student will critique his/her project and share the results with other members of the triad and receive feedback from the teacher on the project.

Activity

Students will critique their own projects using the self assessment questions that follow: What was the purpose of my project? I chose the country of
_____because_____. The best part of the project was_____. I was surprised to learn that_____. If I had to do it all over again, I would_____. The most interesting thing I learned was_____. Upon completing the self assessment the students will discuss their assessment with members of their triad. The teacher will read the self assessments and provide feedback on the project and the self assessment. Student will also complete their participation pie charts at this time.

Assessment

Completion of the project, quality of the project and participation and cooperation within the triad group.

Right Mode—Integrate

Share the project with class. Celebrate with ethnic food and music.

Objective

Students share the projects with the entire class and plan a follow-up celebration.

Activity

Present the projects to the entire class. The presentation should include the required information for the project and sharing part of their self assessment. The class will celebrate their efforts by having a celebration that includes ethnic food and music from some of the countries studied.

Assessment

Participation, quality of the oral presentation, depth of research done by the students.

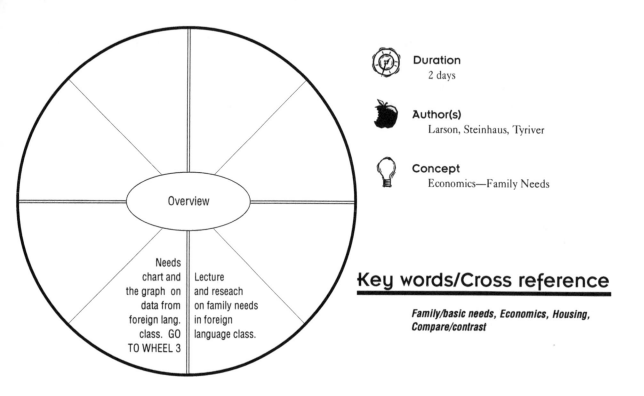

Duration
2 days

Author(s)
Larson, Steinhaus, Tyriver

Concept
Economics—Family Needs

Key words/Cross reference

Family/basic needs, Economics, Housing, Compare/contrast

(Wheel labels: Overview; Needs chart and the graph on data from foreign lang. class. GO TO WHEEL 3; Lecture and reseach on family needs in foreign language class.)

Overview

About the Author
Sid Larson is a Reading/Writing Consultant; Don Tyriver is Principal of Edison Middle School, and Leslie Steinhaus is Assistant Superintendent of Curriculum/Staff Development in the School District of Janesville, Janesville, Wisconsin.

Quadrant 2—Concepts

 ### Left Mode—Define

Lecture and research on family needs in foreign language class.

Objective
TLW complete the social studies chart on family needs using the country of their foreign language class. In addition they will complete a graph that represents data/statistics of their class.

Activity
Complete as a class the social studies chart based on the information given by teacher and found on their own. Basic data/statistics will be collected to use in math and social studies class for their graph.

Assessment
Quality of participation and interest in the information.

Quadrant 3—Applications

 ### Left Mode—Try

Needs chart and the graph on data from foreign lang. class.
GO TO WHEEL 3

Objective
TLW complete the family needs chart and the graph depicting data or statistics from the students foreign language class.

Activity
Students must complete the chart on family needs, the graph and the venn diagram comparing and contrasting their foreign language country with the USA or Japan.

Assessment
Completion of the chart, graph and venn. Quality of the tasks and product.

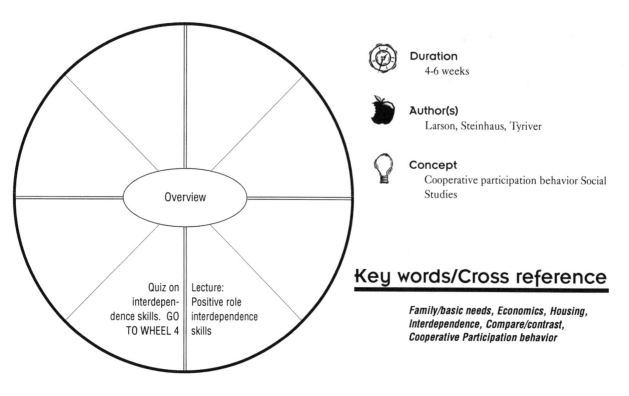

Duration
4-6 weeks

Author(s)
Larson, Steinhaus, Tyriver

Concept
Cooperative participation behavior Social Studies

Key words/Cross reference

Family/basic needs, Economics, Housing, Interdependence, Compare/contrast, Cooperative Participation behavior

Overview

Quiz on interdependence skills. GO TO WHEEL 4

Lecture: Positive role interdependence skills

Overview

Objective
TLW participate in the integrated unit in triad groups using positive interdependence skills.

About the Author
Sid Larson is a Reading/Writing Consultant; Don Tyriver is Principal of Edison Middle School, and Leslie Steinhaus is Assistant Superintendent of Curriculum/Staff Development in the School District of Janesville, Janesville, Wisconsin.

Required Resources
Cooperation in the Classroom. David and Roger Johnson and Edith Holubec, Interaction Book Company, Edina, Minnesota, 1988.

Quadrant 2—Concepts

 ### Left Mode—Define

Lecture: Positive role interdependence skills

Objective
TLW - identify the role skills of positive role interdependence behavior.

Activity
The teacher will review the positive role interdependence skills that specify responsibilities that groups need in order to complete a task. The skills are—Forming, Functioning, Formulating* and Fermenting*. (These are Johnson & Johnson's Cooperative Learning Skills)

*will not be taught until a later unit

Assessment
Accuracy of identification of skills.

Quadrant 3—Applications

 ### Left Mode—Try

Quiz on interdependence skills. GO TO WHEEL 4

Objective
Identify the positive interdependence skills.

Activity
Engage students in the skills of forming and functioning. Rehearse skills with teacher reflecting on feedback provided by the teacher. Practice will continue throughout the unit to move from awkward engagement to routine use.

Assessment
Observation of the skill, feedback, and Quiz.

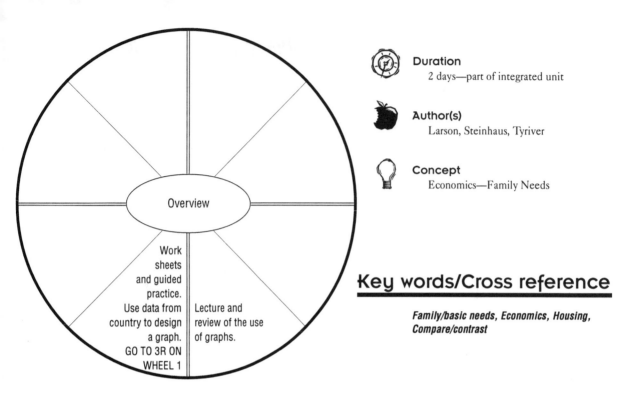

Duration
2 days—part of integrated unit

Author(s)
Larson, Steinhaus, Tyriver

Concept
Economics—Family Needs

Overview

Work
sheets
and guided
practice.
Use data from
country to design
a graph.
GO TO 3R ON
WHEEL 1

Lecture and
review of the use
of graphs.

Key words/Cross reference

*Family/basic needs, Economics, Housing,
Compare/contrast*

Overview

Objective
TLW design a bar, line, pie, or pictorial graph using
research data and /or statistics from the social studies project.

About the Author
Sid Larson is a Reading/Writing Consultant; Don
Tyriver is Principal of Edison Middle School, and
Leslie Steinhaus is Assistant Superintendent of
Curriculum/Staff Development in the School
District of Janesville, Janesville, Wisconsin.

Required Resources
Mathematics Plus, HBO, 1992 or similar math unit
on graphs.

Quadrant 2—Concepts

 ### Left Mode—Define

Lecture and review the use of graphs.

Objective

TLW review the use of graphs to show and interpret data.

Activity

The teacher will review the unit on using data and statistics on pp. 64-65 in HBJ text.

Assessment

Quality of the responses and checking for understanding.

Quadrant 3—Applications

 ### Left Mode—Try

Worksheets and guided practice. Use data from country to design a graph.
GO TO 3R ON WHEEL 1

Objective

TLW use a graph to depict data from Japan or their foreign language class.

Activity

Students will design a bar, pie, line, or pictorial graph from information on Japan or their foreign country. Upon completing their social studies research and the required project, students will use the computer spread sheet to graph their data/statistics. This graph must be shown during the oral presentation.

Assessment

Completion of the graph and accuracy of data portrayed.

Mexican Art 1/4

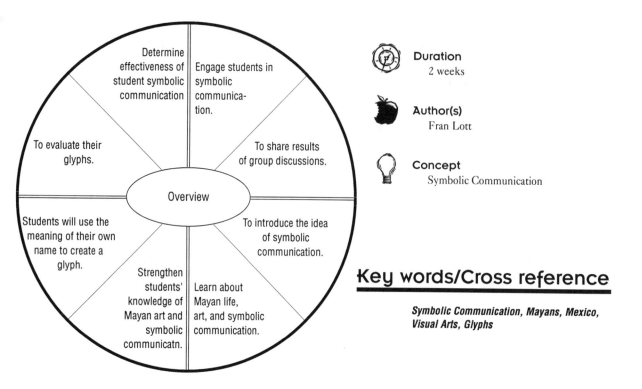

Determine effectiveness of student symbolic communication

Engage students in symbolic communication.

To evaluate their glyphs.

To share results of group discussions.

Overview

Students will use the meaning of their own name to create a glyph.

To introduce the idea of symbolic communication.

Strengthen students' knowledge of Mayan art and symbolic communicatn.

Learn about Mayan life, art, and symbolic communication.

Duration
2 weeks

Author(s)
Fran Lott

Concept
Symbolic Communication

Key words/Cross reference

Symbolic Communication, Mayans, Mexico, Visual Arts, Glyphs

Overview

 Objective

To engage students in an understanding of Symbolic Communication, especially as it relates to ancient Mayan culture.

About the Author

Fran Lott teaches K-12 Art at Polk-Hordville in Polk, NE.

 Required Resources

Copies of symbols, index cards, examples of Mayan art, clay.

 Bibliography

Coe, Michael E. *The Maya*. Thames and Hudson, revised, 1993.
Gardner, Louise. *Art Through the Ages*. Harcourt Brace Jovanovich, revised by Horst de la Croix and Richard G. Tansey, 1976.
Bleeker, Sonia. *The Maya Indians of Central America*. Morrow, 1961.
Stuart, George E. *The Mysterious Maya*. National Geographic Society, 1977.

Quadrant 1—Experience

Right Mode—Connect

Engage students in symbolic communication.

Objective

To interest students in symbolic communication.

Activity

Give small groups of students copies of symbols used today. Examples of symbols - pictographs used on signs such as school crossing, handicapped parking, incline, men and women's restrooms, etc. Groups brainstorm ideas for meanings.

Assessment

Listen to ideas. Which symbols did they know? Are some unfamiliar?

Left Mode—Examine

To share results of group discussions.

Objective

To share results of group discussions.

Activity

Groups share the symbols that they knew and their guesses for those that they didn't know.

Assessment

Student participation in discussion.

Quadrant 2—Concepts

Right Mode—Image

To introduce the idea of symbolic communication.

Objective

To introduce the idea of symbolic communication.

Activity

Each group will create their own set of symbols to be used on signs around the school and/or classroom. Make a list of signs needed: restroom identification, office, classroom identification, library, computer lab, identification of the contents of cupboards and other storage areas. Discuss what makes a successful symbol - the ability for anyone to understand it, will understand, create symbols, draw the symbols on index cards, trade cards with another group and try to identify the symbols. Post some of the new symbols around the classroom or school.

Assessment

The symbols the groups create and the ease with which the other groups identified them.

Left Mode—Define

Learn about Mayan life, art, and symbolic communication.

Objective

To learn about Mayan life, art, and use of symbolic communication. To learn clay relief techniques.

Activity

Lecture on the Mayan civilization. Emphasis on the art and hieroglyphics. *The Maya Indians of Central America,* by Sonia Bleeker and *The Maya,* by Peter Crisp have a description of everyday life and customs at an elementary reading level. Much of Mayan art was done as carved stone reliefs. Some examples to use might be: the Great Dragon from Quirigua, Mexico 6th century A.D.; Stela 7, from Machaquila, Guatemala; the sarcophagus lid, from the tomb of "8 Ahau" at Palenque in Mexico; "Shield Jaguar and Lady Xoc," from Yaxchilan, Mexico A.D. 709. Painted examples could be: wall painting, from Room 1 at Bonampak, Mexico A.D. 790; wall painting, from Room 2 at Bonampak, Mexico. There are four Mayan codices in existence. Codices were written on paper made of cloth made from fibers of the maguey plant or animal skins. They were written or painted with fine brushes on long strips of bark paper that was covered with a layer of chalky paste and when dry, folded like a screen. Some examples of glyphs: glyphs for cycles of the long count (the Mayan calendar) for the earth and heavenly bodies, for directions, for the months, for the colors, for events, for names, for places, for numbers, for the gods. Demonstration of clay relief techniques, roll out a slab of clay about 12" x 8" x 2", draw design onto the slab with a sharp tool, use a loop tool to remove some areas of the design to create the relief.

Assessment
Quiz over Mayan information and steps used to make a clay relief.

Quadrant 3—Applications

 ## Left Mode—Try

Strengthen students' knowledge of Mayan art and symbolic communication.

Objective
To add to students' knowledge of Mayan art and symbolic communication.

Activity
Students will choose several Mayan name glyphs to research. Glyphs are the symbols used in the Mayan written communication. Students will find the meaning of the glyphs they have chosen and write a brief explanation of the meaning and how it is represented symbolically.

Assessment
The students' written explanations.

 ## Right Mode—Extend

Students will use the meaning of their own name to create a glyph.

Objective
Students will create a glyph to symbolically represent their name.

Activity
Use a book of names and meanings to find the meaning of each student's name. Give each student the meaning of their name. Keep these meanings secret. Sketch ideas for a glyph that will represent their name as a symbol. Teacher will work with individual students to choose the best sketch. Students will make their glyph as a clay relief. Allow clay to dry and then fire. After the clay has been fired, finish with glaze, a stain, or acrylic paint. Additional research could be done on the colors used by the Mayas and the meaning of the colors while the clay projects are drying. Green-noblemen, blue-sacrifice, yellow-food, red-blood, black-evil or death.

Assessment
The appearance of the clay projects.

Quadrant 4—Creations

 ## Left Mode—Refine

To evaluate their glyphs.

Objective
Students will evaluate their glyph for appearance and success of symbolic representation.

Activity
Review how to write a critique.

Critique:
Description –
what you see.
Analysis -
how the work is put together - balance, unity, focal point, rhythm and texture.
Interpretation –
what does the work mean and how successfully is the meaning communicated?
Judgment –
do you like the work? why or why not? Which parts were successful? Which parts needed more work?

Assessment
The written critiques.

 ## Right Mode—Integrate

Determine effectiveness of students' symbolic communication.

Objective
To determine how effective the students' symbols are.

Activity
Display the completed glyphs with the student's name. The students will write down what they think the names of their classmates mean by looking at the glyphs. List the guesses under each name on a chart. Each student will explain what their name means and how they represented that meaning symbolically.

Assessment
How easily the glyphs, symbolic meanings were identified.

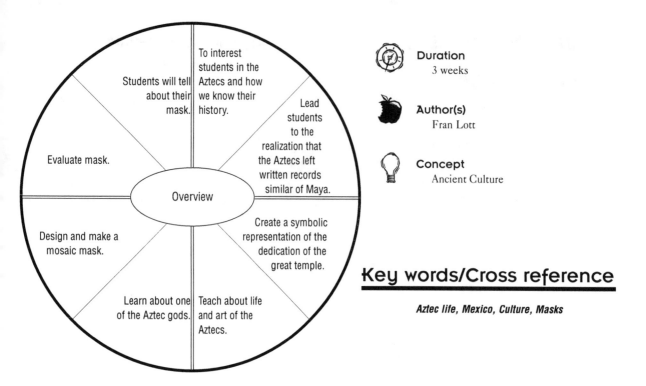

Overview

To interest students in the Aztecs and how we know their history.

Students will tell about their mask.

Evaluate mask.

Design and make a mosaic mask.

Lead students to the realization that the Aztecs left written records similar of Maya.

Create a symbolic representation of the dedication of the great temple.

Learn about one of the Aztec gods.

Teach about life and art of the Aztecs.

Duration
3 weeks

Author(s)
Fran Lott

Concept
Ancient Culture

Key words/Cross reference

Aztec life, Mexico, Culture, Masks

Overview

Objective

Students will explore how we gain understanding of ancient cultures through the medium of the arts of the civilization.

About the Author

Fran Lott teaches K-12 Art at Polk-Hordville in Polk, NE.

Required Resources

Examples of Aztec Art, newspaper, paste, colored paper, research materials.

Bibliography

Gardner, Louise. *Art Through the Ages*. Harcourt Brace Javanovich, revised by Horst de la Croix and Richard G. Tansey,1976.
Pasztory, Esther. *Aztec Art*. H.N. Abrams, 1983.
National Geographic, December 1980. *The Aztecs*. Bart McDowell.

Quadrant 1—Experience

Right Mode—Connect

To interest students in the Aztecs and how we know their history.

Objective
To interest students in the Aztecs and how we know their history.

Activity
Teacher reads the historical account of the dedication of the Aztec's great temple at Tenochtitlan in 1487. An account of this can be found in *The Mighty Aztecs*, by Gene S. Stuart, or an account of the legend of how the Aztec empire came into being could also be used from the same source. Small groups of students discuss how they think historians know these things about the Aztecs.

Assessment
Student interest and group discussion.

Left Mode—Examine

Lead students to the realization that the Aztecs left written records similar of Maya.

Objective
Students will discover that the Aztecs left written records similar to those of the Maya.

Activity
Small groups report their ideas. Compare ideas from small groups to what they know about the Maya's written records. Lead students to the discovery that the Aztecs also used symbolic communication.

Assessment
Students' participation in discussion.

Quadrant 2—Concepts

Right Mode—Image

Create a symbolic representation of the dedication of the great temple.

Objective
Students will create a symbolic representation of the dedication of the temple or the legend.

Activity
Reread story of temple dedication or legend. Generate a list of the most important points of the story. Create an illustration that symbolically represents the facts of the temple dedication or the legend.

Assessment
The illustrations.

Left Mode—Define

Teach about life and art of the Aztecs.

Objective
Students will learn about the life and art of the Aztecs and how to make a paper mache mask decorated with paper mosaic designs.

Activity
Lecture on Aztec life and art. *Everyday Life of the Aztecs*, by Warwick Gray has chapters dedicated to the various aspects of Aztec life. *The Aztec Indians*, by Sonia Bleeker is a good resource at an elementary reading level. *Aztec Art*, by Esther Pasztory has many excellent examples of every type of Aztec art (those of mosaic masks and other objects covered with mosaic designs would be especially useful) as well as drawings of many glyphs. Codex Mendoza with commentaries by Kurt Ross is a reproduction of an Aztec manuscript written shortly after the Spanish conquest using the native symbolic writing. Demonstration of how to make a brown paper mask. Cut brown paper bags into strips about 1" wide. Construct a framework by stretching one piece under the chin of a "model" and gluing it to another piece stretched across the top of their forehead. They should be connected at the sides of the face. Add a strip from one temple to the other molding across the bridge of the nose. Fill in the remaining areas by gluing on very small strips – about 1/4" wide and molding the pieces to the face. After this framework dries, cover it with another layer of brown paper and thin white glue – the glue

can be applied with old brushes both under and over the strips. Demonstration of paper mosaic design – most pieces should be no larger than 2". Art paper that is colored on one side only is better than construction paper. Most Aztec mosaics have little or no spaces between the pieces. Create a design using two or more colors, then glue to mask.

Assessment

Quiz on Aztecs and how to make a brown paper/paper mosaic mask.

Quadrant 3—Applications

 ## Left Mode—Try

Learn about one of the Aztec gods.

Objective

Students will learn about one of the Aztec gods.

Activity

Students will choose one of the Aztec gods to research and write a brief report describing the god and the celebrations to honor him or her – most books on the Aztecs include this type of information. *Everyday Life of the Aztecs*, contains a lengthy chapter on religious life.

Assessment

Reports.

 ## Right Mode—Extend

Design and make a mosaic mask.

Objective

Students will use the information from their report to design a mosaic mask that could be used in a ceremony for that god.

Activity

Draw designs for a mosaic mask. Make a mosaic mask.

Assessment

The mask.

Mexican Art 2/4

Quadrant 4—Creations

 ### Left Mode—Refine

Evaluate mask.

Objective
Students will evaluate their mask and create a short presentation telling about their mask.

Activity
Review form of critique:
Description - what you see.
Analysis – how the work is put together – balance, unity, focal point, rhythm and texture.
Interpretation – what does the work mean and how successfully is the meaning communicated?
Judgment – do you like the work? why or why not? Which parts were successful? Which parts needed more work?
Complete written critique of mask. Create a short presentation about their mask and how they arrived at the design. This could take the form of a display, a speech, a skit, etc.

Assessment
The written critique.

 ### Right Mode—Integrate

Students will tell about their mask.

Objective
Students will share their masks.

Activity
Students will present their masks to the class.

Assessment
The presentations.

Mexican Art 3/4

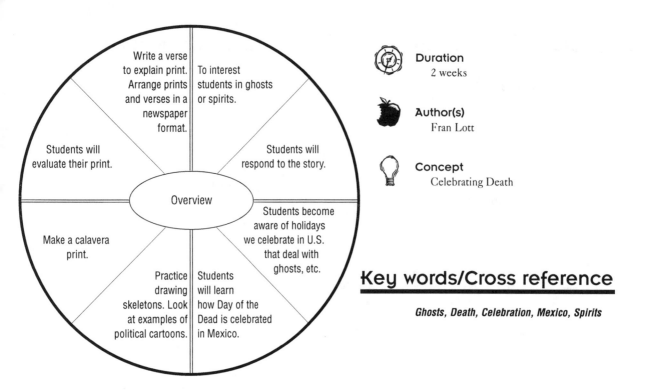

Write a verse to explain print. Arrange prints and verses in a newspaper format.

To interest students in ghosts or spirits.

Students will evaluate their print.

Students will respond to the story.

Overview

Make a calavera print.

Students become aware of holidays we celebrate in U.S. that deal with ghosts, etc.

Practice drawing skeletons. Look at examples of political cartoons.

Students will learn how Day of the Dead is celebrated in Mexico.

Duration
2 weeks

Author(s)
Fran Lott

Concept
Celebrating Death

Key words/Cross reference

Ghosts, Death, Celebration, Mexico, Spirits

Overview

Objective
Students will understand that some cultures had rituals to honor and celebrate those who are dead.

About the Author
Fran Lott teaches K-12 Art at Polk-Hordville in Polk, NE.

Required Resources
Magazines, paper, paste, scissors, a skeleton, or a picture of a skeleton, examples of political cartoons, blocks for printing, carving tools, ink, brayers, examples of calavera art.

Bibliography
Mexico: The Day of the Dead, edited by Chloe Sayer. Shambhala Redstone Editions, 1990.
National Geographic. December, 1980. *The Aztecs*, Bart McDowell.

Quadrant 1—Experience

⊕ Right Mode—Connect

To interest students in ghosts or spirits.

Objective
To interest students in ghosts or spirits.

Activity
Tell a true ghost story, a personal experience if possible, or from a book - *Ghosts and Poltergeists*, by Frank Smyth or *Ghosts*, by Peter Haining, are two possible sources. If time permits, let students tell any personal experiences they have had with ghosts or share a favorite ghost story of their own.

Assessment
Interest of students.

⊕ Left Mode—Examine

Students will respond to the story.

Objective
Students will respond to the story.

Activity
Students will discuss the story in small groups and will report to the large group the number of believers and non-believers.

Assessment
Group discussion.

Quadrant 2—Concepts

⊕ Right Mode—Image

Students become aware of holidays we celebrate in U.S. that deal with ghosts, etc.

Objective
Students will become aware of the holidays we celebrate in the United States that are associated with ghosts, spirits, or the dead and the traditions that go along with those holidays.

Activity
Brainstorm a list of holidays and then eliminate those that do not have anything to do with spirits, ghosts, or the dead. Create a chart of traditions associated with each holiday. Holidays discussed could include Halloween, Veteran's Day, and Memorial Day. Divide into small groups – each group will choose a holiday and make a collage to represent the mood of that holiday. Explain collage to the large group.

Assessment
Discussions and collages.

⊕ Left Mode—Define

Students will learn how Day of the Dead is celebrated in Mexico.

Objective
Students will learn about the Day of the Dead, how it is celebrated in Mexico, the mood of the holiday, and the art that is made for the celebration.

Activity
Lecture on the Day of the Dead. Information and examples can be found in *Portrait of Mexico*, by Diego Rivera, *The Mighty Aztecs*, by Gene S. Stuart, or *Mexico: Day of the Dead*, compiled and edited by Chloe Sayer. Pay particular attention to the calavera prints of Jose Guadalupe Posada Calaveras, or skulls, are witty epitaph written for friends and famous people while they are still alive. They are circulated on printed sheets during the Day of the Dead and are often used for satire and political comment. The people are represented as skeletons. Examples – skeletons fiesta in the Portfirio Diaz Park, calavera of Don Quixote, the Great Pantheon of Lovers, Calaveras employed to serve, who will get what they deserve – all from Mexico: Day of the Dead. Demonstrate steps to make a block print.

Create drawing for the print. Remember the print will be backward. Transfer to the block by coloring the back of the drawing with graphite and then tracing over the lines (I use safety cut blocks which are much easier to cut than linoleum). Use linocut tools to cut out areas that are to remain white – all raised areas will print. Remind students to always cut away from themselves. Ink print with a brayer. Place paper over the block and roll over it with another brayer. Carefully remove paper and allow to dry. Re-ink block each time to make more prints.

Assessment
Quiz on the Day of the Dead and block printing process.

Quadrant 3—Applications

Left Mode—Try

Practice drawing skeletons. Look at examples of political cartoons.

Objective
Students will practice drawing skeletons.

Activity
Students will draw several skeletons from reference photos, drawings, or life.

Assessment
Drawings.

Right Mode—Extend

Make a calavera print.

Objective
Students will make a calavera print.

Activity
Brainstorm ideas for print. Possible subjects could include politicians, celebrities, teachers or other students. Sketch out ideas. Complete final drawing. Make print.

Assessment
Prints.

Quadrant 4—Creations

 ## Left Mode—Refine

Students will evaluate their print.

Objective
Students will evaluate their print.

Activity
Review form of critique:

Description – what you see.

Analysis – how the work is put together - balance, unity, focal point, rhythm and texture.

Interpretation – what does the work mean and how successfully is the meaning communicated?

Judgment – do you like the work? why or why not? Which parts were successful? Which parts needed more work?

Students complete either a written or oral critique.

Assessment
Critique.

Right Mode—Integrate

Write a verse to explain print. Arrange prints and verses in a newspaper format.

Objective
Students will write a verse to go with their print and arrange the prints and verses in a newspaper format to share.

Activity
Read examples of verses that go with calavera prints. The print examples used above have verses printed with them. Discuss the rhythm and/or rhyme used in verse - an English teacher could help with this. Students write a short verse to go with their print. Type verses in small groups. Arrange prints and verses to be photocopied. Copy and distribute prints.

Assessment
How well verses complement the prints and how the final "newspaper" looks.

Mexican Art 4/4

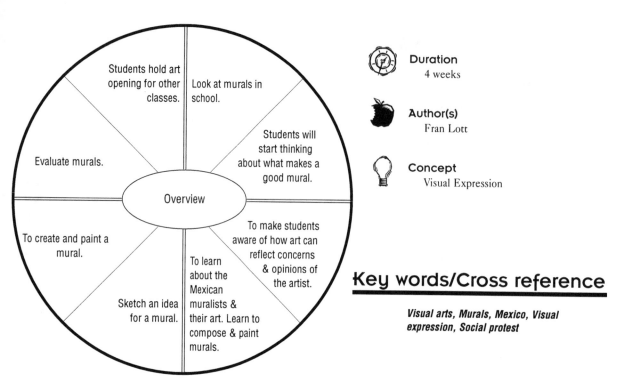

Duration
4 weeks

Author(s)
Fran Lott

Concept
Visual Expression

Overview diagram:
- Students hold art opening for other classes.
- Look at murals in school.
- Students will start thinking about what makes a good mural.
- Evaluate murals.
- Overview
- To make students aware of how art can reflect concerns & opinions of the artist.
- To create and paint a mural.
- To learn about the Mexican muralists & their art. Learn to compose & paint murals.
- Sketch an idea for a mural.

Key words/Cross reference

Visual arts, Murals, Mexico, Visual expression, Social protest

Overview

Objective
Students will explore murals as an art form which has been used as a form of social protest.

About the Author
Fran Lott teaches K-12 Art at Polk-Hordville in Polk, NE.

Required Resources
Murals to critique, paper magazines, paste, paint examples of art from Mexican muralists.

Bibliography
Hartt, Frederick. *Art A History of Painting Sculpture Architecture.* Prentice-Hall, Inc., 1976.
Strickland, Carol. The Annotated Mona Lisa. Andrews and McMeel, 1992.
Rivera, Diego. *Portrait of Mexico.* Covici Friede, 1937.
Scholastic Art. March, 1993. Diego Rivera.

Mexican Art 4/4

Quadrant 1—Experience

 ### Right Mode—Connect

Look at murals in school.

Objective
Students will look at murals already present in their school or community.

Activity
View several murals. Students will choose their favorite mural.

Assessment
Interest of students.

 ### Left Mode—Examine

Students will start thinking about what makes a good mural.

Objective
Students will begin to think about what are the characteristics of a good mural.

Activity
Review process of a critique:
Description – what you see.
Analysis – how the work is put together – balance, unity, focal point, rhythm and texture.
Interpretation – what does the work mean and how successfully is the meaning communicated?
Judgment – do you like the work? why or why not? Which parts were successful? Which parts needed more work?
Divide into groups by favorite mural. Students will complete an oral critique of their favorite mural and report to the large group.

Assessment
Group discussions and reports.

Quadrant 2—Concepts

 ### Right Mode—Image

To make students aware of how art can reflect concerns & opinions of the artist.

Objective
Students will become aware of how art can reflect the concerns and/or heroes of the artist.

Activity
Brainstorm a list of student concerns and/or heroes. Discuss what kinds of visual images would represent these concerns or heroes. Divide students into groups according to the concern or heroes they are interested in portraying. Each group will collect reference pictures that could be used in their portrayal of the concern or heroes. Each group will show their pictures to the large group and tell how each might be used.

Assessment
Reference pictures collected and explanations.

 ### Left Mode—Define

To learn about the Mexican muralists & their art. Learn to compose & paint murals.

Objective
Students will learn about the Mexican muralists, the characteristics of their murals, and how to complete a mural.

Activity
Lecture on the Mexican muralists with emphasis on Diego Rivera. Mural examples:
Agraian Leader Zapata, 1933
Portrait of Morelos
Detroit Industry, 1932-33
Night of the Rich
Exploitation and Insurrection
Social Disorder: Oppression of the Many by the Few
These examples can be found in *Portrait of Mexico* by Diego Rivera and in *Scholastic Art*, March, 1993. Some characteristics of these murals are: simplified figures, figures fill the space, shallow space, space is shown by overlapping figures, figures are heroic and idealized. Steps for painting a mural, draw composition, project on to wall and trace, paint beginning at the top and working to the bottom.

Assessment
Quiz on Mexican muralists.

Quadrant 3—Applications

 ## Left Mode—Try

Sketch an idea for a mural.

Objective

Students will sketch an idea for a mural that reflects a student concern or a hero.

Activity

Using their reference pictures, each group will sketch ideas for a mural. Groups will critique sketches.

Assessment

Sketches and critiques.

 ## Right Mode—Extend

To create and paint a mural.

Objective

To create and paint a mural.

Activity

Groups decide to combine ideas or use one sketch for their mural. Trace drawing on to the wall and paint. Have acrylic or latex colors necessary in small containers with lids (yogurt or similar containers). Put down paper drop cloths that can be thrown away after use. Keep buckets of water to clean brushes nearby. If possible, cover murals after each work session to keep them secret for the opening.

Assessment

Murals.

Quadrant 4—Creations

 ## Left Mode—Refine

Evaluate murals.

Objective

Students will evaluate their mural.

Activity

Groups will critique their murals and turn in a written copy.

Assessment

Critiques.

 ## Right Mode—Integrate

Students hold art opening for other classes.

Objective

Students will share their murals by planning and holding an opening.

Activity

Groups will use their critiques to write a brief monologue about their mural, including how they designed it and why they chose their subject. Create a refreshment committee for the opening. Invite the 7th and 8th grade classes and present the murals using their monologue. Serve refreshments for the opening.

Assessment

The opening.

Globe Skills

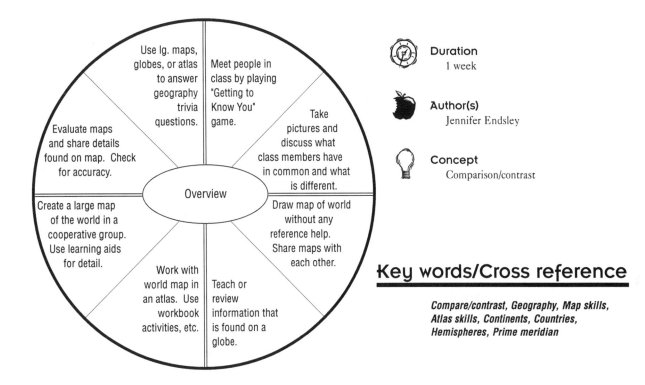

Use lg. maps, globes, or atlas to answer geography trivia questions.

Meet people in class by playing "Getting to Know You" game.

Take pictures and discuss what class members have in common and what is different.

Evaluate maps and share details found on map. Check for accuracy.

Overview

Create a large map of the world in a cooperative group. Use learning aids for detail.

Draw map of world without any reference help. Share maps with each other.

Work with world map in an atlas. Use workbook activities, etc.

Teach or review information that is found on a globe.

Duration
1 week

Author(s)
Jennifer Endsley

Concept
Comparison/contrast

Key words/Cross reference

Compare/contrast, Geography, Map skills, Atlas skills, Continents, Countries, Hemispheres, Prime meridian

Overview

Objective
Review of Globe Skills as a transition to reading an atlas.

About the Author
Jennifer Endsley teaches at Jackson Middle School, Northeast Independent School District, San Antonio, TX.

Required Resources
Camera or camcorder, globe, atlas.

Bibliography
Filmstrips: Available at Jackson Middle School Library
The Globe, Using Maps, Globes, Graphs, Tables and Charts. FR7-912Map. 912.014 UND
Globe Skills, Cultures and Value Systems, Environment Shapes Cultures. 306 His., 306 Env., 306 Dif.

Books:
Hirsh, Abraham, Ph.D, ed. *The World Past and Present.* Dallas: Harcourt Brace Jovanovich.

Workbooks:
Know Your World. McDonald Publishing Co., 1991.

Where in the World. Milliken Publishing Co.
Socials Studies — *Focus on World Regions.* Milliken Publishing Co., 1973.
Maps Unfold The World, Part 2. Milliken Publishing Co., 1982.
Foreman, Dale I., Ph.D and Allen, Sally J. *Using Maps, Charts, and Graphs,* Skillbooster F, Modern Curriculum Press, Inc. 1981.
Map Skills For Today, Book D, A Weekly Reader Practice Book, Columbus, OH: Xerox Education Publications.
Map Skills For Today, Book E, A Weekly Reader Practice Book, Columbus, OH: Xerox Education Publications.

Games:
Junior Trivia
Geography Trivia
Other games with excellent questions that require application, not just recall. Check bookstores, game stores, school supply stores.

Quadrant 1—Experience

Right Mode—Connect

Meet people in class by playing "Getting to Know You" game.

Objective

This unit is used at the beginning of the year. Students will meet people in the class, become more comfortable.

Activity

Play "Getting to Know You" game. Students will interview each other in round robin fashion.

Assessment

Completion of activity.

Left Mode—Examine

Take pictures and discuss what class members have in common and what is different.

Objective

Find differences and similarities among class members.

Activity

Take class picture or video tape. List members of class and what they have in common, former elementary school, favorite subject, pets, TV shows, or other areas. Find differences within class with physical size, family members and so on. Arrange in different poses and take other pictures.

Assessment

Participation and interest in the display of pictures with list of similarities and differences.

Quadrant 2—Concepts

Right Mode—Image

Draw map of world without any reference help. Share maps with each other.

Objective

Imagine a map of the world. (Author's Notes: Students with different backgrounds and interests compose this class. They are both male and female with a variety of all shapes and sizes. They perform and feel differently in the class according to outside factors, such as friends, seating arrangements, interest in subject matter, previous knowledge. This is also true of different continents and countries of the world.)

Activity

Draw a map of the world on a sheet of white paper without any aids. Encourage students to include as many details as possible. Compare pictures of maps. What was important in the pictures? Look at proportion, directions, shapes and sizes of continents, location of continents.

Assessment

Amount of detail in maps can indicate prior knowledge of the world. After a few days, put maps away in individual files to keep until the end of the year.

Left Mode—Define

Teach or review information that is found on a globe.

Objective

Review and use globe skills to read a world map.

Activity

Teach or review hemispheres, special parallels, continents and oceans, directions, prime meridian and equator. Review of locations in the western hemisphere, both bodies of water and land regions. Extend learning basics about eastern hemisphere. What countries are familiar?

Assessment

Globe games that identify continents and individual countries.

Quadrant 3—Applications

Left Mode—Try

Work with world map in an atlas. Use workbook activities, etc.

Objective
Allow students to practice and reinforce knowledge.

Activity
Use of guided practice and workbook activities, note-taking. How are parts of the world alike and different? How are continents alike and different?

Assessment
Correct and grade written work.

Right Mode—Extend

Create a large map of the world in a cooperative group. Use learning aids for detail.

Objective
In cooperative groups, create a large map of the world.

Activity
Draw a world map using globe or atlas. Include continents, bodies of water, seven special parallels, compass finder, countries and major cities, if possible.

Assessment
Display of maps.

Quadrant 4—Creations

Left Mode—Refine

Evaluate maps and share details found on map. Check for accuracy.

Objective
Evaluate maps and share information on other maps.

Activity
Edit and/or include any additional information that could be used to play geography bee or geography jeopardy games.

Assessment
Summarize what was taught. Display maps with pictures of class.

Right Mode—Integrate

Use large maps, globes, or atlas to answer geography trivia questions.

Objective
Use information to answer questions in jeopardy game.

Activity
Play geography bee or geography jeopardy game. May use maps or globes to answer questions.

Assessment
Accumulate points for cooperative groups or individuals. Give winner or winning group certificates of honor at end. Take picture of winning group at end of class. Excellent way to get a class of middle schoolers to interact and review basic facts about geographic locations.

Persecution

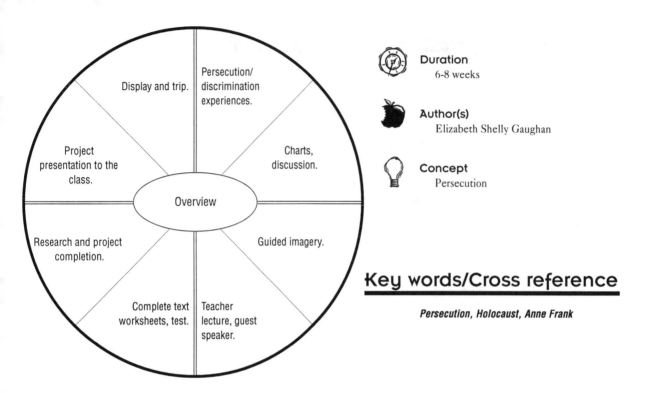

Display and trip.

Persecution/
discrimination
experiences.

Project
presentation to the
class.

Charts,
discussion.

Overview

Research and project
completion.

Guided imagery.

Complete text
worksheets, test.

Teacher
lecture, guest
speaker.

Duration
6-8 weeks

Author(s)
Elizabeth Shelly Gaughan

Concept
Persecution

Key words/Cross reference

Persecution, Holocaust, Anne Frank

Overview

Objective
To provide an understanding of persecution/discrim-
ination throughout history.

About the Author
Elizabeth Shelly Gaughan teaches 8th grade in
Paterson, NJ.

Required Resources
Any library.

Bibliography
The Diary of Anne Frank, by Frances Goodrich and
Albert Hackett, Prentice Hall Literature © 1989,
Englewood Cliff, NJ.

Persecution

Quadrant 1—Experience

Right Mode—Connect

Persecution/discrimination experiences.

Objective

To provide a persecution/discrimination experience.

Activity

Teacher announces to the class: "All people shorter than 5'6" and taller than 5'9" have been proven by scientists to be intellectually inferior. Therefore, if you fall into this category, don't expect anything higher than a D from me." (Clue at least one student in so they can help track reaction.)

Assessment

Student response to teacher announcement.

Left Mode—Examine

Charts, discussion.

Objective

To explore feelings of persecution/discrimination.

Activity

Students write down their individual feelings aroused by the experience from 1R. They gather in small groups to discuss reactions and group creates a chart to share with class. Students should also share personal experience where they felt persecuted.

Assessment

Quality of expression.

Quadrant 2—Concepts

Right Mode—Image

Guided imagery.

Objective

To provide students with a guided imagery of "persecution."

Activity

Students close eyes. Teacher has soft music playing in the background as she takes the students on an imaginary trip where people are cruel to you simply because you are an American, even though you and your family have lived in this imaginary country for as long as anyone can remember. They begin by making fun of you. Then they make you wear an American flag on clothing, etc.

Assessment

When students open eyes, they will illustrate reactions to their treatment. Quality of illustrations will be noted.

Left Mode—Define

Teacher lecture, guest speaker.

Objective

To define persecution/discrimination.

Activity

Teacher lectures on the history of persecution as it relates to the Jewish people during WWII. Invite a Holocaust survivor or family member of a survivor to speak to the class. Students should be encouraged to ask questions.

Assessment

Quality of attention and questions.

Quadrant 3—Applications

Left Mode—Try

Complete text worksheets, test.

Objective
To reinforce the concept of discrimination/persecution.

Activity
Students read *The Diary of Anne Frank* and complete related textbook and workbook activities. Students view the video and complete teacher-made test.

Assessment
Successful completion of related work and test.

Right Mode—Extend

Research and project completion.

Objective
To extend understanding of persecution/discrimination and its origins.

Activity
Working in small groups (2/3), students can complete one activity of their choice.

Assessment
Student effort.
Activity Choices:

1. Find other examples of persecution/discrimination throughout history. Any medium may be used to educate the class on same (i.e. murals, timelines, rap songs—let your imagination fly).

2. Research the War in Bosnia in the 1990's. Create a newspaper page containing several information articles on same. In at least one article, compare/contrast the Bosnian dilemma with that of the Jews in WWII. (*Zlata's Diary* may be helpful, © 1993.)

3. Research concentration camps. Create a news report that will educate the public. Graphics (charts, maps, pictures) should be included. Presentation can be videotaped at home or presented live.

4. Research Adolph Hitler and the Nazis' program to exterminate the Jews and other groups during their reign. Prepare a research report. Include Bibliography and footnotes.

5. The Student As Teacher. Choose any topic from above. Prepare to teach the class for one class period. Student should provide all materials, worksheets, etc.

Quadrant 4—Creations

Left Mode—Refine

Project presentation to the class.

Objective
To refine understanding of persecution/discrimination.

Activity
Small groups share completed projects.

Assessment
Peers judge each other's projects for creativity and completion of goal (content).

Right Mode—Integrate

Display and trip.

Objective
To celebrate freedom from discrimination and persecution.

Activity
Students display projects and unit culminates with a class trip to the Statue of Liberty.

Assessment
Student enjoyment!

Students' Rights

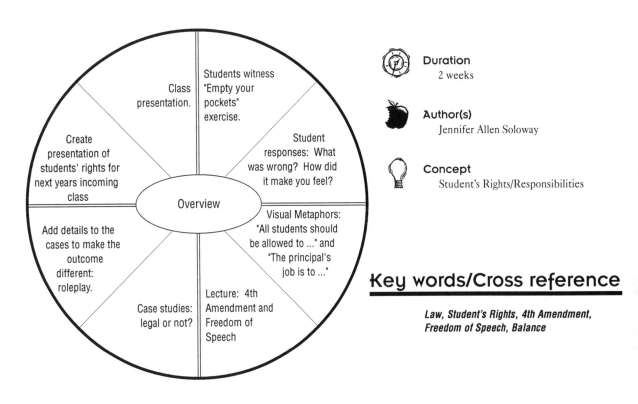

Students witness "Empty your pockets" exercise.

Class presentation.

Student responses: What was wrong? How did it make you feel?

Create presentation of students' rights for next years incoming class

Overview

Visual Metaphors: "All students should be allowed to ..." and "The principal's job is to ..."

Add details to the cases to make the outcome different: roleplay.

Case studies: legal or not?

Lecture: 4th Amendment and Freedom of Speech

Duration
2 weeks

Author(s)
Jennifer Allen Soloway

Concept
Student's Rights/Responsibilities

Key words/Cross reference

Law, Student's Rights, 4th Amendment, Freedom of Speech, Balance

Overview

Objective
To understand the concept of "balance of interests" through the investigation of two court cases and their interpretation of the Bill of Rights.

About the Author
Jennifer Allen Soloway is Principal, Dodd Junior High School, Cheshire, CT. She is Project Leader for the Cheshire 4MAT Implementation Project and a certified 4MAT System trainer.

Bibliography
Camp, William E., Mary Jane Conelly, and Julie K. Underwood, eds., *Current Issues in School Law*. National Organization on Legal Problems of Educators, 1989.
Segel, Naomi, "The Bill of Rights and You," Junior Scholastic, '92, September 22, 1989, pp. 4-7.

Students' Rights

Quadrant 1—Experience

 ### Right Mode—Connect

Students witness "Empty your pockets" exercise.

Objective
To create an experience and the feeling that a student's right to privacy has been violated.

Activity
Per an earlier arrangement, one student enters class late. The teacher demands to know why. Student has no substantive reason, so the teacher forces the tardy student to empty his or her pockets, backpack, handbag, etc. since the student "looks suspicious."

Assessment
Involvement of students; their reaction to the teacher's actions.

 ### Left Mode—Examine

Student responses: What was wrong? How did it make you feel?

Objective
To analyze the experience.

Activity
Teacher leads class discussion focusing on how students felt during the confrontation. What made them uncomfortable about the teacher's demands? Why?

Assessment
The degree to which students are involved in the discussion and the level of their understanding that the issue is an infringement on one student's rights.

Quadrant 2—Concepts

 ### Right Mode—Image

Visual Metaphors: "All students should be allowed to ..." and "The principal's job is to ..."

Objective
To clarify and expand upon the concept of students' rights in contrast to school officials' responsibilities.

Activity
In small groups, students create a visual metaphor of the relationship between a student's rights and a teacher's responsibilities.

Assessment
Students' ability to work within groups; demonstration of a differentiation in and relationship between the two elements.

 ### Left Mode—Define

Lecture: 4th Amendment and Freedom of Speech

Objective
To read case studies of New Jersey v. T.L.O. and Tinker v. Des Moines and to analyze their significance.

Activity
Teacher and students read summaries of the two court cases and discuss the implications of each, focusing on search and seizure, freedom of speech, and balance of interests.

Assessment
Teacher monitoring of student understanding of each case, key terminology, and overall implications.

Quadrant 3—Applications

 ### Left Mode—Try

Case studies: legal or not?

Objective
To develop student understanding further.

Activity
In pairs, students read case studies of school disciplinary actions and decide if each administrative action was legal or illegal. Full class discussion follows.

Assessment
Understanding of fundamental issue in each case and depth of student analysis.

 ### Right Mode—Extend

Add details to the cases to make the outcome different: roleplay.

Objective
To apply what has been learned.

Activity
Students change the details of the case studies (from 3L) to change illegal decisions into legal ones and legal decisions into illegal ones. Students roleplay their revised case studies.

Assessment
Student demonstration of understanding of the need for balance of interests.

Quadrant 4—Creations

 ### Left Mode—Refine

Create presentation of students' rights for next years incoming class

Objective
To extend what has been learned.

Activity
Students create a presentation for next year's incoming seventh grade demonstrating the concept of students rights and the school's responsibility. Presentation may be a play, a brochure, a poster, a rap - anything!

Assessment
Ability to work in a group; individual contributions to group effort.

 ### Right Mode—Integrate

Class presentation.

Objective
To share what has been learned.

Activity
Students share final projects with the rest of the class.

Assessment
Quality of final product; depth of analysis.

Safe Driving Practices

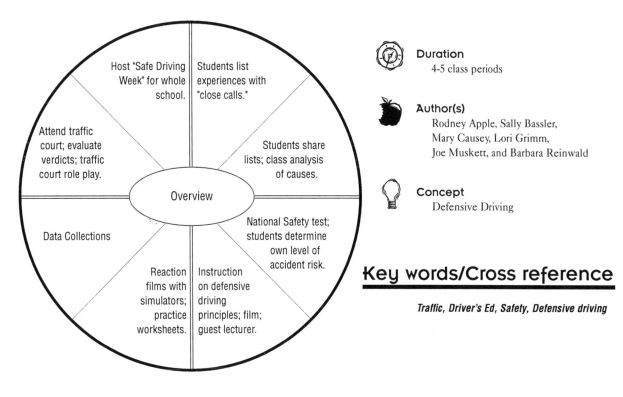

Host "Safe Driving Week" for whole school.

Students list experiences with "close calls."

Attend traffic court; evaluate verdicts; traffic court role play.

Students share lists; class analysis of causes.

Overview

Data Collections

National Safety test; students determine own level of accident risk.

Reaction films with simulators; practice worksheets.

Instruction on defensive driving principles; film; guest lecturer.

Duration
4-5 class periods

Author(s)
Rodney Apple, Sally Bassler,
Mary Causey, Lori Grimm,
Joe Muskett, and Barbara Reinwald

Concept
Defensive Driving

Key words/Cross reference

Traffic, Driver's Ed, Safety, Defensive driving

Overview

 Objective

Students will learn the basic principles and practices of defensive driving and the responsibility of the driver.

 About the Authors

Rodney Apple teaches Driver's Education at Washington-Lee High School, Arlington County Public Schools, Arlington, VA. In his nineteen years experience in education, he has also taught Government, History, Adaptive Physical Education, and Health.

Sally Bassler is an English teacher at Washington-Lee High School. She has twenty years experience as a classroom teacher.

Mary Causey teaches Health and Physical Education at Washington-Lee High School. She has thirty-five years experience as a classroom teacher and coach.

Lori Grimm teaches Health, Physical Education, Adaptive Physical Education, and Driver's

Education at Washington-Lee High School. She has nine years experience as a classroom teacher and coach. Joe Muskett teaches Health, Physical Education, and Driver's Education at Washington-Lee High School. He has thirteen years experience as a classroom teacher and coach.

Barbara Reinwald teaches Health and Physical Education at Washington-Lee High School. In her thirty years experience in education, she has also taught Driver's Education and served as Assistant Athletic Director and coach.

 Required Resources

National Safety Test; guest lecturer(s) and film; worksheets, films and simulators; traffic court video (if necessary); wrecked car for Traffic Safety Week.

Safe Driving Practices

Quadrant 1—Experience

 ### Right Mode—Connect

Students list experiences with "close calls."

Objective

To connect students to their own experiences with hazardous driving.

Activity

Working in small discussion groups, students brainstorm collective lists of the hazardous driving experiences they have had which led to "close calls." They should include experiences both as drivers and passengers.

Assessment

Involvement of students in small group discussion and contributions to the group.

 ### Left Mode—Examine

Students share lists; class analysis of causes.

Objective

To analyze the experiences of the students.

Activity

Groups share their lists with the rest of the class. Teacher conducts class discussion categorizing student experiences as to the causes of the accidents or near accidents (i.e. tail-gating, drinking while driving, attitude problems, etc.).

Assessment

Contributions to large group discussion.

Quadrant 2—Concepts

 ### Right Mode—Image

National Safety test; students determine own level of accident risk.

Objective

To help students connect to the responsibility of the individual for safe driving practice.

Activity

Students will take the National Safety Test to determine their own level of safe driving habits. Using accident reports, they will compare statistics of drivers in northern Virginia with drivers in other areas of the state by age, sex, locale, etc. Students will independently determine their own level of risk for accident based on their safety test score and available statistics. Class members will share their personal evaluation, and the teacher will create a Risk Chart for class members.

Assessment

Involvement in activities and contribution to the class effort.

 ### Left Mode—Define

Instruction on defensive driving principles; film; guest lecturers.

Objective

To learn the principles of defensive driving.

Activity

Teacher will cover basic principles in class using information from textbook, the State Department of Motor Vehicles manual, and a film. Guest lecturers will include a Department of Motor Vehicles officer and a County Traffic officer.

Assessment

Student involvement in presentations, student questions and concerns, teacher verbal checking for understanding.

Quadrant 3—Applications

 ## Left Mode—Try

Reaction films with simulators; practice worksheets.

Objective

To practice what has been learned about defensive driving techniques.

Activity

Using situation and reaction films with simulators, students will practice safe driving techniques in the classroom. In addition, they will complete activities on teacher-prepared worksheets and answer questions in the text.

Assessment

Completion of assigned work and score on text chapter quiz.

 ## Right Mode—Extend

Data Collections.

Objective

To take what has been learned and apply it to the world outside.

Activity

1. Students will stand for one hour at a busy intersection during a heavy traffic time of day and tabulate traffic infractions and "near misses." Each student will create a chart of observations to be shared with the class.
2. Students will tabulate infractions while riding as a passenger in someone else's car. These tabulations will be added in a separate column to the above chart.
3. Students will create posters with slogans which promote safe driving concepts.

Assessment

Quality of student observations and charts; quality of posters.

Quadrant 4—Creations

 ## Left Mode—Refine

Attend traffic court; evaluate verdicts; traffic court role play.

Objective

To analyze the effects of poor driving practice and the reaction of our court system.

Activity

Students will attend traffic court. If not possible, they could view a traffic court video. Their task is to evaluate and respond in writing to the verdicts. Based on this experience, student teams will create and present a traffic court role play.

Assessment

Quality of written analysis and team role play.

 ## Right Mode—Integrate

Host "Safe Driving Week" for whole school.

Objective

To share what has been learned with the rest of the class and the school at large.

Activity

Class will host a Safe Driving Week for the school. A wrecked car will be displayed in the student parking lot to draw attention to the hazards of poor driving. Student posters will be displayed throughout the school. Student role plays will be videotaped and displayed for others to view during the week.

Assessment

Student enjoyment in learning; positive reactions from larger school community.

Essay Revision

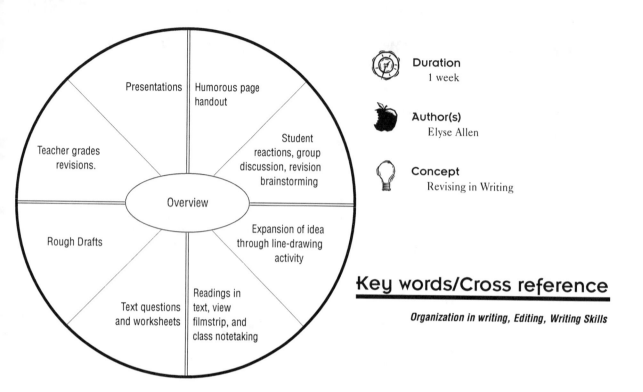

Presentations

Humorous page handout

Teacher grades revisions.

Student reactions, group discussion, revision brainstorming

Overview

Rough Drafts

Expansion of idea through line-drawing activity

Text questions and worksheets

Readings in text, view filmstrip, and class notetaking

Duration
1 week

Author(s)
Elyse Allen

Concept
Revising in Writing

Key words/Cross reference

Organization in writing, Editing, Writing Skills

Overview

Objective

Students will learn the rationale behind revision in writing and appropriate strategies for revising their work.

About the Author

Elyse Allen is a high school English teacher in North East Independent School District, San Antonio, TX. She is a certified 4MAT Trainer as well as a participant in the North East 4MAT Implementation Project led by Fran Everidge and Carol Mendenhall.

Essay Revision

Quadrant 1—Experience

 ### Right Mode—Connect

Humorous page handout.

Objective

To create an experience that shows how some writing can be misconstrued if not written properly.

Activity

Hand out a page of sentences which are funny because they have all kinds of grammatical, usage, and spelling errors. Just let students read and enjoy.

Assessment

Participation of individuals.

 ### Left Mode—Examine

Student reactions, group discussion, revision brainstorming.

Objective

To analyze students' reactions to funny sentences.

Activity

Teacher asks for reactions to sentences. What makes sentences humorous? Ask for suggestions for revision.

Assessment

Participation of individuals; quality of revisions.

Quadrant 2—Concepts

 ### Right Mode—Image

Expansion of idea through line-drawing activity.

Objective

To expand the idea of revision.

Activity

On chalkboard, draw a single line. Now tell each student he/she will come to the board and enhance the creation to make a picture by adding or subtracting something. Rule: No one can erase the entire creation.

Assessment

Quality of student contributions.

 ### Left Mode—Define

Readings in text, view filmstrip, and class note-taking.

Objective

To teach concept of revision.

Activity

Students read text section dealing with revision. View a filmstrip on revision. (Many adequate ones exist.) Take notes.

Assessment

Teacher questioning for student understanding and quality of notes.

Quadrant 3—Applications

Left Mode—Try

Text questions and worksheets.

Objective

To further develop student understanding of revision.

Activity

Students answer questions in text on revision and complete worksheets.

Assessment

Quality of student answers.

Right Mode—Extend

Rough Drafts.

Objective

To apply what has been learned.

Activity

Choice: 1) Have students write the rough draft of an essay, skipping lines to facilitate revision. Then have students exchange papers and revise them. 2) Let students revise an essay you give them.

Assessment

Quality of revision.

Quadrant 4—Creations

Left Mode—Refine

Teacher grades revisions.

Objective

To evaluate students' understanding of revision.

Activity

Grade or check the effectiveness of students' revision. You may or may not have them write a final draft because you are teaching revision.

Assessment

Quality of students' revision.

Right Mode—Integrate

Presentations.

Objective

To share what has been learned.

Activity

Ask certain students to go to the board or use an overhead projector to explain how and why they made revisions.

Assessment

Students' participation both as presenters and listeners.

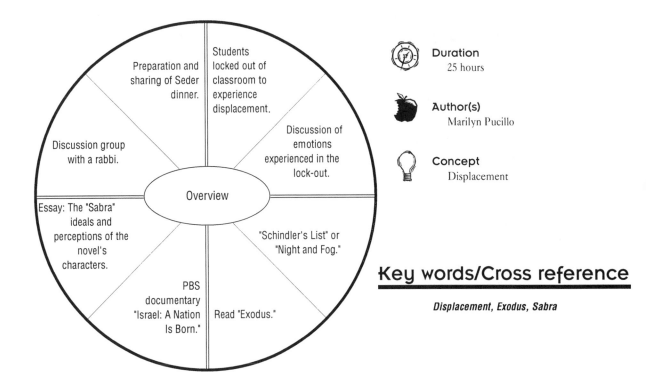

Overview

- Preparation and sharing of Seder dinner.
- Students locked out of classroom to experience displacement.
- Discussion of emotions experienced in the lock-out.
- Discussion group with a rabbi.
- "Schindler's List" or "Night and Fog."
- Essay: The "Sabra" ideals and perceptions of the novel's characters.
- PBS documentary "Israel: A Nation Is Born."
- Read "Exodus."

Duration
25 hours

Author(s)
Marilyn Pucillo

Concept
Displacement

Key words/Cross reference

Displacement, Exodus, Sabra

Overview

Objective
The unit is designed to help students acquire an understanding of the events that made the establishment of Israel so important and how these events created the "Sabra" mentality.

About the Author
Marilyn Pucillo has taught English and Theatre for ten years at High Point Regional High School in Wantage, NJ.

Required Resources
Exodus, by Leon Uris.
Films - *Schindler's List* and/or *Night and Fog.*
PBS documentary - *Israel: A Nation Is Born.*
Input from a rabbi.
Student release time for Seder activities.

Quadrant 1—Experience

 ### Right Mode—Connect

Students locked out of classroom to experience displacement.

Objective

To help students understand the feeling of being completely displaced, of having nowhere to go and of being totally unaccepted.

Activity

With no prior notification, students find the classroom door locked when they arrive and there is a notice posted that they are no longer welcome and they must find somewhere else to go. Faculty and administration are aware of the activity and will not allow students into their classrooms or offices. Restrooms are off limits.

Assessment

Observation of students' actions during the exercise.

 ### Left Mode—Examine

Discussion of emotions experienced in the lock-out.

Objective

To explore and identify the emotions created by being "locked out."

Activity

Open discussion with students.

Assessment

Through the intensity of student's reaction and their willingness to discuss it, a determination can be made of how effective the lock-out was.

Quadrant 2—Concepts

 ### Right Mode—Image

View Schindler's List *or* Night and Fog.

Objective

To help students gain familiarity with the events that made the establishment of a Jewish homeland so important.

Activity

Viewing the film *Schindler's List*, or if that is not available, *Night and Fog*.

Assessment

A student reaction paper to the film — graded for depth of understanding, specificity of emotion.

 ### Left Mode—Define

Read Exodus.

Objective

To gain an understanding of how the State of Israel was established and how the first settlers created the "Sabra" mentality as an outgrowth of God's promise to Abraham.

Activity

Reading the novel *Exodus* with appropriate class discussions of the book and the Biblical history of Palestine.

Assessment

Quizzes on assigned readings, study questions, discussion participation.

Quadrant 3—Applications

Left Mode—Try

PBS documentary Israel: A Nation Is Born.

Objective
To solidify students' concepts and knowledge of the political process involved in establishing the State of Israel.

Activity
Viewing the PBS documentary "Israel: A Nation is Born" (only the hour about the UN vote to establish a Jewish homeland).

Assessment
Student participation in discussion of similarities between the novel and the documentary.

Right Mode—Extend

Essay: The "Sabra" ideals and perceptions of the novel's characters.

Objective
To use their newly acquired knowledge to discuss what the "Sabra" mentality is and how it was formed.

Activity
An essay that discusses the perceptions, behavior and ideas of Ari and Jordana and the other "Sabras" in the novel.

Assessment
Grade essays, evaluating for specificity in defining the characters' ideals and in determining where those ideals were formed and why.

Quadrant 4—Creations

Left Mode—Refine

Discussion group with a rabbi.

Objective
To familiarize students with the Passover ritual, the closing event in the novel.

Activity
Discussion with a local Reformed rabbi.

Assessment
Observing student participation in the discussion.

Right Mode—Integrate

Preparation and sharing of Seder dinner.

Objective
To create the Passover ritual.

Activity
With the rabbi's help, students to prepare Seder dinner and go through the ceremony of eating the meal with the appropriate ritual.

Assessment
Observing the solemnity with which Christian students participated in the Judaic ritual.

Isolationism (Poetry)

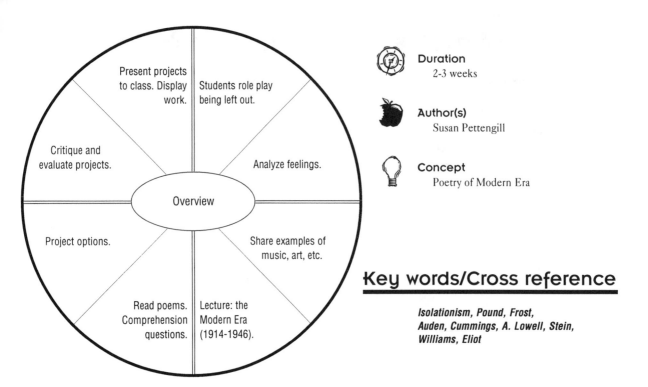

Present projects to class. Display work.

Students role play being left out.

Critique and evaluate projects.

Analyze feelings.

Overview

Project options.

Share examples of music, art, etc.

Read poems. Comprehension questions.

Lecture: the Modern Era (1914-1946).

Duration
2-3 weeks

Author(s)
Susan Pettengill

Concept
Poetry of Modern Era

Key words/Cross reference

Isolationism, Pound, Frost, Auden, Cummings, A. Lowell, Stein, Williams, Eliot

Overview

Objective
Students will gain an understanding of how the poetry of the Modern Era was shaped by historical events.

About the Author
Susan S. Pettengill teaches English at Freehold High School in Freehold, NJ. She has ten years of teaching experience.

Required Resources
Prentice-Hall Literature: *The American Experience.*

Isolationism (Poetry)

Quadrant 1—Experience

 ### Right Mode—Connect

Students role play being left out.

Objective
To create the feeling of being left out by a group or a friend.

Activity
Teacher has students role play situations where someone is excluded from a group or ignored by a friend.

Assessment
Involvement, participation, and reaction of students.

 ### Left Mode—Examine

Analyze feelings.

Objective
To analyze the experience.

Activity
Discussion should focus on how students felt about being part of a group and being left out. How did they feel? Did they react? If so, how and why?

Assessment
Students' comments in discussion.

Quadrant 2—Concepts

 ### Right Mode—Image

Share examples of music, art, etc.

Objective
To have the students identify examples of isolationism and conflict in other media.

Activity
Students bring in video clips, poems, pictures, or songs about conflict or isolationism.

Assessment
Students' examples and enjoyment in sharing and explaining their selections.

Left Mode—Define

Lecture: the Modern Era (1914-1946).

Objective
To explain the historical background of the Modern Era (1914-1946).

Activity
Teacher lectures about the Modern Era: historical perspective; expatriates; Gertrude Stein and Alice B. Toklas; Paris; themes in literature and the arts; samples of representative artists and musicians shared with class.

Assessment
Teacher observation of student understanding. Verbal checking for understanding during instruction.

Isolationism (Poetry)

Quadrant 3—Applications

Left Mode—Try

Read poems. Comprehension questions.

Objective
To give further practice and reinforcement in identifying the theme of isolationism in poetry of the Modern Era.

Activity
Read poems. Record symbols used to express theme in different poems. Complete reading comprehension questions. (Refer to selected poems in literature text.)

Assessment
Quality and completeness of assigned work.

Right Mode—Extend

Project options.

Objective
To allow for personal creative expression.

Activity
Students write their own poems about isolationism or design a piece of music or artwork that illustrates the theme.

Assessment
Quality and participation of students in their own work.

Quadrant 4—Creations

Left Mode—Refine

Critique and evaluate projects.

Objective
To assess and critique the projects.

Activity
Read poems in writing response groups. Get feedback on writing from the group. Write final draft for publication. Show posters/collages/sculpture/music to group for feedback. Make any changes.

Assessment
Student contribution to the group and response to others' criticism.

Right Mode—Integrate

Present projects to class. Display work.

Objective
To complete and share projects with others.

Activity
Students read poems to class or share via class publication (typed on computer, copied & bound). Artwork shared with class. Music performed. Work displayed in classroom – bulletin boards and on shelves.

Assessment
Quality of completed project and enjoyment of learning.

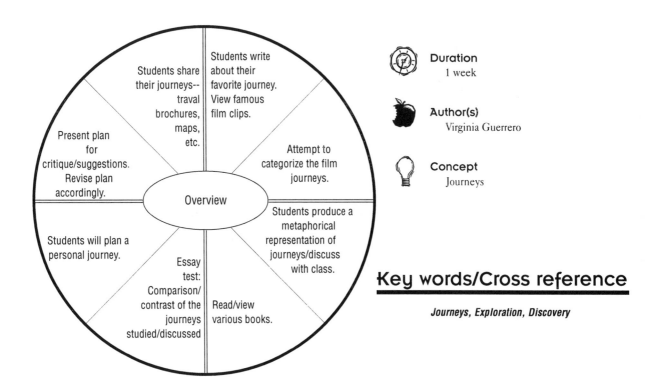

Overview

Students write about their favorite journey. View famous film clips.

Students share their journeys-- traval brochures, maps, etc.

Present plan for critique/suggestions. Revise plan accordingly.

Attempt to categorize the film journeys.

Students will plan a personal journey.

Students produce a metaphorical representation of journeys/discuss with class.

Essay test: Comparison/ contrast of the journeys studied/discussed

Read/view various books.

Duration
1 week

Author(s)
Virginia Guerrero

Concept
Journeys

Key words/Cross reference

Journeys, Exploration, Discovery

Overview

Objective

This lesson provides an introduction to a 7-plan set comprising a full semester or year long study of British Literature for 12th grade students. The lessons included in the set are: (1) This lesson, which introduces the concept of Journeys, (2) The lesson based on Beowulf called "Heroic Journey" and writ-ten by Mary Brent Marks, (3) *The Canterbury Tales* les-son called "Canter Journey," (4) A lesson from the 1992 LessonBank collection called "Maturation from Hamlet," (5) A lesson on Romantic Poets called "Nature Journey," (6) A lesson based on *Pygmalion* called "Change Journey,"(7) And a lesson based on *The Lord of the Flies* called "Inner Journey."

About the Author

Virginia (Ginny) Guerrero is English Department Chair at Churchill High School, in San Antonio, TX. Her accomplishments include a Secondary Teacher of the Year award for the district. She has been teaching for 24 years.

Bibliography

Beowulf; Chaucer, Geoffrey, *Excerpts from The Canterbury Tales*.
Coleridge, Samuel, *Rime of the Ancient Mariner*.
Conrad, Joseph, *The Lagoon*.
Shaw, George Bernard, *Pygmalion*.
All the above are available in The English Tradition: Prentice-Hall Literature. Englewood Cliffs, NJ: Prentice Hall Publishing, 1989.
Frost, Robert. *The Road Not Taken*. From The New Pocket Anthology of American Verse. New York: Washington Square Press, 1966.
Golding, William. *Lord of the Flies*. New York: Perigree Books, 1954.
Heat-Moon, William Least. *Blue Highways*. Boston: Houghton Mifflin Books, 1982.
Picasso, Pablo. *Girl Before the Mirror*. In Art in Action. Dallas; Coronado Publishers, 1987.
Shakespeare, William. *The Tragedy of Hamlet*, Prince of Denmark. New York: Washington Square Press, 1992.
Vivaldi, A. *The Four Seasons*, Musici di San Marcos, Point Productions, 1990.

Quadrant 1—Experience

Right Mode—Connect

Students write about their favorite journey. View famous film clips.

Objective

To initiate thinking about their personal journeys and those of their society.

Activity

1) While listening to "Star Wars" music, students will write about their favorite journey. 2) Students will view film clips of famous film journeys.

Assessment

Student participation.

Left Mode—Examine

Attempt to categorize the film journeys.

Objective

To see various kinds of journeys we all know about.

Activity

Small groups: Try to categorize journeys we've written about and discussed.

Assessment

Group success at categorizing/participation in process.

Quadrant 2—Concepts

Right Mode—Image

Students produce a metaphorical representation of journeys. Discuss with class.

Objective

To understand journey concept in a metaphorical way.

Activity

Students draw metaphoric representations of journey or take a walking journey through the school.

Assessment

Quality of drawings (richness of detail or metaphors)—participation.

Left Mode—Define

Read/view various books.

Objective

To understand the journey concept according to purpose, preparation, value, destination, types, etc.

Activity

Read/view: 1) Erickson's *Carousel of Life.* 2) Excerpts from *Blue Highways.* 3) Frost's *The Road Not Taken.* 4) *Rime of Ancient Mariner.* Invite travel agent to talk about literal journey.

Assessment

Attentiveness, participation.

Quadrant 3—Applications

 ### Left Mode—Try

Essay test: Compare/contrast the journeys studied/discussed.

Objective
To evaluate/synthesize concept of journey.

Activity
Essay test: compare/contrast the journeys we've studied/discussed.

Assessment
Test performance.

 ### Right Mode—Extend

Students will plan a personal journey.

Objective
To internalize concept of journey.

Activity
Plan and conduct personal journey of selected type: discover San Antonio, discover family history, research some intriguing idea, design quest game, find a college, etc.

Assessment
Quality of plan.

Quadrant 4—Creations

 ### Left Mode—Refine

Present plan for critique/suggestions. Revise plan accordingly.

Objective
To apply concept of journey.

Activity
Present plan to small group for critique/suggestions. Revise plans, based on group suggestions.

Assessment
Quality of plan revision/product.

 ### Right Mode—Integrate

Students share their journeys—travel brochures, maps, etc.

Objective
To share learning.

Activity
Travel fair: students share travel brochures, maps, written summaries, photo essays, quest games, etc.

Assessment
Quality of presentation.

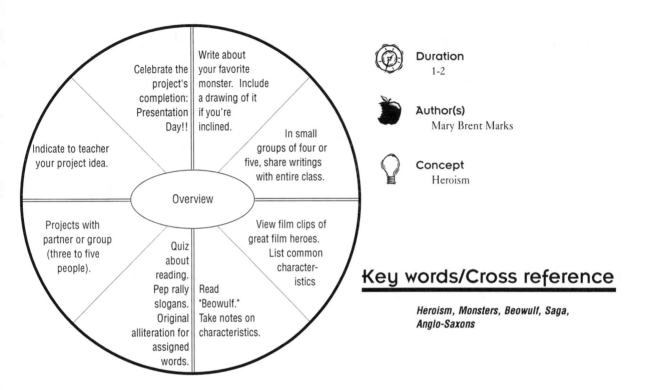

Celebrate the project's completion: Presentation Day!!

Write about your favorite monster. Include a drawing of it if you're inclined.

Indicate to teacher your project idea.

In small groups of four or five, share writings with entire class.

Overview

Projects with partner or group (three to five people).

Quiz about reading. Pep rally slogans. Original alliteration for assigned words.

Read "Beowulf." Take notes on characteristics.

View film clips of great film heroes. List common characteristics

 Duration
1-2

 Author(s)
Mary Brent Marks

Concept
Heroism

Key words/Cross reference

Heroism, Monsters, Beowulf, Saga, Anglo-Saxons

Overview

 Objective
See the Overview notes in the lesson entitled "Journey s (1 of 7)."

 About the Author
An English teacher for 23 years, Mary Brent Marks has spent the last 16 years at Madison High School in San Antonio, TX. Currently, she teaches a semester course in British Literature and a semester course in Media which she designed. 4MAT has come easily to Mary Brent. Her career highs include the publishing of a Foxfire-type magazine about Southern Maryland and student film-making of documentaries, and public service announcements and literary parodies.

Required Resources
Video clips of film, television, cartoon heroes (about 15 minutes worth), and teaching video on Beowulf, filmstrip *Heroes and Heroines in Literature Part One* - Guidance Associates, Celtic (or any!) harp music.

Bibliography
Beowulf. *The English Tradition*. Prentice Hall: Englewood Cliffs, NJ, 1989.
For complete bibliography, see lesson entitled "Journeys (1 of 7)."

Quadrant 1—Experience

Right Mode—Connect

Write about your favorite monster. Include a drawing of it if you're inclined.

Objective
To recognize and write about the identity and characteristics of a favorite monster with heroic characteristics.

Activity
Write about your favorite monster hero in a couple of paragraphs.

Assessment
Credit as class activity—students write on spot.

Left Mode—Examine

In small groups of four or five, share writings with entire class.

Objective
To share personal writing about favorite monster hero.

Activity
In groups of four or five, share writings. Choose one or two to be shared with entire class.

Assessment
Teacher collects writings—gives credit as class activity.

Quadrant 2—Concepts

Right Mode—Image

View film clips of great film heroes. List common characteristics.

Objective
To recognize common characteristics of heroes; to realize for every great monster there is a hero who conquers.

Activity
View 15-min. film clips of great heroes; discuss/list common characteristics these heroes share. Explain they will now study a hero from an earlier age who uses his own unique characteristics to save the day.

Assessment
Class participation.

Left Mode—Define

Read Beowulf. Take notes on characteristics.

Objective
To become knowledgeable about Beowulf, characteristics of Anglo-Saxons, and epic heroes-(Beowulf's characteristics).

Activity
Read *Beowulf*, answer questions and discuss, notetaking on characteristics of Anglo-Saxons and their lives.

Assessment
Question/answer in class, written answers to questions, notetaking evaluated for class credit.

Quadrant 3—Applications

Left Mode—Try

Quiz about reading. Pep rally slogans. Original alliteration for assigned words.

Objective

To become knowledgeable about entire Beowulf saga; to demonstrate knowledge via quiz/test; to have fun with poetic devices found in Beowulf; to become familiar with etymologies.

Activity

1) Beowulf quiz over assigned reading. 2) Make up pep rally slogans using accented syllables and caesura found in Beowulf; make up Kennings and turn in etymologies and funsheet on Beowulf beat; demonstrate knowledge by passing quiz and test.

Assessment

Student products and performance on written assignments.

Right Mode—Extend

Projects with partner or group (three to five people).

Objective

To create a new superhero and describe his/her characteristics based on unit learning; students will choose from five projects and work with partner or small group.

Activity

Meet in groups: 1) Create a cartoon superhero in comic strip form. 2) Create a new superhero and videotape his exploits.

Assessment

Each student will choose a project.

Quadrant 4—Creations

Left Mode—Refine

Indicate to teacher your project idea.

Objective

To demonstrate student progress on chosen project; student will refine project.

Activity

Check points: 1) Choice of project has been made. 2) Progress report written to teacher detailing what has been made.

Assessment

Each student must complete check points to receive full credit for project.

Right Mode—Integrate

Celebrate the project's completion: Presentation Day!!

Objective

To present superhero projects.

Activity

Each student will present his project; each student will praise project/make suggestion for refining.

Assessment

Teacher will assign a grade for project based on product presented.

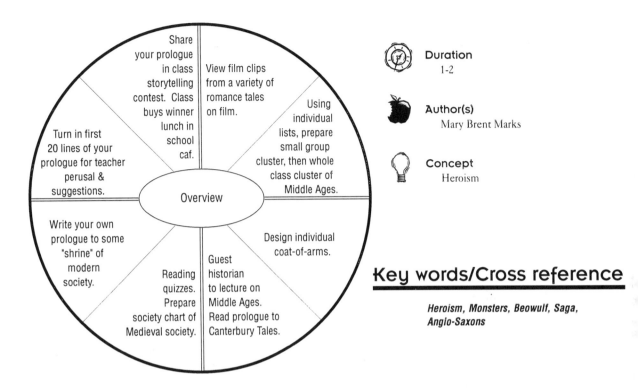

Duration
1-2

Author(s)
Mary Brent Marks

Concept
Heroism

The wheel diagram contains, clockwise from top:

- Share your prologue in class storytelling contest. Class buys winner lunch in school caf.
- View film clips from a variety of romance tales on film.
- Using individual lists, prepare small group cluster, then whole class cluster of Middle Ages.
- Design individual coat-of-arms.
- Guest historian to lecture on Middle Ages. Read prologue to Canterbury Tales.
- Reading quizzes. Prepare society chart of Medieval society.
- Write your own prologue to some "shrine" of modern society.
- Turn in first 20 lines of your prologue for teacher perusal & suggestions.

Center: Overview

Key words/Cross reference

Heroism, Monsters, Beowulf, Saga, Anglo-Saxons

Overview

Objective
See the Overview notes in the lesson entitled "Journeys (1 of 7)."

About the Author
Virginia (Ginny) Guerrero is English Department Chair at Churchill High School, in San Antonio, TX. Her accomplishments include Secondary Teacher of the Year award for the district. She has been teaching for 24 years.

Bibliography
See bibliography in lesson entitled "Journeys (1 of 7)."

Quadrant 1—Experience

 ## Right Mode—Connect

View film clips from a variety of romance tales on film.

Objective
To initiate student interest in Middle Ages.

Activity
1) Show filmclips from a variety of Medieval romance tales on film—Robin Hood, Ivanhoe, Lion in Winter, etc. 2) Ask students to list everything they associate with the Middle Ages.

Assessment
Level of participation/involvement.

 ## Left Mode—Examine

Using individual lists, prepare small group cluster, then whole class cluster of Middle Ages.

Objective
To ascertain preconceptions of Middle Ages; to compare preconceptions.

Activity
1) Using individual lists, prepare small group clusters of the Middle Ages. 2) Prepare a class cluster of the Middle Ages.

Assessment
Individual participation/involvement, complexity of clusters.

Quadrant 2—Concepts

 ## Right Mode—Image

Design individual coat-of-arms.

Objective
To connect own characteristics to the customs of the Middle Ages.

Activity
1) Discuss example coats-of-arms on Medieval shields. 2) With colored pens, white paper, and other ornamented items, students design own shield insignia and write explanation.

Assessment
Individual involvement/originality and complexity of shield.

 ## Left Mode—Define

Guest historian to lecture on Middle Ages. Read prologue to Canterbury Tales.

Objective
To learn about Medieval culture, and Chaucer's satire of that culture.

Activity
1) Guest lecturer—historian to lecture on life in the Middle Ages. 2) Read prologue and selected tales from The Canterbury Tales. 3) Review literary methods of characterization. 4) Discuss characteristics of satire.

Assessment
Attentiveness, notetaking.

Quadrant 3—Applications

 ### Left Mode—Try

Reading quizzes. Prepare society chart of Medieval society.

Objective
To demonstrate acquired knowledge about Middle Ages, Canterbury Tales, and satire.

Activity
1) Reading quizzes after each tale. 2) Character charts reflecting Medieval class structure. 3) Collaborative essays—character sketches of travelers.

Assessment
1) Quiz scores. 2) Accuracy of character charts. 3) Insight demonstrated by character sketches.

 ### Right Mode—Extend

Write your own prologue to some "shrine" of modern society.

Objective
To apply Chaucer's method and style to own culture.

Activity
Pairs of students write prologue for mock pilgrimage to a "shrine" of our society. Travelers should include family, friends, famous persons, etc. (at least 50 lines).

Assessment
1) Individual involvement. 2) Closeness to Chaucer style. 3) Insight shown into modern society, people.

Quadrant 4—Creations

 ### Left Mode—Refine

Turn in first 20 lines of your prologue for teacher perusal & suggestions.

Objective
To check progress.

Activity
1) Turn in first 20 lines of prologue for teacher perusal. When the lines are returned, appropriate revision/editing should occur. 2) Complete prologue.

Assessment
1) Individual involvement. 2) Incorporation of noted editing, revisions.

 ### Right Mode—Integrate

Share your prologue in class story-telling contest. Class buys winner lunch in school cafe.

Objective
To allow publication/celebration of new understanding/accomplishment.

Activity
Share prologues with class in a story-telling contest. Winner?—free lunch in cafeteria.

Assessment
1) Effectiveness of oral communication. 2) Cleverness and satiric quality.

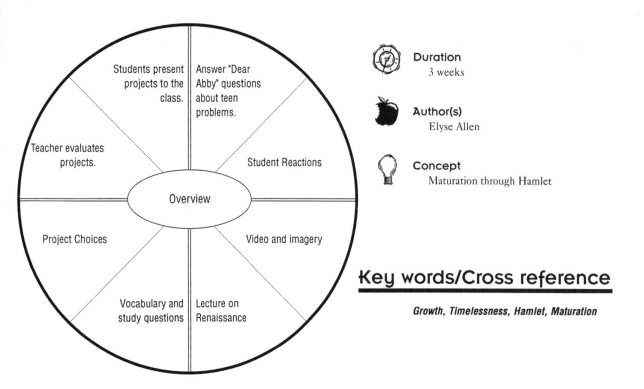

Duration
3 weeks

Author(s)
Elyse Allen

Concept
Maturation through Hamlet

Key words/Cross reference

Growth, Timelessness, Hamlet, Maturation

Overview

Objective
To use the concept of "maturation" as a vehicle for understanding the character of Hamlet.

About the Author
Elyse Allen is a high school English teacher in North East Independent School District, San Antonio, TX. She is a certified 4MAT Trainer as well a participant in the North East 4MAT Implementation Project led by Fran Everidge and Carol Mendenhall.

Optional Resources
Psychologist guest lecturer.

Quadrant 1—Experience

Right Mode—Connect

Answer "Dear Abby" questions about teen problems.

Objective
To connect students to the idea of life leading us to "maturation."

Activity
Hand out "Dear Abby" questions and have students write a response on 3x5 cards. Questions: 1) What would you do if your girlfriend/boyfriend returned all your gifts with no explanation? 2) What would you do if your two best friends betrayed you by supporting your parents (in some way) rather than you? 3) How would you respond to your mother if she married your uncle less than a month after your father's death? 4) How would you react to a friend telling you s/he had seen a ghost of your dead father?

Assessment
Quality of student participation.

Left Mode—Examine

Student Reactions

Objective
To formulate a conception of maturity.

Activity
On board, teacher groups students' reactions under 1-4 (for questions). At bottom of board, draw a horizontal line with 10 vertical lines equally spaced on it to represent a maturity chart. Let students rate answers ("1=immature" to "10=very mature").

Assessment
Student participation and effort; contribution to group.

Quadrant 2—Concepts

Right Mode—Image

Video and imagery.

Objective
To link maturation of Hamlet to students' lives.

Activity
Use guided imagery to stimulate students' awareness of their past so they can create their own timeline.

Assessment
Quality of sharing.

Left Mode—Define

Lecture on Renaissance.

Objective
To read and analyze the play with a focus on maturation.

Activity
Lecture on Renaissance in England, the life of Shakespeare, the Globe theater, etc. If possible, arrange a psychologist guest lecturer to speak about maturation. Read Hamlet.

Assessment
Student notetaking; teacher checking for understanding through questioning.

Quadrant 3—Applications

 ## Left Mode—Try

Vocabulary and study questions.

Objective
To practice concepts learned in 2L.

Activity
Vocabulary, study questions, quizzes, tests, compositions, culminating with a timeline of Hamlet's maturation (act by act).

Assessment
Quality of written work.

 ## Right Mode—Extend

Project Choices.

Objective
To further focus on maturation.

Activity
Project choices to show Hamlet's maturation process: 1) Hamlet newspapers (groups). 2) Write a parody or poem about Hamlet. 3) Design a graveyard with epitaphs on the tombs for all major characters. 4) Interview major characters in any style (i.e., Oprah, Arsenio, Carson, etc.).

Assessment
Intensity of student effort.

Quadrant 4—Creations

 ## Left Mode—Refine

Teacher evaluates projects.

Objective
To analyze for originality.

Activity
Student/teacher evaluation of projects.

Assessment
Quality of student work.

 ## Right Mode—Integrate

Students present projects to the class.

Objective
To extend the joy of the projects.

Activity
Students present projects to the class.

Assessment
Quality of final products and celebration of work.

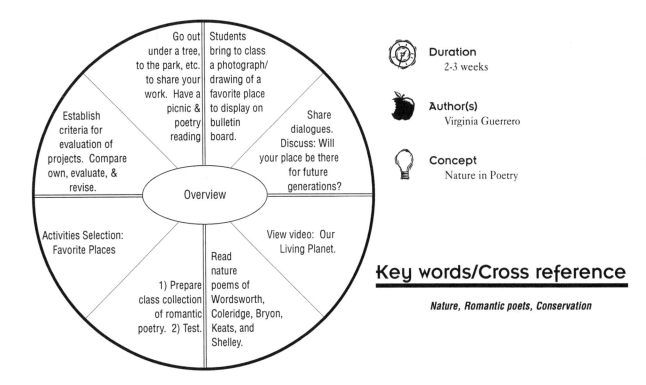

Duration
2-3 weeks

Author(s)
Virginia Guerrero

Concept
Nature in Poetry

Key words/Cross reference

Nature, Romantic poets, Conservation

Circle content:

Overview (center)

- Students bring to class a photograph/ drawing of a favorite place to display on bulletin board.
- Go out under a tree, to the park, etc. to share your work. Have a picnic & poetry reading
- Share dialogues. Discuss: Will your place be there for future generations?
- View video: Our Living Planet.
- Read nature poems of Wordsworth, Coleridge, Bryon, Keats, and Shelley.
- 1) Prepare class collection of romantic poetry. 2) Test.
- Activities Selection: Favorite Places
- Establish criteria for evaluation of projects. Compare own, evaluate, & revise.

Overview

Objecitve
See the Overview notes in the lesson entitled "Journeys (1 of 7)."

About the Author
Virginia (Ginny) Guerrero is English Department Chair at Churchill High School, in San Antonio, TX. Her accomplishments include a Secondary Teacher of the Year award for the district. She has been teaching for 24 years.

Bibliography
See lesson entitled "Journeys (1 of 7)."

Quadrant 1—Experience

 ## Right Mode—Connect

Students bring to class a photograph/ drawing of a favorite place to display on bulletin board.

Objective
To discover personal connections to favorite places.

Activity
1) Students bring to class for display a photograph or drawing of a favorite place. 2) Write short dialogue taking persona of grandparent talking to grandchild about this place.

Assessment
Individual involvement/participation.

 ## Left Mode—Examine

Share dialogues. Discuss: Will your place be there for future generations?

Objective
To see future possibilities in our environment.

Activity
1) Share dialogue. 2) Discuss probability or possibility of such dialogue—will your future place be there for your grandchild?

Assessment
Involvement/responses.

Quadrant 2—Concepts

 ## Right Mode—Image

View video: Our Living Planet.

Objective
To discover our own aesthetic stake in our environment.

Activity
1) View Our Living Planet video. 2) While watching, note places you would like to visit and show your grandchild.

Assessment
Attentiveness/response/involvement.

Left Mode—Define

Read nature poems of Wordsworth, Coleridge, Bryon, Keats, and Shelley.

Objective
To learn about the romantic poets, time period, ideas, and attitude toward nature.

Activity
1) Read: Wordsworth's *"My Heart Leaps Upon"* or *"The World Is Too Much With Us;"* Coleridge's *"Rime of Ancient Mariner,"* Byron's *"Apostrophe to the Ocean,"* Shelly's *"Ode to the West Wind,"* *"To a Skylark,"* Keat's *"Ode to a Nightingale,"* *"Bright Star,"* and *"I Would I Were."*
2) Lecture: Life and Times of Romantic Poets.

Assessment
Teacher checking for understanding; students' level of involvement in discussion.

Quadrant 3—Applications

 ### Left Mode—Try

1) Prepare class collection of romantic poetry. 2) Test.

Objective
To provide practice in reading, understanding, analyzing poetry of the Romantics.

Activity
Prepare poetry study collection of Romantic poets. Small groups will prepare study guide for assigned Romantic poem.

Assessment
Quality of worksheet, activities in poetry study collection.

 ### Right Mode—Extend

Activities Selection: Favorite Places.

Objective
To apply own understanding of relationship between Man and Nature.

Activity
Choose an activity: 1) Write a poem(s) to immortalize your favorite place. 2) Write a narrative about an experience in your favorite place. 3) If your place is endangered, research this danger and take some action to save it—write a letter, attend a meeting, etc. 4) Design a children's picture book about your place.

Assessment
Intensity of student effort.

Quadrant 4—Creations

 ### Left Mode—Refine

Establish criteria for evaluation of projects. Compare own, evaluate, & revise.

Objective
To evaluate effectiveness of selected activity.

Activity
1) As a class, establish criteria for evaluation of activities. 2) Compare own project to criteria and make adjustment.

Assessment
Degree of application of evaluation criteria to own project.

 ### Right Mode—Integrate

Go out under a tree, to the park, etc. to share your work. Have a picnic & poetry reading.

Objective
To celebrate your own understanding of Romantic attitude toward nature.

Activity
1) Go out under a tree, to the park, etc. to share your work. 2) Have a picnic and read favorite romantic poems as well.

Assessment
Quality of project as effective communication of idea.

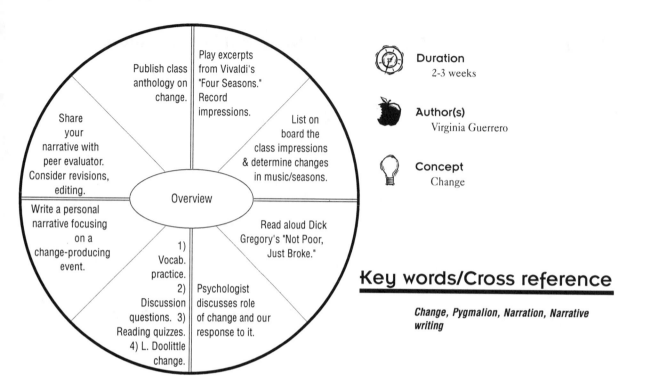

Duration
2-3 weeks

Author(s)
Virginia Guerrero

Concept
Change

Key words/Cross reference

Change, Pygmalion, Narration, Narrative writing

Overview

Objecive
See the Overview notes in the lesson entitled
"Journeys (1 of 7)."

About the Author
Virginia (Ginny) Guerrero is English Department
Chair at Churchill High School, in San Antonio, TX.
Her accomplishments include a Secondary Teacher
of the Year award for the district. She has been
teaching for 24 years.

Bibliography
See lesson entitled "Journeys (1 of 7)."

Quadrant 1—Experience

Right Mode—Connect

Play excerpts from Vivaldi's "Four Seasons." Record impressions.

Objective
To introduce concept of change.

Activity
1) Listen to excerpts from various parts of Vivaldi's "Four Seasons." 2) Students should record images and impressions from various parts/seasons of music.

Assessment
Involvement.

Left Mode—Examine

List on board the class impressions & determine changes in music/seasons.

Objective
To compare impressions with rest of class.

Activity
A scribe should list on board all impressions of each season. Ask class to determine changes/differences in musical seasons.

Assessment
Involvement.

Quadrant 2—Concepts

Right Mode—Image

Read aloud Dick Gregory's Not Poor, Just Broke.

Objective
To connect changes to causes.

Activity
1) Read aloud Dick Gregory's *Not Poor, Just Broke*,
2) Discuss the changes which Gregory attributes to this incident. 3) Students prepare list of important changes in own lives.

Assessment
Student responses.

Left Mode—Define

Psychologist discusses role of change and our response to it.

Objective
1) To examine change as a part of life. 2) To study Pygmalion as an example of change. 3) To learn skills of narrative writing.

Activity
1) Guest speaker—psychologist speaking on role/effect of change in our lives. 2) Read Pygmalion. 3) Study "Writing with a Narrative Focus" (attached).

Assessment
Involvement, notetaking.

Quadrant 3—Applications

Left Mode—Try

1) Vocab. practice. 2) Discussion questions. 3) Reading quizzes. 4) L. Doolittle change.

Objective

To practice and increase understanding of concept of change, the play Pygmalion, and the skills of narrative writing.

Activity

1) Vocabulary. 2) Reading quizzes. 3) Time line or character map for Liza Doolittle.

Assessment

Grades on quizzes, accuracy of map.

Right Mode—Extend

Write a personal narrative focusing on a change-producing event.

Objective

To apply concept of change to own life.

Activity

1) Write a personal narrative in which you focus on an event or moment which precipitated change in your life. 2) Accompany your narrative by one of the following: a) photo essay, b) illustrative or symbolic artwork, c) personal timeline, d) interview with a witness to your event—how it appeared to them.

Assessment

1) Effective narration. 2) Communication of change in accompanying work.

Quadrant 4—Creations

Left Mode—Refine

Share your narrative with peer evaluator. Consider revisions, editing.

Objective

To evaluate narrative.

Activity

With peer evaluator using class-established criteria, discuss your narrative/consider discussion in making revisions.

Assessment

Application of discussion in revision.

Right Mode—Integrate

Publish class anthology on change.

Objective

To celebrate and demonstrate learning.

Activity

Publish class anthology on change using students' narratives and accompanying materials.

Assessment

Effectiveness of communication concerning cause and effects of change.

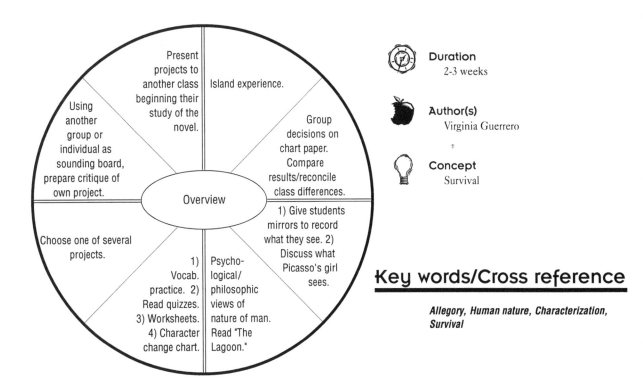

Author(s)
Virginia Guerrero

Concept
Survival

Key words/Cross reference

Allegory, Human nature, Characterization, Survival

Overview

Objecitve

See the Overview notes in the lesson entitled "Journeys (1 of 7)."

About the Author

Virginia (Ginny) Guerrero is English Department Chair at Churchill High School, in San Antonio, TX. Her accomplishments include a Secondary Teacher of the Year award for the district. She has been teaching for 24 years.

Bibliography (for the set of seven lessons)

See lesson entitled "Journeys (1 of 7)."

Quadrant 1—Experience

Right Mode—Connect

Island experience.

Objective

To initiate thinking about survival and what it demands and shows about the inner self.

Activity

Guided imagery "Deserted Island" experience with an emphasis on survival feelings.

Assessment

Participation.

Left Mode—Examine

Group decisions on chart paper. Compare results/reconcile class differences.

Objective

To find similarities, differences, and reasoning in group decisions.

Activity

Present group discussions on flip chart paper. Compare results with other groups. Defend reasoning.

Assessment

Quality of discussion.

Quadrant 2—Concepts

Right Mode—Image

1) Give students mirrors to record what they see. 2) Discuss what Picasso's girl sees.

Objective

To examine own ideas about inner nature.

Activity

1) Give students mirrors and ask them to record what they see—outer image. 2) Examine/discuss Picasso's "Girl Before the Mirror." 3) Draw personal "Girl/Boy Before a Mirror" reflecting inner self/feelings.

Assessment

Detail/complexity of drawings.

Left Mode—Define

Psychological/philosophical views of nature of man. Read The Lagoon.

Objective

To study theories on nature of man; to study allegory *The Lagoon* and *The Lord of the Flies.*

Activity

1) Lecture—various psychological/philosophical views of nature of man. 2) Read Conrad's *The Lagoon.*
3) Read *Lord of the Flies.* 4) Lecture: Concept of the Allegory.

Assessment

Notetaking/completion of reading.

Quadrant 3—Applications

Left Mode—Try

1) Vocab. practice. 2) Read quizzes. 3) Worksheets.
4) Character change chart.

Objective
To practice concepts learned in lectures and reading.

Activity
1) Vocabulary. 2) Reading quizzes. 3) Worksheet. 4) Character changes chart. 5) Essay test focusing on Golding's symbols.

Assessment
Scores made on quizzes and tests.

Right Mode—Extend

Choose one of several projects.

Objective
To apply concept of inner journey to self.

Activity
Choose one of the following projects: 1) Construct model of Golding's Macrocosm of Soul. 2) Write poetic allegory of human society. 3) Produce symbolic wall mural of our society. 4) Inquiry/trial into guilt or innocence of characters. 5) Write a monologue for one of character's reflecting character's internal conflict and change.

Assessment
Intensity of student effort.

Quadrant 4—Creations

Left Mode—Refine

Using another group or individual as sounding board, prepare critique of own project.

Objective
To evaluate own application of learning.

Activity
Use another group as a sounding board to prepare critique of own projects.

Assessment
Thoroughness of critique.

Right Mode—Integrate

Present projects to another class beginning their study of the novel.

Objective
To demonstrate/celebrate learning.

Activity
Display/present projects to another class beginning their study of the novel.

Assessment
Effective communication of concept.

Crime and Punishment

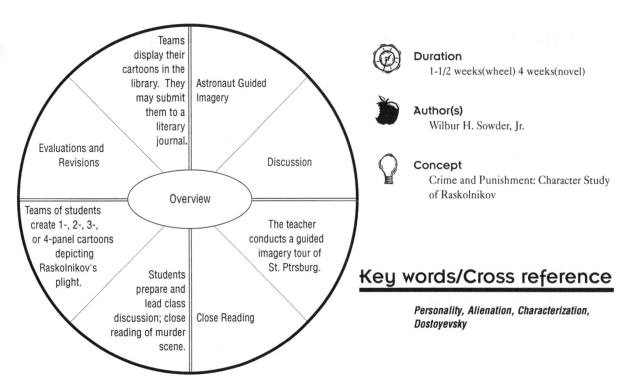

Teams display their cartoons in the library. They may submit them to a literary journal.

Astronaut Guided Imagery

Evaluations and Revisions

Discussion

Overview

Teams of students create 1-, 2-, 3-, or 4-panel cartoons depicting Raskolnikov's plight.

The teacher conducts a guided imagery tour of St. Ptrsburg.

Students prepare and lead class discussion; close reading of murder scene.

Close Reading

Duration
1-1/2 weeks(wheel) 4 weeks(novel)

Author(s)
Wilbur H. Sowder, Jr.

Concept
Crime and Punishment: Character Study of Raskolnikov

Key words/Cross reference

Personality, Alienation, Characterization, Dostoyevsky

Overview

Objective
To teach the art of character study through Crime and Punishment and the development of Raskolnikov.

About the Author
Bill Sowder is a high school English teacher in Ridgefield Park Public Schools, Ridgefield Park, NJ. He is a certified 4MAT Trainer.

Crime and Punishment

Quadrant 1—Experience

 Right Mode—Connect

Astronaut Guided Imagery.

Objective

To immerse the class in a shared experience of a character whose dreams reveal his mind and his emotions, expose his world, and suggest his fate.

Activity

(Pre-assignment: for homework the students have read the first section of *Crime and Punishment*.) Have students close their eyes and imagine that they are astronauts, that it is the night before blast-off, and that this is their dream. Then play David Bowie's "Space Oddity" ("Ground control to Major Tom ...").

Assessment

A brief discussion of how powerful the experience was (it should be very powerful).

 Left Mode—Examine

Discussion.

Objective

To verbalize responses to a powerful aural, imaginative stimulus. To acknowledge and explore the value of a contemporary art form. To compare/contrast art forms. To begin understanding and evaluating Raskolnikov.

Activity

The class discusses its responses to the song and compares/contrasts Major Tom and Raskolnikov as he was introduced in the first section of *Crime and Punishment*.

Assessment

The thoroughness, quality, excitement, and originality of the discussion.

Quadrant 2—Concepts

 Right Mode—Image

The teacher conducts a guided imagery tour of St. Petersburg.

Objective

To continue defining/exploring Raskolnikov's personality.

Activity

Ask students to close their eyes and listen and imagine that they are Raskolnikov and describe one of his walks through St. Petersburg. (He often loses contact with sensory reality, retreating into memories and dreams.) Alternately display the wanderings of his mind (as he sleepwalks through the city) and evoke the sordid sights, foul odors, harsh sounds, and jarring incongruities of the city (beggars, bureaucrats, and aristocracy, garbage and gardens, pubs and palaces). Try to create a sense of disorientation, of alienation, which is an essential part of Raskovnikov's personality.

Assessment

The quality and depth of the follow-up discussion: How did it feel to "be" Raskolnikov?

 Left Mode—Define

Close Reading.

Objective

To model a critical method: close reading.

Activity

Lead a class discussion: a "close reading" of Raskolnikov's dream the day before the murder. Emphasize how elements of the dream reveal his personality, reflect his environment and his childhood, and suggest themes Dostoyevsky will explore.

Assessment

Contribution to, participation in the seminar discussion.

Quadrant 3—Applications

 ## Left Mode—Try

Students prepare and lead class discussion; close reading of murder scene.

Objective

To demonstrate complex and creative understanding of a central scene in the novel.

Activity

A team of students lead a class discussion: a close reading of Raskolnikov's murders, focusing on how symbolic actions and objects and the dream-like atmosphere further reveal Raskolnikov's character, forecast his future, and suggest Dostoyevsky's themes.

Assessment

The quality of both preparation and presentation.

 ## Right Mode—Extend

Teams of students create 1-, 2-, 3-, or 4-panel cartoons depicting Raskolnikov's plight.

Objective

To demonstrate personal "ownership" of Dostoyevsky's ideas, characters, style.

Activity

Teams and/or individuals create a 1, 2, 3 or 4-panel cartoon depicting the essence of Raskolnikov's personality or dilemma.

Assessment

Effort and serious purpose observed by the teacher; questions raised by the students; evidence of trial-and-error learning and risk taking.

Quadrant 4—Creations

 ## Left Mode—Refine

Evaluations and Revisions.

Objective

To develop thoroughness, a desire and respect for excellence.

Activity

The teams present their cartoons for class evaluation, comments, suggestions. They may revise.

Assessment

Teacher observation of effort, serious purpose, thoroughness.

 ## Right Mode—Integrate

Teams display their cartoons in the library. They may submit them to a literary journal.

Objective

To demonstrate that we are a community of creative, divergent (and critical) thinkers. To celebrate ourselves.

Activity

The teams display their cartoons in the library. They mail them to a literary publication (e.g., *The English Journal*).

Assessment

The quality of the final product.

Gender Stereotypes

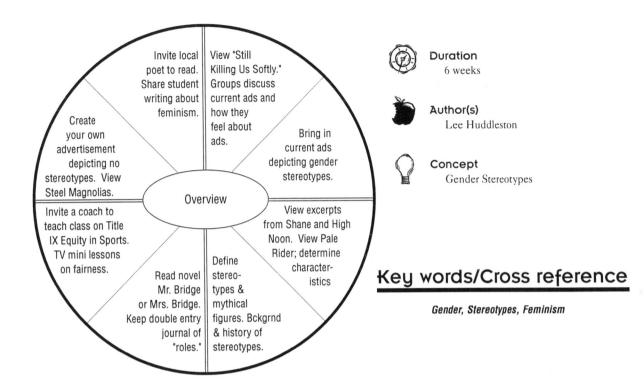

Overview

- Invite local poet to read. Share student writing about feminism.
- View "Still Killing Us Softly." Groups discuss current ads and how they feel about ads.
- Bring in current ads depicting gender stereotypes.
- Create your own advertisement depicting no stereotypes. View Steel Magnolias.
- Invite a coach to teach class on Title IX Equity in Sports. TV mini lessons on fairness.
- Read novel Mr. Bridge or Mrs. Bridge. Keep double entry journal of "roles."
- Define stereotypes & mythical figures. Bckgrnd & history of stereotypes.
- View excerpts from Shane and High Noon. View Pale Rider; determine characteristics.

Duration
6 weeks

Author(s)
Lee Huddleston

Concept
Gender Stereotypes

Key words/Cross reference

Gender, Stereotypes, Feminism

Overview

Objective

To generate awareness and tolerance as well as ideas and subject matter for writing, students will focus on material which evinces some of the common gender stereotypes, from Submissive Woman to Western Man. Students will review literature, film, television, and print media to recognize and identify the characteristics of and changes in these stereotypes.

About the Author

Lee Huddleston is a high school English teacher at Winston Churchill High School in San Antonio, TX.

Required Resources

Still Killing Us Softly (documentary available for rental or purchase).
Mr. Bridge or Mrs. Bridge (paperback by Evan Connell or another novel portraying stereotypes - like *A Doll's House).*
Videos for clips *Shane, High Noon,* and all of *Pale Rider.* CNN's video Battle of the Sexes or any other current TV specials.

Select articles from periodicals concerning sex stereotyping and when it begins . . . see the SIRS file in your school library.
For background reading, check out a copy of *Women in Literature* from the library and a new 1994 book called *Failing at Fairness: How American Schools Cheat Girls.*

Bibliography

CNN, *Battle of the Sexes,* video, 1994.
Connell, Evan. *Mr. Bridge.* San Francisco: North Point Press, 1969.
Connell, Evan. *Mrs. Bridge.* San Francisco: North Point Press, 1959.
Cutright, Melissa. *"Sex Stereotyping Hurts All Kids."* PTA Today, Vol. 4, Mar. 1991, pp. 13-15.
Fairbanks, Carol. *Women in Literature.* Metuchen, NJ: Scarecrow Press, 1976.
Kilbourne, Jean. *Still Killing Us Softly.* Cambridge, MA: Cambridge Documentary, 1987.
Sadker, Myra. *Failing at Fairness: How American Schools Cheat Girls.* New York: Chas. Scribner, 1994.

Quadrant 1—Experience

Right Mode—Connect

View "Still Killing Us Softly." Groups discuss current ads and how they feel about ads.

Objective

To connect stereotypes in documentary with current advertisements. To compare and contrast roles of males and females. To discuss impact of ads on individuals' lives.

Activity

Ask students what advertisements they notice most. Ask which (if any) are offensive. View *Still Killing Us Softly*. In small groups, discuss the documentary's representation of stereotypical ads. Debrief in class discussion.

Assessment

Active participation in small groups. Contribution to constructive, positive discussion.

Left Mode—Examine

Bring in current ads depicting gender stereotypes.

Objective

To reflect on personal experience with advertisements. Connect ads to other real world experiences. Define and explain terms/definitions.

Activity

Ask students to recall terms or titles of specific gender stereotypes. Teacher should explain or clarify terms and add definitions (ex: Mythical Western Man has certain characteristics . . .). Students are to cut out, mount, and title advertisements from current magazines, newspapers, etc. that show gender stereotypes. Title must be of a known gender stereotype.

Assessment

Clean copy of an ad, mounted for presentation or display. Title clearly reflects recognition of a gender stereotype. Discussion of personal feelings as students selected these ads.

Quadrant 2—Concepts

Right Mode—Image

View excerpts from Shane and High Noon. View Pale Rider; determine characteristics.

Objective

To understand the "myth" in the Mythical Western Man. To compare the ideal (as seen in this stereotype) to a real figure.

Activity

For class notes teacher will give definition of the Mythical Western Man (MWM), including all the characteristics normally expected. View film clips of Shane and High Noon for understanding of characteristics. View all of Pale Rider. Students will list characteristics of the mythical Western Man and give examples from Pale Rider.

Assessment

Student ability to determine which characteristics of the MWM are evident in Pale Rider.

Left Mode—Define

Define stereotypes & mythical figures. Background & history of stereotypes.

Objective

To recall characteristics of MWM. Write a Siskel and Ebert style critique (Thumbs Up or Thumbs Down).

Activity

Teacher will review the definition of the Mythical Western Man. Ask students to recall all the characteristics of this MWM. Teacher will extend learning to definitions of other gender stereotypes (Supermom, Macho Man, Dominating Woman, Submissive Woman, etc.). Students will take notes on the titles of these well known stereotypes and take notes on the characteristics of each. Students will write a "Siskel & Ebert" style critique of Pale Rider and Clint Eastwood as a Mythical Western Man in the film.

Assessment

Writing reflects understanding of the MWM and his mythical characteristics.

Quadrant 3—Applications

Left Mode—Try

Read novel Mr. Bridge or Mrs. Bridge. Keep double entry journal of "roles."

Objective

Determine society's role in creating or perpetuating gender stereotypes. Practice close reading skills. Write about the effects of living one's life as a stereotype.

Activity

Students read either Mr. Bridge or Mrs. Bridge. Keep a double-entry journal (two entries per 30-40 pages) with a short passage from the novel on left and on the right side of the journal, a personal reaction to or memory evoked by the passage from novel. Student skit of one episode.

Assessment

Double entry journal reflects personal emotions, memories. Reflects understanding of limits imposed by stereotyping. Participation in/originality of skit.

Right Mode—Extend

Invite a coach to teach class on Title IX Equity in Sports. TV mini lessons on fairness.

Objective

Students to think objectively about topics that affect them personally. View both sides of an argument and come to a conclusion based on facts, not emotion.

Activity

Ask a football coach to come in and speak to class about the effects of the Title IX issue: equity in sports (a federal law). Coach should lead discussion on the reduction of college football scholarships as well as other scholarships for boys' sports in order to provide more money for girls' scholarships in sports. May also address new state rulings which allow girls to play football.

Assessment

Ability to listen actively to others. Ability to participate constructively in "hot" topic.

Quadrant 4—Creations

Left Mode—Refine

Create your own advertisement depicting no stereotypes. View Steel Magnolias.

Objective

To gain tolerance and awareness of the origins of stereotyping. To reflect on origin of students' own ideas of the roles of males and females.

Activity

Handout of *Sex Stereotyping Begins at Birth* for students to read quietly. View film clips dealing with fairness in school or read selections from Failing at Fairness. View CNN's Battle of the Sexes. Discuss the origins of stereotypes and what perpetuates these attitudes. Discuss all the issues raised in the handouts and film clips. Ask "How can we benefit from simply being aware of stereotypes?"

Assessment

Quiz over handout. Class discussion and individual participation.

Right Mode—Integrate

Invite local poet to read. Share student writing about feminism.

Objective

Students to work cooperatively on projects outside the classroom. To create an advertisement that sells the product in an unbiased manner.

Activity

Group assignment of creating an advertisement that is free of gender stereotypes (video, radio, magazine, newspaper). View Steel Magnolias or Lonesome Dove. Films that portray real people and few stereotypes. Invite local poet to read feminist poetry, etc. and poetry that binds and heals: Example – *Councils* by Marge Piercy. Conclude with group presentations of ads followed by class response and questions.

Assessment

Students demonstrate appreciation for variety of viewpoints. Ads reflect positively on male and female roles, no stereotypes. Quality of work involved in creating the ads.

Grapes of Wrath

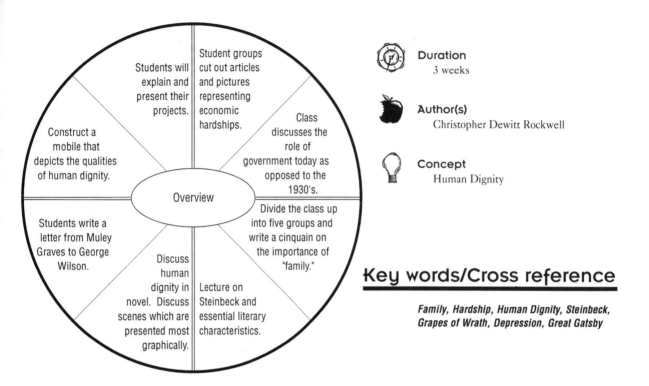

- Student groups cut out articles and pictures representing economic hardships.
- Students will explain and present their projects.
- Construct a mobile that depicts the qualities of human dignity.
- Overview
- Class discusses the role of government today as opposed to the 1930's.
- Divide the class up into five groups and write a cinquain on the importance of "family."
- Lecture on Steinbeck and essential literary characteristics.
- Discuss human dignity in novel. Discuss scenes which are presented most graphically.
- Students write a letter from Muley Graves to George Wilson.

Duration
3 weeks

Author(s)
Christopher Dewitt Rockwell

Concept
Human Dignity

Key words/Cross reference

Family, Hardship, Human Dignity, Steinbeck, Grapes of Wrath, Depression, Great Gatsby

Overview

Objective
To foster understanding of human dignity and self worth through the plight of the Joad Family.

About the Author
Christopher Dewitt Rockwell teaches English at Robert E. Lee High School in Staunton, VA.

Bibliography
Dezoe, Dr. Thelma. *"The Grapes of Wrath."* Mass: Sundance Publishers & Distributors Inc., 1987.

Grapes of Wrath

Quadrant 1—Experience

 ### Right Mode—Connect

Student groups cut out articles and pictures representing economic hardships.

Objective

To foster understanding of the economic conditions of today.

Activity

Divide class into five groups and distribute magazines and newspapers. Each group is responsible for cutting out articles and pictures that represent the economic hardships of today. Class presentations will be in collage form.

Assessment

Quality of group effort and enthusiasm.

 ### Left Mode—Examine

Class discusses the role of government today as opposed to the 1930's.

Objective

To compare and contrast hardships of today with those of the Great Depression.

Activity

Students will brainstorm conditions of the 1930's. Class discussion on the role of the government today as opposed to the 1930's.

Assessment

Quality of student participation.

Quadrant 2—Concepts

 ### Right Mode—Image

Divide the class up into five groups and write a cinquain on the importance of "family."

Objective

For students to understand the importance of the family and its role in survival.

Activity

Divide the class up into five groups and write a cinquain on the importance of "family." Individually write a journal entry on what your family means to you and include how you contribute or interact with your family.

Individual Activity

You suddenly have to leave your house or apartment. You must leave your belongings behind, and, aside from a few clothes, you can take only four of your possessions. What would you take? Draw these four possessions. In addition, in a letter to a friend, explain what those items mean to you and why you chose as you did. Include your feelings about the items you had to leave behind and any anger or frustration that you felt, as well as sadness.

Group Activity

Mindmap of Chapters 1-12

1. Divide class up into six groups.
2. Distribute poster paper and markers.
3. Create a mindmap of chapters 1-12. (Incorporate plot, characterization, symbolism, themes.)

Visual Activity

1. Divide class into groups.
2. Class will choose one of the following:
A) Draw an enlarged map of the travels of the Joads. Place symbols on the map to indicate key events that happened at different locations. In addition, write a cinquain under the map on "plight."
B) Draw the "great valley" of California as witnessed by the Joad family for the first time. Create a logo that sums up its vast possibilities. (Include a statement referring to land ownership.)
C) Draw a Hooverville from the details provided in the novel and/or from photographs of the time. Label your pictures with descriptive adjectives. In addition, write a simile that symbolizes the living conditions.

Individual Activity

Ma says, "We're the people that live . . . why, we're the

people —- we go on." Read Carl Sandburg's poem, I *Am The People, The Mob* and from *The People, Yes.* Compare its message to what Ma is saying about the Migrants. Present in the form of a short essay.

The Charade Activity

1. Divide the class into two teams.
2. A student from one of the teams approaches the board; the other team decides on the character or the situation. The student has one minute to convince his or her team what the subject is. The student can only draw or act. No talking.
3. The winning team gets two extra points on the test.

Assessment
Group and individual effort.

Left Mode—Define

Lecture on Steinbeck and essential literary characteristics.

Objective
To read and study *The Grapes of Wrath*.

Activity
Lecture on Steinbeck's life, writing style, the introduction to the novel. A class discussion after assigned chapters. The students will identify the essential literary characteristics (plot, setting, theme, etc.). A reading quiz everyday. Three vocabulary activity sheets to complete. Group activities after every class discussion. A test at the completion of the novel. The class will be assigned a three- to five-page paper.

Assessment
Successful completion of above.

Quadrant 3—Applications

Left Mode—Try

Discuss human dignity in novel. Discuss scenes which are presented most graphically.

Objective
To foster an understanding of the theme of human dignity and its role of survival in the novel.

Activity
A discussion on the need for and struggle for human dignity in the novel. Discuss those scenes or statements which are presented most graphically.

Assessment
Student participation in discussion.

Right Mode—Extend

Students write a letter from Muley Graves to George Wilson.

Objective
To deepen understanding of and appreciation for human dignity through a written exercise.

Activity
In letter form, each student will write a letter from Muley Graves to George Wilson (The Great Gatsby) explaining how the banks have stripped him of his human dignity. In addition, each student will write a response from George, who explains how the corrupting upper-class ruined his life. (Incorporate his home "Valley of Ashes" and his wife.)

Assessment
Quality and creativity of letter.

Grapes of Wrath

Quadrant 4—Creations

 ### Left Mode—Refine

Construct a mobile that depicts the qualities of human dignity.

Objective
For students to creatively present their understanding of the value of human dignity.

Activity
Construct a mobile that depicts the qualities of human dignity. Represent people, ideals, and/or quotes.

Assessment
Student interest, creativity, and effort.

 ### Right Mode—Integrate

Students will explain and present their projects.

Objective
To complete and share mobiles.

Activity
Students will explain and present their projects.

Assessment
Quality of effort and presentation.

Perspectives in Catcher

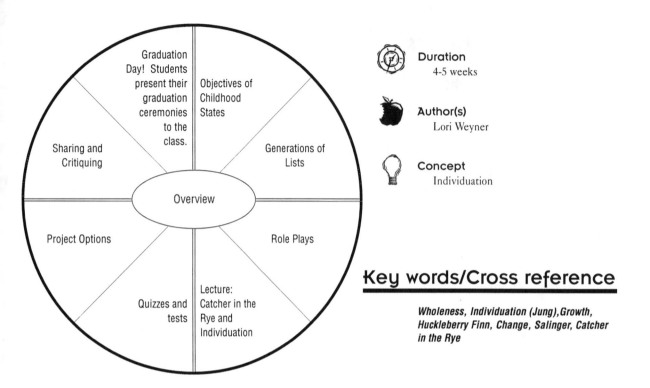

Duration
4-5 weeks

Author(s)
Lori Weyner

Concept
Individuation

Key words/Cross reference

Wholeness, Individuation (Jung), Growth, Huckleberry Finn, Change, Salinger, Catcher in the Rye

Overview

Objective
To recognize the importance of "perspective" as an ongoing concept in junior English through the study of *Catcher in the Rye* and the process of "individuation" as described by Carl Jung.

About the Author
Lori Weyner teaches English at Ridgewood High School, Ridgewood, NJ. She is a certified 4MAT Trainer.

Perspectives in Catcher

Quadrant 1—Experience

 ### Right Mode—Connect

Objectives of Childhood States.

Objective
To recognize the difference between perspectives viewed as a child and those viewed as an adult.

Activity
Students bring in objectives that represent the states of childhood and adulthood. In groups, they share objects and discuss importance of them in their lives.

Assessment
Student participation

 ### Left Mode—Examine

Generations of Lists.

Objective
To become aware of the typical words one usually associates with these states: innocence, freedom (childhood); experience, responsibility (adulthood) as examples.

Activity
Students generate a list of childhood and adulthood words that seemed to recur in the descriptions above.

Assessment
Group list evaluated for completeness.

Quadrant 2—Concepts

 ### Right Mode—Image

Role Plays.

Objective
To see the words come alive in typical adult/child situations.

Activity
With the generated list of adulthood and childhood words, students role play typical situations associated with these words. Non-role-playing students are asked to keep a list of the "gains" and "losses" they've noticed as individuals move from one state to another.

Assessment
Graded as a writing exercise, "gains and losses" is checked for completeness as well as for student's insight as an observer.

 ### Left Mode—Define

Lecture: Catcher in the Rye and Individuation.

Objective
To study *Catcher in the Rye* by J.D. Salinger as a novel which centers around perspective, the journey, and the growth of Holden Caulfield.

Activity
Teach Carl Jung's theory of individuation which is referred to as the process by which we become whole. Also refer to Mark David Chapman, the man who killed former Beatle John Lennon. (He was reported to have been reading Catcher shortly after he shot Lennon. What did he see in this book?)

Assessment
Quality of discussion.

Quadrant 3—Applications

Left Mode—Try

Quizzes and tests.

Objective

To test students' comprehension of novel, Jung, and the sociological impact of the novel.

Activity

Quizzes, tests, paper on:
1) Jungian analysis of Holden's individuation process.
2) Letter to Holden's parents explaining Holden's problems as you see them.
3) "Huck and Holden: An American Journey".**

Assessment

Quality of student work.
** The unit before this one is The Adventures of Huckleberry Finn.

Right Mode—Extend

Project Options.

Objective

For students to visualize Holden's journey through Manhattan. For students to recreate his footsteps through one portion of the journey.

Activity

For students to understand Holden's desire to keep things "as they are" and to understand the need for growth or change.
1) Students create map of entire journey through N.Y.C., noting the important positive and negative influences along the way.
2) For students in the metropolitan New York City area, a field trip to:
a) Museum of Natural History
b) Skating rink
c) Carousel in Central Park (Students ride carousel for 25¢).
3) Write a letter to Holden describing the experience at the museum, the rink, and the carousel.

Assessment

Visual: metaphoric ability and completeness of journey.
Letter: conceptual understanding of growth and change.

Quadrant 4—Creations

Left Mode—Refine

Sharing and Critiquing.

Objective

To see the gains and losses of moving from one state to another, and to "take" Holden with them.

Activity

Students are divided into three groups to share their letters, noting commonalities among them. As a designated group (either primary, middle or high school), they must create a graduation ceremony featuring Holden in some prominent role (teacher, principal, parent, former student, guest speaker, etc.).

Assessment

Conceptual understanding, originality, completeness.

Right Mode—Integrate

Graduation Day! Students present their graduation ceremonies to the class.

Objective

For students to "graduate" Holden and, in so doing, move on to themselves.

Activity

Students present their graduations to the larger group.

Assessment

Quality and enjoyment of student presentations.

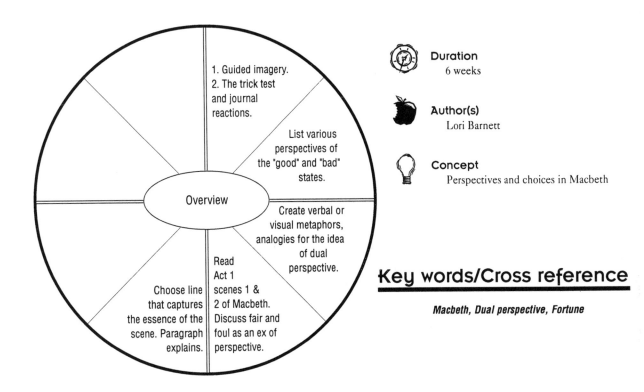

1. Guided imagery.
2. The trick test and journal reactions.

List various perspectives of the "good" and "bad" states.

Overview

Create verbal or visual metaphors, analogies for the idea of dual perspective.

Read Act 1 scenes 1 & 2 of Macbeth. Discuss fair and foul as an ex of perspective.

Choose line that captures the essence of the scene. Paragraph explains.

Duration
6 weeks

Author(s)
Lori Barnett

Concept
Perspectives and choices in Macbeth

Key words/Cross reference

Macbeth, Dual perspective, Fortune

Overview

Objective
To introduce students to the concept of perspective as an ongoing theme in the junior English curriculum using the Royal Shakespeare Company's production of Macbeth on video.

About the Author
Lori Barnett is a High School English teacher and Staff Development Leader in the Ridgewood, New Jersey schools. She is a certified 4MAT Trainer and consultant.

Required Resources
Macbeth, by William Shakespeare
Acting Shakespeare, video by Ian McKellan.

Quadrant 1—Experience

Right Mode—Connect

1. Guided imagery.
2. The trick test and journal reactions.

Objective

Students will begin to recognize the importance of perspective in their own lives.

Activity

1) Guided imagery: Imagine having something you always coveted, but obtaining it would be hard work. Think of the steps you might take to attain your goal. Imagine the same goal, only this time, obtaining it more easily would require some "shady maneuvering." 2) Teacher distributes a blank test on Act One of Macbeth; in groups, students are asked to come up with strategies they might employ to insure a good grade on this test. At random, teacher collects one group of four tests and announces that this group gets an automatic "A" and will not have to attend class on exam day. After the outbreak of protest is contained, students are asked to record all feelings in their journals they are experiencing at having been presented with such "good" or "bad" fortune.

Assessment

Student involvement, engagement, and quality of student insights as expressed in journal entries.

Left Mode—Examine

List various perspectives of the "good" and "bad" states.

Objective

Students will begin to recognize how situations can be viewed differently, depending on one's perspective.

Activity

The next day, students are asked to reflect on the previous day's activity. How could the "good" fortune be viewed as "bad" and vice-versa? In groups, students come up with examples from current events or fiction, movies in which "good" fortune could be viewed as "bad" and vice versa.

Assessment

Quality of discussion, group examples.

Quadrant 2—Concepts

Right Mode—Image

Create verbal or visual metaphors, analogies for the idea of dual perspective.

Objective

Students will be introduced to the concept of dual perspective or equivocation.

Activity

Students will create visual metaphors or written analogies for the idea of dual perspective.

Assessment

Strength of metaphor or analogy.

Left Mode—Define

Read Act 1 scenes 1 & 2 of Macbeth. Discuss fair and foul as an example of perspective.

Objective

To introduce "fair and foul" as the first of many examples of perspective in Macbeth.

Activity

Read Act One scenes one and two. Discuss fair and foul as an example of dual perspective.

Assessment

Understanding of language, quality of discussion.

Quadrant 3—Applications

 Left Mode—Try

Choose line that captures the essence of the scene. Paragraph explains.

Objective

In writing, students will be able to articulate the "essence" of perspective as it is depicted in opening scenes.

Activity

Students choose the line that captures the essence of these two scenes, and they write a paragraph defending their choice. (These lines may be chosen by the teacher in less advanced classes. All lines usually point nicely to the perspective issue that permeates the play.)

Assessment

Quality of written discussion.

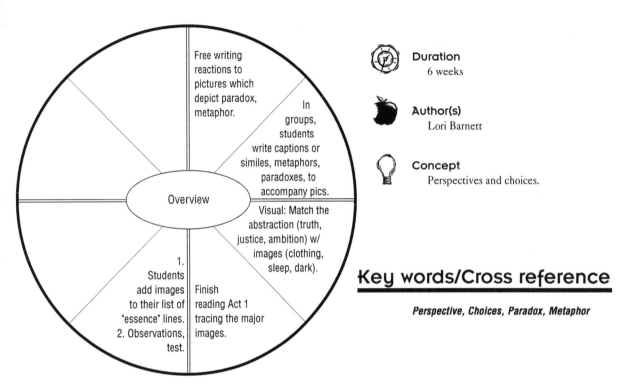

Duration
6 weeks

Author(s)
Lori Barnett

Concept
Perspectives and choices.

Key words/Cross reference

Perspective, Choices, Paradox, Metaphor

Overview

Objective
To introduce students to the concept of perspective as an ongoing theme in the junior English curriculum using the Royal Shakespeare Company's production of Macbeth on video.

About the Author
Lori Barnett is a high school English teacher and staff development leader in the Ridgewood, New Jersey, schools. She is a certified 4MAT Trainer and consultant.

Required Resources
Royal Shakespeare Company's version of Macbeth on video
Macbeth, by William Shakespeare
Acting Shakespeare, video by Ian McKellan.

Quadrant 1—Experience

 ### Right Mode—Connect

Free writing reactions to pictures which depict paradox, metaphor.

Objective
To introduce students to metaphor, simile, paradox, oxymoron.

Activity
Students free-write reactions to: Picture of an American flag composed of unlit matches about to be lit by a stray match already lit and teacher selected pictures, cartoons depicting metaphor, paradox, oxymoron.

Assessment
Completion of task.

 ### Left Mode—Examine

In groups, students write captions or similes, metaphors, paradoxes, to accompany pictures.

Objective
Students will begin to understand the concept of paradox, oxymoron, metaphor as viewed from a visual perspective.

Activity
In groups, students write captions consisting of similes, metaphors, paradoxes to accompany pictures.

Assessment
Quality of captions.

Quadrant 2—Concepts

 ### Right Mode—Image

Visual: Match the abstraction (truth, justice, ambition) w/ images (clothing, sleep, dark).

Objective
Students will begin to understand how abstraction is explained through concrete imagery.

Activity
Teacher distributes a list of words which represent abstractions (truth, justice, ambition, loyalty) with a list of words that represent images (clothing, sleep, dark, light). Students are then asked to match an abstraction with an image and show in a visual way why the two go together.

Assessment
Quality of understanding depicted in the visual as well as the ability to articulate the relationship between the image and the abstraction.

 ### Left Mode—Define

Finish reading Act 1 tracing the major images.

Objective
Students will be able to trace the major images in the play.

Activity
Finish reading Act 1 of Macbeth, tracing the major images. Key scenes will be viewed on R.S.C. version of play. Discussion of how image was depicted on the stage.

Assessment
Quality of discussion.

Quadrant 3—Applications

 ## Left Mode—Try

1. Students add images to their list of "essence" lines.
2. Observations, test.

Objective
Students will begin to see the relationship between the images and themes in the play.

Activity
1) Students add images to their "essence" lines.
2) Paragraphs on the essence lines and quote test.

Assessment
Quality of writing, ability to identify quotes for speaker, and image.

Macbeth 3/3

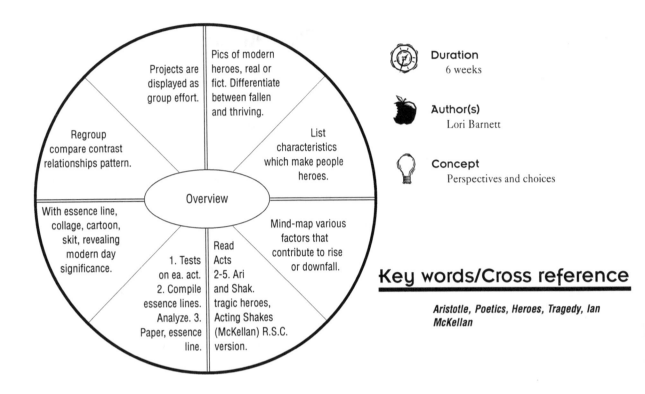

Overview

- Pics of modern heroes, real or fict. Differentiate between fallen and thriving.
- Projects are displayed as group effort.
- Regroup compare contrast relationships pattern.
- With essence line, collage, cartoon, skit, revealing modern day significance.
- 1. Tests on ea. act. 2. Compile essence lines. Analyze. 3. Paper, essence line.
- Read Acts 2-5. Ari and Shak. tragic heroes, Acting Shakes (McKellan) R.S.C. version.
- Mind-map various factors that contribute to rise or downfall.
- List characteristics which make people heroes.

Duration
6 weeks

Author(s)
Lori Barnett

Concept
Perspectives and choices

Key words/Cross reference

Aristotle, Poetics, Heroes, Tragedy, Ian McKellan

Overview

Objective

To introduce students to the concept of perspective as an ongoing theme in the junior English curriculum Royal Shakespeare Company's production of Macbeth on video.

About the Author

Lori Barnett is a High School English teacher and Staff Development Leader in the Ridgewood, New Jersey schools. She is a certified 4MAT Trainer and consultant.

Required Resources

Macbeth, by William Shakespeare
Acting Shakespeare, video by Ian McKellan.

Quadrant 1—Experience

 ## Right Mode—Connect

Pics of modern heroes, real or fictional. Differentiate between fallen and thriving.

Objective
Students will begin to examine the thriving and fallen heroes in our own lives.

Activity
Students will bring in pictures of modern heroes, real or fictional and differentiate between ones who fell from hero status and ones who have retained hero status.

Assessment
Completion of task.

 ## Left Mode—Examine

List characteristics which make people heroes.

Objective
To recognize the characteristics of the fallen hero.

Activity
In groups, choose a fallen and a thriving hero and list characteristics which make these people who they are.

Assessment
Completion of task.

Quadrant 2—Concepts

 ## Right Mode—Image

Mind-map various factors that contribute to rise or downfall.

Objective
To examine factors which contribute to rise or downfall.

Activity
Mind-map various factors which contribute to rise or downfall.

Assessment
Quality of mindmap.

 ## Left Mode—Define

Read Acts 2-5. Ari and Shak. Tragic heroes, Acting Shakes (McKellan) R.S.C. version.

Objective
To compare and contrast Aristotle's, Shakespeare's and our own idea of the tragic hero.

Activity
Read Acts 2-5. Read Aristotle's description of tragic hero. View Macbeth portion of Acting Shakespeare by Ian McKellan. View key scenes in R.S.C. production.

Assessment
Completion of tasks, degree of involvement.

Quadrant 3—Applications

 ### Left Mode—Try

1. Tests on each act. 2. Compile essence lines. Analyze. 3. Paper, essence line.

Objective
Students will view play as a complex intertwining of images and themes.

Activity
1) Tests on each act. 2) Compilation of essence lines which will be analyzed for completeness and figurative power. 3) Students will write a paper on the single line that captures the essence of the play.

Assessment
Completeness, writing ability.

 ### Right Mode—Extend

With essence line, create collage, cartoon, skit, revealing modern day significance.

Objective
To show how Shakespeare's language has meaning in our lives today.

Activity
Using the essence line they chose for their papers, students will create a collage, cartoon, or skit, which explains how the line holds significance in our lives today.

Assessment
Accuracy of example, creativity, quality of presentation.

Quadrant 4—Creations

 ### Left Mode—Refine

Regroup; compare/contrast relationships pattern.

Objective
Students will see how their own ideas relate to those of others.

Activity
Students with similar lines will group together to compare/contrast and point to patterns/relationships among the lines depicted in their projects.

Assessment
Ability to see patterns and connections.

 ### Right Mode—Integrate

Projects are displayed as group effort.

Objective
To celebrate understanding of the play and the thematic significance in our lives today.

Activity
Groups invent a new way to share individual efforts to present or display to class.

Assessment
Quality of group effort.

A Man for All Seasons

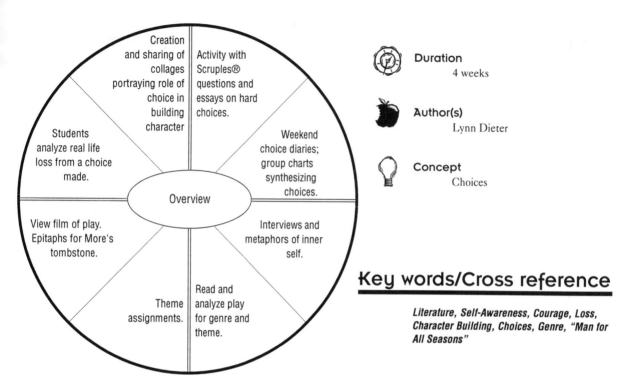

Creation and sharing of collages portraying role of choice in building character

Activity with Scruples® questions and essays on hard choices.

Students analyze real life loss from a choice made.

Weekend choice diaries; group charts synthesizing choices.

Overview

View film of play. Epitaphs for More's tombstone.

Interviews and metaphors of inner self.

Theme assignments.

Read and analyze play for genre and theme.

Duration
4 weeks

Author(s)
Lynn Dieter

Concept
Choices

Key words/Cross reference

Literature, Self-Awareness, Courage, Loss, Character Building, Choices, Genre, "Man for All Seasons"

Overview

Objective
To connect students to the concept of personal choice and ethical decisions as evidenced in the play, *A Man for All Seasons.*

About the Author
Lynn P. Dieter, Ph.D., is an English teacher at Maine East High School, District 207, Park Ridge, IL. She has over twenty years teaching experience.

Required Resources
The game, "Scruples®", published by Milton-Bradley Co.

Bibliography
The film, *A Man for All Seasons,* starring Paul Scolfield, is available on RCA/Columbia Home Video, 120 minutes.

Author's Notes
For the English teacher who is concerned with teaching elements of a genre, the comparison of the film and the book, which are significantly different, allows the lesson to focus on how the genre and its elements alter the readers' perceptions. This play has continually been a favorite of my students. One measure of this is that as seniors applying to college one year later, many choose to write about this play as the work of literature which made the most impact upon them. Many also write about More as a hero. The play itself, because it breaks so many of the conventions of the genre, allows the teacher to focus upon these. The writing is laden with metaphors and comparisons, and this allows many possibilities in Quadrant Two, Right Mode.

A Man for All Seasons

Quadrant 1—Experience

 ### Right Mode—Connect

Activity with Scruples® questions and essays on hard choices.

Objective
To connect students to the idea of making choices: how we make choices, why we feel guilt, and how our values dictate our choices.

Activity
Students work in groups of three. Each group is given a set of three Scruples® (Milton-Bradley game) questions, with the same set of questions going to at least two groups. After 10-15 minutes of group discussion, each group must reach consensus on action and present their positions to the whole class for discussion. After all groups have presented, for homework students will write a brief discussion of the hardest choice they have made in life, why it was difficult, and what part guilt and/or other people played in the decision, what was lost through the choice and what was gained.

Assessment
Intensity of small group and whole class discussions; depth of individual essays.

 ### Left Mode—Examine

Weekend choice diaries; group charts synthesizing choices.

Objective
To formulate a concept of how choices are made and how we rank our values.

Activity
For one weekend, students will keep a diary of choices they make. For the next class, they must prioritize their choices in terms of importance, identifying which actions really were choices. In class, again in groups, they will share their choices and create a group composite chart, identifying hardest choices, the function of guilt in choices, the influence of our values in the choices we make, and what was lost and gained in each choice. Teacher leads class discussion, hopefully helping students recognize that choices are usually "gray" and within each person is that part of the self which determines who and what we are.

Assessment
Student participation and effort; contribution to the group.

Quadrant 2—Concepts

 ### Right Mode—Image

Interviews and metaphors of inner self.

Objective
To preface the drama by helping students see that in our times we see ourselves by what we do, as opposed to a criterion such as "Renaissance Man" or "Christian Humanist."

Activity
Each student will ask 5 people, "Who are you?" and write down their responses. The class as a whole will read ahead in the play to the metaphor that More uses to describe himself, "...it is an area no bigger than a tennis court to him." Students will write or sketch a metaphor to express that which is their self: the part of themselves they will not change or alter for anyone. How often is that part of themselves involved in a decision or choice?

Assessment
Contributions to class discussion and sharing of personal metaphors.

 ### Left Mode—Define

Read and analyze play for genre and theme.

Objective
To read and analyze the play with a focus on its genre and the choices made by the characters.

Activity
Students read the play, keeping track of page numbers of events on which More makes a choice. Class discussion focuses on the genre and thematic ideas running throughout the play, particularly the Common Man as antagonist to More and the idea that "No man is an island."

Assessment
Student notetaking and teacher checking for understanding through objective quiz.

Quadrant 3—Applications

Left Mode—Try

Theme assignments.

Objective
To analyze how the disregard of usual play conventions and genre format helps convey the characterization and involve the audience to a greater extent.

Activity
1. Students take each convention in the play, trace its use through the drama, and show how Bolt's manipulation of it did or did not work with a focus on his manipulation of character.
2. Traditional theme assignment to focus on structure and function, comparing these to the play Hamlet.
3. Students will write a theme based on an article in which Albert Speer asserts that the Nazis were just following orders. They must relate this stance to the play and the idea of individual choices. In addition, they will research one real-life incident in which someone took a stand or did not (e.g., Kitty Genovese case in NY or the mass rape of the woman in the New Bedford, Massachusetts bar).

Assessment
Quality of all written work.

Right Mode—Extend

View film of play. Epitaphs for More's tombstone.

Objective
To further focus on choices made and the revelation of self.

Activity
1. Students will select one character and show how outcome of play would have been different if another choice had been made.
2. Class will watch Paul Scofield movie of the play. Class discussion will concern whether "seeing" the play alters our opinions. The discussion will refer back to the idea of the metaphor for "self" and analyze the techniques of metaphor creation and use.
3. Students will develop epitaphs for More's tombstone, each of which must be in metaphorical form, e.g., "Here lies the fly from which the little boy tore the wings."

Assessment
Student contributions to discussion and caliber of epitaphs.

Quadrant 4—Creations

Left Mode—Refine

Students analyze real life loss from a choice made.

Objective
To transfer understanding of personal choices to real life situations.

Activity
Students will select a living example of someone who lost something by making a choice. This person may be a friend, family member, teacher, acquaintance, or themselves. Their subject must be analyzed in terms of the concepts of guilt and sorrow and the ability to live with the outcome of the choice s/he made. What did they gain through the choice? How did what they gained affect their ability to live with their choice? The analysis will be presented in theme form.

Assessment
Quality of personal analysis and written work.

Right Mode—Integrate

Creation and sharing of collages portraying role of choice in building character.

Objective
To extend the expression of what has been learned.

Activity
In triads, using pictures and appropriate newspaper/magazine articles and/or headlines, students will create collages to symbolically portray how our characters are built by the choices we make. These will be shared with the school in a display.

Assessment
Quality of final products.

Man's Inhumanity to Man

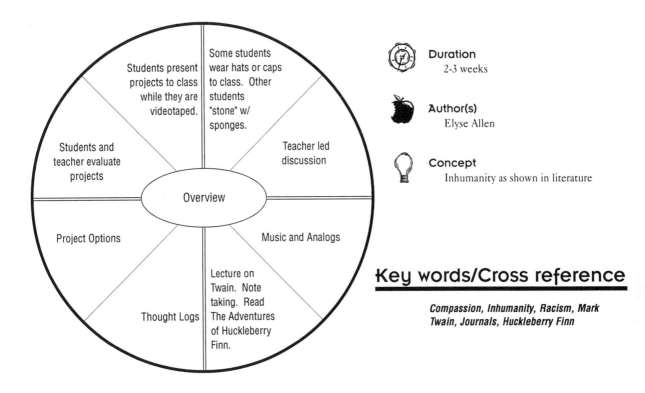

Overview

- Some students wear hats or caps to class. Other students "stone" w/ sponges.
- Teacher led discussion
- Music and Analogs
- Lecture on Twain. Note taking. Read The Adventures of Huckleberry Finn.
- Thought Logs
- Project Options
- Students and teacher evaluate projects
- Students present projects to class while they are videotaped.

Duration
2-3 weeks

Author(s)
Elyse Allen

Concept
Inhumanity as shown in literature

Key words/Cross reference

Compassion, Inhumanity, Racism, Mark Twain, Journals, Huckleberry Finn

Overview

Objective

To use the concepts of prejudice and inhumanity to teach *The Adventures of Huckleberry Finn*.

About the Author

Elyse Allen is a high school English teacher in North East Independent School District, San Antonio, TX. She is a certified 4MAT System trainer and a participant in the North East Independent School District 4MAT Implementation Project led by Fran Everidge and Carol Mendenhall.

Required Resources

Appropriate filmstrips and/or video; recording of the musical score from the play, Big River; videotape equipment.

Quadrant 1—Experience

Right Mode—Connect

Some students wear hats or caps to class. Other students "stone" w/ sponges.

Objective

To create an experience of man's inhumanity to man.

Activity

Ask several students to wear a hat or cap to class the next day. Teacher cuts up inexpensive sponges in one inch pieces. In class, hand out "movie prop rocks" to students not wearing hats and let them "stone" those who are.

Assessment

Student participation.

Left Mode—Examine

Teacher-led discussion.

Objective

To discuss experience of 1R.

Activity

Teacher leads discussion of absurdity of stoning or otherwise harming someone because he is different.

Assessment

Quality of discussion; student participation.

Quadrant 2—Concepts

Right Mode—Image

Music and Analogs.

Objective

To integrate experience of man's inhumanity to man.

Activity

Play discordant music (Stravinsky works well) while students draw two analogs, one of compassion and one of inhumanity. Post on bulletin board.

Assessment

Quality of analogs.

Left Mode—Define

Lecture on Twain. Note taking. Read The Adventures of Huckleberry Finn.

Objective

To teach novel and concept.

Activity

Lecture on Mark Twain and background of novel. Also show appropriate filmstrips or videos on the life and works of Mark Twain: many good ones are available in most media centers and provide interesting background for Twain's work. Students take notes. Read *The Adventures of Huckleberry Finn*.

Assessment

Students listening and quality of notes.

Quadrant 3—Applications

 ### Left Mode—Try

Thought Logs.

Objective
To practice information learned in Quadrant Two, Left Mode.

Activity
Listen to two songs per day from musical, Big River, and then ask students to respond in a "Thought Log." Students complete study questions, vocabulary, tests, compositions, etc.

Assessment
Quality of students' work.

 ### Right Mode—Extend

Project Options.

Objective
To add student to novel's reading.

Activity
Choices: 1) Write (a number) of journal entries from Jim's viewpoint, emphasizing his feelings during the trip. 2) Research and write a report on an area in the world currently experiencing "man's inhumanity to man." 3) Make a AAA triptik of the raft trip. 4) Write a play version of one significant scene in the novel and act out.

Assessment
On-task behavior.

Quadrant 4—Creations

 ### Left Mode—Refine

Students and teacher evaluate projects.

Objective
To evaluate projects.

Activity
Student teams refine and edit projects. Teacher evaluates projects.

Assessment
Quality of student work.

 ### Right Mode—Integrate

Students present projects to class while they are videotaped.

Objective
To share and celebrate projects.

Activity
Students present projects to the class as they are videotaped. Show videotape to other classes.

Assessment
Student participation and enjoyment of projects.

Ordinary People

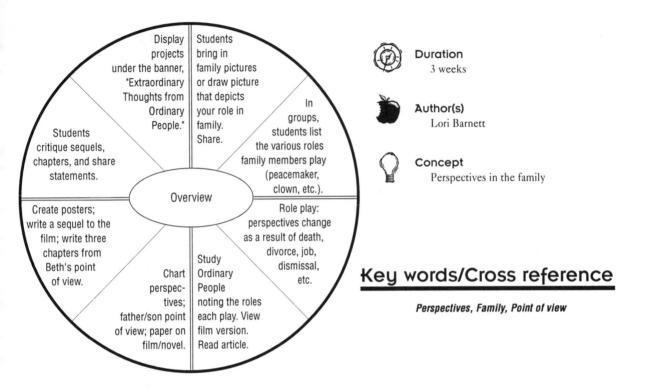

Display projects under the banner, "Extraordinary Thoughts from Ordinary People."

Students bring in family pictures or draw picture that depicts your role in family. Share.

Students critique sequels, chapters, and share statements.

In groups, students list the various roles family members play (peacemaker, clown, etc.).

Overview

Create posters; write a sequel to the film; write three chapters from Beth's point of view.

Role play: perspectives change as a result of death, divorce, job, dismissal, etc.

Chart perspectives; father/son point of view; paper on film/novel.

Study Ordinary People noting the roles each play. View film version. Read article.

Duration
3 weeks

Author(s)
Lori Barnett

Concept
Perspectives in the family

Key words/Cross reference

Perspectives, Family, Point of view

Overview

Objective
Students will be able to investigate the ongoing concept of perspective, as illustrated in the changing roles of the family in the novel and movie, *Ordinary People.*

About the Author
Lori Barnett is an English teacher and staff development leader in the Ridgewood, NJ, schools. She is a certified 4MAT Trainer and consultant.

Bibliography
Ordinary People, by Judith Guest; video of film, *Ordinary People*, directed by Robert Redford Handout of *"A Problem of Dislike,"* by Eda LeShan; *Working Parents Magazine*, Feb./March, 1987; poster-board for projects.

Ordinary People

Quadrant 1—Experience

 ### Right Mode—Connect

Students bring in family pictures or draw picture that depicts their role in family. Share.

Objective
For students to examine the individual roles people play in their own families.

Activity
Students bring in a photo or draw a depiction of their families and the roles each member plays within the family unit (peacemaker, doer, clown, disciplinarian, etc.). In groups, students share their pictures and describe the different roles to the group.

Assessment
As a group activity: level of involvement in response to students' pictures.

 ### Left Mode—Examine

In groups, students list the various roles family members play (peacemaker, clown, etc.).

Objective
To recognize the variety of roles people play in family (the organizer, the clown, the peacemaker, the problem solver, etc.) and when roles conflict with one another.

Activity
In groups, students: 1) generate a list of the various roles described in Q1 activity, 2) speculate on roles that might come in conflict with one another.

Assessment
Group involvement, ability to speculate on possible conflicts.

Quadrant 2—Concepts

 ### Right Mode—Image

Role play: perspectives change as a result of death, divorce, job, dismissal, etc.

Objective
For students to investigate events which change the roles we play in our families.

Activity
Role play scenarios in which perspectives change as a result of death, divorce, job loss, college, relocation, etc. Students write a short paragraph explaining how the various roles altered when an unexpected event changed the way the family operated as a unit.

Assessment
Quality of student roleplays and accompanying paragraphs.

 ### Left Mode—Define

Study Ordinary People noting the roles each play. View film version. Read article.

Objective
To study the difference in point of view as depicted in the chapters written in the father's voice and the chapters written in the son's voice. To discuss the different perspectives created by the film version. To introduce the idea of "dislike" as characterized in the article, "*A Problem of Dislike,*" as a possible motivation for Beth in the film version.

Activity
Read novel, choosing metaphors and axioms from each character's point of view; view film, read article.

Assessment
Homework, group activities, discussion, quote tests which identify speaker and describe the significance of the particular metaphor or axiom.

Quadrant 3—Applications

 ### Left Mode—Try

Chart perspectives; father/son point of view; paper on film/novel.

Objective
To show how each character's perspective changes during the course of the novel/film.

Activity
Quote text to identify the different voices and to discuss the significance of the lines, metaphors, axioms; comparison/contrast paper on novel. In this paper, the students will explore why the screenwriter and director chose to change the perspective in the film based on the following topics: Beth Jarrett: A Problem of Dislike?; Calvin Jarrett: Passive or Active?; The Jarrett Family: a Breakdown in Communication.

Assessment
Grades based on: ability to identify point of view, significance of chosen lines from novel, film; comprehensiveness of exploration in two genres; writing ability.

Right Mode—Extend

Create posters; write a sequel to the film; write three chapters from Beth's point of view.

Objective
Students will explore the "missing" perspective in the novel (Beth's); students will speculate on a happier ending to the film; students will extract the most meaningful statements, metaphors, or axioms as ones we can all remember to help us through rough times.

Activity
1) Students write an epilogue to the film showing what happened to the Jarrett family. 2) Students write three chapters from Beth's point of view and indicate where in the novel they would be most suitable. 3) Students create posters to show how our own perspectives have changed as a result of *Ordinary People.*

Assessment
Grades based on creativity, comprehensiveness.

Quadrant 4—Creations

 ### Left Mode—Refine

Students critique sequels, chapters, and share statements.

Objective
To see the importance of perspective in genre, character, future situations.

Activity
Students will critique each others' projects with perspective in mind. Students will create new situations which could relate to the axioms chosen in the novel.

Assessment
Peer editing, visual impact.

Right Mode—Integrate

Display projects under the banner, "Extraordinary Thoughts from Ordinary People."

Objective
To celebrate: the changing perspectives of the characters in both novel and film, and our own awareness of the possibility for change in perspective in our own future situations.

Activity
Display of original work under the overall heading "Extraordinary Thoughts from Ordinary People."

Assessment
Quality of individual and group display as well as the ability to articulate how the messages in the novel and film can be integrated in our own lives and the lives of others.

Our Town

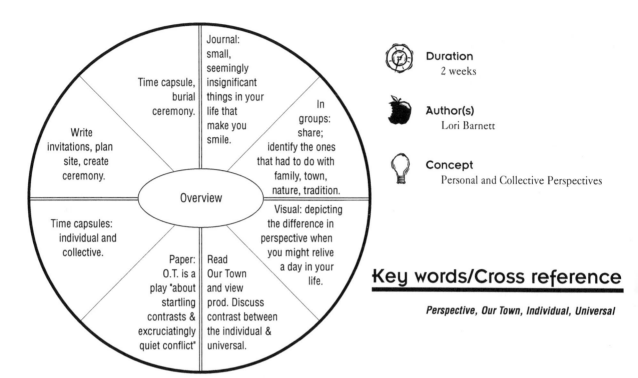

Duration
2 weeks

Author(s)
Lori Barnett

Concept
Personal and Collective Perspectives

The wheel diagram contains:

- **Overview** (center)
- Time capsule, burial ceremony.
- Journal: small, seemingly insignificant things in your life that make you smile.
- In groups: share; identify the ones that had to do with family, town, nature, tradition.
- Write invitations, plan site, create ceremony.
- Visual: depicting the difference in perspective when you might relive a day in your life.
- Time capsules: individual and collective.
- Paper: O.T. is a play "about startling contrasts & excruciatingly quiet conflict"
- Read Our Town and view prod. Discuss contrast between the individual & universal.

Key words/Cross reference

Perspective, Our Town, Individual, Universal

Overview

Objective
As part of an ongoing study of the concept of perspective in junior English, students will examine the contrast between the individual and the universal as depicted in *Our Town* by Thorton Wilder and as it is depicted in the students' individual lives and the culture of their time.

About the Author
Lori Barnett is an English teacher and Staff Development Leader in the Ridgewood, NJ, schools. She is a certified 4MAT Trainer and consultant.

Required Resources
New York Times theatre reviews from prominent productions.

Bibliography
Our Town, by Torton Wilder; Hal Holbrook version of play on video; individual time capsule contents; school burial site.

Quadrant 1—Experience

Right Mode—Connect

Journal: small, seemingly insignificant things in your life that make you smile.

Objective
Students will begin to identify the simple things in their lives that reverberate with meaning.

Activity
In journals, students will make an exhaustive list of the small, seemingly insignificant things in their lives that make them smile. Students will share lists in groups, noting similarities, if any.

Assessment
Completion of task, level of group involvement.

Left Mode—Examine

In groups: share; identify the ones that had to do with family, town, nature, tradition.

Objective
Students will begin to analyze the significance of the small, everyday events in their lives that have meaning to them individually.

Activity
After students have shared lists, they will classify their lists under the headings: House, Family, Town, Nature, Other. Groups will report summary of classifications to larger group.

Assessment
Completion of task, group involvement.

Quadrant 2—Concepts

Right Mode—Image

Visual: depicting the difference in perspective when you might relive a day in your life.

Objective
Students will imagine the difference in perspective one might have if one were to relive a day in one's life.

Activity
If you were to relive any day in your life, good or bad, which would it be? Create a representational or non-representational visual depicting the difference in perspective between the two states of "knowing": each visual must show the day as it was lived the first time and the day as it was relived the second time.

Assessment
Strength of visual, ability to articulate the different states of perspective.

Left Mode—Define

Read Our Town and view production. Discuss contrast between the individual & universal.

Objective
Students will read and view Our Town, discussing the role of the stage manager as a character representing multiple states of "knowing"; students will read and discuss various reviews of the play: some critics view it as a tribute to small town life, others see it as a very dark play; students will discuss the contrast between the individual and the universal and how it is depicted in the play through language, character, set design, miming, overall structure. Students will discuss the difference in perspectives between the living and the dead as depicted in the play.

Activity
Class presentations of key scenes, group discussions, analyses of reviews.

Assessment
Dramatic ability, caliber of discussion, caliber of writing.

Quadrant 3—Applications

 ### Left Mode—Try

Paper: O.T. is a play "about startling contrasts & excruciatingly quiet conflict."

Objective
Students will examine the often painful realization of our place in the scheme of things as well as the beauty of our individuality.

Activity
Students will: compile lists of the contrasts and conflicts in the play; analyze the contrast between the universal and the individual in the stage manager's speeches; write a major paper on the statement: "Our Town is a play about startling contrasts and excruciatingly quiet conflicts."

Assessment
Caliber of writing.

 ### Right Mode—Extend

Time capsules: individual and collective.

Objective
Students will celebrate the individual and the collective in their lives.

Activity
After having reread the speech in which the stage manager describes the time capsule Grovers Corners buried in the cornerstone of the bank, students will: 1) create individual mini-capsules they are to hide for a period of time, 2) create a large time capsule which typifies the life of a Ridgewood High School student living in the present time in the state of New Jersey. Students are to include music, literature, art, photographs, objects, etc.

Assessment
Completion of task, quality of contents.

Quadrant 4—Creations

 ### Left Mode—Refine

Write invitations, plan site, create ceremony.

Objective
Students will evaluate the capsule as a true representation of themselves and their culture.

Activity
In committees, students will create a time capsule ceremony with: appropriate contents and protection against the elements, invitations to the present burial as well as the future unearthing, burial site and necessary approval, appropriate speeches and music, town publicity and yearbook notification.

Assessment
Committee contribution to overall project.

 ### Right Mode—Integrate

Time capsule, burial ceremony.

Objective
To celebrate: the individual as well as the collective; the small as well as the large; the present as well as the future.

Activity
Students will conduct the burial ceremony and invite guests to the unearthing to take place in 25 years.

Assessment
Quality and smoothness of presentation.

Poetic Devices

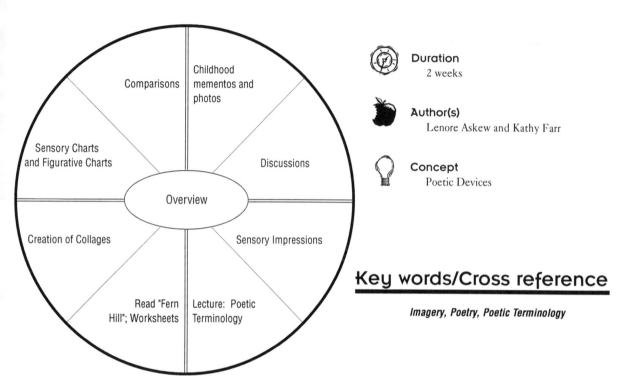

Comparisons

Childhood mementos and photos

Sensory Charts and Figurative Charts

Discussions

Overview

Creation of Collages

Sensory Impressions

Read "Fern Hill"; Worksheets

Lecture: Poetic Terminology

Duration
2 weeks

Author(s)
Lenore Askew and Kathy Farr

Concept
Poetic Devices

Key words/Cross reference

Imagery, Poetry, Poetic Terminology

Overview

Objective
Students will be able to identify and apply poetic devices.

About the Authors
Lenore Askew and Kathy Farr are high school teachers at Shikellamy High School, Shikellamy School District, Northumberland, PA. The are participants in the Shikellamy 4MAT Implementation Project led by Tim and Trudy Shannon.

Required Resources
Chart paper and markers.

Bibliography
Thomas, Dylan. *Fern Hill*,
James Applegate, Ed., *Adventures in World Literature*,
New York: Harcourt, Brace, Jovanovich, 1970.

Poetic Devices

Quadrant 1—Experience

 ### Right Mode—Connect

Childhood mementos and photos.

Objective
To connect students with childhood memories.

Activity
Write a brief description of the incident surrounding a childhood photo or memento that they bring to class.

Assessment
Completion of descriptive passage.

 ### Left Mode—Examine

Discussions.

Objective
To share the childhood experience.

Activity
In small (or large) groups, students will attempt to match the photos or mementos with the appropriate student. Then they will share their recollections with the group.

Assessment
Student participation and effort.

Quadrant 2—Concepts

 ### Right Mode—Image

Sensory Impressions.

Objective
To recall sensory impressions surrounding the incident.

Activity
Students will try to re-create the incident by recalling all sensory impressions and recording them on a chart under the appropriate columns for sound, sight, taste, touch, and smell.

Assessment
Number of sensory impressions recorded.

 ### Left Mode—Define

Lecture: Poetic Terminology.

Objective
To define poetic terminology.

Activity
The teacher will present and define the following poetic devices: free association, dream images, half-rhyme, consonant chime, alliteration, imaginative symbolism, puns.

Assessment
Student note taking and objective quiz on terminology.

Quadrant 3—Applications

 ### Left Mode—Try

Read "Fern Hill"; Worksheets.

Objective

To read the poem *"Fern Hill"* and identify the poetic devices.

Activity

Students will complete a worksheet finding examples of the poetic devices listed in *"Fern Hill."*

Assessment

Appropriateness and completeness of examples of poetic devices on worksheets.

 ### Right Mode—Extend

Creation of Collages.

Objective

To extend student understanding of imagery.

Activity

Students will create, in small groups, a collage representing Thomas' imagery in *"Fern Hill."*

Assessment

Student participation and effort as evidenced in the collages.

Quadrant 4—Creations

 ### Left Mode—Refine

Sensory Charts and Figurative Charts.

Objective

To apply the concept of imagery to individual experience.

Activity

Students will use their sensory charts (from activity 2R) to create their own figurative language to describe their initial experience in prose or poetry.

Assessment

The originality and appropriateness of the figurative language to convey the experience.

 ### Right Mode—Integrate

Comparisons.

Objective

To share and compare their second "figurative" versions with their original versions of the childhood recollection.

Activity

Students will read their figurative versions and their original versions and will compare the two versions in a small group discussion.

Assessment

The quality of personal analyses and insights.

Rich in Love

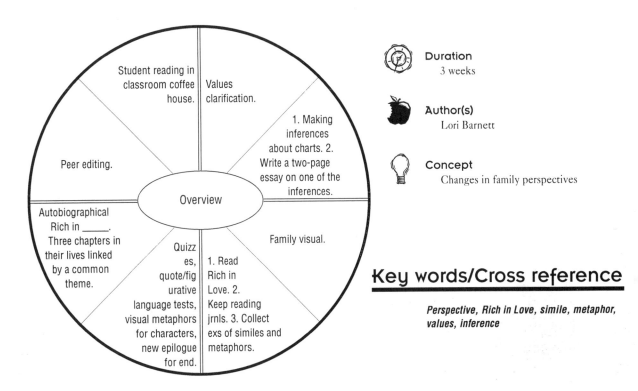

Student reading in classroom coffee house.

Values clarification.

1. Making inferences about charts. 2. Write a two-page essay on one of the inferences.

Peer editing.

Overview

Autobiographical Rich in ____. Three chapters in their lives linked by a common theme.

Family visual.

Quizzes, quote/figurative language tests, visual metaphors for characters, new epilogue for end.

1. Read Rich in Love. 2. Keep reading jrnls. 3. Collect exs of similes and metaphors.

Duration
3 weeks

Author(s)
Lori Barnett

Concept
Changes in family perspectives

Key words/Cross reference

Perspective, Rich in Love, simile, metaphor, values, inference

Overview

Objective
As part of an ongoing study of the concept of perspective in junior English, students will explore changing family values as illustrated in the novel, *Rich in Love*, by Josephine Humphreys. Students will explore the idea that as individual family members change, we learn more about our own perspectives on things. Families can weather these changes and surprise us with their resilience. Moreover, bad experiences, as well as good, strengthen our values and make us stronger people.

About the Author
Lori Barnett is a high school English teacher and Staff Development Leader in the Ridgewood, New Jersey schools. She is a certified 4MAT Trainer and consultant.

Required Resources
Rich in Love by Josephine Humphreys, journals, materials for book making.

Bibliography
Values Clarification by Simon, Howe, Kirschenbaum.

Quadrant 1—Experience

Right Mode—Connect

Values clarification.

Objective

Students will examine their own value systems.

Activity

Using Strategy #1 in the Values Clarification book, students are to make a list of 20 things, small or large, they love to do. Using the left hand margin of the paper, students are to code their responses in the following manner: $: anything that costs more than $5-7 (amount may vary) every time it is done; The letter A placed next to items the students prefer to do alone; The letter P next to those items the student prefers to do with people, and A-P next to those items for which he has no preference (alone or with people); The letters PL are to be placed next to items which require planning; The code N-5 is to be placed next to those items which would not have been listed 5 years ago; The numbers 1-5 are to be placed beside the five most important items in descending order of preference. (5 least favorite, and so on) Students share results in groups. For homework, students are to give the activity to one or more family members to fill out, and they are to bring in the results for homework.

Assessment

Completion of task.

Left Mode—Examine

1. Making inferences about charts. 2. Write a two-page essay on one of the inferences.

Objective

To encourage students to make inferences about themselves and others in their families.

Activity

Students share individual charts with group members, noting similarities and differences. Students are asked to speculate on whether differences in group are based on varying likes or dislikes or real differences in value systems. Students then make a few inferences based on the information listed on their own charts and the charts of their families. Students write a 2-page essay on one of those inferences for homework.

Assessment

Degree of participation, strength of writing.

Quadrant 2—Concepts

Right Mode—Image

Family visual.

Objective

To explore the similarity and differences in students' individual and family values systems.

Activity

Create a visual of your family showing how the information from yours and your family members' charts differ or intertwine. You may use representational or non-representational images to communicate your ideas.

Assessment

Thoroughness, ability to visualize a values system.

Left Mode—Define

1. Read Rich in Love. 2. Keep reading journals. 3. Collect examples of similes and metaphors.

Objective

To identify Lucille's values and how they differ from those of her family and peers.

Activity

Read the first 6 chapters and keep a reading journal which keeps track of Lucille's "philosophy" on things. Locate similes and metaphors which relate to her philosophies. Finish the novel.

Assessment

Completion of reading and journal assignments.

Quadrant 3—Applications

 ### Left Mode—Try

Quizzes, quote/figurative language tests, visual metaphors for characters, new epilogue for end.

Objective

To appreciate the novel for its figurative and thematic power. To encourage students to see figurative language as a means of recognizing a character's voice.

Activity

Quizzes, figurative language/quote tests, visual metaphors for characters in the novel, new epilogue for the end.

Assessment

Varies according to activity.

 ### Right Mode—Extend

Autobiographical Rich in _____. Three chapters in their lives linked by a common theme.

Objective

As Lucille realizes that she is "rich in love," students will realize that they, too, are "rich" in a quality maybe unbeknownst to them.

Activity

Students are to take the short essay written in 1L, expand it, and examine it for thematic potential. They are to determine what about themselves is "rich" (in laughter, recklessness, curiosity, etc.) and write three chapters from their own lives that illustrate this idea. Students are to include figurative language in their writing in the way that Humphreys employs it in the first person with Lucille.

Assessment

Quality of writing, ability to see common themes developing.

Quadrant 4—Creations

 ### Left Mode—Refine

Peer editing.

Objective

Students will celebrate similarities and differences among their "books" and provide support through peer editing.

Activity

Students read each others "books," and regroup according to similar themes. Students peer-edit each others' work. Students pick the single best effort from the individual groups.

Assessment

Level of group involvement.

 ### Right Mode—Integrate

Student reading in classroom coffee house.

Objective

For students to celebrate themselves and their work.

Activity

Having chosen five of the best examples, authors hire: publishers to print copies, illustrators, promotional people and organizers to present a "coffee house reading" in the classroom to which the public can be invited. Books are displayed in classroom/library after reading.

Assessment

Smoothness of each part of preparation/presentation.

Symbolism

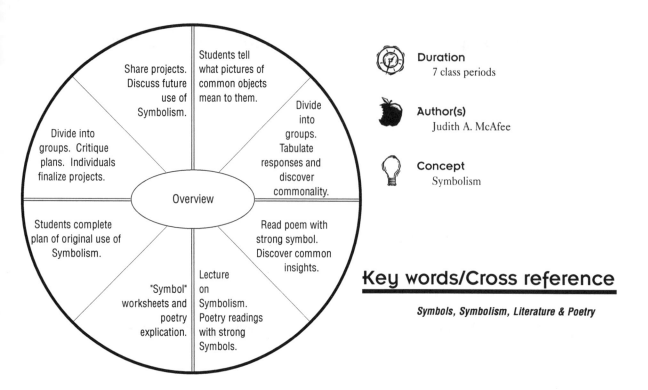

Duration
7 class periods

Author(s)
Judith A. McAfee

Concept
Symbolism

Key words/Cross reference

Symbols, Symbolism, Literature & Poetry

Overview

Objective
Students will understand that a symbol enhances the meaning of any art form, especially literature.

About the Author
Judith A. McAfee teaches English at Newburgh Free Academy, Newburgh City School District, Newburgh, NY. She is a certified 4MAT System Trainer for her school district.

Author's Notes
This unit has been particularly effective with low-achieving high school students.

Quadrant 1—Experience

 Right Mode—Connect

Students tell what pictures of common objects mean to them.

Objective

To help students see that symbols are all around them as part of everyday life.

Activity

Divide the board into four quadrants, and have students divide and number 4 pieces of paper. Put a drawing of a common symbol in each quadrant of board (suggestions: heart, scales, skull and crossbones, stork) and have students write word or phrase describing it on paper of same number. Teacher answers also, and tapes his/her responses face down on board for later use.

Assessment

Completed sheet divided into parts and submitted as requested.

 Left Mode—Examine

Divide into groups. Tabulate responses and discover commonality.

Objective

To show that we have similar to identical ideas of what some things mean. To introduce common thought patterns on which Symbolism is based.

Activity

Divide students into four groups and assign each a drawing from the board. Give group the submitted papers for what drawing means to classmates. Record-keepers tabulate answers on board by drawing. Discuss results. Group spokespersons present conclusions to class. Uncover teacher answers and compare.

Assessment

Behavior appropriate to task. Logical conclusions.

Quadrant 2—Concepts

 Right Mode—Image

Read poem with strong symbol. Discover common insights.

Objective

To read a poem with a symbol. To see the symbol and realize that it means about the same thing to everyone who reads that poem.

Activity

Students read poem, *"Mother to Son"* by Langston Hughes. Working independently, students draw an interpretive symbol for the poem and write a word or phrase explaining its meaning. Have them tape on tack board as they finish, allowing them to see the similarities in their work.

Assessment

Identification of symbol and understanding of its meaning.

 Left Mode—Define

Lecture on Symbolism. Poetry readings with strong symbols.

Objective

To see that symbols enrich meaning. To analyze poem for symbolic meaning.

Activity

Teacher lectures on Symbolism including definition, purpose, famous examples. Use *"Mother to Son"* to show students how to analyze a poem. Students read *"Brown Baby"* by Oscar Brown, Jr. and "Johnny" by M. Merchant.

Assessment

Attentiveness. Note taking (periodic notebook checks).

Symbolism

Quadrant 3—Applications

Left Mode—Try

"Symbol" worksheets and poetry explication.

Objective

To reinforce understanding by working with symbols. To develop a symbol bank (a glossary of common symbols).

Activity

Symbol worksheet (pictures provided and students give meaning). Check own answers when complete. Students choose either "Brown Baby" or "Johnny" to analyze using system provided by teacher.

Assessment

Poem analysis.

Right Mode—Extend

Students complete plan of original use of Symbolism.

Objective

To personalize symbolism and use it effectively in original work.

Activity

Plan the use of a symbol in art or literature. Music lyric acceptable. Plan should include theme and subject matter as well as what the Symbol is and how it will be used.

Assessment

Completion of plan.

Quadrant 4—Creations

Left Mode—Refine

Divide into groups. Critique plans. Individuals finalize projects.

Objective

To improve student ability to analyze the use and appropriateness of symbols.

Activity

Divide into four groups. Share individual plan with group for analysis of symbol validity in context used. Using suggestions, make complete plan into finished project.

Assessment

Quality of analysis. Quality of finished project.

Right Mode—Integrate

Share projects. Discuss future use of Symbolism.

Objective

To understand the value of Symbolism in visual art. To encourage the use of symbols in original student work.

Activity

Posting or publication of projects and gallery time for viewing/reading. Come together for class discussion of symbolism and how it leads to conceptualizing of our ideas.

Assessment

Essay exam on symbolism as a visual reinforcement which enhances and extends meaning.

Creating An Environment

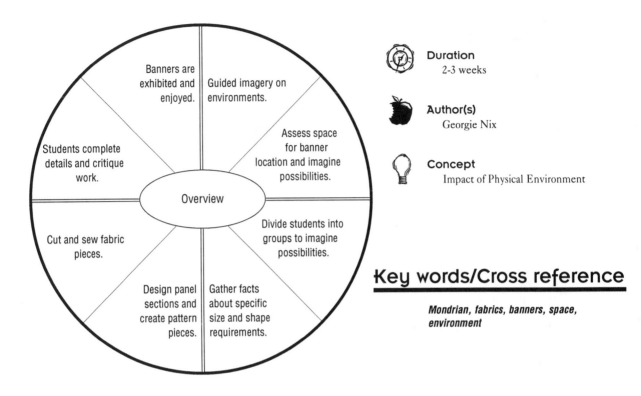

Overview

- Banners are exhibited and enjoyed.
- Guided imagery on environments.
- Assess space for banner location and imagine possibilities.
- Divide students into groups to imagine possibilities.
- Gather facts about specific size and shape requirements.
- Design panel sections and create pattern pieces.
- Cut and sew fabric pieces.
- Students complete details and critique work.

Duration
2-3 weeks

Author(s)
Georgie Nix

Concept
Impact of Physical Environment

Key words/Cross reference

Mondrian, fabrics, banners, space, environment

Overview

Objective

The spaces around us help to determine the way we feel and the way we act. Creating a positive learning environment is a goal of all exemplary schools. Following discussion on the characteristics of environments, the students will create fabric banners based on the paintings of artist Piet Mondrian. The banners will be hung in the school hallways, library, cafeteria, stairways or any space deemed appropriate by the students, to be enjoyed by one and all.

About the Author

Georgie Nix teaches both Visual and Performing Arts at Franklin Regional Junior High School, Murrysville, Pennsylvania. In addition to twenty-two years experience as a mid-level arts teacher, she has two years teaching experience at the elementary level. For the past four years she has been involved in the Getty Center for Education in the Arts discipline-based art instruction.

Required Resources

Graph paper, Colored pencils, Scissors, Roll paper, Pins, Nylon flag material, Thread, Sewing machine, Metal grommets, Wire

Bibliography

Examples of the works of artist Piet Mondrian.

Creating An Environment

Quadrant 1—Experience

Right Mode—Connect

Guided imagery on environments.

Objective

Using guided imagery, the students will discuss the effect environment has on the mood, motivation and attitudes of people.

Activity

Ask the students to close their eyes and think about:
1. The way they feel in a variety of environments: Hospitals, Disney World, school, home, church, the beach, etc.
2. Why environmental elements make space feel the way it does.
   • How colors effect us.
   • How sounds effect us.
   • How smells effect us.
   • How movement effects us.

Assessment

Reflection on types of spaces (Aesthetics).

Left Mode—Examine

Assess space for banner location and imagine possibilities.

Objective

The students will explore spaces in the school and try to brainstorm ideas for a banner installation.

Activity

As students tour the school they will:
1. Consider how banners might change the environment of an area in the school.
2. Brainstorm about banner characteristics to be used.
3. Consider various banner shapes, sizes, colors, etc.

Assessment

Shared ideas on existing spaces and the changes banners might make to it. (Aesthetics).

Quadrant 2—Concepts

Right Mode—Image

Divide students into groups to imagine possibilities.

Objective

The students will transfer the idea of creating an environment to banners, based on geometric designs.

Activity

1. View examples of the geometric paintings by artist Piet Mondrian.
2. Divide class into groups of 2-4.
3. Assign each group to a panel.
4. Explain how panels will be connected to form banners.
5. Discuss in small groups how the work of Piet Mondrian might be an inspiration for their banner panel.

Assessment

Quality of student translating the work of Mondrian into a design for a banner panel (Art History).

Left Mode—Define

Gather facts about specific size and shape requirements.

Objective

The students will collect information on banner requirements as they review the entire banner building process.

Activity

1. Review banner process:
   • Working on graph paper, use squares, triangles and rectangles to create a design for a banner panel.
   • Check designs with the design of the group(s) on either side of their panel.
   • Color in graph paper design.
   • Check color scheme with the colors of the group(s) on either side of their panel.

Assessment

Developing banner criteria through Art Production and Art Criticism.

Creating An Environment

Quadrant 3—Applications

Left Mode—Try

Design panel sections and create pattern pieces.

Objective

The students will create a 2' x 3' drawing of their panel design to be used as a pattern.

Activity

1. Complete 2' x 3' colored panel design on graph paper.
2. Using a 2' x 3' piece of white roll paper, enlarge and transfer design.
3. Trace over each shape using black marker.
4. Write color name on each shape.

Assessment

Complete patterns for banner panel (Art Production).

Right Mode—Extend

Cut and sew fabric pieces.

Objective

The students will build their banner panel.

Activity

1. Carefully cut out one pattern piece from paper.
2. Pin paper pattern piece to the matching fabric color.
3. Cut out the fabric pieces as precisely as possible.
4. Repeat for all pieces of fabric.
5. As each piece of fabric is cut, lay it out on a table as you would put together a puzzle.
6. When all fabric pieces have been cut out and laid on the table, have them checked by the teacher.
7. You are now ready to begin sewing the banner panel (Sewing may be completed by the students, the teacher or a parent - depending on sewing skills.)
8. Place two fabric pieces together, one on top of another overlapping about 1/8 inch.
9. Pin the pieces together.
10. Using a small zig-zag stitch, sew the fabric pieces together.
11. Continue to pin and sew until all pieces are assembled.

Assessment

Cooperative learning through Art Production.

Quadrant 4—Creations

Left Mode—Refine

Students complete details and critique work.

Objective

The students will complete finishing details on individual panels, attach panels together and critique work.

Activity

1. Trim excess fabric from seams on individual panels.
2. Sew banner panels together.
3. Sew fabric strip to top of banner.
4. Attach metal grommets to top of fabric strip for hanging.
5. Critique group panel designs, craftsmanship of work and completed banners.

Assessment

Group discussion on completed work (Art Production and Art Criticism).

Right Mode—Integrate

Banners are exhibited and enjoyed.

Objective

The banners will be hung in the school to be enjoyed by everyone.

Activity

After banners are exhibited, students will complete a short writing on the banner making experience.

Assessment

Comments on the experience from a discipline-based point of view.

American Revolution

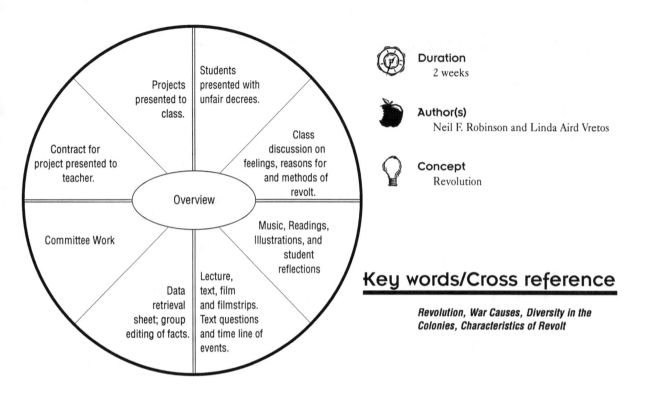

Projects presented to class.

Students presented with unfair decrees.

Contract for project presented to teacher.

Class discussion on feelings, reasons for and methods of revolt.

Overview

Committee Work

Music, Readings, Illustrations, and student reflections

Data retrieval sheet; group editing of facts.

Lecture, text, film and filmstrips. Text questions and time line of events.

Duration
2 weeks

Author(s)
Neil F. Robinson and Linda Aird Vretos

Concept
Revolution

Key words/Cross reference

Revolution, War Causes, Diversity in the Colonies, Characteristics of Revolt

Overview

Objective
To teach students the concept of "Revolution" and its affect on the American colonies break with England at the time of the Revolutionary War.

About the Author
Neil F. Robinson is a classroom teacher at West Potomac High School, Fairfax County Schools, Alexandria, VA. He has been a teacher for over fifteen years. Linda Aird Vretos is Head Librarian at West Potomac High School. She has over twenty years experience in education. They are participants in the Fairfax County 4MAT Implementation Project led by Dr. June Price.

Required Resources
Selections of 18th Century music, artwork and illustrations, and original writings.

Editor's Note
This plan was originally published in 1990. We recognize that the A/V suggestions are dated; however, the plan is still a good example of 4MAT in action.

Bibliography
Sound Filmstrips:
Where Historians Disagree: Origins of the American Revolution. Random House/Educational Enrichment Materials Production, 1986. Order N. 537-69905-8.
The Oncoming Revolution, 1775-1776. New York Times: Filmstrip Current Affairs, 1975. Library of Congress Card No. 75-734557.
Silent Filmstrips:
American Revolution. Life, 1950.
A History of the American People: The American Revolution. Society for Visual Education, Inc., 1948.

Authors' Note
Although copyrighted 40 years ago, these filmstrips are used to reinforce the content with students who read below grade level.
16mm Film:
The American Revolution, 1770-1783 - "A Conversation with Lord North."
Phoenix, 1971.

Quadrant 1—Experience

 ### Right Mode—Connect

Students presented with unfair decrees.

Objective

To create a direct experience engaging students in the concept of "revolt."

Activity

Students are presented with the following two major "decrees" which have been sent down from the central school administration.

SCHOOL DISTRICT DECREES:

The following actions are effective immediately!

1. Students will pay a tax on all denim apparel!
2. Students may not wear Reeboks®, Adidas®, Nike®, or Fila® apparel!
3. Students may not wear any type of jewelry!
4. Students may not wear make-up, perfume, cologne, hair spray, or mousse!
5. Students may not wear Benetton®, Guess®, or LA Gear® apparel!

By order of the School District, there will be no appeal of this directive!

FURTHER SCHOOL DISTRICT DECREES:

The following actions are effective immediately:

1. Students must pay a daily locker fee!
2. Students must pay a daily cafeteria fee! Students may not bring bag lunches.
3. Students must pay a daily parking fee!
4. Students must drive automobiles manufactured in the United States of America!
5. Students must pay a building entrance fee upon arrival in the morning!
6. Students must pay a building exit fee upon departure in the afternoon!
7. Students must pay a daily school bus rider fee!
8. Students must pay a daily library fee!
9. Students must pay a daily soft drink machine rental fee!

All revenues collected as a result of this directive will be sent immediately and directly to the School District Central Office!

By order of the School District, there will be no appeal of this Directive!

The teacher presents in a serious manner the rationale for each decree, hoping to convince the class that these new rules are real and in effect immediately.

Assessment

Engagement of students; reaction to unfairness of decrees.

 ### Left Mode—Examine

Class discussion on feelings, reasons for and methods of revolt.

Objective

To develop listening skills and group discussion techniques. To distinguish between violent and non-violent revolt.

Activity

Teacher leads student discussion analyzing feelings and reaction to the two decrees. Working in small groups, students discuss the characteristics of revolt, focusing on methods of protest for both violent and non-violent revolt. Small group findings are shared with the class as a whole.

Assessment

Contributions to small and large group discussion.

Quadrant 2—Concepts

 ### Right Mode—Image

Music, readings, illustrations, and student reflections.

Objective

To create a feeling on the part of the students for the diversity of American society in the years leading up to the Revolutionary War.

Activity

While listening to music from the Revolutionary Period and viewing original artwork portraying communities and cities of the time, students will listen as teacher reads excerpts from original diaries and letters. In small group discussion, students will try to capture the feelings of the people during those times. Each group will create a mindmap to be shared with the rest of the class.

Assessment

Involvement of students in guided imagery. Quality of group mindmap.

Left Mode—Define

Lecture, text, film and filmstrips. Text questions and timeline of events.

Objective
To comprehend the structure of the institutions and events of the period preceding the Revolutionary War.

Activity
Students read assigned text chapters. Teacher lecture covers significant events, with accompanying filmstrips and film. Students answer questions in text and create a timeline for chronicling significant events. In addition, they will complete filmstrip and movie worksheets.

Assessment
Student notetaking and teacher checking for understanding through class discussion and completion of text/worksheet questions.

Quadrant 3—Applications

 ## Left Mode—Try

Data retrieval sheet; group editing of facts.

Objective
To analyze the actions of Parliament which affected the Colonists, 1763-1775.

Activity
Using information from class notes and the text assignment, students will complete a data retrieval sheet. They are responsible for identifying key dates and actions. Individual students will refine and edit their completed data in cooperation with three other students.

Assessment
Completion of assigned data retrieval sheet.

 ## Right Mode—Extend

Committee Work.

Objective
To extend and apply what has been learned.

Activity
The class is subdivided into Committees of Correspondence. Based on research in the media center,

each Committee will compile a list of its colonial grievances, adopt and replicate its own sign and flag, select a song from the era, and create an original diary entry and letter.

Assessment
Group plans for project completion. Individual student contributions to group effort.

Quadrant 4—Creations

 ## Left Mode—Refine

Contract for project presented to teacher.

Objective
To edit and refine projects.

Activity
Each team presents its contractual project plan to the teacher. Each plan must include activities for which individual members are responsible as well as criteria for evaluation, both for a team grade as well as for individual grades.

Assessment
Quality of team proposals.

 ## Right Mode—Integrate

Projects presented to class.

Objective
To share and enjoy what has been learned.

Activity
Student Committees of Correspondence present their final projects to each other. Presentation must include: music, skits or role play, and written work which expresses why the Committee does or does not desire revolt.

Assessment
Quality of team final efforts and enjoyment of each other's work.

Slavery

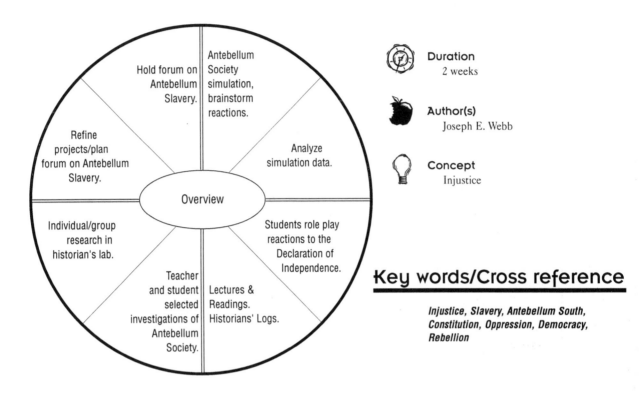

Overview

- Antebellum Society simulation, brainstorm reactions.
- Analyze simulation data.
- Students role play reactions to the Declaration of Independence.
- Lectures & Readings. Historians' Logs.
- Teacher and student selected investigations of Antebellum Society.
- Individual/group research in historian's lab.
- Refine projects/plan forum on Antebellum Slavery.
- Hold forum on Antebellum Slavery.

Duration
2 weeks

Author(s)
Joseph E. Webb

Concept
Injustice

Key words/Cross reference

Injustice, Slavery, Antebellum South, Constitution, Oppression, Democracy, Rebellion

Overview

Objective

Students will investigate the divisive impact of slavery on the economic, political and social life of America during the Antebellum Era.

About the Author

Joseph E. Webb is an Instructional Specialist with the North Carolina Department of Public Instruction. He is a certified 4MAT trainer working in the department's Southeast Technical Assistance Center in Jacksonville, North Carolina.

Required Resources

Wrapped candies, newsprint, art supplies, primary source materials, artifacts and reference materials.

Bibliography

Books:

Bishop, Jim. *The Day Lincoln Was Shot.* New York: Harper & Row Publishers, 1964.

Chesnutt, Mary B. *A Diary From Dixie.* ed. C. Vann Woodward, 1981. New Haven, CT, Yale University Press, 1981. Provides the perspective of a southern woman whose world is falling apart.

Davidson, Margaret. *Frederick Douglass Fights for Freedom.* New York: Scholastic, Inc., 1968.

Faulkner, William J. *The Days When the Animals Talked.* New York: Modern Curriculum Press, Inc., 1977. Focuses on folktales.

Nash, Gary B., ed. *Retracing the Past: Readings in the History of the American People.* New York: Harper & Row, 1990. An excellent source of primary source documents. See chapters 12 and 13 for folktales and European travel journals.

Nash, Gary B., et al. *The American People: Creating a Nation and a Society.* New York: Harper and Collins, 1990. An excellent college text, which interweaves primary source material.

Olmstead, Frederick B. *A Journey in the Back Country.* New York: Mason Bros., 1863. An excellent reference containing the insights of a northerner traveling through the antebellum south.

Phillips, U.B. *American Negro Slavery.* 1918.

Joyner, Charles. *Down by the Riverside*. Urbana, Illinois, University of Illinois Press, 1984. An excellent monograph focusing on the daily life, customs and religion in the ante-bellum slave community.

Sandburg, Carl. *Abraham Lincoln: The Prairie Years and the War Years*. New York: Harcourt, Brace, Jovanovich, 1974.

Sherwood, Robert. *Abe Lincoln in Illinois*. New York: Charles Scribner and Sons, 1939.

Stampp, Kenneth. *The Peculiar Institution*. 1956.

Tise, Larry E. Confronting the Issue of Slavery (Chap. 9). in *The North Carolina Experience: An Interpretive and Documentary History*, eds. Lindsay S. Butler and Alan D. Watson. Chapel Hill: The University of North Carolina Press, 1984. An excellent collection of diaries, letters and public documents including the Slave Code of 1741.

Documentaries/Films/Slides:

American History Slide Collection, group H.

Roots, e.g., "Uprooted" (50 mins.) focuses on the black family and the plight of slave women.

Slavery (30 mins) uses spirituals and testimony of former slaves.

Journal:

Metcalf, Fay. *"Teaching with Historic Places: When Rice Was King."* Social Education 56 (November/December, 1992) insert following p. 408. Part of a series of activity packets produced by the National Park Service and the National Trust for Historic Preservation.

Quadrant 1—Experience

 Right Mode—Connect

Antebellum Society simulation, brainstorm reactions.

Objective

To create an experience to help students apprehend the impact of slavery on individuals living in southern ante-bellum society.

Activity

Involve students in a classroom simulation of a society based on slavery and conditions of inequality.

1) Before class scatter a large quantity of wrapped candy mints around the room to represent the wealth of the society within the classroom. They will be "harvested" and consumed by students. Some of the candy should be hard to reach imperiling the lives of those who might attempt to harvest it.

2) Play selected samples of plantation songs/spirituals as students enter the classroom.

3) Divide the students into the following groups representing various elements of antebellum society: a) plantation owner and his family, b) field slaves, c) household slaves, d) free blacks, e) abolitionist(s), f) Yeomen (white non-slave holding farmers), g) overseer(s) [to be selected by the Plantation Owner from among the Yeomen].

Apportion the students among the groupings such that the slave groups comprise the majority of the students. Select a small group to role-play the plantation owner and his family. Assign them to a privileged space in the classroom to represent the "big house" and surrounding plantation. The Yeomen and free blacks should be confined to the perimeter of the classsroom space to represent their relative status in antebellum southern society. The Yeomen should have a designated space to "harvest." Make sure their space is limited and supplied with relatively few pieces of candy. The space for free blacks should be far more limited and contain fewer pieces of candy. Select one or two students to role-play the overseer looking after the interest of the plantation owner. Also, select one or two students to observe the scene from the perspective of an abolitionist.

4) Initiate the simulation helping students assume their respective roles as the field hands "harvest the wealth of the plantation" under the watchful eye of the overseer and the household slaves serve the plantation owner and his family. The remaining

groups enact their roles on the fringes of the classroom society.

5) Interact with role players as needed to encourage and sustain the experience. Monitor the emotional tone and note key events for the post-simulation debrief.

6) After all the "wealth has been harvested," the candy should be collected into three piles of distinctly unequal portions. The largest pile should be before the plantation owner, the next largest should be before the Yeoman, and the smallest should be before the free blacks. The abolitionists do not share in the wealth. At this point, the plantation owner pays his overseer(s) and feeds his slaves. Encourage the students to eat of the fruits of their labor and enjoy.

7) Form reaction groups to brainstorm and record on newsprint a list of feelings and thoughts engendered by the experience. As each group reports out, post their responses.

Assessment
The degrees of student involvement and the emotional response of the role players in the simulation. e.g., Did the mood among the slaves shift from laughter to somber, passive acceptance of their status in life or to violent rebellion? Did the overseer(s) assume a demanding, cruel demeanor?

 ## Left Mode—Examine

Analyze simulation data.

Objective
To process/analyze the experience.

Activity
1) Conduct a debrief of the simulation in which students analyze the simulation using the K-W-L charting procedure. a) Label a sheet of newsprint, "What we know" or hypothesize about slavery and antebellum society. Label a second sheet, "What we want to know" about slavery and antebellum society. Label a third sheet, "What we learned" about slavery and antebellum society. Record and save student responses. Leave the third sheet blank for later use. b) To foster maximum student involvement and to illicit the broadest possible range of student responses, use the think/pair/share technique.

2) Raise questions to help students examine personal connections between the experience and their prior knowledge of slavery and its influence on the lives of individuals living before the civil war. For example: a) Several of you who played the role of slaves expressed hostility toward the plantation owner when he limited you to one piece of candy for all your work, while a few of you said nothing. How do you account for this difference in reaction? What does it suggest about how slaves might have coped with their enslavement? b) Continue the inquiry in like manner focusing on such issues as the relationship that seemed to emerge between and among various groups within the simulation. What does this suggest about the relationships that existed in antebellum society? What can we hypothesize about the impact of slavery on antebellum society in general? What do we need or want to know?

3) Tell the students that they will have an opportunity to be historians as they seek answers to these questions during this unit of study.

Assessment
Level of student involvement in discussion and quality of contributions to the group.

Quadrant 2—Concepts

Right Mode—Image

Students role play reactions to the Declaration of Independence.

Objective

To help students imagine the incompatibility between slavery and the political ideals of liberty and equality expressed in the Declaration of Independence.

Activity

1) Proclaim the following excerpt from the Declaration of Independence: "We hold these truths to be self-evident that all men are created equal and are endowed by their creator with certain unalienable rights; that among these are life, liberty, and the pursuit of happiness; that, to secure these rights, governments are instituted among men, deriving their just powers from the consent of the governed; that whenever any form of government becomes destructive of these ends, it is the right of the people to alter or to abolish it . . . ." Conclude by saying that our forefathers used these words to justify rebellion against oppression.

2) Have students dramatically or graphically represent the inconsistencies between these words and the inequalities experienced in the simulation.

or

3) Re-enact the responses of slaves, free blacks, Yeomen, plantation wives, and other hypothetical individuals upon hearing this proclamation.

Assessment

Variety of responses, intensity of emotions; engagement of students and quality of individual contributions.

Left Mode—Define

Lectures & Readings. Historians' Logs.

Objective

To define and characterize the "peculiar institution of slavery" that buttressed southern antebellum society betraying the ideals of liberty and equality expressed in the Declaration of Independence.

Activity

1) Teacher structures mini-lectures, leads class discussions, and employs a variety of media in order to provide learning experiences accommodating the

need for and interest in specific information generated in Quadrant 1. As questions raised during the K-W-L process are answered, expanded or discarded, note the changes. As new questions arise, add them to the "Want to Know" column. Major Concepts/Themes: the institution of slavery as the foundation of southern antebellum society; the lifestyles, roles and status of individuals and groups living within that society; modes of social control and the means of coping, avoiding, and/or rebelling employed by master and slave, the role of religion in plantation life, and the conflicting attitudes and viewpoints toward the ideals of liberty and equality inherent in antebellum society.

2) To increase student comprehension of how historians approach the study of history, pose questions that enable students to compare divergent views expressed by the experts and the manner in which each supports his/her arguments. e.g., Was the institution of slavery an essentially benign system or one that perpetuated racial injustice? Read or have students read brief excerpts from the *American Negro Slavery* by U.B. Phillips (1918) or *The Peculiar Institution* by Kenneth Stampp (1956). What factors might account from their widely divergent views on slavery? Invite a historian to give a guest lecture on some aspect of slavery and to discuss his/her work as a historian.

3) Students maintain a "historians log" in which they record basic factual information presented, answers to questions raised in the K-W-L process and additional ones raised in class, personal reflections and notes to guide individual research/study, etc.

Assessment

Teacher checking for understanding/level of student questions; notebooks.

Quadrant 3—Applications

Left Mode—Try

Teacher and student-selected investigations of Antebellum Society.

Objective

To reinforce the unit concepts and to provide opportunities for students to engage in historical research.

Activity

1) Teacher-selected activities structured to provide opportunities for students to practice the skills of information acquisition, information processing, and historical interpretation. For example: a) Visit a plantation site, e.g., Somerset Place located in Creswell, N.C. b) Explore life on the Chicora Wood Plantation using the primary source documents contained in an activity packet compiled by Fay Metcalf. See bibliography. c) Read Abraham Lincoln's essay, "On Defining Liberty" and his speech, "A House Divided"; have students construct a graphic organizer comparing the divergent viewpoints of an abolitionist and a proponent of slavery.

2) History Lab

   Establish a variety of learning stations supplied with learning materials that will allow students in small work groups or individually to expand their conceptual knowledge and to experiment with the work of history. The stations should include a wide selection of materials and questions or discussion starters such as: a) A collection of maps depicting the concentration of slave populations from 1820 to 1860 and the areas where various crops such as rice and cotton were produced. Ask students to draw conclusions about the relationship between the concentration of slave populations and the production of a given crop. b) Statistical data such as population distribution charts for each state showing the percentage of white, slave, and free black inhabitants. Based on this data, which states would most strongly favor the preservation or abolition of slavery? c) Diaries, letters and other personal items representing a particular point of view, e.g., slave narratives and the diary of Mary Chesnutt. d) Public and private estate documents, e.g., copy of the slave codes for various slave states, bills of sale for slaves bought and sold. e) Photographs depicting various aspects of slave culture. f) Recordings of spirituals and other period music. g) Literary collections, e.g., fictional and non-fictional accounts of slavery and plantation life, e.g., Uncle Tom's Cabin, published speeches of various abolitionists and proponents of slavery. As students work through the materials, facilitate their exploration through open-ended questions. Provide opportunities for brief mini-conferences in which you encourage your student historians to share some new insight or interest gleaned from the history lab. Student choice is paramount in lab activities to ensure balance between teacher direction and student initiative.

3) In cooperative groups, students construct web charts on slavery and antebellum society. Students post and share web charts.

Assessment

Quality of individual and group work, individual contributions to the web charts, and engagement of students with choice activities.

Right Mode—Extend

Individual/group research in historian's lab.

Objective

To extend and apply concepts learned.

Activity

1) Students in small groups or individually select a topic for further investigation. At this point, the "history lab" activities assume greater importance as students focus on specific areas of inquiry. Teacher and students collaboratively add to the resources in the "history lab."

2) Students select a mode of project presentation suited to their particular learning style preference and interest. A wide variety of art supplies and other production materials should be available for student use.

3) Hold large group mini-conferences affording students opportunities to share their "work in progress" and to learn from each other. The teacher facilitates such conferences by diverting student questions to one another whenever possible and linking students with similar interests and needs.

Assessment

Quality and efficiency of project planning; the degree and quality of student participation in mini-conferences.

Quadrant 4—Creations

Left Mode—Refine

Refine projects/plan forum on Antebellum Slavery.

Objective
To edit and revise projects.

Activity
1) Teachers and students develop a planning/evaluation checklist tailored to this unit of study. 2) Teachers and students collaboratively evaluate, edit and revise projects as needed. 3) Teachers and students collaboratively plan the format and logistics of a public forum that would showcase their learnings. Planning and logistical tasks are divided among small groups and individuals. The teacher interacts to facilitate and support student initiatives as needed.

Assessment
Quality of student projects and public forum planning.

Right Mode—Integrate

Hold forum on Antebellum Slavery.

Objective
To share and celebrate learnings.

Activity
1) Hold a public forum on slavery in the antebellum era featuring student projects for invited guests. 2) Make a videotape of the forum to be included in the school library. 3) Re-play and enjoy the video. 4) The teacher and students affirm and celebrate their learnings in the unit by summarizing new insights about slavery on "post-it" notes. The notes are then posted on the sheet of newsprint entitled, "What we learned about slavery and Antebellum Society" as students leave the classroom.

Assessment
Quality of student presentations and degree of student engagement in the forum; variety and quality of learning reflected in the "post-it" notes. These notes provide an excellent source of ideas for the next 4MAT cycle focusing on the American Civil War and the emancipation of slaves.

Revisionist History

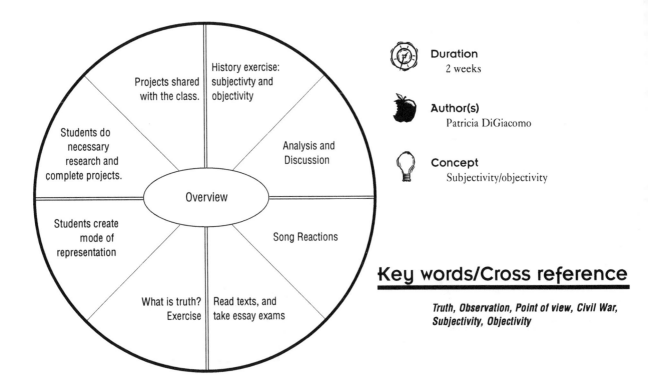

Projects shared with the class.

History exercise: subjectivty and objectivity

Students do necessary research and complete projects.

Analysis and Discussion

Overview

Students create mode of representation

Song Reactions

What is truth? Exercise

Read texts, and take essay exams

Duration
2 weeks

Author(s)
Patricia DiGiacomo

Concept
Subjectivity/objectivity

Key words/Cross reference

Truth, Observation, Point of view, Civil War, Subjectivity, Objectivity

Overview

Objective
Students will involve themselves in the writing of history to understand that no historical writing is free from subjectivity.

About the Author
Patricia DiGiacomo teaches at Dodd Junior High School, Cheshire, CT. She is a certified 4MAT Trainer for her school district.

Required Resources
Musical selections, film clips.

Quadrant 1—Experience

Right Mode—Connect

History exercise: subjectivity and objectivity.

Objective

To increase student understanding that history is not a mathematical science, but rather a constantly changing and vibrant blend of subjectivity and objectivity.

Activity

1) Class divided into four sections with each section facing a different wall. 2) One student sent out of room. 3) Teacher goes about the room doing usual and unusual things. 4) Student returns; all students face front.

Assessment

Each student writes down what he or she witnessed.

Left Mode—Examine

Analysis and Discussion.

Objective

To have students reflect on this experience.

Activity

1) The absent student attempts to piece together what actually happened from student lists. 2) Absent student shares with the class his/her perception of what happened. 3) Class determines "accuracy" of that moment of history. 4) Students discuss why their narrowed viewpoint made getting the "big picture" so difficult and perhaps then impossible.

Assessment

Students will hand in their original list and a rewrite when all of the knowledge has been pooled together.

Quadrant 2—Concepts

Right Mode—Image

Song Reactions.

Objective

To integrate the personal reflections with artistic expressions of the 1960's and 1860's.

Activity

1) Play 1960's pro-war music (Barry Sadler, "Ballad of the Green Beret"; Merle Haggard, "Okie from Muskoqee"). Anti-war (Country Joe and the Fish "We're All Going to Die Rag"; Barry Maquire, "Eve of Destruction". 2) Play "Dixie" and "Battle Hymn of the Republic."

Assessment

Students discuss their "reaction" to these musical examples.

Left Mode—Define

Read texts, and take essay exams.

Objective

To increase student knowledge of various published histories of the time period.

Activity

1) Students read their text. 2) Students read "traditional" Southern historians William Archibald Dunning and James Ford Rhodes. 3) Students read revisionist historian W.E.B. DuBois.

Assessment

Essay exam.

Quadrant 3—Applications

Left Mode—Try

What is truth? Exercise.

Objective
To reinforce concept of different "truths."

Activity
Show brief parts of video/films that show different aspects and point of view of the Civil War. Possible sources: "Gone With the Wind," "Red Badge of Courage," "Dances With Wolves," "They Died With Their Boots On," Ken Burns' "The Civil War." Students will write essays on the questions of point of view of each film, drawing their own conclusions as to the "truth" about the American Civil War.

Assessment
Student essays.

Right Mode—Extend

Students create mode of representation.

Objective
1) To personalize learning experience. 2) To increase students' ability to analyze and evaluate data. 3) To enhance students' understanding that they must seek the "truth."

Activity
Students choose to write, film, speak, perform, etc. a historical analysis of the Civil War. While the implementation must be "factual" the presentation will have a point of view.

Assessment
Student obtains approval of teacher for his/her project upon the submission of a written proposal.

Quadrant 4—Creations

Left Mode—Refine

Students do necessary research and complete projects.

Objective
To aid students in formulating their opinions and supporting them with relevant details.

Activity
1) Teacher guides completion of project. 2) Teacher provides library opportunities.

Assessment
Teacher checks progress of students.

Right Mode—Integrate

Projects shared with the class.

Objective
1) To bring full circle the students' personal learning experience. 2) To share what they have learned with others.

Activity
1) Presentation of student projects. 2) Discussion of the various points of view presented. 3) Class writes a consensus history.

Assessment
Projects will be graded by teacher.

Graphing Sinusoids

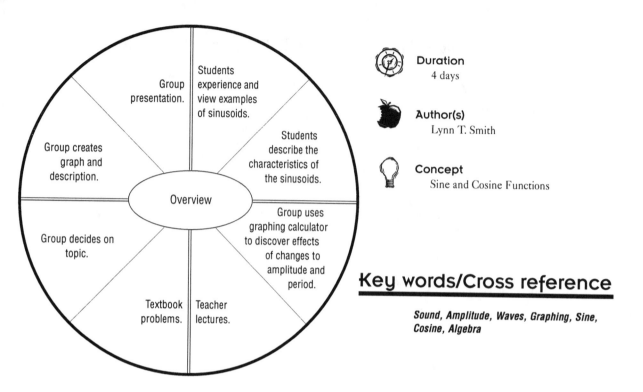

Group presentation.

Students experience and view examples of sinusoids.

Group creates graph and description.

Students describe the characteristics of the sinusoids.

Overview

Group decides on topic.

Group uses graphing calculator to discover effects of changes to amplitude and period.

Textbook problems.

Teacher lectures.

Duration
4 days

Author(s)
Lynn T. Smith

Concept
Sine and Cosine Functions

Key words/Cross reference

Sound, Amplitude, Waves, Graphing, Sine, Cosine, Algebra

Overview

Concept Statement Objective
The students will be able to analyze the sinusoid graph and its applications.

About the Author
Lynn Smith is a mathematics teacher at Academic Magnet High School, Charleston, SC. She is a certified 4MAT T.rainer.

Required Resources
Visuals of sinusoid waves which appear in nature; graphing calculators; teacher prepared worksheets.

Graphing Sinusoids

Quadrant 1—Experience

 ### Right Mode—Connect

Students experience and view examples of sinusoids.

Objective
The student will be able to visualize a sinusoid graph.

Activity
The students will do the "wave" (the kinesthetic wave that is done by fans at a football game). The students will also view pictures and physical examples of the sinusoid wave in nature.

Assessment
Student participation.

 ### Left Mode—Examine

Students describe the characteristics of the sinusoids.

Objective
The students will be able to compare and contrast the examples of the waves.

Activity
The students will list descriptions that compare and contrast the different waves and establish the patterns.

Assessment
The students' ability to construct a Venn diagram comparing and contrasting the waves.

Quadrant 2—Concepts

 ### Right Mode—Image

Group uses graphing calculator to discover effects of changes to amplitude and period.

Objective
The students will describe amplitude and period and the effects they have on the sinusoid graph.

Activity
The students will help the teacher construct the sine and cosine graph with the coordinates from the circle graph. The students will work in groups with the graphing calculator and discover patterns in changing the amplitude and period. (A teacher-designed worksheet will guide the students in this activity.)

Assessment
The ability of the students to discover the effect of changing the amplitude and period of the graph.

 ### Left Mode—Define

Teacher lectures.

Objective
The student will be able to graph the sine and closing functions. The student will be able to determine the amplitude and period of the sine and cosine functions.

Activity
The teacher will lecture.

Assessment
The ability of the students to answer the teacher's questions.

Graphing Sinusoids

Quadrant 3—Applications

 ## Left Mode—Try

Textbook problems.

Objective

The student will be able to construct the graphs of the sinusoid functions indicating period and amplitude.

Activity

Textbook problems.

Assessment

Completion of assignment.

Right Mode—Extend

Group decides on topic.

Objective

The students will be able to determine their own sinusoid graph.

Activity

The students will work in groups to pick an area of interest to them and find an example of a sinusoid graph. Some suggestions are music, tide tables, temperature over a period of time, moon changes, oscillator, or any other area the student may notice the sinusoid occurring.

Assessment

The students' ability to find a problem.

Quadrant 4—Creations

 ## Left Mode—Refine

Group creates graph and description.

Objective

The student will be able to determine the characteristics of the graph he chose to investigate.

Activity

The students will work in groups to graph their sinusoid function and to label its amplitude and period. They will make a chart depicting their investigations and results.

Assessment

The students' work.

 ## Right Mode—Integrate

Group presentation.

Objective

The student will be able to demonstrate his knowledge of the sinusoid function.

Activity

The students will present their function to the class and discuss its properties. The student will take a test on graphing the sine and cosine functions.

Assessment

Student presentation and test.

Patterns

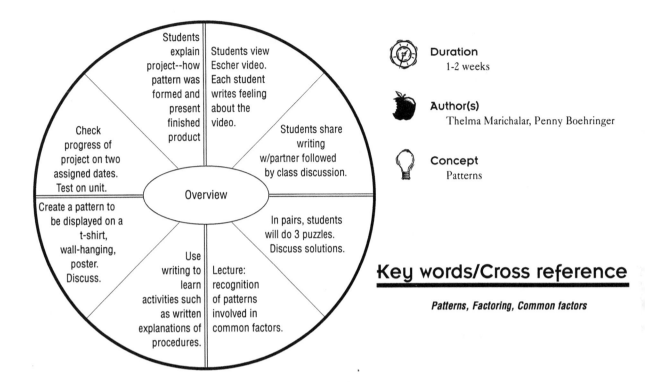

Duration
1-2 weeks

Author(s)
Thelma Marichalar, Penny Boehringer

Concept
Patterns

Key words/Cross reference

Patterns, Factoring, Common factors

Overview

Objective

About the Author(s)

Penny Boehringer has been a teacher for 25 years, the last 8 with Churchill High School in San Antonio, TX. Among her accomplishments, she was awarded Teacher of the Year in 1991 and 1992. Thelma Marichalar has taught for 20 years and was awarded Teacher of the Year in 1987. She currently teaches Algebra and Algebra II Honors as well as an SAT prep course for Churchill HS in San Antonio, TX.

Bibliography

Algebra II with Trigonometry, Merrill, 1990.
Algebra II with Trigonometry, Harcourt, Brace, Jovanovich, 1983.

Quadrant 1—Experience

Right Mode—Connect

Students view Escher video. Each student writes feeling about the video.

Objective

To help students understand the importance of patterns in life and everyday mathematics.

Activity

Students will be arranged in pairs or groups of four to view video. Ask students to write about their reactions/thoughts to the video. (Note: We created a seven minute video based on the work of artist M.C. Escher.)

Assessment

Quality of writing, participation and interest.

Left Mode—Examine

Students share writing w/partner followed by class discussion.

Objective

To enhance students' ability to discuss what they have seen, felt, and experienced. To arouse their curiosity for the material to be presented. To develop listening skills, group discussion techniques and opinion giving.

Activity

Students will discuss their thoughts with a partner. Students will share ideas with the class. Teacher will list thoughts, ideas, on board, being mindful that there is not a right or wrong response to any of the things discussed. The role of the teacher is to encourage discussion and thought.

Assessment

Quality of discussion. Were the students engaged? How many ideas were generated?

Quadrant 2—Concepts

Right Mode—Image

In pairs, students will do 3 puzzles. Discuss solutions.

Objective

To integrate the previous experience and discussion into the concept of patterns. To experience the importance of finding a pattern as a solution to a problem. To experience a solution which involves "seeing" from a different viewpoint.

Activity

Students work in pairs to solve three puzzles. Envelopes containing puzzle pieces are identified on the outside as "circle," "square," and "horse." Each group of students is asked to take an envelope labeled "circle" and empty the pieces onto their desk. They are told to work together to find a way to arrange the pieces and form a circle. Teacher monitors student progress. After all or most pairs have completed the puzzle, the teacher can demonstrate the solution using pre-cut pieces on an overhead projector. Follow the same procedure for the "square" puzzle which is a tangram and then the "horse" puzzle. The horse puzzle is an ancient Chinese puzzle which involves placing two riders which are in the proper position on the horses. No flipping or overlapping is allowed. This puzzle involves being able to visualize the given pieces in several ways. Follow up discussion on what is important in working the puzzles: Does looking for patterns help work the puzzles? Where have they seen or worked with patterns before (in math or elsewhere)? Examples: Art, English (Poetry), Chemistry, History ("History repeats itself"), Algebra II (patterns seen in multiplication unit just completed, in problem solving in math courses, geometry). Focus attention on the importance of patterns in life, jobs/careers where patterns are important—Electrician (circuit design), Fabric/wallpaper designs, Architect (building designs), Civil Engineer, Accountant, Music (Symphony), etc.

Assessment

Quality of discussion and participation. Creativity in finding solutions to puzzles. Quality of understanding of pattern concept in math and daily life.

Patterns

 ## Left Mode—Define

Lecture: recognition of patterns involved in common factors.

Objective
To enhance knowledge of factoring and to understand factoring as a concept of pattern. To listen to lectures. To increase notetaking skills. To ask relevant questions. To write analytically.

Activity
Teacher will teach factoring: 1) Identify types.
2) Recognize patterns.
3) Understand concepts using "writing-to-learn" activities. Students will identify: 1) Common factors,
2) Difference of two squares, 3) Sum and difference of two cubes, 4) Perfect square trinomials, and 5) Grouping. Teacher will demonstrate patterns involved in all processes.

Assessment
Students will identify and explain in writing the types of factoring and methods involved in factoring.

Quadrant 3—Applications

 ## Left Mode—Try

Use writing to learn activities such as written explanations of procedures.

Objective
To allow students to practice concepts and reinforce learning.

Activity
Teacher generated worksheets, factor puzzles (steps to problems written on separate 3" x 5" cards which students in groups of four must arrange in order), MATHO (math bingo), more writing assignments designed for clarity of explanations, quizzes.

Assessment
Quality and accuracy of above.

 ## Right Mode—Extend

Create a pattern to be displayed on a t-shirt, wall-hanging, poster. Discuss.

Objective
To personalize unit material. To enhance student creativity.

Activity
The students are required to choose a project which will involve creating a pattern to be displayed on a poster, a t-shirt, or wall hanging. This step is the planning step. Teacher will provide a timeline and completion date.

Assessment
Individual personalized plans.

Quadrant 4—Creations

Left Mode—Refine

Check progress of project on two assigned dates. Test on unit.

Objective

To enable students to make the connection between mathematics and everyday applications. To enhance student's ability to plan a learning project. To enhance ability to find resource material. To refine skills.

Activity

Students hand in project plans including description of project, outline of progress, and 8" x 10" sketch of pattern. Teacher checks plans making revisions as necessary. Students continue review of unit material using worksheets, games, writing activities.

Assessment

Quality of plans. Unit test.

Right Mode—Integrate

Students explain project—how pattern was formed—and present finished product

Objective

To enhance students' ability to complete a project. To share projects with class and have classmates teach each other what they have learned about patterns.

Activity

Each student presents a project to the class. The students must explain how the pattern used was created and how the finished product was achieved. Teacher will display all projects in classroom.

Assessment

How well each project meets previously established criteria. Quality of presentations and sharing.

Student Evaluation of 4MAT Process

I believe the 4MAT Method of teaching helps students understand by using a less structured, less strict way of teaching and learning. The old way taught that math was hard work and old and crotchety people loved it (don't ask me how I got that idea, but math teachers should have blue hair, arthritis and a metal edged ruler to swack knuckles with). Math is still hard, but this new way of organizing teaching helps a lot.

Sequences

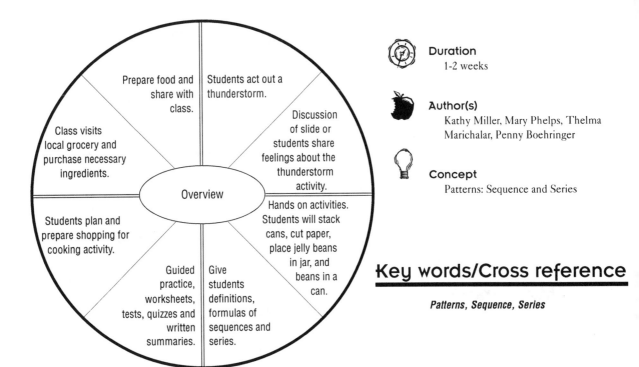

Duration
1-2 weeks

Author(s)
Kathy Miller, Mary Phelps, Thelma Marichalar, Penny Boehringer

Concept
Patterns: Sequence and Series

Key words/Cross reference

Patterns, Sequence, Series

Overview

Objective
Students will learn different types of sequences and series and the corresponding formulas.

About the Author(s)
Penny Boehringer has been a teacher for 25 years, the last 8 with Churchill High School in San Antonio, TX. Among her accomplishments, she was awarded Teacher of the Year in 1991 and 1992. Thelma Marichalar has taught for 20 years and was awarded Teacher of the Year in 1987. She currently teaches Algebra and Algebra II Honors as well as an SAT prep course for Churchill High School in San Antonio, TX. Kathy Miller has been teaching for 11 years, the last 8 with Churchill High School, part of Northeast ISD, in San Antonio, TX.

Bibliography
Algebra II with Trigonometry, Merrill, 1990.
Algebra II with Trigonometry, Harcourt, Brace, Jovanovich, 1983.

Quadrant 1—Experience

Right Mode—Connect

Students act out a thunderstorm.

Objective

To create an awareness for students regarding mathematical progression.

Activity

Separate students into five groups and have them re-create a thunderstorm using sound and movement; or show slide presentation from "The Powers of Ten."

Assessment

Quality of reactions and participation of students.

Left Mode—Examine

Discussion of slide or students share feelings about the thunderstorm activity.

Objective

To enhance students' ability to discuss what they have seen or experienced based on their perceptions.

Activity

Discuss the thunderstorm activity and how the activity relates to mathematics; or have students discuss and analyze the slide presentation.

Assessment

Willingness to participate in discussion and ability to listen to comments from classmates.

Quadrant 2—Concepts

Right Mode—Image

Hands-on activities. Students will stack cans, cut paper, place jelly beans in jar, and beans in a can.

Objective

To add to the students' understanding of the concept of sequence.

Activity

Students working in five groups will be given a bag or box with instructions for completing four tasks. The tasks include stacking cans, placing jelly beans in a jar, placing beans in a can, and cutting paper. (Two groups will stack cans.) Instructions for the tasks are as follows: Allow each group 6 to 8 minutes to complete a task before moving to the next.

Jelly Beans:

Determine how many jelly beans you want to put in the jar to start. Continue putting the same number in the jar until the jar is filled or the jelly beans are gone.

How many did you decide to put in each time?

How many "additions" were made to the jar?

What is the total number of jelly beans in the jar?

Is there a way to determine this without counting all the jelly beans?

Beans:

Put one bean in the jar. Put twice as many beans in the jar. Continue putting twice as many beans in the jar as previously. Continue until all the beans are gone.

What starts happening to the number of beans put in each time?

How does the "number" of beans compare?

What is the total number of beans in the jar?

How did you arrive at this figure?

How many times did you "add" beans to the jar?

Stacking Cans (or Cups):

Stack the cans (cups) given to you to form a pyramid.

How did you start?

How many cans (cups) in each row?

How does the number of cans in the bottom row compare to the number of cans in the top row?

What is the total number of cans in the stack?

Is there a way to figure it out without counting all the cans?

Assessment

Group participation, adherence to guidelines and ability to complete each task.

Sequences

 ## Left Mode—Define

Give students definitions, formulas of sequences and series.

Objective
To define sequence and series, discuss the different types of sequences and series, and their related formulas.

Activity
Teacher presents vocabulary, new information, formulas using lecture, demonstration and discussion.

Assessment
Student notetaking and teacher checking for understanding.

Quadrant 3—Applications

 ## Left Mode—Try

Guided practice, worksheets, tests, quizzes and written summaries.

Objective
To reinforce understanding by practice.

Activity
Students will work sample problems in text and teacher-prepared worksheets using prescribed procedures, take quizzes and tests, and write test summaries.

Assessment
Quality and accuracy of worksheets, quizzes, tests and written summaries.

 ## Right Mode—Extend

Students plan and prepare shopping for cooking activity.

Objective
To enhance student creativity and ability to work together as a group.

Activity
Students will be divided into groups. Each group will be given a recipe to increase/decrease sequentially (at least three changes). They must conclude with a required number of servings for which they will prepare a shopping list. Mathematical calculations will be required and will be shared with the class.

Assessment
Enthusiasm of students and accuracy of shopping list.

Quadrant 4—Creations

 ## Left Mode—Refine

Class visits local grocery store and purchases necessary ingredients.

Objective
To follow plan in real life activity.

Activity
Take students to a local grocery store with their shopping lists. Each group will determine quantities needed and most cost effective way to purchase supplies.

Assessment
Quality of group interaction.

 ## Right Mode—Integrate

Prepare food and share with class.

Objective
To prepare recipe and share with class.

Activity
Take class to food lab, prepare recipe, and share product with the class.

Assessment
Contribution to group effort and level of enjoyment.

Conic Sections

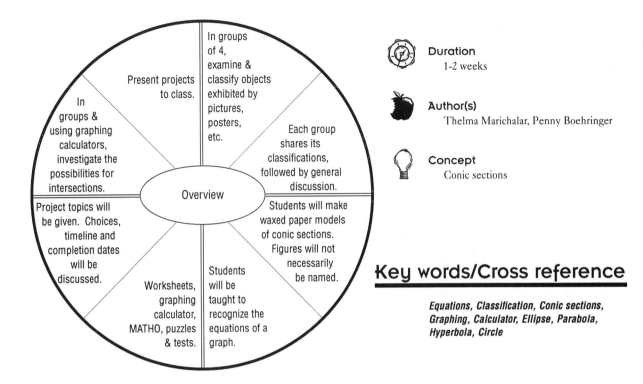

In groups of 4, examine & classify objects exhibited by pictures, posters, etc.

Each group shares its classifications, followed by general discussion.

Students will make waxed paper models of conic sections. Figures will not necessarily be named.

Students will be taught to recognize the equations of a graph.

Worksheets, graphing calculator, MATHO, puzzles & tests.

Project topics will be given. Choices, timeline and completion dates will be discussed.

In groups & using graphing calculators, investigate the possibilities for intersections.

Present projects to class.

Overview

Duration
1-2 weeks

Author(s)
Thelma Marichalar, Penny Boehringer

Concept
Conic sections

Key words/Cross reference

Equations, Classification, Conic sections, Graphing, Calculator, Ellipse, Parabola, Hyperbola, Circle

Overview

Concept Statement
Students will learn the basic mathematical concepts necessary to understanding conic sections.

About the Author(s)
Penny Boehringer has been a teacher for 25 years, the last 8 with Churchill High School in San Antonio, TX. Among her accomplishments, she was awarded Teacher of the Year in 1991 and 1992. Thelma Marichalar has taught for 20 years and was awarded Teacher of the Year in 1987. She currently teaches Algebra and Algebra II Honors as well as an SAT prep course for Churchill High School in San Antonio, TX.

Bibliography
Algebra II with Trigonometry, Merrill, 1990.
Algebra II with Trigonometry, Harcourt, Brace, Jovanovich, 1983.

Conic Sections

Quadrant 1—Experience

Right Mode—Connect

In groups of 4, students examine & classify objects exhibited by pictures, posters, etc.

Objective

To create student curiosity about conic sections as they appear in real life situations.

Activity

Students working in groups of four examine numbered exhibits. Exhibits will be posters containing pictures (found in magazines or newspapers) of conic sections as seen in real life, and objects (e.g., a horseshoe, ball, egg, vase, etc.) displayed on tables. Each group will classify the exhibits by grouping together similar pictures and objects. You will find that students will use different methods to classify your display.

Assessment

Involvement of students and their ability to work together.

Left Mode—Examine

Each group shares their classifications, followed by general discussion.

Objective

To enhance student ability to discuss what they have observed. To arouse curiosity for the material to be presented.

Activity

One student from each group reports on how his group classified the exhibits. The teacher lists the classifications on the board. General discussion follows after all groups have reported. It is not necessary to name all the conic sections at this point.

Assessment

Quality of discussion and participation.

Quadrant 2—Concepts

Right Mode—Image

Students will make waxed paper models of conic sections. Figures will not necessarily be named.

Objective

To create the conic sections using waxed paper.

Activity

Following are the instructions for creating an ellipse, hyperbola, and parabola using waxed paper. Since students are familiar with the construction of a circle, it is not necessary to perform this construction.

1) Ellipse - Draw a circle of ink in the middle of a sheet of waxed paper. Fold the circle in half and crease the paper. On the fold line (diameter of the circle), mark a point about one inch inside the circle. Fold the waxed paper so that a point on the circle lies on the point. Crease the waxed paper. Rotate the paper keeping the circle on the point at all times, creasing the paper with each successive move until an ellipse is formed.

2) Hyperbola - Draw a circle in the middle of a sheet of waxed paper. Fold the circle about one inch outside the circle. Fold the waxed paper so that the circle lies on the point. Crease the paper. Rotate the paper keeping the circle on the point at all times, creasing the paper with each move until a hyperbola is formed.

3) Parabola - Draw a line across the middle of the waxed paper. Mark a point about one inch above the line. Fold the waxed paper so that the line lies on the point and crease. Rotate the paper keeping the line on the point at all times, creasing the paper after each move until a parabola is formed.

After students have created their conic models, discuss the similarities between these shapes and the exhibits they previously classified in Activity 1.

Assessment

Student participation and attention.

Conic Sections

 ## Left Mode—Define

Students will be taught to recognize the equations of a graph.

Objective

To teach concepts needed in order to understand conic sections.

Activity

Teach the following concepts: recognition of the equations and graphs of circles, ellipses, hyperbolas, and parabolas; graph the four conic sections; write the equations of the four conic sections. The graphing calculator may be easily used with this material.

Assessment

Student notetaking and level of questions, and teacher checking for understanding.

Quadrant 3—Applications

 ## Left Mode—Try

Worksheets, graphing calculator, MATHO, puzzles & tests.

Objective

To allow students to practice concepts and reinforce learning.

Activity

Students will work individually and in groups on problem sets, puzzles and play MATHO. They will write test summaries before each test.

Assessment

Quality of problem solving. Ability of students to work together and contribute to group effort.

 ## Right Mode—Extend

Project topics will be given. Choices, timeline and completion dates will be discussed.

Objective

Students will increase their ability to choose from options based on curiosity and interest, and apply the concepts they have learned while enhancing their ability to plan a personalized learning project.

Activity

Students will be given project choices and timeline. These will be discussed in class.
CONICS PROJECTS:

1. Create a video, slide presentation, or photo album which illustrates the use of conics in everyday life. Material must be original, i.e., photographs instead of pictures cut from magazines. Know the type of conic you are videotaping or photographing. Minimum of 15 examples with at least three obvious examples of each of the four conic sections.

2. Investigate and explain the use of conics in the real world: conics used in construction (e.g., how to build a suspension bridge, build a whisper chamber or an amphitheater, etc.); satellite tracking; conics in space (missiles, astronomy, etc.); modern military use (role conics played in Desert Storm, etc.). Report should be a minimum of two pages, typed (double spaced) or four pages, handwritten with mandatory bibliography.

3. Create a skit, poem, story, or video using definitions and properties of conics, history of conics, and/or applications of conics. A parody (just inserting conic terms) will not be accepted.

4. Do a presentation using visuals to explain an application of conics. Visuals must be large enough for the class to read (poster, overlays for the overhead, etc.), or a handout needs to be provided for each student.

Assessment

Level of student participation and enthusiasm.

Quadrant 4—Creations

Left Mode—Refine

In groups & using graphing calculators, investigate the possibilities for intersections.

Objective

To extend and apply what has been learned.

Activity

In groups, students will investigate (by sketching and/or using the graphing calculator) the possible intersections of combinations of two conic sections. They will make a table or chart showing the possible combinations of conic sections and the number of points of intersection. Students will learn to solve systems of quadratic equations or systems of quadratic/linear equations algebraically. Progress on student projects will be monitored.

Assessment

Quality of student questions/responses and evidence of understanding of the extended concepts.

Right Mode—Integrate

Present projects to class.

Objective

To share what was learned and created.

Activity

Students will present their completed projects including an explanation demonstration, and/or exhibit to their classmates.

Assessment

Quality of completed projects, presentations, participation, and enjoyment of the learning.

Exponents

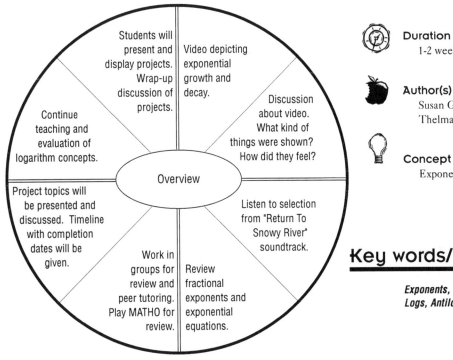

Circle diagram:

- Students will present and display projects. Wrap-up discussion of projects.
- Video depicting exponential growth and decay.
- Discussion about video. What kind of things were shown? How did they feel?
- Continue teaching and evaluation of logarithm concepts.
- **Overview**
- Listen to selection from "Return To Snowy River" soundtrack.
- Project topics will be presented and discussed. Timeline with completion dates will be given.
- Work in groups for review and peer tutoring. Play MATHO for review.
- Review fractional exponents and exponential equations.

Duration
1-2 weeks

Author(s)
Susan Gude, Otto Kurth, Roland Rios, Thelma Marichalar, Penny Boehringer

Concept
Exponential Equations

Key words/Cross reference

Exponents, Decay, Equations, Logarithms, Logs, Antilogs, Growth

Overview

Concept Statement

Students will understand the basic concept of exponents, with an emphasis on real-life application.

About the Author(s)

Penny Boehringer has been a teacher for 25 years, the last 8 with Churchill High School in San Antonio, TX. Among her accomplishments, she was awarded Teacher of the Year in 1991 and 1992. Thelma Marichalar has taught for 20 years and was awarded Teacher of the Year in 1987. She currently teaches Algebra and Algebra II Honors as well as an SAT prep course for Churchill High School in San Antonio, TX. Otto Kurth holds a B.S. in Mathematics. He has taught for 22 years, the last 7 at Churchill High School in San Antonio, TX. Roland Rios is currently in his second year of teaching at Churchill High School in San Antonio, TX. He was nominated for the Sallie Mae First Year Teacher of the Year award. His Algebra students placed second in the American Statistical

Association's poster competition. Susan Gude is at the Nimitz Academy, part of the Northeast I.S.D., San Antonio, TX.

Bibliography

Algebra II with Trigonometry, Merrill, 1990.
Algebra II with Trigonometry, Harcourt, Brace, Jovanovich, 1983.

Exponents

Quadrant 1—Experience

 ### Right Mode—Connect

Video depicting exponential growth and decay.

Objective
To see examples of exponential/logarithmic growth in everyday life.

Activity
Video depicting exponential growth and decay.

Assessment
Attentiveness.

 ### Left Mode—Examine

Discussion about video. What kind of things were shown? How did they feel?

Objective
To analyze the video.

Activity
Teacher leads discussion about video. What kind of things were shown? How did they feel?

Assessment
Quality of and participation in discussion.

Quadrant 2—Concepts

 ### Right Mode—Image

Listen to selection from "Return To Snowy River" soundtrack.

Objective
To hear, feel, and express changes in sound.

Activity
Listen to a selection from "Return to Snowy River" soundtrack. Do analog of how the music makes each student feel. Display and discuss analogs. Discuss the roles of exponents in mathematics.

Assessment
Depth and quality of analogs; ideas generated by discussion.

 ### Left Mode—Define

Review fractional exponents and exponential equations.

Objective
To teach unit on logarithms.

Activity
Teach the following concepts: Review fractional exponents and exponential equations; teach meaning of logarithms, laws of logos, solve logarithm equations, use table of logs, find antilogs.

Assessment
Quality of response and understanding of concepts taught.

Exponents

Quadrant 3—Applications

Left Mode—Try

Work in groups for review and peer tutoring. Play MATHO for review.

Objective
To practice concepts being taught.

Activity
Students will work in cooperative groups for review and peer tutoring. Students will play MATHO*, do worksheets, write summaries for tests, and take quizzes and tests.

Assessment
Participation in group activities and performances on quizzes and tests.
- MATHO board attached. List at least 40 answers on board or overhead. Ask students to copy 24 answers (random) onto their gamesheets. Write a problem on board or overhead. Students work problem and place a square over the answer. Continue to play as BINGO.

Right Mode—Extend

Project topics will be presented and discussed. Timeline with completion dates will be given.

Objective
To allow students to personalize the material.

Activity
Give students project options and due dates. Discuss options with students.
I. RESEARCH PAPER suggested topics:
- Business applications of exponents or logarithms
- Use of exponents and logarithms in carbon dating
- Development of the Richter Scales
- History of logarithms (Napier)
- Another pre-approved topic

II. WORK OUT A LOGARITHMIC OR EXPONEN-TIAL FUNCTION — This project involves the application of an established function using logs or exponents. You will supply data for each type of problem and show the result in a change in data. For example, show how different interest rates yield different returns on the same investment. For added clarity, results could be graphed or illustrated. Some

suggestions include:
- Growth and Decay
- Compound Interest
- Appreciation/Depreciation
- Decibel Computation

III. ILLUSTRATING EXPONENTIAL GROWTH
— This project involves graphically and/or artistically representing some sort of exponential or logarithmic growth. This growth is not limited to established logarithmic functions. Examples include:
- Since the invention of the airplane our ability to go higher and higher into space has grown exponentially. In the few short years since the invention we have traveled millions and millions of miles into space. This growth could easily be graphed using interesting pictures or drawings.
- The number of hamburgers served in the U.S. by major restaurant chains has increased dramatically. This could also be illustrated graphically.
- Your own pre-approved idea.

IV. CREATIVE IDEAS (Limited only by your imagination and our approval. Think of fun and exciting ways to illustrate logs and exponents.) Suggestions include:
- A poem about logs and/or exponents
- Song or rap about logs and/or exponents
- Video showing exponents and logs in use
- "Sales ad" showing the many uses of logs.

Assessment
Commitment to project choice.

Quadrant 4—Creations

Left Mode—Refine

Continue teaching and evaluation of logarithm concepts.

Objective
To transfer understanding of personal choices to real life situations. To improve understanding through additional practice.

Activity
Submit written explanation of chosen project. Continue teaching and evaluating concepts.

Assessment
Level of student involvement.

Right Mode—Integrate

Students will present and display projects. Wrap-up discussion of projects.

Objective
To allow students to share what has been learned regarding logarithms.

Activity
Students complete their contracted projects and present, explain, and display them to their classmates.

Assessment
Enjoyment and participation in the experience.

Algebraic Properties

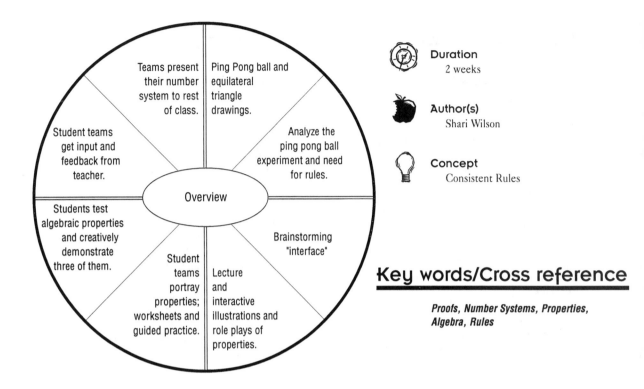

Overview

Teams present their number system to rest of class.

Ping Pong ball and equilateral triangle drawings.

Student teams get input and feedback from teacher.

Analyze the ping pong ball experiment and need for rules.

Students test algebraic properties and creatively demonstrate three of them.

Brainstorming "interface"

Student teams portray properties; worksheets and guided practice.

Lecture and interactive illustrations and role plays of properties.

Duration
2 weeks

Author(s)
Shari Wilson

Concept
Consistent Rules

Key words/Cross reference

Proofs, Number Systems, Properties, Algebra, Rules

Overview

Objective

To teach students the concepts of algebraic functions as universal rules that have transferability and application to life.

About the Author

Shari Wilson is the Executive Director of the Arkansas Education Renewal Consortium, a position she has held since 1991. Prior to this position, she was the Mathematics Curriculum Coordinator for Pulaski County Special School District in Little Rock, AR, for four years. In addition, Shari has ten years experience as a teacher. In 1987 she received the Presidential Award for Excellence in Teaching Mathematics.

Required Resources

Ping-pong balls and felt tip pens.

Quadrant 1—Experience

Right Mode—Connect

Ping Pong ball and equilateral triangle drawings.

Objective

To create an interest in the "rules" not working and a need to create new truths.

Activity

Each student is given a ping pong ball and a fine-point felt tip marker. Students are instructed to draw a small equilateral triangle, and to observe its sides, angles, and the sum of the angles. Next they will draw progressively larger triangles around the first one until frustration is reached.

Assessment

Involvement of each student. Teacher conversations with individual students including comments of "I can't do it," "What do I do with these curved lines?", "Where are the angles?," and observations about the triangle becoming a circle are shared with the rest of the class.

Left Mode—Examine

Analyze the ping pong ball experiment and need for rules.

Objective

To analyze the ping pong experience. Students will realize that the term "triangle" is relative to the system and that Euclidean geometry only works in two dimensional space. "Rules" are therefore relative: new situations demand new rules.

Activity

Teacher leads class discussion. What is a triangle? What is the range of the sum of the angles of a spherical triangle? How can "hunches" about this range be tested?

Assessment

Students' recognition of the need for developing new rules and testing them.

Quadrant 2—Concepts

Right Mode—Image

Brainstorming "interface."

Objective

To see how we adapt to the need for creating anew in our own lives. That algebraic language and algebraic properties have transferabilities into everyday language and properties.

Activity

This activity will use metaphor to help students see that algebraic language has transferability to everyday use. Working in small groups, students are asked to brainstorm an example of a time when they needed to describe something for which there was not an adequate word. Have they ever created a new word? What would make a new word or term reach a level of acceptance in society? Teacher gives definition of INTERFACE and its origin in computer terminology. Have a group of students kinesthetically act out "interface." Working in small groups, students brainstorm everyday examples of how "interface" is used. Teacher charts all examples in mindmap format.

Assessment

Ability of students to relate to language experience and "interface" activity.

Left Mode—Define

Lecture and interactive illustrations and role plays of properties.

Objective

To teach algebraic properties through student involvement, demonstration, and visual images.

Activity

The following properties are introduced and defined by the teacher: Reflexive, Symmetric, Transitive, Identity, Inverse, Commutative, Associative, Distributive, Substitution, and Closure. For each property and definition, a team of students is involved in a kinesthetic or visual representation of that property. For example: The Reflexive property (a=a) is demonstrated by the teacher using a mirror as the "=" sign.

The Symmetric property (a=b) (b=a) is demonstrated with hands. If you were to write "a=b" on the backs of each of your hands, and then fold them together, the

Algebraic Properties

"a" would match with the "b" and the "b" would match with the "a" — thumb to thumb and pinky to pinky.

The Transitive property — If (a=b) and (b=c) then (a=c) is likened to crossing a creek. To cross a creek is to transfer from one side to the other by way of steps in between.

The Associative property (a+b) + c = a + (b+c) is demonstrated using a boy and two girls from the class. The boy's arms are the parentheses. Associative comes from the root word Associate. This boy "Associates" with two different girls on different days. Have students physically demonstrate this equation.

The Distributive property a (b+c+d) = ab + ac + ad is illustrated by a truck distributing Nintendo sets to the various WalMart stores on his route.

Students work in small groups to generate their own kinesthetic, metaphorical, and visual examples of each algebraic property as it is introduced.

Assessment

Interest and enjoyment of students in teacher-led activities and ability of students to generate and share their own examples.

Quadrant 3—Applications

Left Mode—Try

Student teams portray properties; worksheets and guided practice.

Objective

To reinforce student understanding of algebraic properties.

Activity

1. Divide class into two teams. Each team has a colored set of cards consisting of the following: 2 "a"; 2 "b"; 2 "c"; 3 "="; 2 "+"; 2 "-"; 2 "("; 2 ")"; 1 "if"; 1 "and"; 1 "then"; 2 "•". As a property is called out by the teacher, teams must assemble to form an algebraic sentence that shows the property. A designated team member raises her hand when the team is ready. Teams face one another and cross correct their sentences. A point system is established for scoring each team's efforts.

2. Students will complete worksheets with arithmetic problems as well as algebraic proofs. They must supply the reasoning for each step in 2-column formal form.

Assessment

Student ability to demonstrate algebraic properties; completion and correctness of assigned work.

Right Mode—Extend

Students test algebraic properties and creatively demonstrate three of them.

Objective

To create representations of the algebraic properties using various modalities.

Activity

1. Student teams will find or invent a number system and an operation in which at least one of the properties studied does not hold true. They will use a matrix to chart the operations of their system within the set. They will demonstrate whether or not the algebraic properties they have learned hold true in their new system. They may create a new property for their system, name it, and demonstrate it in some way.

2. Working in cooperative groups, students will create a song, poem, rap, sculpture, painting, dance, or role play to demonstrate three of the properties. All properties must be divided up by the class so that each is demonstrated in at least one form.

Assessment

Ability of students to work together on group project. Quality of projects.

Quadrant 4—Creations

Left Mode—Refine

Student teams get input and feedback from teacher.

Objective
To apply the principles of the algebraic properties.

Activity
Students will be given the opportunity to test their number system projects with the teacher to verify workability. Those teams that are not quite on track will be given a second attempt at the correct completion of their project.

Assessment
Individual student contributions to team effort; teacher monitoring for understanding and application.

Right Mode—Integrate

Teams present their number system to rest of class.

Objective
To share in final form what has been learned with the rest of the class.

Activity
Student teams present their new system, matrix, and perform their property.

Assessment
Quality of student demonstration of understanding; enjoyment of team presentations.

Binary Systems

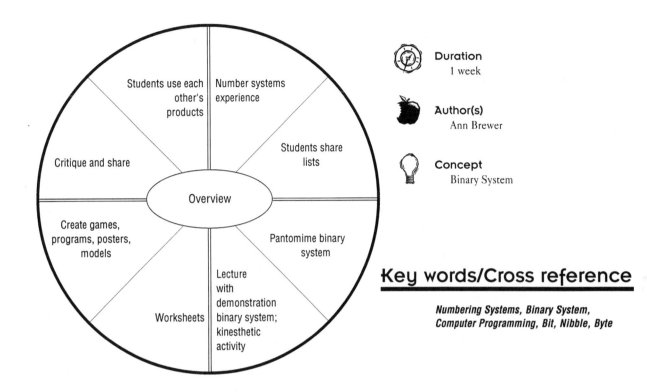

Students use each other's products

Number systems experience

Critique and share

Students share lists

Overview

Create games, programs, posters, models

Pantomime binary system

Worksheets

Lecture with demonstration binary system; kinesthetic activity

Duration
1 week

Author(s)
Ann Brewer

Concept
Binary System

Key words/Cross reference

Numbering Systems, Binary System, Computer Programming, Bit, Nibble, Byte

Overview

Objective
Students will learn the concept behind the numbering systems necessary for computer programming and strategies for converting one system to another.

About the Author
Ann Brewer teaches Computer Science at Tucker Area Vocational-Technical Center, Marion Community Schools, Marion, IN. She has been a participant in the Marion Community Schools 4MAT Implementation Project led by Carol Secttor.

Required Resources
Chart paper and markers; teacher-prepared "neck signs"; worksheets; cut and paste materials for student projects.

Quadrant 1—Experience

Right Mode—Connect

Number systems experience.

Objective
To interest students in the various numbering systems and in translations.

Activity
1) Break students into groups of four or five. Ask students to imagine they are system programmers employed by IBM, they are 30 years old, and they are on a company trip to Europe. Using chart paper and markers, brainstorm and write the different numbering systems (bases) they might encounter during the trip. Examples: U.S. money is base 10 (decimal). The clock at the airport is base 60. Gasoline is in liters. Mileage is kilometers, etc.
2) Speak to the students in a combination of Spanish and Pig Latin: "Buenos Dias, Amigos. e-wa are earning-la about ecimal-da, inary-ba, and exi-ha ecimal-da, etc."

Assessment
Students' curiosity and reaction to teacher behavior.

Left Mode—Examine

Students share lists.

Objective
To analyze why we have different numbering systems and how our minds can translate.

Activity
Using chart paper and markers, 1) Students share their lists of the numbering systems encountered on the trip to Europe. 2) Students translate what the teacher said.

Assessment
Quality of group lists.

Quadrant 2—Concepts

Right Mode—Image

Pantomime binary system.

Objective
To familiarize students with Base 2 and foster a desire for more information about numbering systems.

Activity
Each group should pantomime an activity or thing that demonstrates a use of Base 2 and/or reminds us of Base 2. Examples:
1. Nod head/shake head — Yes/No
2. Flip light switch — On/Off
3. Sit/Stand — Up/Down
4. Close eyes/open eyes — Asleep/Awake
5. Shiver/Perspire — Cold/Hot
Which example of Base 2 do you think is most like the computer? (On/Off)

Assessment
Level of student contribution to activity.

Left Mode—Define

Lecture with demonstration; binary system kinesthetic activity.

Objective
To explain how computers use the binary system. To explain how and why programmers use the hexidecimal system. To explain how to convert from decimal to binary to hexidecimal.

Activity
1) Tape eight signs to the wall that read "1, 2, 4, 8, etc." Have eight students wear signs that read "0" and "1" and stand under the signs on the wall. The teacher then physically places the eight students into a line and by turning their cards over, constructs binary numbers and explains how to translate those binary numbers into decimal numbers. The teacher can then illustrate how each group of four students is a "nibble," while all eight students represent a "byte." The teacher then uses each nibble to explain how binary can be converted to hexidecimal.
2) Teacher does conventional lecturing and diagramming at the board for emphasis.
3) Students read textbook.

Assessment
Teacher checking for understanding; quality of student questions and involvement in interactive lecture/discussion.

Quadrant 3—Applications

Left Mode—Try

Worksheets.

Objective

To gain skill in creating and converting numbers in the three numbering systems.

Activity

There are many interactive worksheets in game formats available on the market which present opportunities for students to convert number systems.

Assessment

Quality of student worksheets.

Right Mode—Extend

Create games, programs, posters, models.

Objective

To experiment with binary and/or hexidecimal by creating a project.

Activity

Students create a game (Bingo, Dominoes), card trick, puzzle, picture, poster, model, song, teaching tool, computer program, etc. that utilizes either Base 2 or Base 16. Students are encouraged to use individuality in selection and design of their project.

Assessment

Quality of student project plans.

Quadrant 4—Creations

Left Mode—Refine

Critique and share.

Objective

To critique the project from 3R.

Activity

Students trade projects and another student completes a form listing the strengths and weaknesses of the project.

Assessment

Students' ability to critique the effectiveness of the assignment. Did they understand the concept well-enough to critique another's work?

Right Mode—Integrate

Students use each other's products.

Objective

To share their knowledge of binary and hexidecimal with others.

Activity

Students play the games, work the puzzles, sing the songs, etc. that were prepared in 3R (and then improved in 4L). (Possible Alternate Activity — if the project lends itself, perhaps the presentation of the project could go school-wide on closed-circuit TV.)

Assessment

Student enjoyment of shared learning.

Boundaries

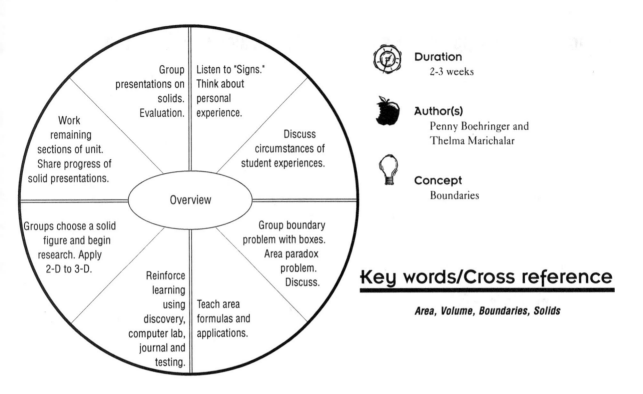

Group presentations on solids. Evaluation.

Listen to "Signs." Think about personal experience.

Work remaining sections of unit. Share progress of solid presentations.

Discuss circumstances of student experiences.

Overview

Groups choose a solid figure and begin research. Apply 2-D to 3-D.

Group boundary problem with boxes. Area paradox problem. Discuss.

Reinforce learning using discovery, computer lab, journal and testing.

Teach area formulas and applications.

Duration
2-3 weeks

Author(s)
Penny Boehringer and
Thelma Marichalar

Concept
Boundaries

Key words/Cross reference

Area, Volume, Boundaries, Solids

Overview

Objective
To use the concept of boundaries in teaching the area and volume units.

About the Author
Penny Boehringer has been a teacher for 26 years, the last nine at Churchill High School in San Antonio, Texas. She currently teaches geometry and math analysis. She is a district 4MAT trainer, serves on several district curriculum committees, and is a presenter at district inservices. In 1991 and 1992, she was selected Teacher of the Year. Several of her lessons are included in the 1993 LessonBank. Thelma Marichalar has taught for 25 years, the last 20 at Churchill High School in San Antonio, Texas. She currently teaches Algebra II as well as an S.A.T. Prep course. She is a district 4MAT Trainer, serves on several district curriculum committees, and is a presenter at district inservices. In 1987, she was selected Teacher of the Year. Several of her lesson plans are included in the 1993 LessonBank.

Required Resources
Copy of song "Signs," group sets of 15 boxes of varying sizes and shapes, copy of area paradox problem.

Bibliography
"Signs" recorded by Five Man Electric Band.

Boundaries

Quadrant 1—Experience

Right Mode—Connect

Listen to "Signs." Think about personal experience.

Objective

To focus thoughts on the concept of area.

Activity

Class will listen to song "Signs" recorded by Five Man Electric Band (a song concerning social boundaries). Ask students to discuss their reactions and feelings to the song. Ask students to think of a situation where they have been made to feel uncomfortable, unwanted, rejected, unacceptable, etc.

Assessment

Level of interest.

Left Mode—Examine

Discuss circumstances of student experiences.

Objective

To examine a personal experience.

Activity

Discuss the circumstances of their experiences.

Assessment

Level of participation and willingness to share.

Quadrant 2—Concepts

Right Mode—Image

Group boundary problem with boxes. Area paradox problem. Discuss.

Objective

To experiment with the concept of boundaries in a problem solving situation.

Activity

In groups of four, choose a secretary to record the problem solving process. Each group will receive a set of boxes (approximately 15 boxes) of varying shapes and sizes.

1. Ask the groups to arrange the boxes to cover the largest space possible. Share solutions with the groups.
2. Ask the groups to arrange the boxes to cover the smallest space possible. Share solutions with the groups.
3. Do area paradox problem. Give each student a sheet of centimeter paper. Cut an 8x8 square from one corner. Using an overhead transparency, show students where to cut their square into four pieces. Then ask students to work together to rearrange these four pieces into a rectangle. If they want, students may draw another 8x8 square and their new 13x5 rectangle on the remaining centimeter paper. Have students find the area of the square (64 sq. units) and then the area of the rectangle (65 sq. units). Ask questions such as: Are the areas correct? Why or why not? Is something wrong? What basic property have we contradicted? (whole = sum of parts)

Assessment

Involvement and creativity in group activities.

Boundaries

Left Mode—Define

Teach area formulas and applications.

Objective

To teach concepts of area and volume and their applications.

Activity

Teacher will give and/or derive area formulas and methods of solving different types of problems. Students will be made aware that they will need to find missing measurements before using the area formulas. They will need to recall many geometric facts learned earlier in the course.

Assessment

Quality of participation and level of student discussion and contributions.

Quadrant 3—Applications

Left Mode—Try

Reinforce learning using discovery, computer lab, journal and testing.

Objective

To focus attention on the concepts of area and volume.

Activity

Students will work individually and in groups on computer activities (Supposer or Sketchpad software if available), group discovery activities, journal entries, and written test summaries to reinforce concepts. Tests and quizzes will follow.

Assessment

Level of participation in group work. Quality and accuracy of assessment activities.

Right Mode—Extend

Groups choose a solid figure and begin research. Apply 2-D to 3-D.

Objective

To enhance student creativity and develop decision-making process.

Activity

Students will be divided into groups of six. Each group must investigate a solid figure (prisms, pyramids, cones, cylinders, spheres) and prepare a presentation for the class. The presentation must include: 1) A creative representation which examines the solid and includes particular vocabulary and/or formulas, applications, etc. 2) A demonstration including instruction on drawing the solid formulas and their applications. 3) An assignment for the class due the next class period.

Assessment

Quality of discussion about connections between learned concepts and application to assignment.

Boundaries

Quadrant 4—Creations

 Left Mode—Refine

Work remaining sections of unit. Share progress of solid presentations.

Objective
To evaluate student progress and extend area/volume concepts.

Activity
Teach remaining sections of area/volume unit (except those topics which will be taught by student groups). Encourage students to share questions and thoughts about their projects with each other. Prepare students for their final presentation.

Assessment
Group interaction and excitement about the projects. Evidence that concepts learned during the teaching of the unit are being applied.

 Right Mode—Integrate

Group presentations on solids. Evaluation.

Objective
To share their newly acquired knowledge.

Activity
Each group will present information on its solid and give class assignment. Each student will complete an individual and class evaluation.

Assessment
The level of enjoyment reached by the class during the presentation. Students will be evaluated on their method of presentation, meeting criteria, creativity, validity, and enthusiasm.

Optimization

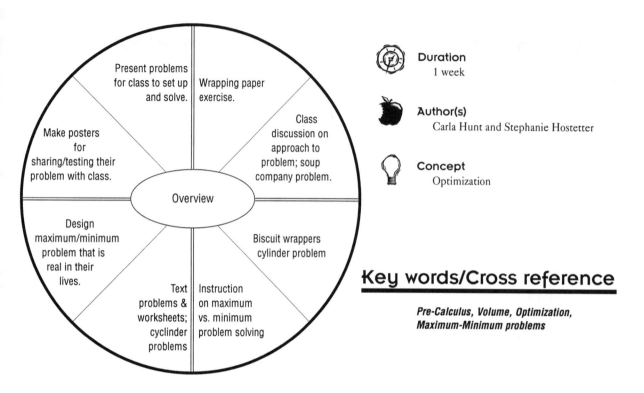

Present problems for class to set up and solve.

Wrapping paper exercise.

Make posters for sharing/testing their problem with class.

Class discussion on approach to problem; soup company problem.

Overview

Design maximum/minimum problem that is real in their lives.

Biscuit wrappers cylinder problem

Text problems & worksheets; cyclinder problems

Instruction on maximum vs. minimum problem solving

 Duration
1 week

Author(s)
Carla Hunt and Stephanie Hostetter

Concept
Optimization

Key words/Cross reference

Pre-Calculus, Volume, Optimization, Maximum-Minimum problems

Overview

 Objective
To teach the concept of optimization and its application in daily life.

 About the Author
At the time this plan was first published in 1990, Stephanie Hostetter was Foreign Language chair and Spanish teacher at South Lakes High School, Fairfax County Schools, Reston, VA. Carla Hunt taught mathematics at South Lakes High School for six years. This unit plan was developed when Carla and Stephanie were team partners in the Fairfax County 4MAT Course.

 Required Resources
Boxes and wrapping paper; sample biscuit cans.

Authors' Note
This lesson can be used with a pre-calculus class when presenting and introducing the concept of maximum/minimum value problems. It is also appropriate for a Calculus AP or Basic class; however, the teacher may want to change the presentation order of the activities "on the wheel." I have used this lesson successfully in both Pre-calculus and AP Calculus.

Optimization

Quadrant 1—Experience

 Right Mode—Connect

Wrapping paper exercise.

Objective
To form an image of doing the most with the least.

Activity
Working in cooperative learning groups, students are given a sheet or two of wrapping paper and several boxes to wrap. They must get the most wrapped with the least amount of paper. Think of the best way to proceed to wrap all packages.

Assessment
Ability to solve the problem.

 Left Mode—Examine

Class discussion on approach to problem; soup company problem.

Objective
Based on the wrapping paper experience, to define what is meant by maximizing and minimizing.

Activity
Teacher leads discussion eliciting feedback on how groups solved the problem. Connect problems to real world: a department store which provides gift wrap service would want to use the least amount of paper to provide the service yet maximize its profit. Another problem for groups to solve: a soup company wants to make soup cans to hold a given amount with the least amount of manufacturing material. How would soup cans be designed to maximize profit? What factors must be considered?

Assessment
Discussion from the students.

Quadrant 2—Concepts

 Right Mode—Image

Biscuit wrappers cylinder problem.

Objective
To broaden students' understanding of maximum/minimum with an emphasis on conditions set for the problem.

Activity
Working in pairs, students are given two Hungry Jack® biscuit wrappers or traced copies. Students are to roll wrappers back up to make two different sizes of cylinders. Tape these two cylinders to hold their shape. One is shorter and fatter. The other is longer and thinner. The teacher should have two cylinders of the two different sizes prepared as discussion models to expedite the student activity. Problem: determine if the two cylinders hold the same amount.

Assessment
Ability of student teams to create the two cylinders and to find a way to solve the problem.

 Left Mode—Define

Instruction on maximum vs. minimum problem solving.

Objective
To learn to set up and work a maximum/minimum problem.

Activity
Using overhead transparencies, teacher presents problem solving strategies for mathematically determining maximum and minimum under given conditions. Problems are presented for class to set up and solve together using realistic examples from business and industry.

Assessment
Students' involvement during instruction and teacher checking for ability to solve sample problems.

Quadrant 3—Applications

Left Mode—Try

Text problems & worksheets; cylinder problems.

Objective

To develop proficiency in setting up and solving a variety of maximum/minimum problems.

Activity

1. Students work sample problems in text and teacher-prepared worksheet using a prescribed procedure.
2. Student pairs will use Hungry Jack® cylinders made in Quadrant Two Right and seal off the bottom with cardboard and tape. Remembering that the two cylinders have the same lateral area, students will mathematically predict the volume. Using rice or dried beans, they will test and verify their predictions.
3. Each team will bring a sample food can from home. The team task is to design an ideal can to hold a given volume but using the least amount of material for total outer surface area.

Assessment

Completion and correctness of assigned work. In-class quiz to check for understanding.

Right Mode—Extend

Design maximum/minimum problem that is real in their lives.

Objective

To develop a project applying what has been learned.

Activity

1. Working in teams, students will design a maximum/minimum problem that exists in their own experience. For example, the SGA wants to sell tickets to the faculty talent show to groups to get the most people to attend, and also to make the most money. If they give a discount of 20¢ for each number of tickets sold over 10 tickets with a single ticket price of $5.00, how many must be sold to maximize profit?
2. Students will write to a major can company to find out how they do or do not use the "ideal can" and what factors determine the size of the can that they do use.

Assessment

Student on-task behavior.

Quadrant 4—Creations

Left Mode—Refine

Make posters for sharing/testing their problem with class.

Objective

To complete project assignments.

Activity

Students make posters for testing their real-life problems with the rest of the class. Findings of correspondence with can companies are put into a brief report.

Assessment

Quality of sample problems and posters.

Right Mode—Integrate

Present problems for class to set up and solve.

Objective

To share in final form what has been learned with the rest of the class.

Activity

Students make a presentation to the class of their self-designed problem, including a visual. The rest of class will set up and solve each team problem presented. Responses from can companies are posted in a composite chart and will be shared orally with the rest of the class.

Assessment

Evaluation, peer evaluation, self-evaluation done orally with class.

The Cell

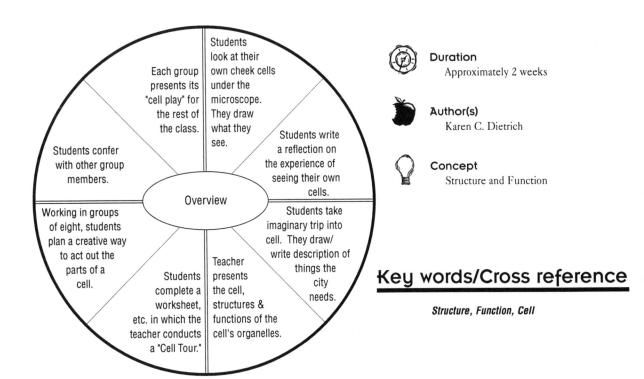

Duration
Approximately 2 weeks

Author(s)
Karen C. Dietrich

Concept
Structure and Function

Key words/Cross reference

Structure, Function, Cell

Overview

Objective
The students will show an understanding of the importance of the cell and its organelles.

About the Author
Sr. Karen Dietrich SSJ has been a classroom teacher of all levels of biology for over 20 years. In 1991 she was Awarded the Presidential Award for Excellence in Science Teaching representing the state of NJ.

Bibliography
The Invisible World. 60 min. VHS. National Geographic Society. Vestron Video. P.O. Box 4000, Stanford, Connecticut 06907. (Video used in conjunction with the cell and introduction to the microscope.)
The Biology Coloring Book. Robert D. Griffin. Barnes and Noble Books (available at most mall bookstores).

Quadrant 1—Experience

Right Mode—Connect

Students look at their own cheek cells under the microscope. They draw what they see.

Objective

To have students personally realize that all living things, including themselves, are made up of cells.

Activity

The students begin this unit by looking at the basic structure of their bodies by doing the classic "cheek cell" lab. Having reviewed the parts and techniques of using a light microscope, the students gently rub the inside of their cheeks with toothpicks. They then make wet mounts and stain their specimens with methylene blue. They should see flat, irregularly roundish squamous cells with lavender cytoplasm and dark purple nuclei. They will also see strange foreign particles and even bacteria. The students should be provided with the materials necessary to draw what they see and color it. (It proves useful to provide students with a worksheet which has circles approximately 6cm in diameter representing the microscope field.)

Assessment

Attentiveness of the class to the activity, success in finding their cheek cells and excitement at looking at a piece of themselves.

Left Mode—Examine

Students write a reflection on the experience of seeing their own cells.

Objective

To have the students reflect on the experience of seeing some of their own cheek cells; to have them realize that in that dark, purple, central spot are all the directions for making them uniquely themselves.

Activity

Students are given the opportunity to reflect on a series of guiding questions, first independently and then as a class. Sample questions would include: What did the cells look like? Were they all exactly the same? How big are your cells? Do you think all your body cells look alike? What are some special types of body cells you know about? Did you see anything besides your cheek cells on the slide? Do you think bacteria are cells? Why

is it appropriate to define a cell as a building block? Does each person have a structure in common? How are we the same? How are we different?

Assessment

Quality and appropriateness of student answers.

The Cell

Quadrant 2—Concepts

 ### Right Mode—Image

Students take imaginary trip into cell. They draw/write descriptions of the things the city needs.

Objective

The students will identify some of the functions of the organelles by working with the metaphor of the cell as a city.

Activity

Students have only seen cytoplasm and a nucleus when they looked at their cheek cells. For homework, they are asked to take an imaginary trip into the cell. They are told that the cell is like a city. The assignment asks them to identify the things that every functioning city needs and then to record those things in drawing or in words. The next class begins with generating a composite list. Then the teacher generates some thought questions: What would happen in a city where there were no water reservoirs; no garbage trucks; no transport system? Can you see why a cell would need similar structures?

Assessment

Quality of student responses: their ability to identify all the critical structures that keep a city functioning and to take the metaphorical leap to see that a cell would need similar structures and functions.

 ### Left Mode—Define

Teacher presents the cell, structures & functions of the cell's organelles.

Objective

To provide the students with the names, structures and functions of the organelles of the cell and to show their universality as well as the link to specialization.

Activity

Using electron micro graphs of real cells, a 3D model, and the metaphor that links the organelles to the parts of a city, the teacher presents the STRUCTURES and FUNCTIONS of the cell's organelles.

Assessment

Quality of students' notes; their ability through verbal checking to identify organelles and their functions.

Quadrant 3—Applications

 ### Left Mode—Try

Students complete a worksheet, etc. in which the teacher conducts a "Cell Tour."

Objective

To confirm the students' ability to visually identify both drawings and electron micro graphs of cell organelles; to check that they can verbally identify the organelles and match them with their unique and yet interrelated function in the cell; to have the students identify examples of protozoa, plant and animal cells under the microscope.

Activity

For this octant, students

1) complete a worksheet where they label the parts in a drawing of the cell,
2) take a quiz of simple matching columns for structure and function,
3) participate in a practice review in which the teacher conducts a "CELL CITY TOUR" (this is one of the highlights of the year. The teacher can get dressed up in a slicker, galoshes, umbrella and carry a picket sign that says 'CELL TOURS." She/he greets the students at the door and welcomes them into a cell. Tacked up around the room are simple, large, colorful drawings typically used to designate the different organelles. Members of the "tour group" are invited to come up and describe in detail a random "site" on the tour),
4) look at micro viewer slides of real cell organelles,
5) bring in samples of water, plants, etc. that they chose to look at under the microscope.

Assessment

Quality of student involvement in the activities: their success in labeling the diagram and matching structures and functions; their enthusiasm and accurate, active participation in the "Tour"; their ability to draw and identify organelles on the micro viewer slides.

Right Mode—Extend

Working in groups of eight, students plan a creative way to act out the parts of a cell.

Objective

To have the students own and "play with" the functioning parts of the cell.

Activity

Working in approximately three groups of eight, the students plan a creative way to act out the parts of a cell. Essentially, they are designing one or more metaphors in which they act out their understanding of the cell and its organelles. They can write a play and get dressed up to match the functions of the organelles, or they can write a rap song or a long rhyming poem, or even become a living model.

Assessment

Creativity and participation of the group members.

Quadrant 4—Creations

Left Mode—Refine

Students confer with other group members.

Objective

To have the students check their productions for technical accuracy.

Activity

Students confer with other group members and the teacher to check the accuracy of their ideas and to hone the presentations.

Assessment

Faithfulness of the creative metaphors to the structures and/or functions of the organelles.

Right Mode—Integrate

Each group presents their "cell play" for the rest of the class.

Objective

Have the students share what they have learned about the cell and its organelles and "teach it" in yet another way.

Activity

Groups present their "Cell Productions" for the rest of the class.

Assessment

Quality of productions; enthusiasm and enjoyment of the performers and audience.

Classification

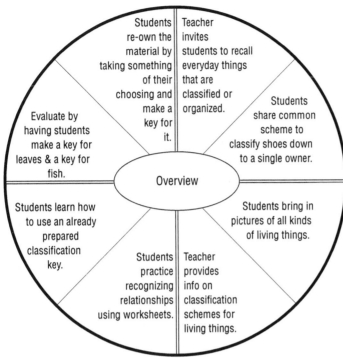

 Duration
Approximately 2 weeks

 Author(s)
Karen C. Dietrich

 Concept
Classification of Living Things

Key words/Cross reference

Classification, Living things, Patterns, Relationships

Overview

 Objective
The students will show an understanding of the need for organization; the ability to interpret classification schemes; use dichotomous keys to identify unknown organisms and design their own keys to classify.

 About the Author
Sr. Karen Dietrich has been a classroom teacher of all levels of biology for over 20 years. In 1991 she was awarded the Presidential Award for Excellence in Science Teaching representing the state of NJ.

 Bibliography
Five Kingdoms Classification Kit. Ward's Biology. 5100 West Henrietta Rd., P.O. Box 92912, Rochester, NY 14692-9012. Order #32W2209 (hands-on, paper/sticker kit that allows students to build a 5 kingdom scheme and see evolutionary relationships).
Just about every lab manual that goes with commonly used textbooks has at least one classification lab which involves using a key. For a good one that includes the pictures of leaves and fish from which the students can design their own key, try the *Laboratory Manual for Living Systems* by Merrill.

Classification

Quadrant 1—Experience

Right Mode—Connect

Teacher invites students to recall everyday things that are classified or organized.

Objective

To have students actively realize that many things in their everyday experience are classified or organized so that they may be used/found more readily and then to create a class experience in which the students devise a scheme to classify a common object.

Activity

The students begin this concept by surfacing as many things in their everyday experiences as they can which are classified or organized. They are usually very good at contributing items such as: dictionaries, supermarkets, libraries, department stores, class schedules, etc. Then they are asked to make a large circle around the periphery of the room; remove their left shoe and push it into the center of the circle. (At this point, they're not sure what is going to happen.) The teacher asks for three volunteers, one to go to the board and two to separate the shoes. The task is to devise a scheme, based on similarity of structure, by which the shoes can be broken down into smaller and smaller piles until each student receives her/his own shoe.

Assessment

Participation of the students in contributing examples of everyday things which are classified and their cooperation in joining in the show activity.

Left Mode—Examine

Students share common scheme to classify shoes down to a single owner.

Activity

The scheme that appears on the board almost always looks something like the example below:
LEFT SHOES
LACES   NO LACES
NOT PENNY LOAFERS   PENNY LOAFERS
Students freely contribute suggestions for identifying the categories and become more attentive to subtle distinguishing features.

Assessment

Quality and degree of student involvement.

Quadrant 2—Concepts

Right Mode—Image

Students bring in pictures of all kinds of living things.

Objective

The students will begin to make the bridge between the classification of ordinary objects and the task of classifying millions of living things.

Activity

For homework, the students are asked to find pictures of living things. Any living thing is acceptable, so some even bring in photographs of their family members or pets. They bring these pictures to class the next day and the teacher goes around looking at what they've brought, making comments, etc. Before the next class period, these contributions will be hung around the classroom as a visual reminder of the variety of living things. (And this is only a small sampling.) After the presentation of Aristotle and Linnaeus' Schemes, the teacher comes back to this Quadrant 2, Right Mode and puts out on a desk representative members of the different kingdoms. For example, photographs of magnified bacteria, a sample of pond water, a few mushrooms from the supermarket, the classroom pet hamsters and a handy plant, moldy bread, a goldfish, a flower, etc. can be gathered. Then the students are again asked to group these living things based on similarities of features.

Assessment

Quality of student responses: their willingness to bring in pictures and critically identify distinguishing structures/features in living things.

Classification

Left Mode—Define

Teacher provides info on classification schemes for living things.

Objective

To provide the students with the historical basis of biological classification, giving Aristotle's simple scheme, Linnaeus' contributions of levels of organization and binomial nomenclature and Whittaker's presently recognized five kingdom scheme.

Activity

Using the blackboard, colored chalk and imitating the same type of scheming patterns that the students used for the shoe activity, the teacher shows the progression and increasing complexity of how scientists have attempted to put living things in some kind of order so that they can be studied. When doing binomial nomenclature, many examples are given with a little explanation of why Latin was chosen. When explaining the Levels of Organization (Kingdom, Phylum, Class, Order, Family, Genus, Species) an analogy is drawn using the location of the teacher, i.e., Kingdom = country, Phylum = state, Class = city, Order = street, Family = #, Genus = last name, Species = first name. The most important point is that the more of these levels two organisms share in common, the more closely related they are. Finally, Whittaker's Five Kingdom Scheme is presented.

Assessment

Quality of students' notes; their ability to correctly answer class questions involving analysis of relationship charts and identification of the key characteristics and example organisms of each of the Kingdoms.

Quadrant 3—Applications

Left Mode—Try

Students practice recognizing relationships using worksheets.

Objective

To confirm the students' ability to identify degree of relationships among living things and to check that they can properly place organisms in the kingdom to which they belong based on their characteristics.

Activity

For this octant, students 1) complete a worksheet where they fill-in appropriate levels of organization to establish closeness of relationships among four different organisms, and 2) work on a small group activity which involves them placing a number of different organisms in the appropriate kingdoms based on structural features and characteristics.

Assessment

Quality of students' involvement in the activities: their success in completing the chart; their active participation in completing the activity.

Right Mode—Extend

Students learn how to use an already prepared classification key.

Objective

To have the students learn how to use an already prepared tool for identification of living things, a classification key.

Activity

Working in pairs, the students discover how to use a prepared classification key. Most lab books contain at least one exercise where the students are taught to use a key to identify a series of unknown organisms. Some books provide pictures of families of fish, or sharks, or dinosaurs, or even imaginary monsters.

Assessment

Success of the students in correctly identifying the unknown organisms by using the key provided.

Quadrant 4—Creations

 Left Mode—Refine

Evaluate by having students make a key for leaves & a key for fish.

Objective

To have the students confirm their understanding of classification keys by constructing their own keys for leaves or fish or some other small sampling of living things.

Activity

Now that they have used and studied keys, the students are given a set of pictures of fish or leaves (something different than what they have already used), and asked to construct their own dichotomous key. They then swap the key with a partner to ensure that it is true to the form and that it works.

Assessment

Students' ability to successfully construct and use a dichotomous classification key.

 Right Mode—Integrate

Students re-own the material by taking something of their choosing and making a key for it.

Objective

To have the students re-own the material by taking some objects of interest to them and organizing/classifying them by similarity of structure and then devising a key so that others may identify them.

Activity

The students are asked to take something of their own choosing (cars, tapes, silver patterns, sports balls, cereals) and make a key for their identification. Usually this is given as a homework assignment. They usually draw or cut out pictures of the items with which they are working. Then they construct a key so that someone not knowing the items can correctly identify the items. In class the next day, students exchange keys and test them for accuracy.

Assessment

Quality of students' choice of items, numbers of objects used and accuracy of the key in terms of form and purpose.

Decay

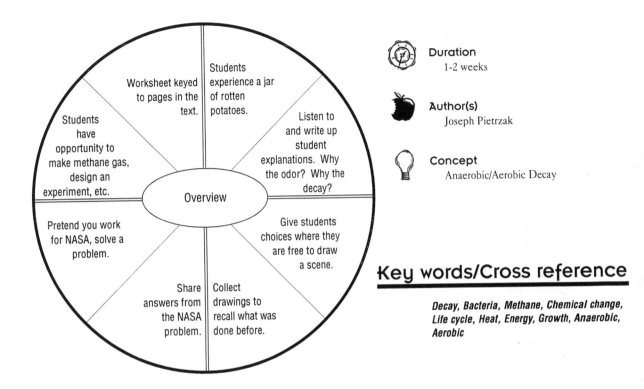

Duration
1-2 weeks

Author(s)
Joseph Pietrzak

Concept
Anaerobic/Aerobic Decay

Key words/Cross reference

Decay, Bacteria, Methane, Chemical change, Life cycle, Heat, Energy, Growth, Anaerobic, Aerobic

Overview

Objective
Introduce bacteria through a process of decay.

About the Author
Joe Pietrzak teaches science at Oliver Middle School in Brockport, NY.

Required Resources
Material presented here has been invented, created and planned by the teacher. Any beginning biology textbook chapter about bacteria can give a background. One may have to read about aerobic/anaerobic decay.

Quadrant 1—Experience

Right Mode—Connect

Students experience a jar of rotten potatoes.

Objective

Motivate students. Something's going on in the room. They have no idea what it is that I want to study at this point. Get them interested.

Activity

Students to experience a jar of rotten potatoes after I set up the class by saying that I've made something for you . . . , it took me six days to make . . .. Students to line up to observe (especially smell) the potatoes.

Assessment

Increased participation, fun, smiles, controlled noise. The number of volunteers that line up. All usually try it once someone starts. If not, diffusion will get to them.

Left Mode—Examine

Listen to and write up student explanations. Why the odor? Why the decay?

Objective

Analysis of the activity. Solicit answers from as many students as possible.

Activity

Why the odor? Why the decay? Listen to and write up student explanations. All answers are "good," given positive reinforcement.

Assessment

Students directed and are pleased to take all the input and generally agree on 2-3 ideas. 1) Potatoes are changing into NEW materials that include solids and gases, the change causes odor for one . . . 2) Bacteria are responsible, something microscopic and invisible is "eating" the potatoes and this results in change. 3) A third idea emerges too—decay needed for plants to live.

Quadrant 2—Concepts

Right Mode—Image

Give students choices where they are free to draw a scene.

Objective

Students to agree that decay process is good. Decay is a part of a cycle of renewed life.

Activity

What would the "world" (a scene) look like if things did not decay? Students to draw a scene showing this idea and can choose from Lake Ontario, Niagara Falls, a thruway, farm yard, Eric Canal, backyard, cemetery, or a scene they "invent."

Assessment

Show off the great ideas. Hang up all posters as they arrive to evaluate ideas. Artists explain what they thought too.

Left Mode—Define

Collect drawings to recall what was done before.

Objective

Time to teach. What is it I want them to know about bacteria?

Activity

Lecture. Name three groups and shapes of bacteria. Define anaerobic, aerobic decay. Explain how anaerobic decay makes Methane, not odorous gases. How are bacteria both helpful and harmful? Sample how they reproduce. True life stories about beach closings/food poisoning. Discuss how a friend made a Methane gas operated farm truck with cow manure.

Assessment

Randomly select to check understanding. Also tell their math teacher to practice fission math problems.

Decay

Quadrant 3—Applications

 ### Left Mode—Try

Share answers from the NASA problem.

Objective
Practice.

Activity
Worksheet keyed to pages in text. Read the text chapter Analysis Sampling. Ditto on keying bacteria to practice types and whether they are helpful. Puzzles, groups can help check keys.

Assessment
Quiz and walking around to help solve problems.

 ### Right Mode—Extend

Pretend you work for NASA, solve a problem.

Objective
An opportunity to tinker.

Activity
1) Extra credit given for anyone making Methane gas in a 2 liter plastic bottle. 2) Design an experiment to test this question, "Which room in my home has the most bacteria?" 3) Each class to work in groups of four. Where would you expect to find A LOT of bacteria? Come up with a list of four.

Assessment
1) Will a pinhole in the bottle result in a flame? 2) Read off ideas planned. Students desiring to actually do this are given a jar for culturing bacteria. Talk about disposal/safety. 3) Students given cotton swabs. Go collect your bacteria. Place samples in a jar. Culture samples (do not open again). Check out ideas.

Quadrant 4—Creations

 ### Left Mode—Refine

Students have opportunity to make methane gas, design an experiment, etc.

Objective
Solving a unique problem. Apply methods to solve a problem. Take the learning and apply it.

Activity
Pretend you work for NASA (ditto). Astronauts return from the moon. Are they safe to release? What if they bring back a new strain of bacteria that is harmful? Problem: give at least four things you can do to astronauts, their equipment and samples to make certain no new harmful bacteria are present. Oh yes, you can not kill them to make sure they're safe.

Assessment
Student answers, solicited. List solutions on board, discuss.

 ### Right Mode—Integrate

Worksheet keyed to pages in the text.

Objective
Show that unit of study is related in other subject areas.

Activity
Inform team members of study beforehand. My social studies colleague will read with students how disease was introduced to Native Americans and may have led to a decay in health, leadership, culture lifestyle, etc.

Assessment
Generally, answers given to discussion, reading and questions led by instructor.

Enzymes

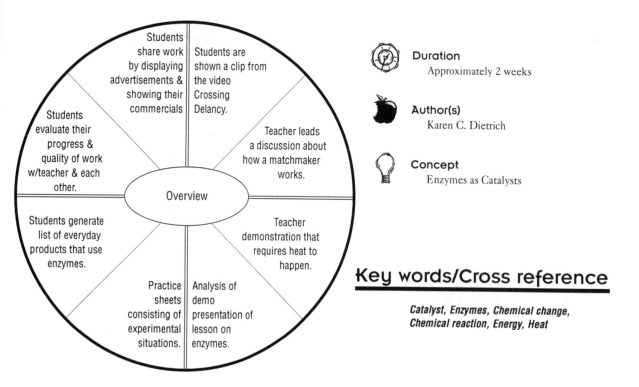

Duration
Approximately 2 weeks

Author(s)
Karen C. Dietrich

Concept
Enzymes as Catalysts

Key words/Cross reference

*Catalyst, Enzymes, Chemical change,
Chemical reaction, Energy, Heat*

Overview

 Objective

The students will show an understanding of the
purpose and mechanism of action of enzymes by
being able to explain their effect on chemical reactions.

 About the Author

Sr. Karen Dietrich has been a classroom teacher of
all levels of biology for over 20 years. In 1991 she
was awarded the Presidential Award for Excellence
in Science Teaching representing the state of NJ.

 Required Resources

Video — Crossing Delancy.

Enzymes

Quadrant 1—Experience

 Right Mode—Connect

Students are shown a clip from the video Crossing Delancy.

Objective

To allow the students to become intrigued with a chemical catalyst or enzyme by an initial introduction which compares it to a matchmaker in the movies (or real life).

Activity

The students are shown a clip from the movie Crossing Delancy which is currently available in video rental stores. The clip is about twenty minutes into the film and features an old-fashioned matchmaker who brings a "nice girl" and a "good boy" together. They meet at a kitchen table. While the couple interact, the matchmaker (and the girl's grandmother) leave and go into the kitchen. The connection with enzymes works well, because two substrates (the girl and boy) are brought together so that they can react. They may have gotten together eventually, but it may have taken seventy years. The kitchen table is the active site and the matchmaker leaves and does not become part of the final reaction. The video is timely and currently available, but if it is impossible or impractical to show, this is also the perfect time for the teacher to become storyteller and make up a fascinating five minute story about a kind, nosy neighbor who brings two young people together.

Assessment

Attentiveness of the students during the movie clip or story.

 Left Mode—Examine

Teacher leads a discussion about how a matchmaker works.

Objective

To have students analyze the role of a matchmaker, guiding them to the aspects that will be appropriate when discussing enzymes.

Activity

As a whole class, students participate in a brief analysis of how a matchmaker "works." The teacher may supply some leading questions such as: "What is the job of a matchmaker?" "Does there need to be a meeting place?" "Does the matchmaker stay around after the couple are happy together?"

Assessment

Quality of class attention and participation.

Quadrant 2—Concepts

 Right Mode—Image

Teacher demonstration that requires heat to happen.

Objective

To perform a demonstration of a chemical reaction which requires a boost of energy (heat) to happen; to begin the bridge into enzymes which lower activation energy without heat.

Activity

The teacher does a demonstration of a chemical reaction that requires heat in order to occur. A simple and appropriate example might be the Benedict's Test for the presence of glucose. This is an indicator reaction which is commonly used in the average biology class. It is also good because it can be used again in a lab experience as a test for the action of an enzyme. After the demonstration, the students are asked to draw the set up and indicate with colored pencils what happened.

Assessment

Success of the students in observing and understanding the role of heat in supplying energy for a reaction to happen.

 Left Mode—Define

Analysis of demo presentation of lesson on enzymes.

Objective

To teach the structure and function of enzymes in lowering activation energy so that substrates can be joined or separated in a chemical reaction without the addition of heat.

Activity

The students need to answer some questions. 1) What is heat? 2) What does heat provide for this reaction? 3) How was heat like a matchmaker? 4) What is the physical color change an indication of? 5) Can a reaction that needs a boost always make use of heat? At this point the teacher introduces the concept of a catalyst or enzyme, defining the action of bond breaking and forming, activation energy, substrates, end products, specificity, active site. During these potentially abstract concepts, it is helpful to use visual aids. Most traditionally, enzymes are described as lock and keys or puzzle pieces. Cut out large puzzle pieces from different color poster boards or actually take your key and fit it in the classroom door, then take someone else's house key and try it. What makes a key specific is its shape. Enzymes are proteins that also have a specific shape. If something de-shapes the enzyme, it doesn't fit anymore.

Assessment
A short quiz on enzyme structure and function.

Quadrant 3—Applications

Left Mode—Try

Practice sheets consisting of experimental situations.

Objective
To have the students practice their understanding of enzymes through paper problem analysis and actual lab experimentation.

Activity
Students work on practice sheets which consist of varied experimental situations involving the use of enzymes. They get together in small groups to discuss and compare answers. At this point, it is also good for the students to actually try some experimentation which indirectly shows that action of an enzyme on a substrate. Many books use the example of sucrose acting on sucrose to facilitate its breakdown into glucose and fructose. Yeast cells make sucrose. A few grains or a small piece of yeast can stand in a cup of water for about twenty minutes. Then it should be filtered and the filtrate kept. The filtrate has the enzyme sucrose. To check for the presence of sucrose, the students fill two test tubes 1/4 full of sugar solution. Test one with Benedict's solution for the presence of glucose. Put about 6ml of the enzyme extract in the second tube. Let it set for an hour and test it with Benedict's; it will be positive showing sucrose was changed to glucose and fructose. The students can write a formal lab, or do a flow chart of what took place, or draw it in terms of a metaphor like the puzzle pieces.

Assessment
Quality of student work on problem situation sheets and lab activity.

Right Mode—Extend

Students generate list of everyday products that use enzymes.

Objective
To have the students take what they have learned about enzymes and apply it in a creative way that capitalizes on their understanding.

Activity
Working in groups of five, the students generate a list of everyday products which they know or suspect use enzymes. Detergents and contact lens cleansers are obvious and excellent examples. One large whole-class list is compiled and different students volunteer to write to some of the different manufacturers of the products for information on the enzyme activity, and if possible, the process used to test for it. While waiting for the manufacturing companies to respond, the groups are given, in class, one lab period to design a new commercial/advertisement for a product of their choice in which the role of the enzymes is emphasized. The commercial should have a brief segment which explains to the public what an enzyme is. Out-of-class time may be used to actually video the commercial or if it's for a magazine, the layout can possibly be done on a desktop publishing computer. This project allows for a variety of talents: writing, drawing, video-making, computer expertise, acting to be utilized.

Assessment
Diligence, progress, and involvement of each member of the group in working on the commercial.

Enzymes

Quadrant 4—Creations

 ### Left Mode—Refine

Students evaluate their progress & quality of work w/teacher & each other.

Objective
To have the students evaluate their progress and quality of work with the teacher and each other.

Activity
The groups check in with each other and the teacher to confirm the accuracy of their commercials/advertisements as far as the enzyme information is concerned and to have any "technical" questions answered.

Assessment
Students' ability to complete and critique their project.

 ### Right Mode—Integrate

Students share work by displaying advertisements & showing their commercials.

Objective
To have the students share their commercials/advertisements.

Activity
Advertisements are displayed and commercials are shown. An "Emzy Award" is presented for the best in each medium. An award can be given for most creative, most accurate, best layout, best video.

Assessment
Quality of student presentations.

Living/Non-living Things

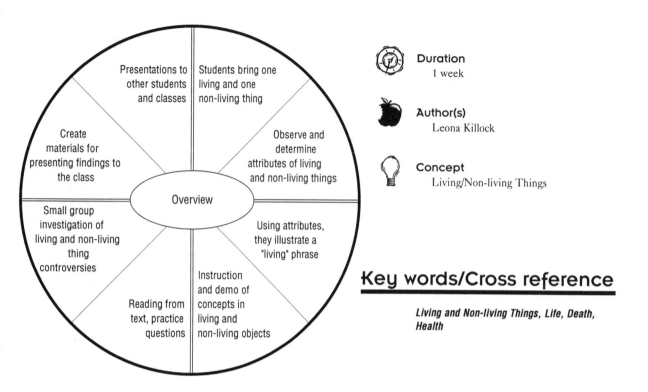

Duration
1 week

Author(s)
Leona Killock

Concept
Living/Non-living Things

Wheel sections (clockwise from top):
Students bring one living and one non-living thing

Observe and determine attributes of living and non-living things

Using attributes, they illustrate a "living" phrase

Instruction and demo of concepts in living and non-living objects

Reading from text, practice questions

Small group investigation of living and non-living thing controversies

Create materials for presenting findings to the class

Presentations to other students and classes

Center: Overview

Key words/Cross reference

Living and Non-living Things, Life, Death, Health

Overview

Objective
To introduce students to the characteristics of living vs. non-living forms.

About the Author
Leona Killock is Principal of Thomas Jefferson Elementary School, Kenmore Town of Tonawanda Union Free School District, Tonawanda, NY. Her previous experience includes twenty-one years as a secondary classroom science teacher. She has also been a staff development team member responsible for developing a program in her district for system-wide implementation of 4MAT. Leona is a member of the Excel Consultants Group.

Required Resources
Video equipment.

Author's Notes
This plan was used successfully as the first unit to introduce students to Biology.

Living/Non-living Things

Quadrant 1—Experience

 ### Right Mode—Connect

Students bring one living and one non-living thing.

Objective

To have students think about the similarities and differences between living and non-living objects.

Activity

Students are assigned to bring to class one living and one non-living object. (Living objects must be contained in a humane environment and returned to their natural environment no later than the end of the school day.)

Assessment

Quality and diversity of objects brought in.

Author's Notes

This unit is taught within the first week of school. One incentive to encourage participation is by giving 10 homework points for the living and another 10 points for the non-living objects. An additional 10 points may be earned if the object is unique, that is, no other student in the class brought in the same type of object.

 ## Left Mode—Examine

Observe and determine attributes of living and non-living things.

Objective

To have students observe and determine the attributes of living and non-living objects.

Activity

1. Place students in groups of 4.
2. Each member of the group places his/her living object in the center of the table. After observing the 4 living objects in their group, a list of similarities found in all of the objects is compiled. Repeat this process for the non-living objects.
3. Each group shares their lists with the whole class.
4. One list of common attributes is compiled for the living objects and another for the non-living objects.

Assessment

Quality of student involvement and lists of attributes.

Quadrant 2—Concepts

 ### Right Mode—Image

Using attributes, they illustrate a "living" phrase.

Objective

To express in color and shape some common phrases associated with living and non-living things.

Activity

Using chart paper and colored markers, each group of students is instructed to select one of the following. They must illustrate their choice while incorporating the characteristics that were listed in Step Two.
- "Teeming with life."
- "Living from hand to mouth."
- "A breath of life."
- "Living on the edge."
- "Fit for life."
- "Living beyond your means."
- "Nine Lives."
- "Living the good life."
- "Over my dead body."
- "Dead as a door nail."
- "In the dead of winter."
- "Light of my life."

Assessment

Quality of art work and discussion while sharing their impressions.

 ## Left Mode—Define

Instruction and demo of concepts in living and non-living objects.

Objective

To provide students with the 'scientific ' interpretation of the characteristics/attributes of living things.

Activity

Teacher presents vocabulary and new information using lecture, demonstration, and discussion.

Assessment

Level of student interest and the quality of questions and comments.

Quadrant 3—Applications

 ## Left Mode—Try

Reading from text, practice questions.

Objective
To have students practice the new information.

Activity
Assign reading from the text and appropriate questions for students to answer.

Assessment
Quality of student responses to text questions and grades on an objective test.

 ## Right Mode—Extend

Small group investigation of living and non-living thing controversies.

Objective
To have students explore the fact that the line between living and non-living is not well defined.

Activity
Students are to select a topic from a list that contains the following choices to investigate and report on. They may work in groups of 3 and only one group may report on a given topic.
1. Are viruses considered to be living or non-living?
2. When does life begin for humans?
3. When does human life end?
4. Design and conduct an experiment that will show if radish seeds are alive or non-living according to the defined characteristics of life.
5. What are the issues associated with the use of tissue from aborted human fetuses for research and treatment of human conditions?
6. What are the issues associated with using organs for transplant from infants born with only a brain stem?

Assessment
Level of student participation and enthusiasm.

Quadrant 4—Creations

 ## Left Mode—Refine

Create materials for presenting findings to the class.

Objective
Student will determine the modes of presentation they will use, assign tasks, and complete their projects.

Activity
Students will decide the method(s) to be used when presenting their findings. Some form of visual and oral presentation must be included.

Assessment
Monitoring of student progress and level of interest. Accuracy of content.

 ## Right Mode—Integrate

Presentations to other students and classes.

Objective
To celebrate the students new understanding of the significance and delicacy of life.

Activity
Students present their projects to the class. All presentations are video-taped. Appropriate presentations are placed in showcases, others may be presented to health classes or English classes as an example of the controversy in our world today over living vs. non-living things.

Assessment
Creativity and accuracy of content in the presentations.

Models

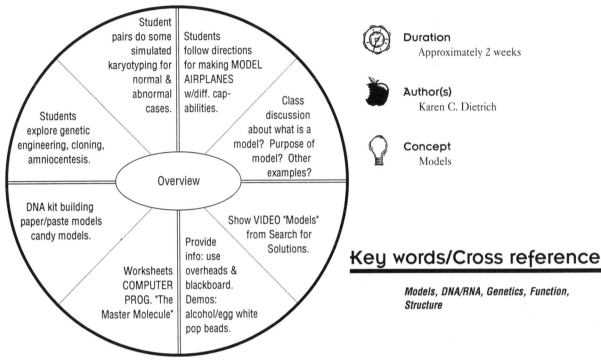

Overview

- Student pairs do some simulated karyotyping for normal & abnormal cases.
- Students follow directions for making MODEL AIRPLANES w/diff. capabilities.
- Class discussion about what is a model? Purpose of model? Other examples?
- Students explore genetic engineering, cloning, amniocentesis.
- DNA kit building paper/paste models candy models.
- Worksheets COMPUTER PROG. "The Master Molecule"
- Provide info: use overheads & blackboard. Demos: alcohol/egg white pop beads.
- Show VIDEO "Models" from Search for Solutions.

Duration
Approximately 2 weeks

Author(s)
Karen C. Dietrich

Concept
Models

Key words/Cross reference

Models, DNA/RNA, Genetics, Function, Structure

Overview

Objective
The students will show an understanding of the structure and function of the DNA molecule.

About the Author
Sister Karen Dietrich SSJ has been a classroom teacher of all levels of biology for over 20 years. In 1991 she was awarded the Presidential Award for Excellence in Science Teaching representing the state of NJ.

Bibliography

The World's Greatest Paper Airplane and Toy Book, Keith R. Laux. TAB Books, Inc. 1987. Blue Ridge Summit, PA 17294.

The Search for Solutions. Videocassettes c/o Phillips Petroleum Co., C-25 Phillips Bldg., Bartlesville, OK 74004 (for free duplication set, request on school letterhead).

DNA – The Master Molecule. William W. Currier. E.M.E., Old Mill Plain Rd., P.O. Box 2805, Danbury, CT 06813-2805 (computer software program).

The Molecular Model of DNA and its Replication Kit. LAB-AIDS Inc. 249 Trade Zone Drive, Ronkonkoma, NY 11779 (hands-on plastic building kit for teams of students).

Human Chromosome Analysis Bio Kit. Carolina Biological Supply Company. Burlington, NC 27215 (student worksheets with normal and abnormal chromosome photographs that can be cut out and karyotyped).

Quadrant 1—Experience

Right Mode—Connect

Students follow directions for making model airplanes w/different capabilities.

Objective

To have students experience a common example of a model by actually building a model paper airplane and paying attention to how its structure affects its flying pattern.

Activity

Teamed with a partner, the students are given a piece of scrap Xerox paper, a piece of good colored Xerox paper, and a set of directions for making a paper airplane. Without explanation, they are instructed to read the directions to teach themselves to make the airplane and then to make their own, good model. This takes approximately twenty minutes. Of course they may practice to make sure it flies. There are many books available in libraries and book stores which contain a wide variety of paper planes which, because of their structural features, perform different stunts. It's preferable to give each team a different flyer to produce. This adds to the fun and lays the groundwork for the idea that structure determines function. The teacher can then take ten to fifteen minutes to have a contest where each team comes up, describes the plane's structural features, and what trick they hope it will perform. One set of directions follows at the end of the cycle.

Assessment

Quality of student interest, participation and model planes.

Left Mode—Examine

Class discussion about what is a model? Purpose of model? Other examples?

Objective

To have students analyze what a model is, what are some different kinds of models, and why models are useful.

Activity

After the contest, the teacher can lead the class in an analysis of the experience. Some questions which may be discussion starters are included at the end of the cycle. Obviously, they center around the nature of a model, what a model is, and why models are useful. The students can also be encouraged to share other models with which they are familiar.

Assessment

Quality of discussion and students' ability to express the purpose of models.

Models

Quadrant 2—Concepts

 Right Mode—Image

Show VIDEO "Models" from Search for Solutions.

Objective

To have the students move from the general idea of a model to the special use of models in science by showing a video that shares several specific examples of scientific models.

Activity

To make the bridge to scientific models, specifically that of Watson and Crick's DNA model, the students are shown the Search for Solutions segment on Modeling. This segment is one of nine, twenty minute segments which are readily available on a free-loan basis and may be copied by the school. In this segment on Modeling, several examples, both historical and current are shown. One of these features Linus Pauling, and how he made a paper model of the alpha helix while recovering from a cold. Oodles of noodles (found in the supermarket and very inexpensive) can be brought in their package—tightly coiled to fit. Then boil them right before their very eyes. They relax and you can start to spread them out a strand at a time to show that chromatin, about a meter of it, must be VERY tightly coiled to fit inside the nucleus of a cell.

Assessment

Student attention and response to the video.

 Left Mode—Define

Provide info: use overheads & blackboard. Demos: alcohol, egg white, pop beads.

Objective

To give the students the basic features of DNA as explained by Watson and Crick's model and to show how those structures explain its role in replication and protein synthesis by lecturing and critical questioning.

Activity

The teacher presents the classical, structural features of Watson and Crick's model of DNA. The important underlying concept is: Structure determines Function. This critical information lays the foundation for an understanding of replication, protein synthesis and genetic engineering. While the purpose of this octant is to provide the learner with the facts, this does not mean that many visual means are not employed to make those facts as clear as possible. Demonstrations are particularly helpful in a topic that is abstract. A little egg white in a beaker, mixed with a bit of rubbing alcohol and stirred with a glass rod is also an excellent simulation of what extracted DNA looks like. Pop beads and a long zipper are also invaluable when teaching DNA and its functions.

Assessment

A short test on the material presented.

Quadrant 3—Applications

Left Mode—Try

Worksheets, computer program: "The Master Molecule"

Objective
To make sure students not only know the facts about DNA structure, but to see if they can use that information by using paper and computer problem simulations related to DNA replication and protein synthesis.

Activity
In this octant, the students work as a class on a computer program called The Master Molecule. The menu for this program provides choices which allow the review of DNA structure, replication and finally introduces mRNA, tRNA and ribosomes and their roles in protein synthesis. By using a large screen TV monitor and gathering the whole class around, this proves to be an enjoyable activity that is confirming for the students and their confidence in the material. This can be followed up with a paper/pencil assignment for class or for homework that involves transcription and translation, and results in the primary structure of a piece of imaginary protein. A copy of the worksheet follows at the end of the cycle.

Assessment
Student participation and quality of answers in the computer simulation, and then successful completion of the worksheet.

Right Mode—Extend

DNA kit building paper, paste models, candy models.

Objective
To have the students now build their own model of DNA which will allow them to visualize the helical formation and the way its structure permits replication and then how it serves as a template for mRNA in protein synthesis.

Activity
Just about every lab manual or teacher reference book has directions for students to build paper models of the nucleotide parts which can be assembled into a model of DNA. There are also some inexpensive, completely re-usable plastic kits for DNA/RNA modeling which have the advantage of twisting and showing a three-dimensional representation. It is also fun, and a bit more creative to let the students decide what material they'd like to use to make their model. Different kinds of candy has been a favored choice. They can use five different kinds of candy to represent each of the nitrogen bases, another type for the sugars and another for the phosphates. Gum drops work well!

Assessment
Quality of the model in its representation of the facts.

Models

Quadrant 4—Creations

 ### Left Mode—Refine

Students explore genetic engineering, cloning, amniocentesis.

Objective
To begin to have students explore some of the current research being done which requires the understanding of the molecule called DNA.

Activity
Students do some out-of-class research on topics such as amniocentesis, cloning, genetic engineering and genetic counseling. A possibility for this last section (which serves as a very good lead-in to a next chapter on DNA research today) is to have a guest speaker come in who is a technician with an expertise in karyotyping. The guest could explain the purpose and procedure and show some real examples.

Assessment
Quality of discussion.

 ### Right Mode—Integrate

Student pairs do some simulated karyotyping for normal & abnormal cases.

Objective
To have students explore current techniques and research being done which is built on the foundations of the material they have just studied.

Activity
There are a number of lab manuals which provide very realistic chromosome pictures which carry different abnormalities. The students can do a karyotype themselves by cutting and pasting, identify the genetic abnormality which they have found to be present, and then do some research on that disease, its severity and consequences, and share that in an oral report to the class.

Assessment
Quality of the karyotype, proper identification of the chromosomal abnormality and resulting syndrome, research and class presentation.

The Mole

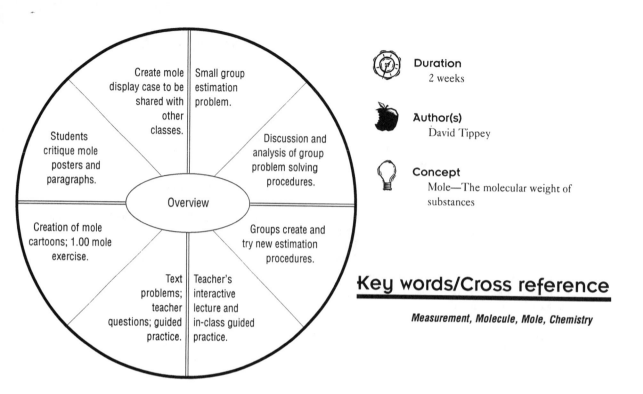

Create mole display case to be shared with other classes.

Small group estimation problem.

Students critique mole posters and paragraphs.

Discussion and analysis of group problem solving procedures.

Overview

Creation of mole cartoons; 1.00 mole exercise.

Groups create and try new estimation procedures.

Text problems; teacher questions; guided practice.

Teacher's interactive lecture and in-class guided practice.

Duration
2 weeks

Author(s)
David Tippey

Concept
Mole—The molecular weight of substances

Key words/Cross reference

Measurement, Molecule, Mole, Chemistry

Overview

Objective
Students will understand the concept of mole and its use in calculating mass.

About the Author
David Tippey teaches chemistry at Marion High School, Marion Community Schools, Marion, IN. He has been a classroom teacher for over eighteen years. He is a participant in the Marion 4MAT Implementation Project led by Carol Secttor.

Required Resources
Variety of objects for estimation; teacher prepared worksheets; materials for student display.

The Mole

Quadrant 1—Experience

Right Mode—Connect

Small group estimation problem.

Objective

To gain an appreciation for the importance of being able to estimate the number of particles in a sample of a substance.

Activity

The teacher labels and displays jars containing 150 of each of the following: marbles, paper clips, grains of rice, pennies, BB's, iron filings, etc. Additional jars have samples of elements and compounds such as zinc, water, and magnesium, or multiple units of 2 to 3 connected items. Students work in small groups. Each group is given a different jar and must follow the appropriate directions from the following:

1. Estimate the number of particles in your sample, or
2. Estimate the number of atoms in your sample, or
3. Estimate the number of molecules in your sample.

Assessment

Involvement of students in activity and contributions to the efforts of their group.

Left Mode—Examine

Discussion and analysis of group problem-solving procedures.

Objective

To analyze the effectiveness of their estimation.

Activity

Each group displays its sample and explains how they arrived at their estimates. Teacher leads discussion focusing on the following:

1. Difficulties experienced in trying to estimate.
2. Types of particles which were easier to estimate and which were hardest.
3. Is it possible to know how many atoms or molecules are in a sample?
4. Which jars contain samples which could be called "singles" and which could be called multiple units?
5. What problems would occur if a sample contains an exceedingly huge number of particles?

Teacher tells students with countable samples (marbles, pennies, etc.) how many particles were really in their sample.

Ask students to name units they are familiar with which are used to count pieces in a sample; examples are pair, dozen, score, etc. Have them generate as many terms as possible.

Assessment

Contributions to small group effort and large group discussion.

Quadrant 2—Concepts

 ### Right Mode—Image

Groups create and try new estimation procedures.

Objective

To learn other ways to determine the number of particles in a sample without counting them.

Activity

Continuing to work with the same group, students are asked to determine the number of particles in a different sample without counting. They must devise an actual procedure to carry out and test their idea, with proper equipment (such as balance and/or ruler) provided by the teacher. Each group experiment is guided by the following questions:

1. What do you assume about each particle? (Must you assume that each particle is equal?)
2. Is that a valid assumption?
3. Would it help to know how much 1 dozen particles of the sample weighs? How?

Each group shares its results with the class.

Assessment

Ability of students to try to solve the problem.

 ### Left Mode—Define

Teacher's interactive lecture and in-class guided practice.

Objective

To introduce and teach related terms.

Activity

Using overhead projector, teacher introduces term "mole" as the SI unit of measuring the quantity of a substance. Lecture on Avogadro's Number and its meaning. Compare and relate the terms molar mass, gram atomic mass, gram formula mass, and gram molecular mass. Draw simple diagrams of atoms, ionic compounds, molecules and moles to relate to the definition of each term. Check for student understanding with a matching exercise on the overhead. Teach mole-mass calculations and provide guided practice for students using sample problems for them to solve in class with their own calculators.

Assessment

Student involvement during lecture and ability of students to solve in-class problems.

Quadrant 3—Applications

 ### Left Mode—Try

Text problems; teacher questions; guided practice.

Objective

To use new vocabulary and practice new calculations.

Activity

1. Students complete assigned problems in text.
2. Students answer teacher-prepared questions, such as:
   "How many fingers are on a mole of hands?"
   "How many legs are on a mole of insects?"
   "How many moles of toes would be on 50 million frogs?"
3. Students are given an iron nail and a balance. Their task is to determine the number of atoms in the nail.
4. Working in pairs, each is given a sample of a common element or compound. They must calculate the number of grams in exactly 1 mole of their substance. Then they will measure this amount of the substance in a beaker. Students then observe and compare the various 1.00 mole samples that were measured by each group. They should see that 1.00 mole of one substance does not weigh the same nor take up the same volume as 1.00 mole of another substance. They should be reminded of the previous activity when they wondered if it was possible to know the number of atoms or molecules in an element or compound.

Assessment

Completion of assigned work.

 ### Right Mode—Extend

Creation of mole cartoons; 1.00 mole exercise.

Objective

To apply and internalize what they have learned about the mole.

Activity

Student teams will do the following:
Devise a cartoon which has to do with the term "mole."
Create a description of what they could do if someone gave them 1.00 mole of pennies.

Assessment

Student on-task behavior.

The Mole

Quadrant 4—Creations

Left Mode—Refine

Students critique mole posters and paragraphs.

Objective
To complete project assignments.

Activity
Student posters and paragraphs are shared with the class and critiqued. Each group has the opportunity to edit or refine its work.

Assessment
Quality of projects and ability to critique the work of oneself and others.

Right Mode—Integrate

Create mole display case to be shared with other classes.

Objective
To share in final form what has been learned with the rest of the class and the school at large.

Activity
Students will prepare a display case with the following:
- 1 mole samples of various elements and compounds.
- Cartoons on the mole.
- Sample written work on what can be done with 1.00 mole of pennies.
- Samples of 1 dozen, 1 ream, 1 gross, etc.
- A real mole animal (preserved specimen) from the biology department!

Assessment
Student enjoyment in learning; student contributions to the class display effort.

Geological Features

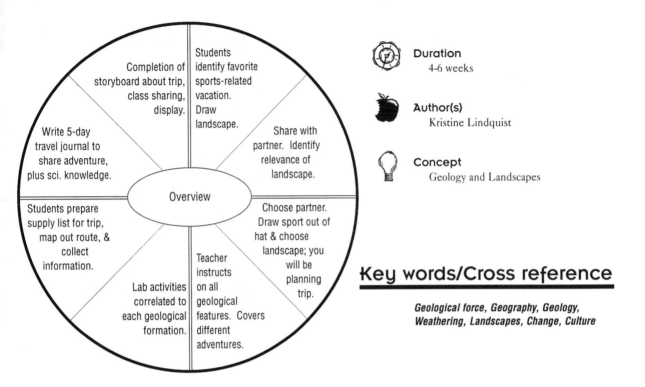

Students identify favorite sports-related vacation. Draw landscape.

Completion of storyboard about trip, class sharing, display.

Share with partner. Identify relevance of landscape.

Write 5-day travel journal to share adventure, plus sci. knowledge.

Overview

Choose partner. Draw sport out of hat & choose landscape; you will be planning trip.

Students prepare supply list for trip, map out route, & collect information.

Teacher instructs on all geological features. Covers different adventures.

Lab activities correlated to each geological formation.

Duration
4-6 weeks

Author(s)
Kristine Lindquist

Concept
Geology and Landscapes

Key words/Cross reference

Geological force, Geography, Geology, Weathering, Landscapes, Change, Culture

Overview

Objective
Over time, forces that have attacked the earth have changed it dramatically, creating geological features uniquely suited to allow humans to enjoy the landscape recreationally.

About the Author
Kristine Lindquist has taught both junior and senior high for Atascadero Unified School District (4 years). She was staff development mentor for this district, training as many teachers as possible in 4MAT design. She currently resides in Phoenix, Arizona.

Required Resources
Maps of 50 states (number depends on scope), travel books (free to AAA members) and school library with strong geology section.

Bibliography
Earth Science, Namowitz/Spaulding. D.C. Heath & Co., 1989 and their Earth Science Lab Investigations.

Authors' Note
In this thematic unit, there is one Quadrant 1 & 4, but several Quadrants 2 & 3. The time frame is from 4-6 weeks depending on grade level and scientific detail provided during teacher instruction portion (Q2 & 3).

Geological Features

Quadrant 1—Experience

 ### Right Mode—Connect

Students identify favorite sports-related vacation. Draw landscape.

Objective

To motivate students to visit a unique landscape in the U.S.

Activity

Have students visualize, then write down their favorite sports-related vacation and briefly sketch the landscape.

Assessment

Teacher observation.

 ### Left Mode—Examine

Share with partner. Identify relevance of landscape.

Objective

Allow students to focus on how the geological features of the land allowed the sporting activity to be possible.

Activity

Share with partner sketch and story. Discuss unique feature of land that allowed vacation and sporting enjoyment.

Assessment

List on board best adventures in class. Example: rafting rapids in Grand Canyon Gorge, wind sailing off cliffs in Monterey, caving in Carlsbad, scuba diving in Australia. Skiing in Colorado.

Quadrant 2—Concepts

 ### Right Mode—Image

Choose partner. Draw sport out of hat & choose landscape; you will be planning trip.

Objective

Students link with an adventure that will require knowledge of landscape to participate in.

Activity

Have students pair up in "adventure teams" and choose an activity (sport).

Assessment

Students with partner brainstorm three possible locations in U.S. to plan 5-day trip.

 ### Left Mode—Define

Teacher instructs on all geological features. Covers different adventures.

Objective

Over 4-6 week time period, students receive instruction on Forces That Attack The Earth, weathering, mass movements, underground H2O systems, cavern formation, stream erosion, creation of river valleys, waterfalls, glacial movements, wind and waves as agents of change, and all geological land features associated with these forces.

Activity

Lectures, videos, laser discs, computer research, outdoor observations, etc.

Assessment

Students responsible for covering one chapter in text related to their geological landscape plus quizzes interspersed to check for understanding.

During the 4-6 week Q2, 3 period, students are taking one day a week to gather information from library resources.

Geological Features

Quadrant 3—Applications

 ### Left Mode—Try

Lab activities correlated to each geological formation.

Objective
Students gain hands-on experiences in Q2 material covered in class and library.

Activity
Various labs—campus tour of weathering (mechanical and chemical), soil type lab, porosity lab, making stalactites, Play-doh activities (forming valleys, gorges, etc.), glacial analysis, map exercises on H2O basins, and drainage gaps, etc.

Assessment
Lab conclusions, quizzes, teacher observations.

Right Mode—Extend

Students prepare supply list for trip, map out route, & collect information.

Objective
Students (pairs) plan out 5-day adventure to a national park in U.S. that allows their sporting activity due to its geological features.

Activity
Library time (several days spread over 4-6 week period). Students provide outlines of areas to research as prompt to journal writing.

Assessment
Completion of supply list—all necessary items for 5-day adventure including expense list, sporting equipment, personals, lodging, and map of area.

Quadrant 4—Creations

 ### Left Mode—Refine

Write 5-day travel journal to share adventure, plus scientific knowledge.

Objective
Students compose a 5-day travel journal of their adventure.

Activity
Write a 5-page travel journal with partner covering how geological features of landscapes were created (scientific background) and how those features allowed them to participate in a particular sporting activity (class instruction and library research).

Assessment
Graded on accuracy of scientific information, inclusion of key vocabulary terms from text, and creativity of adventure.

Right Mode—Integrate

Completion of storyboard about trip, class sharing, display.

Objective
Encourage uniqueness of their trip and have students share as experts, their knowledge of a particular recreational activity and national park in the U.S.

Activity
Prepare story board that includes travel journal, hand drawn map, supply list, and five views of geological features of land.

Assessment
Graded by inclusion of set criteria and vote from class of favorite adventure. Poster boards cover the entire walls of classroom.

Glaciation

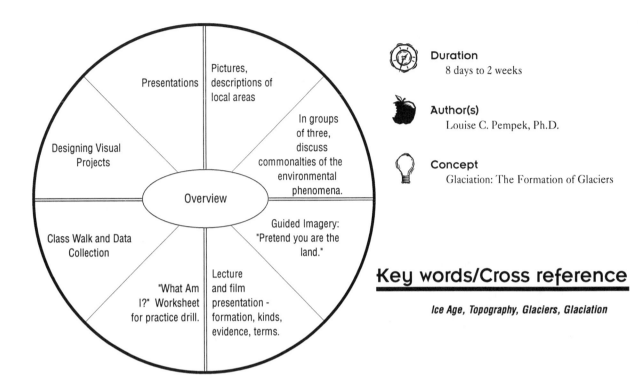

Duration
8 days to 2 weeks

Author(s)
Louise C. Pempek, Ph.D.

Concept
Glaciation: The Formation of Glaciers

Key words/Cross reference

Ice Age, Topography, Glaciers, Glaciation

Overview

Objective

Glaciers carve(d) the earth's surface which has resulted in a characteristic topography.

About the Author

Louise Pempek, Ph. D., is the Adminsitrator of Remedial/Compensatory Education in Killingly, CT. She also serves as Adjunct Professor of Education at the following: Sacred Heart University, Bridgeport, CT; Rhode Island College, Providence; and Eastern Connecticut State University, Willimantic. In addition to numerous awards for outstanding service, Dr. Pempek received the Connecticut Educator Award in 1989. She is a certified 4MAT Trainer and a member of the Excel Consultants Group.

Quadrant 1—Experience

Quadrant 2—Concepts

Right Mode—Connect

Pictures, descriptions of local areas

Objective
To identify three landforms from local area. (Predicated on fact that local area is in glaciated region.)

Activity
Draw, take pictures, or describe three land features near home, on the way from school, or a favorite place in town. Bring to class.

Assessment
Photos, sketches, etc. presented in class.

Left Mode—Examine

In groups of three, discuss commonalties of the environmental phenomena.

Objective
To compare landforms from local glaciated region.

Activity
In groups of three, discuss commonalties of the environmental phenomena which each group member has brought to class. List those features which might not be present in Florida or some other non-glaciated region familiar to students.

Assessment
Quality of lists.

Right Mode—Image

Guided Imagery: "Pretend you are the land."

Objective
To experience vicariously the growth and erosive power of glaciers.

Activity
Conduct a detailed Guided Imagery: (main parts of script). "Pretend you are the land. Think of continual snow for a whole year; a thousand years. The snow piles up; you are "squished." Like an ice cube, the icy snow moves, recedes, melts. Think about what is happening to you. How do you feel? Any scars?"

Assessment
Participation in Guided Imagery.

Left Mode—Define

Lecture and film presentation - formation, kinds, evidence, terms.

Objective
To define "Glaciation" and identify related terminology.

Activity
Teacher lecture and accompanying film or slide presentation (many appropriate A/V programs are available through most media centers)
a) glacier formation
b) kinds of glaciers
c) glacier evidence
d) terms.

Assessment
Objective Quiz after each section.

Quadrant 3—Applications

 ### Left Mode—Try

"What Am I?" Worksheet for practice drill.

Objective
To identify glacier features and evidence.

Activity
Teacher created term worksheet "What Am I?" for practice and drill.

Assessment
Check for understanding by correcting worksheets.

 ### Right Mode—Extend

Class Walk and Data Collection

Objective
To identify glacial features in neighborhood of school.

Activity
Class walk around school to find, sketch, and list evidence of glaciation: esker, kame, kettle, striae, moraine, tiel, drumlin. Write a paragraph on how the glacier affected and continues to affect life in our town.

Assessment
Amount of evidence presented in sketches. Quality of paragraphs on effects.

Quadrant 4—Creations

 ### Left Mode—Refine

Designing Visual Projects

Objective
To design presentation to teach others about glaciation.

Activity
In groups of four, plan and design a slide or video presentation, using their own environment.
e.g. "Our Town's Latest Visitor"
"One Thousand Feet Under Ice."

Assessment
Critique of plans.

 ### Right Mode—Integrate

Presentations

Objective
To teach someone else about glaciation and to celebrate new learning.

Activity
Present slide or video show to a middle school science class or at an Open House at high school.

Assessment
Quality of show or videotape. Audience survey on reactions.

Scientific Method

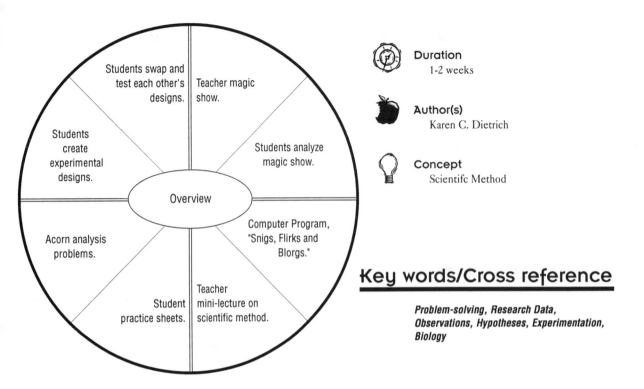

- Students swap and test each other's designs.
- Teacher magic show.
- Students create experimental designs.
- Students analyze magic show.
- Overview
- Acorn analysis problems.
- Computer Program, "Snigs, Flirks and Blorgs."
- Student practice sheets.
- Teacher mini-lecture on scientific method.

Duration
1-2 weeks

Author(s)
Karen C. Dietrich

Concept
Scientifc Method

Key words/Cross reference

Problem-solving, Research Data, Observations, Hypotheses, Experimentation, Biology

Overview

Objective
To introduce student to the Scientific Method as a strategy for successful problem-solving.

About the Author
Sr. Karen Dietrich SSJ has been a classroom teacher of all levels of biology for over 20 years. In 1991 she was awarded the Presidential Award for Excellence in Science Teaching representing the state of NJ.

Required Resources
Materials for teacher "Magic Show" presentation; TV monitor and computer terminal; acorns and other materials for lab.

Scientific Method

Quadrant 1—Experience

Right Mode—Connect

Teacher magic show.

Objective
To actively involve students in an enjoyable "non-scientific" experience that requires observation of patterns and hypothesis formation.

Activity
The teacher performs a Magic Show of science-based and non science-based tricks. The tricks have been gathered from a variety of Science Magic books and also from an exciting trip to the local magic store. Simple, cheap tricks are easily mastered by the teacher; for example, "Chinese laundry ticket," "ball and cups," "multiplying rabbits," etc. The experience can be enhanced with background music, top hat and cape, assistants from the "audience," and so forth. As students observe each trick, the students must record their observations about how the trick was done. A sample student observation sheet contains the following:
THE MAGIC SHOW
Trick:
Observations:
Repeated Actions:

Assessment
Quality of class participation and attention to experience.

Left Mode—Examine

Students analyze magic show.

Objective
To have the students analyze what they have just observed, recognize patterns and then test "educated guesses".

Activity
In small groups, students analyze a given trick, pool ideas and write a procedure to do one of the tricks. Groups are then given the materials needed and attempt to perform the trick for their classmates.

Assessment
Ability of the group to correctly perform its given trick.

Quadrant 2—Concepts

Right Mode—Image

Computer Program, "Snigs, Flirks and Blorgs."

Objective
To connect students to the understanding that science involves observing patterns, too.

Activity
Using a large screen TV monitor and computer terminal, the whole class joins in an activity of identifying patterns and forming hypotheses about those patterns. There are a number of software companies that have good scientific method programs. One that is conducive to large group participation is "Snigs, Flirks, and Blorgs" by Focus Media. This program presents three problems in levels of increasing difficulty.

Assessment
Quality of class participation and success of the class in solving the three problem sets.

Left Mode—Define

Teacher mini-lecture on scientific method.

Objective
To teach the traditional steps of the scientific method.

Activity
Using overhead, chalkboard, and examples, the teacher provides the framework of a scientific process for problem solving, emphasizing that science is a creative process in addition to a critical one. Particular attention is paid to controlled experiments and their impact on hypothesis formation and identification of the variable. More than memorizing a set of steps, time is taken to explore the difficulty in identifying a problem; examples such as Flemming and the discovery of penicillin are examined.

Assessment
Short objective quiz.

Quadrant 3—Applications

Left Mode—Try

Student practice sheets.

Objective

To have students practice recognition of a problem, hypothesis, observation based on experimentation, etc.

Activity

1. Before going into the lab, students work first in whole class, then in cooperative groups, and finally, alone on practice sheets which consist of varied experimental situations which are related to biology. The paragraphs contain the elements learned in the lecture such as problem, hypothesis, data, observation, conclusion.
2. Students get hands-on experience in performing a pre-designed "wet lab" which provides them with all the information they need to successfully complete the lab. Most high school biology books contain at least one such lab on the scientific method.

Assessment

Students' ability to correctly complete the practice sheets and understand the experimental design in the lab activity.

Right Mode—Extend

Acorn analysis problems.

Objective

To have students take what they have learned about the scientific process and write their own experimental design for an identified problem.

Activity

Students are given the following problem involving acorns:

To the student: Select ten different acorns from the trays provided in class. They should be different in that they have caps or don't have caps, different shapes and different sizes. Record the similarities and differences on a chart you construct for the data section in your report. Fill a glass bowl or beaker nearly full of water and place one acorn in the container of water. Allow the acorn to sit for approximately 30 seconds. Determine if the acorn sinks or floats. Remove the acorn from the container and place it in a bag labeled either "sinker" or a bag labeled "floater". Repeat this procedure with the other nine acorns.

Using your observations, form a hypothesis as to why you think the acorns float or sink. State your hypothesis as "If... , then..." Use the steps of the scientific process as described in class and the text. Use proper controls and variables for your experiment. When you are finished with the experiment, write a report about your findings. Include data charts and graphs to show your data.

Author's note: This lab works well because acorns are so readily available at the beginning of the school year. There is a little worm which infiltrates acorns and eats the meat inside. Then the worm leaves by boring a hole. When acorns first fall from trees they are still filled with their meat; when these are dropped in water, they will sink. Those acorns which have been on the ground for a week or so which have been infiltrated by worms will float, if they are hollow. This becomes a fascinating observation/problem for those who do not know about the little worms. Why do some acorns float and others sink? It is important for the students to share their experimental hypotheses/results with each other.

Assessment

Quality of student reports, their ability to describe the problem, state a hypothesis, and design and perform an experiment.

Scientific Method

Quadrant 4—Creations

 ### Left Mode—Refine

Students create experimental designs.

Objective
To have the students and the teacher evaluate the lab activity for the criteria presented in the lecture.

Activity
In a whole-class format, the students analyze their lab activity for the steps in the scientific method. Their task is to identify how the scientific method format helps insure the validity and accuracy of their experiment.

Assessment
Quality of class discussion.

 ## Right Mode—Integrate

Students swap and test each other's designs.

Objective
To share individual experimental designs.

Activity
Each student will swap her/his acorn experimental designs with a classmate who will verify the findings by following each other's experimental procedures.

Assessment
Quality of lab procedures designed especially by their adherence to the steps of the scientific process and the ability of other students to get the same results.

Index

Index

Index

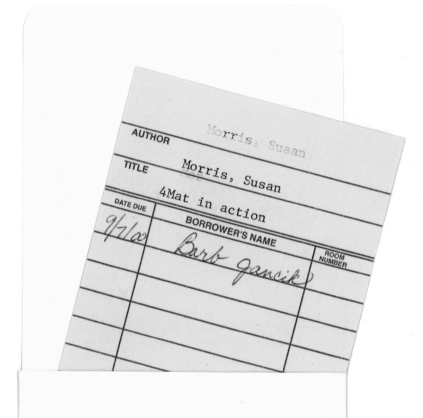

Morris, Susan

4Mat in action